School mental health

Global challenges and opportunities

School mental health

Global challenges and opportunities

Edited by

Stan Kutcher
Dalhousie University and the IWK Health Centre, and WHO/PAHO Collaborating Centre in Mental Health Training and Policy Development, Halifax, NS, Canada

Yifeng Wei
Dalhousie University and the IWK Health Centre, Halifax, NS, Canada

Mark D. Weist
Department of Psychology, University of South Carolina, SC, USA

CAMBRIDGE
UNIVERSITY PRESS

CAMBRIDGE
UNIVERSITY PRESS

University Printing House, Cambridge CB2 8BS, United Kingdom

Cambridge University Press is part of the University of Cambridge.

It furthers the University's mission by disseminating knowledge in the pursuit of education, learning and research at the highest international levels of excellence.

www.cambridge.org
Information on this title: www.cambridge.org/9781107053908

© Cambridge University Press 2015

First published 2015

Printed in the United Kingdom by Clays, St Ives plc

A catalogue record for this publication is available from the British Library

ISBN 978-1-107-05390-8 Hardback

Stan
To my wife and family, for putting up with me.

Yifeng
I dedicate my first book to Dr. Kutcher and Dr. Weist for their guidance, support, and mentorship.

Mark
For Dixie and Stan, with love and gratitude for your guidance and support.

Contents

Contributors

Sanjay Agarwal
Department of Psychiatry, Tata Main
Hospital, Jamshedpur, India

AbdulKareem AlObaidi, MD, MPH
Visiting Scholar at the Institute
of International Education, NY, USA

Faten Alshazly, MA
Sun Life Financial Chair in Adolescent
Mental Health Team, Dalhousie
University/IWK Health Centre, Halifatx,
Nova Scotia, Canada

Keli Anderson
President and CEO, National Institute
of Families for Child & Youth Mental Health

Ary G. Araripe Neto
Projeto Cuca Legal, Departamento de
Psiquiatria, Universidade Federal de São
Paulo, Brazil

Alexa Bagnell, MD, FRCPC
Associate Professor, Dalhousie University,
Halifax, NS, Canada

Susan Barrett
Director of the PBIS Regional Training
and Technical Assistance Center at
Shepard Pratt Health System
Baltimore, MD, USA

Margaret M. Barry, PhD
Professor of Health Promotion and Public
Health, Health Promotion Research
Centre, National University of Ireland
Galway, Ireland

Srikala Bharath
Department of Psychiatry, National
Institute of Mental Health and Neuro
Sciences, Bangalore, India

Ann Blackwood
English Program Services, Education
and Early Childhood Development,
Halifax, NS, Canada

Jillian Boon
Institute of Mental Health, Buangkok,
Singapore

Isabel A. S. Bordin
Departamento de Psiquiatria, Universidade
Federal de São Paulo, Brazil

Rodrigo A. Bressan
Projeto Cuca Legal, Departamento de
Psiquiatria, Universidade Federal de São
Paulo, Brazil

Vanessa Bruce, MA
Sun Life Financial Chair in Adolescent
Mental Health Team, Dalhousie
University/IWK Health Centre, Halifax,
Nova Scotia, Canada

Steve Cairns, M.Ed
School Administrator (retired), BC School
Centred Mental Health Coalition, and
Director of the F.O.R.C.E. Society for Kid's
Mental Health, West Vancouver, BC, Canada

Michelle Cianfrone, MPH
Project Manager, Health Literacy, BC
Mental Health and Substance Use Services,
Vancouver, BC, Canada

Aleisha M. Clarke, B.Ed, M.Ed, PhD
Postdoctoral researcher, Health Promotion
Research Centre, National University
of Ireland Galway, Ireland

Connie Coniglio R.Psych., Ed.D.
Provincial Executive Director, Children
and Women's Mental Health and

Substance Use Program, BC Mental Health and Substance Use Services

Linyuan Deng, PhD
Assistant Professor of Psychology at the Faculty of Education, Beijing Normal University, Beijing, China

Pauline Dickinson, PhD
Researcher and Evaluation Team Leader at SHORE and Whariki Research Centre, School of Public Health, Massey University, Auckland, New Zealand

Yasong Du, MD, PhD
Professor of Psychiatry and Director of Department of Child and Adolescent Psychiatry, Shanghai Mental Health Center, Shanghai Jiaotong University, School of Medicine

Lucille Eber, Ed.D.
Statewide Director, Midwest PBIS Network, Westmont, IL, USA

Gustavo M. Estanislau
Projeto Cuca Legal, Departamento de Psiquiatria, Universidade Federal de São Paulo, Brazil

Steven W. Evans, PhD
Professor of Psychology, Assistant Chair for Graduate Studies and Co-Director at the Center for Intervention Research in Schools at Ohio University, Athens, OH, USA

Xiaoyi Fang, PhD
Yangzi-River Professor of Psychology, Institute of Developmental Psychology, Beijing Normal University, Beijing, China

Paul Flaspohler
Associate Professor of clinical psychology at Miami University, Oxford, OH, USA

Daniel Fung MBBS, MMed (Psychiatry)
Chairman Medical Board, Institute of Mental Health, Buangkok View, and

Adjunct Associate Professor at Yong Loo Lin School of Medicine, Duke NUS Graduate Medical School, Singapore

Julia Gallegos-Guajardo, PhD
Professor of Psychology, Center for Research and Treatment of Anxiety (CETIA), Universidad de Monterrey, Mexico

Deborah Garrity
Parent Partner, BC School Centred Mental Health Coalition, BC, Canada

Don Glover
English Program Services, Education and Early Childhood Development, Halifax NS, Canada

Uma Hirisave
Department of Clinical Psychology, National Institute of Mental Health and Neuro Sciences, Bangalore, India

Muriel Halpern, MD Mg
Assistant Professor of Child and Adolescent Psychiatry, School of Medicine, University of Chile, Santiago, Chile

Kenneth Hamwaka, PhD
Executive Director, Guidance, Counselling and Youth Development Centre for Africa, Lilongwe, Malawi

Moshe Israelashvili, PhD
Associate Professor of Counseling, Tel Aviv University, School of Education, Ramat Aviv, Tel Aviv, Israel

Jill Johnson
Illinois PBIS Network, Westmont, IL, USA

Selin Karacam, Ed.M.
School Psychologist at Ozel Guzel Gunler Poliklinigi, Istanbul, Turkey

Charlene King
Project Manager, Health Literacy, BC Mental Health and Substance Use Services, Vancouver, BC, Canada

Devvarta Kumar, PhD
Associate Professor, Department
of Clinical Psychology, National Institute
of Mental Health and Neuro Sciences,
Bangalore, India

Stan Kutcher, MD, FRCPC, FCAHS
Professor of Psychiatry and Sun Life
Financial Chair in Adolescent Mental
Health at Dalhousie University and the
IWK Health Centre, and Director of the
WHO/PAHO Collaborating Centre in
Mental Health Training and Policy
Development, Halifax, NS, Canada.

Amanda Lee BS/BA
Intern/Fellow at BasicNeeds, Tamale
Northern Region, Ghana, and Directed
Research Assistant at the 3D Shape Lab,
Brown University, Providence, RI, USA

Amy MacKay, CAPM
Sun Life Financial Chair in Adolescent
Mental Health Team, Dalhousie
University/IWK Health Centre, Halifax,
Nova Scotia, Canada

Heather McDaniel
Undergraduate Research Assistant, School
Mental Health Team, Department of
Psychology, University of South Carolina,
SC, USA

Tomiko Miki, BSc
Professor at the Research Laboratory of
Practical Yogo Science, Kagawa Education
Institute of Nutrition, Sakado, Saitama,
Japan

Taís S. Moriyama
Projeto Cuca Legal, Departamento de
Psiquiatria, Universidade Federal de São
Paulo, Brazil

Yasutaka Ojio, PHN, MSc
Department of Physical and Health
Education, Graduate School of Education,
University of Tokyo, Tokyo, Japan

Kumiko Ohnuma, MA
Department of Pediatrics, Graduate
Medical School, Tokyo Medical and Dental
University, Tokyo, Japan

A. Raisa Petca, MSc
Graduate Research Assistant/Psychology
Trainee at Ohio University, Athens, OH,
USA

Rebecca Peterson, BA BASc
Population Health Advisor, Hawke's Bay
District Health Board, Napier Health
Centre, Napier, New Zealand

Louise Rowling PhD(S'ton)
Honorary Associate Professor in Health
Promotion, University of Sydney, Sydney,
NSW, Australia

Norma Ruvalcaba-Romero, PhD
Professor-Researcher at the Department of
Mental Health Clinics, University of
Guadalajara, Mexico

Darcy Santor, PhD
Professor, School of Psychology, University
of Ottawa, Ottawa, ON, Canada

Tsukasa Sasaki, MD, PhD
Professor in Psychiatry at the Graduate
School of Education, University of Tokyo,
Tokyo, Japan

Hemang Shah
Department of Psychiatry, GMERS
Medical college, Sola, Ahmedabad,
India

Wan Hua Sim
Institute of Mental Health, Singapore

Mitchell Shea
Sun Life Financial Chair in Adolescent
Mental Health Team, Dalhousie
University/IWK Health Centre

Marissa Smith-Millman
Miami University, Oxford, OH, USA

Jeff Stewart, BA Hons, B.Ed., MA
District Principal, Distributed Learning,
Comox Valley School District, Vancouver
Island, BC, Canada

Jessica Swain-Bradway, PhD
Midwest PBIS Network, Westmont, IL, USA

Marlene A. Vieira
Departamento de Psiquiatria, Universidade
Federal de São Paulo, Brazil

Yuko Watabe, PhD
Department of Psychology,
Ohio University, Athens,
OH, USA

Katherine Weare
Emeritus Professor, School of Education
University of Southampton, and Honorary
Visiting Professor, School of Psychology,
University of Exeter, UK

Cynthia Weaver
Adolescent Services, Ontario Shores Centre
for Mental Health Sciences, Whitby, ON,
Canada

Yifeng Wei, MA, PhD Candidate
Sun Life Financial Chair in Adolescent
Mental Health Team, Dalhousie
University/IWK Health Centre, Halifax,
Nova Scotia, Canada

Mark D. Weist, PhD
Professor and Director of the
Clinical-Community Program at the
Department of Psychology, University
of South Carolina, SC, USA

Ardath Whynacht, PhD Candidate
Assistant Professor at the Department of
Sociology, Mount Allison University,
Halifax, NS, Canada

Yuhuan Xie, MBBS MS
Consutant Psychiatrist at the Institute of
Mental Health, Singapore, and Assistant
Professor in Psychiatry at the Child and
Adolescent Division, Department of
Psychiatry, School of Medicine, Queen's
University, Kingston, ON, Canada

Peter Yaro, MA
Executive Director at BasicNeeds, Tamale
Northern Region, Ghana

Yanki Yazgan, MD
Clinical Director at Ozel Guzel Poliklinigi,
Istanbul, Turkey; Professor (E) at Marmara
University Faculty of Medicine, Istanbul,
Turkey; and Assistant Professor, Adjunct at
Yale Child Study Center, New Haven, CT,
USA

Nataliya Zhabenko, MD, PhD
Research Assistant at State Establishment
"The Lugansk State Medical University,"
Lugansk, Ukraine

Olena Zhabenko, MD, PhD
Researcher, Ukrainian Research Institute of
Social and Forensic Psychiatry and Drug
Abuse, Ukraine

Allison K. Zoromski, MS
Graduate Student/Research Associate,
Psychology (Arts and Sciences), Ohio
University, Athens, OH, USA

Chapter

1

The global advancement of school mental health for adolescents

Mark D. Weist, Stan Kutcher, and Yifeng Wei

Adolescence is a time of significant development across all dimensions – physical, cognitive, emotional, behavioral, and social. It is also a time of significant vulnerability to life stress; negative family, peer, and neighborhood influences; and the development of mental illness, with around one in five youth showing signs of notable emotional/behavioral impairment (see Merikangas *et al.*, 2010; Romero *et al.*, 2014; Strang, Pruessner, & Pollack, 2011; Weist, Ginsburg, & Shafer, 1999).

The school mental health (SMH) field is growing around the world (Kutcher & McLuckie, 2013; President's New Freedom Commission, 2003; Rowling & Weist, 2004; Wei & Kutcher, 2012; Weist & McDaniel, 2013; Weist, Lever, Bradshaw, & Owens, 2014), related to fundamental recognition that: (1) children, adolescents, and families usually make no or very poor connections to specialty mental health (Atkins *et al.*, 1998; Catron, Harris, & Weiss, 1998); (2) schools are where children and youth are; and (3) many advantages accrue when education, mental health, and other youth-serving systems join together to better meet the mental health needs of students, in ways that reflect reducing and removing barriers to learning (Andis *et al.*, 2002; Weist, 1997). National and global networks are increasingly recognizing the centrality of the SMH agenda as reflected in increasing funding, growing training opportunities, key policy initiatives, and an advancing research base that involves localities, states, regions, and countries pursuing common themes. Sadly, in some countries this agenda is receiving increased support through school shootings and the concomitant recognition of students' need for mental health services and missed opportunities for early identification and intervention (United States White House, 2013).

A critically important agenda, and reflecting the public health approach (see Blau, Huang, & Mallery, 2010) is to develop a full continuum of effective promotion, prevention, early intervention, and treatment for adolescents in schools, and for this agenda to consider unique cultural, socioeconomic, and governmental factors as reflected in differences across nations. That is the purpose of this book, which we hope will spur advancements in research, practice, and policy in SMH for adolescents around the world.

In this regard, it should be noted that much of the literature on SMH reflects the experience of developed nations, and there is a need for global dialogue that includes the experience of low- and middle-income nations. For example, Wei and Kutcher (2012) emphasize that a challenge faced by many countries is to provide adequate human resources for delivery of essential mental health interventions, and in many nations, even in developed ones, these resources are not adequate. Given these realities, new strategies for SMH need to

School Mental Health: Global Challenges and Opportunities, ed. Stan Kutcher, Yifeng Wei and Marc D. Weist. Published by Cambridge University Press. © Cambridge University Press 2015.

be developed consistent with other strategies such as working in primary care and with other community-based programs (e.g., in recreation centers, through sports) and empowering and equipping non-specialist providers, such as healthcare workers, consumers of care, caregivers, teachers, and others with the skills to identify and assist youth with mental health challenges, as well as help to spur broader mental health promotion initiatives (Wei & Kutcher, 2012, Weare, 2004).

Related to these recognitions, international organizations including the United Nations, World Health Organization, World Federation for Mental Health, and the Global Consortium for Promotion and Prevention in Mental Health have endorsed the need for effective school mental health promotion and intervention (Vince-Whitman *et al.*, 2007). Beginning early in the 2000s, the International Alliance for Child and Adolescent Mental Health and Schools (INTERCAMHS) began to advance a global network for SMH, including national leaders from Australia, Canada, Germany, Great Britain, Ireland, Jamaica, and Norway. INTERCAMHS organized a series of global conferences on SMH promotion in conjunction with World Conferences for Mental Health Promotion led by the Clifford Beers Foundation and collaborators (see worldcongress2014.org) held in London (2002), Auckland (2004), Oslo (2006), Melbourne (2008), Washington, DC (2010), and Perth (2012).

Emerging from INTERCAMHS, the School Mental Health International Leadership Exchange (SMHILE) is bringing together leaders from regions and countries across the world to share knowledge; co-create dissemination and leadership strategies; and signal best research, policy, and practice directions for the field (Short, Weist, & McDaniel, 2014). SMHILE aims to offer a credible and authoritative international resource on topics related to SMH leadership, including a focus on workforce development; interdisciplinary and cross-system collaboration; family, student, and stakeholder involvement; implementation of evidence-based practices; and quality assurance. Working with the Clifford Beers Foundation, SMHILE coordinated a set of 30 presentations on SMH held at the Eighth World Conference on Mental Health Promotion held in London in September 2014, and is preparing an even larger program focused on SMH to be held at the Ninth World Conference to be held in Columbia, South Carolina in September 2015.

There are many issues being confronted across nations in the emerging SMH field. In addition to resource limitations reviewed above (Wei & Kutcher, 2012), a critical challenge is to convince policy makers of the value of mental health in schools. For example, school leaders may not support this agenda based on the view that schools are not in "the mental health business" and/or concern of taking on a responsibility that will be burdensome in terms of time and cost (Weist *et al.*, in press). In addition, education administrators uniformly endorse the value of academic success, but may not see the value of positive emotional/behavioral functioning in contributing to it (Klern & Connell, 2004).

In many nations, a significant problem is high variability in governmental approach and associated initiatives for children, adolescents, and families across jurisdictions and regions, contributing to a hodge-podge of experiences and programs that lack coherence. A challenge is that SMH initiatives should reflect local culture and characteristics, while moving to some level of uniformity and consistency. This is particularly difficult given site-based decision making and high organizational fluidity in schools; for example, as shown by high rates of mobility and turnover among administrators, teachers, and other school personnel (Guarino Santibañez, Daley, & Brewer, 2004). For the establishment and growth of effective SMH programs within nations, working agreements regarding roles, functions, and communication between mental health staff and schools typically need to be negotiated and maintained on a building-by-building basis (Weist *et al.*, in press). Further, as mentioned above, in some nations there will not be a mental health workforce, and the press will then become one of empowering others, such as teachers and healthcare providers, to attain skills to move this agenda forward (Wei & Kutcher, 2012). A very significant concern is limited resources in nations for education, let alone supportive programs and services for students in schools such as SMH. This is a monumental challenge in impoverished developing nations (see Chapter 17, detailing experiences in northern Ghana), and one that is present even in highly developed nations. For example, a survey of SMH programs in the United States (likely the global leader in this field) indicated that more than 70% of district leaders reported an increase in need for services, while experiencing funding levels that were actually decreasing (Foster *et al.*, 2005). This connects to a related social marketing agenda for SMH, for communities to rally around the message that this may be *the most important* set of actions to engage in, since effective mental health in schools is about promotion of positive emotional, behavioral, and social functioning; engagement in school; improved learning; and improved achievement and contribution to society (Kutcher & McLuckie, 2013; Weist *et al.*, 2014).

As some of the above policy-related challenges are navigated, schools, communities, and governments should focus on building capacity for effective SMH, including strategies for training, coaching, and ongoing implementation support, evidence-based practice, family and youth engagement and empowerment, quality assessment and improvement, assuring cultural competence, and evaluation (Fixsen, Naoom, Blasé, Friedman, & Wallace, 2005; Weist *et al.*, 2014). A major irony in the SMH field is that *when done well* – that is when programs pay significant attention to these dimensions – services actually lead to valued outcomes, including improved student behavior, emotional functioning, and academic performance, and positive evaluation findings can be used to leverage increased resources and capacity for the field (Weist, Evans, & Lever, 2003). However, many programs will not focus on these dimensions, continue to engage in reactive, ineffective practices, resulting in no change, and consequent failure to document positive outcomes and build policy support.

A way forward is for systematic sharing of experiences across communities, states/regions and nations, for example, through a National Community of Practice on SMH such as in the United States (Cashman, Rosser, & Linehan, 2013; Wenger, McDermott, & Snyder, 2002) and through SMHILE, mentioned earlier.

We are enthused to bring you this volume – *School Mental Health: Global Challenges and Opportunities*. The book builds from and amplifies themes from prior books on SMH (Clauss-Ehlers, Serpell, & Weist, 2013; Evans, Weist & Serpell, 2007; Robinson, 2004; Weist *et al.*, 2003; 2014) and is the first to emphasize international themes and experiences particularly relevant for adolescents. Chapters include those from developed nations and reflecting relatively advanced experiences in SMH (e.g., Chapter 2, Australia; Chapters 4, 5, and 6, Canada; Chapter 11, Ireland; Chapter 12, Israel; Chapter 16, New Zealand; Chapter 21, the United Kingdom; and Chapters 22 and 23, United States); from developed nations with more recent but growing initiatives (Chapters 13 and 14, Japan; Chapter 15, Chile; Chapter 18, Singapore; Chapter 19, Turkey); and programs that are just emerging in countries experiencing economic, sociodemographic, and/or racial/ethnic challenges (Chapter 3, Brazil; Chapters 7 and 8, China; Chapter 9, India; Chapter 10, Iraq; Chapter 17, northern Ghana; Chapter 20, Ukraine). Diverse themes in this book (reflecting some presented in this brief review and many others) underscore the potential for a global agenda for SMH for adolescents and strategies to move forward. As shown in all chapters of the book, this work is hard and challenging, but of the highest promise for adolescents and their families, schools, and other youth-serving systems.

References

Andis, P., Cashman, J., Praschil, R., Oglesby, D., Adelman, H., Taylor, L., & Weist, M. D. (2002). A strategic and shared agenda to advance mental health in schools through family and system partnerships. *International Journal of Mental Health Promotion*, 4, 28–35.

Atkins, M. S., McKay, M. M., Arvanitis, P., London, L., Madison, S., Costigan, C., Haney, M., Hess, L., Zevenbergen, A., & Bennett, D. (1998). An ecological model for school-based mental health services for urban low-income aggressive children. *The Journal of Behavioral Health Services & Research*, 25, 64–75.

Blau, G. M., Huang, L. N., & Mallery, C. J. (2010). Advancing efforts to improve children's mental health in America: A commentary. *Administration and Policy in Mental Health*, 37, 140–144.

Cashman, J., Rosser, M., & Linehan, P. (2013). Policy, practice, and people: Building shared support for school behavioral health. In S. Barrett, L. Eber, & M. Weist (Eds.), *Advancing education effectiveness: An interconnected systems framework for Positive Behavioral Interventions and Supports (PBIS) and school mental health* (pp. 96–112). Eugene, Oregon: University of Oregon Press.

Catron, T., Harris, V. S., & Weiss, B. (1998). Posttreatment results after 2 years of services in the Vanderbilt School-Based Counseling Project. In M. H. Epstein & K. Kutash (Eds.), *Outcomes for children and youth with emotional and behavioral disorders and their families: Programs and evaluation best practices.* (pp. 633–656). Austin, TX: PRO-ED, Inc.

Clauss-Ehlers, C., Serpell, Z., & Weist, M. D. (2013). *Handbook of culturally responsive school mental health: Advancing research, training, practice, and policy.* New York: Springer.

Evans, S. W., Weist, M. D., & Serpell, Z. (2007). *Advances in school-based mental health interventions: Best practices and program models* (Vol. II). New York: Civic Research Institute.

Fixsen, D. L., Naoom, S. F., Blasé, K. A., Friedman, R. M., & Wallace, F. (2005).

Implementation research: A synthesis of the literature. Tampa, FL: University of South Florida, Louis de la Parte Florida Mental Health Institute, The National Implementation Research Network.

Foster, S., Rollefson, M., Doksum, T., Noonan, D., Robinson, G., & Teich, J. (2005). *School mental health services in the United States 2002–2003.* Rockville, MD: Center for Mental Health Services, Substance Abuse and Mental Health Services Administration.

Guarino, C., Santibañez, L., Daley, G., & Brewer, D. (2004). *A review of the research literature on teacher recruitment and retention.* Santa Monica, CA: RAND Corporation.

Klern, A. M., & Connell, J. P. (2004). Relationships matter: Linking teacher support to student engagement and achievement. *School Mental Health*, 74, 262–273.

Kutcher, S., & McLuckie, A. (2013). Evergreen: Creating a child and youth mental health framework for Canada. *Psychiatric Services*, 64(5), 479–482.

Merikangas, K., He, J., Burstein, M., Swanson, S., Avenevoli, S., Cui, L., Benjet, C., Georgiades, K., & Swendsen, J. (2010). Lifetime prevalence of mental disorders in U.S. adolescents: Results from the National Comorbidity Survey Replication – Adolescent Supplement (NCS-A). *Journal of the American Academy of Child & Adolescent Psychiatry*, 49 (10). doi: 10.1016/j.jaac.2010.05.017

President's New Freedom Commission. (2003). *Achieving the promise: Transforming mental health care in America.* Washington, DC: President of the United States (http://govinfo.lib rary.unt.edu/mentalhealthcommission/reports/ reports.htm, accessed July 3, 2014)

Robinson, R. (Ed.). (2004). *Advances in school-based mental health interventions: Best practices and program models* (1st ed.). Kingston, NJ: Civic Research Institute.

Romero, C., Master, A., Paunesku, D., Dweck, C. S., & Gross, J. J. (2014). Academic and emotional functioning in middle school: The role of implicit theories. *Emotion*, 14(2), 227–234.

Rowling, L., & Weist, M. D. (2004). Promoting the growth, improvement and sustainability of school mental health programs worldwide. *International Journal of Mental Health Promotion*, 6, 3–11.

Short, K., Weist, M. D., & McDaniel, H (2014). The School Mental Health International Leadership Exchange: First foundations. Unpublished manuscript.

Strang, N. M., Pruessner, J., & Pollak, S. D. (2011). Developmental changes in adolescents' neural response to challenge. *Developmental Cognitive Neuroscience*, 1(4), 560–569.

United States Whitehouse. (2013). *Now is the time: The President's plan to protect our children and our communities by reducing gun violence*. Washington, DC: President of the United States (www.whitehouse.gov/now-is-the-time, accessed July 3, 2014).

Vince-Whitman, C., Belfer, M., Oommen, M., Murphy, S., Moore, E., & Weist, M. D. (2007). The role of international organizations to promote school-based mental health. In S. Evans, M. Weist, & Z. Serpell (Eds.), *Advances in school-based mental health interventions* (pp. 22:1–22:14). New York: Civic Research Institute.

Weare, K. (2004). The International Alliance for Child and Adolescent Mental Health and Schools (INTERCAMHS). *Health Education*, 104(2), 65–67.

Wei, Y., & Kutcher, S. (2012). International school mental health: Global approaches, global challenges, and global opportunities. *Child and Adolescent Psychiatric Clinics of North America*, 21(1), 11–27.

Weist, M. D. (1997). Expanded school mental health services: A national movement in progress. In T. H. Ollendick & R. J. Prinz (Eds.), *Advances in clinical child psychology* (pp. 319–352). New York: Plenum.

Weist, M. D., Evans, S. W., & Lever, N. (2003). *Handbook of school mental health: Advancing practice and research*. New York: Kluwer Academic/Plenum Publishers.

Weist, M. D., Flaherty, L. T., Lever, N., Stephan, S., Van Eck, K., & Albright, A. (in press). The history and future of school mental health. In S. Evans, B. Schultz, & J. Harrison (Eds.), *School mental health services for adolescents*. New York: Oxford University Press.

Weist, M. D., Ginsburg, G. S., & Shafer, M. (1999). Progress in adolescent mental health. *Adolescent Medicine: State of the Art Reviews*, 10, 165–174.

Weist, M. D., Lever, N., Bradshaw, C., & Owens, J. (2014). *Handbook of school mental health: Research, training, practice, and policy*, (2nd ed.). New York: Springer.

Weist, M. D., & McDaniel, H. L. (2013). The international emphasis of Advances in School Mental Health Promotion. *Advances in School Mental Health Promotion*, 6, 81–82.

Wenger, E., McDermott, R., & Snyder, W. (2002). *Cultivating communities of practice: A guide to managing knowledge*. Boston, MA: Harvard Business School Press.

Developing and sustaining mental health and wellbeing in Australian schools

2

Louise Rowling

Introduction

This chapter documents the evolution of a suite of mental health promotion interventions designed and implemented nationally over a 15-year period. Three noteworthy themes that emerged from this work are: the critical role of the implementation context; the linking of school mental health and educational research and practice; and the utilization of a public health approach.

In the 1990s in Australia, significant mental health reform began at a national level. The first two national mental health plans involved a shift in thinking about mental health service delivery from institutionalized care to supporting individuals in the community, and included recognition of the need for increasing attention to be given to promoting mental health and preventing mental illness (Parham, 2007). The first National Mental Health Plan (Australian Health Ministers [AHM] 1992) had as some of its priorities: consumer rights; the relationship between mental health services and the general health sector; linking mental health services with other sectors; and a service mix. However, the plan acknowledged that treatment interventions alone could not significantly reduce the burden of mental illness and that prevention and promotion approaches were important. The Second National Mental Health Plan (AHM, 1998) had three priority areas: promotion and prevention; partnerships in service reform and delivery; and quality and effectiveness. However, it was widely recognized there was little understanding within the mental health sector about how to progress this agenda (Parham, 2007). The national-level policy making included multi-disciplinary debate and discussion around areas of policy and practice such as identifying areas of focus: including promoting wellbeing of populations; promoting mental health of individuals with existing mental health problems; intervening early to promote mental health and prevent mental health problems; developing population approaches to improve the mental health status of all; as well as developing appropriate strategies to ensure that all of these domains are addressed (Walker and Rowling, 2007). The re-conceptualization of mental health from an illness perspective to a positive concept of resilience and wellbeing was also a challenge, given that professional groups were trained to focus on risk and disease. To address this, the Australian government established the National Promotion and Prevention Working Party to guide and oversee the development of a National Action Plan for Promotion, Prevention and Early Intervention for Mental Health. The Working Party consisted of representatives from key groups leading the mental health and public health sectors in Australia at that time. This collaboration between sectors was an important step

School Mental Health: Global Challenges and Opportunities, ed. Stan Kutcher, Yifeng Wei and Marc D. Weist. Published by Cambridge University Press. © Cambridge University Press 2015.

recognizing that the mental health sector alone could not achieve desired outcomes (Parham, 2007). Additional discussions focused on the aims of actions to be taken. Should the focus be on building resilience at the individual level, or should we be concerned with altering social and economic environments and in so doing focus on the prevention of illness at its source? In addition, if we are to build resilience while at the same time addressing the environments that impact negatively on health, then which professions have a role to play in this work? The resultant framework addressed a spectrum of required policies, programs, organizations, and workforce development in order to promote mental health and prevent escalating levels of mental illness, as well as identify the range of required services.

This breadth of national mental health policy development that included mental health promotion was a unique characteristic of the Australian focus. Capacity mapping for mental health promotion in four European countries in early 2000 did not find this breadth of action (Jané-Llopis and Anderson, 2005). While these researchers did identify policies about mental health, it was established that mental health promotion was less a priority than the policies indicated, with low levels of resources available in all but one of the countries. For young people, within this policy and strategic approach, concern has not only been about service provision, but early intervention, awareness-raising promotion, and prevention. Additionally, unlike many other countries' approaches, mental health promotion focusing on mental health and wellbeing (rather than mental illness) for populations as well as individuals, has been an integral component. This expands the more traditional clinical service models to actions that address whole populations, settings, and determinants of mental health and wellbeing.

A number of key themes will be interwoven through this chapter, which explores the multidisciplinary theoretical and empirical frameworks that have been utilized to guide planning, implementation, and evaluation in Australia. These themes – context, linking school mental health and educational research and practice, implementation, and a public health population approach – together helped to establish a new science base for school mental health promotion and contribute to sustainability of actions. Important national government-funded school mental health interventions will be described to exemplify significant issues.

Context

There are a variety of ways of conceptualizing context as it applies to school mental health. These include reference to surroundings, circumstances, environment, and background, or settings which determine, specify, or clarify meaning (wiktionary [http://en.wiktionary.org/wiki/context]). Context is an important consideration in implementation. A focus on the support context addresses structures, strategies, and practices that stimulate smooth and efficient implementation of actions and activities (Weiner *et al.*, 2009). The following brief review of the contexts within which early school mental health promotion was initiated places national initiatives within a specific disciplinary culture and practices.

Political, social, and psychological environments

The Australian political structural context involves a federation of states and territories. Education and health are shared responsibilities between state and commonwealth (national) level. National programs need to gain the "buy in" of state jurisdictions to ensure successful implementation. Many health and social problems have been found to be connected, so addressing mental health has impacts wider than for the health sector. For example, in the early 1990s these links were obvious in etiological data internationally that show connections between factors that affect mental health and factors associated with crime (National Crime Prevention, 1999), drug abuse (Resnick *et al.*, 1997) and academic achievement (Zubrick *et al.*, 1997). These factors include school attendance, connectedness to school and community, and opportunities for success at school. The resultant multidisciplinary foci involving varying ideologies, language and practice means mental health can be the purview of other disciplinary areas (Rowling, 2002). In this context the horizontal linking of practice, research, and development of policy, benefits from drawing on the different sectors' perspectives (Rowling and Taylor, 2005). Horizontal linking involves creating ties between equals – for example health sector research on policy development and implementation, and educational in the same areas. It can also link mental health with the health, education, employment, social welfare, justice, and family sectors. Additionally, a World Health Organization mental health report (WHO, 2004) recommended that programs should address multiple outcomes. One aspect of practice that was emphasized in Australian national policy was the role of consumers in decision-making about policy and their own care. These understandings were important elements for the development of effective interventions to maximize the connections of the preventive actions with young people's lives. This was consistent with the approach recommended by Durlak and Wells (1997), recognizing that mental health and mental disorders need to be conceptualized within communities of care and support, not solely as an individual's problem.

This emphasis continued. In early 2000 this need for partnership development was being utilized in the implementation of prevention programs in the United States. Ialongo (2002) argued for partnerships with those organizations for whom programs were designed and who would be responsible for their ongoing implementation. Further, prevention programs (see review by Greenberg *et al.*, 2001) that focused individually on the child were not as effective as those that simultaneously focused on the child, the school, and the family. Additionally, school health promotion research of the 1990s consistently found that greatest impact on pupils' health was achieved by a comprehensive approach (e.g., Olweus, 1995).

This contextual description provides an outline of the political, social, and psychological environments that formed the theoretical and empirical base to the conceptualization of school mental health promotion and prevention. This focus on the need to understand and engage with young people and their contexts for quality school mental health promotion established that using research on educational change as a theoretical and empirical base would be required.

Creating a new science base for school mental health promotion

Linking school mental health with educational change

The second theme that is interwoven into this chapter is the health–education nexus that has increasingly come to be utilized in assessing outcomes for school mental health (see Dix *et al.*, 2012). A complex dynamic of group behaviors and system changes operates within a school by staff and students, in collaboration with external stakeholders. Recent work on school health promotion has highlighted how critical an understanding of the complexity of quality practice in education is to school health programs (Samdal and Rowling, 2013).

Hoyle *et al.* (2010) have called for a re-focus, from getting support for health programs to "finding the niche of the [mental] health promotion process in on-going school improvement efforts" (p. 165). From this perspective the ultimate health-promoting aim of increased subjective wellbeing and behaviors conducive to health is not only an end-point, but also a premise for educational aims and educators (Samdal and Rowling, 2013). Recently a World Health Organization report (Suhrcke and de Paz Nieves, 2011) highlighted this need to shift perspective from seeing improved health as a product of education to seeing it as a factor that could determine educational outcomes. Subjective wellbeing may in this perspective be seen as an important prerequisite for learning and academic achievement in school (Basch, 2010).

It is only in the last few years that the importance of utilizing educational research about schools changing to promote teaching and learning for academic achievement combined with improving health outcomes, has been accepted as a key focus area. Prior to this, much health promotion implementation was designed from a health behavior change perspective, without any link or motivation to improve student academic performance in school (Valois *et al.*, 2011).

The gradual shift in approaches that has followed now involves research building on the premises and acknowledgment of: educational aims; school as an institution in constant change; and the development of integrating the principles of empowerment and participation in health promotion, to simultaneously promote both health and learning (Samdal and Rowling, 2013). This nexus between health and education disciplinary bases is a crucial element in the take-up by schools of interventions and their sustainability. The outcome involves building on existing school policies and activities, not treating schools as a vacuum for interventions.

Implementation

The third key theme is implementation. In considering the breadth of population groups (e.g., students, their teachers and parents, and health personnel), organizational systems (e.g., schools, mental health services, educational services) and the different epistemological positions of the health and education sectors about how to bring about and measure health behavior change, the complexity of implementation for school mental health becomes evident.

The population health approach for schools is operationalized as a "settings" approach to health promotion, namely health-promoting schools (WHO, 1998), and healthy schools (Department for Education and Employment (DfEE) and Department of Health, 1999). The importance of a whole-school approach is evident in addressing wellbeing which involves "mapping the whole of life and considering each life event or social context that has the potential to affect the quality of individual lives or the cohesion of society" (Trewin, 2001: 6).

For nearly two decades schools in Australia, Canada, England, Scotland, and other parts of Europe have been implementing a settings approach to school health, creating health-promoting schools. However, quality implementation has not been achieved despite the development of guidelines and indicators (Samdal and Rowling, 2011). This was the implementation context within which school mental health promotion was initiated in Australia. Implementation issues of acknowledging educational aims; seeing schools as institutions in constant change; and integrating the principles of empowerment and participation emerge as important influencing factors in school mental health promotion implementation in Australian national strategies (see descriptions in "A review of nationally funded Australian interventions" below).

Public health approach

A fourth theme in this chapter is one which globally was quite unique in the early 1990s, that the national policy makers took a public health perspective. The influence of public health is evident in the policy framework. The conceptual framework embraces a social view of health including defining mental health in terms of wellbeing, and articulating the social and economic determinants that influence mental health. Public health policy supports a health-promotion framework which emphasizes that health is created within the settings of everyday life (i.e., family, school, workplace, community); thereby locating mental health within a holistic framework of health (Parham, 2007). The underlying principle is that mental health is integral to overall health and therefore has universal relevance. Rather than a sole focus on prevention of specific health problems through teaching, or for mental health, through short-term interventions for at-risk young people, school health promotion in recent years has come to focus on the whole-school community.

Taken together the themes of context, health and education nexus, implementation and public health approach can inform a new science base for school mental health promotion.

A review of nationally funded Australian interventions

Australia's innovations in school mental health promotion and prevention over 15 years illustrate essential elements of a quality planning, implementation, evaluation, and dissemination of school mental health promotion and prevention. One of the first challenges in the 1990s was deciding on the language to be used, mental health (which was synonymous with mental illness and carried a great deal of stigma) or wellbeing. Program developers decided that while the use of the term mental health with its connotation of mental illness might present a barrier to implementation in school settings, de-stigmatizing language and concepts was viewed as an important and necessary process in awareness-raising among school personnel and parents.

Within the public health mental health policy context of partnerships, population health and mental health as positive concepts, a number of national initiatives were funded, including for school mental health promotion, MindMatters (Rowling, 2007). The MindMatters initiative began in 1997, and drew upon the then current knowledge about exemplary practice in education, including student engagement and alienation (Cumming, 1996); strategies need to "fit" the "growth" state of a particular school (Hopkins *et al.*, 1997); adequacy of implementation time (Huberman and Miles, 1984); variability of schools to engage in innovation (Fullan and Steigelbauer, 1991); building teacher efficacy (Ross *et al.*, 1996); and the research finding that varying support strategies are needed at different stages of school change (Hopkins *et al.*, 1997). This knowledge influenced the decisions about the curriculum, the professional development and the format of the trialing of the materials, although some decisions, such as the period of time available for trialing materials, were determined by the funding body.

MindMatters

MindMatters is a unique example of long-term implementation of school mental health and wellbeing promotion, prevention, and early intervention. It has broken new ground in a number of ways. In just over a decade, it has contributed to changing how mental health and wellbeing is addressed in secondary schools across Australia. The MindMatters materials provided the first comprehensive whole-school approach to the promotion of mental health globally and for young Australians (Wyn *et al.*, 2000). The initial trial materials were developed in consultation with a team of practicing teacher and mental health professionals during 1997. The year-long national implementation pilot occurred in 1998. Schools identified their areas of concern and priority for attention as part of this audit. Each school had a member of the project team who acted as their "critical friend," supporting them to implement specific elements they had chosen to trial and give feedback on.

From a mental health perspective, while it was recognized that a 12-month trial was too short a time frame to measure mental health outcomes, one of the key desired aims of the funding body was that no harm should result from this trial. This represented the fear by mental health professionals of other sectors' involvement in the psychology field. Interestingly, "do no harm" has been identified as a criterion to demonstrate efficacy before larger scale dissemination (Flay *et al.*, 2005). For the education sector the shift to a health-promotion approach for school mental health involved a re-shaping of roles for teachers and a re-conceptualization of partnerships with the mental health sector from being the recipient of programs developed by outsiders to approaches based on school community involvement and ownership. At a school level it required teachers being:

1. convinced of the link between the mental health of students, connectedness to school, and academic achievement;
2. provided with the training and resources to recognize their role and enhance and refine their work to include whole-school change for mental health and wellbeing.

The implementation of MindMatters was grounded in the understanding that the professional development of teachers is fundamental to the success of any innovation (Fullan and Steigelbauer, 1991). Additionally, the approach taken in MindMatters focuses on the importance of the organizational structures, the social environment, and the individual within this context. MindMatters implementation can be distinguished from single-topic health education projects because it places mental health within the core educational business of schools rather than identifying it as a "health topic." This marks a significant shift away from approaches that emphasize individual deficits of young people, and individually focused behavior-change models (Sheehan *et al.*, 2002).

The curriculum materials are based on the understanding that young people need to engage actively with ideas and concepts in order to learn. The classroom materials frequently place the student at the center of activities, positioning the teachers as a facilitator. Many of the sessions use experiential and interactive teaching strategies to promote learning and skills development. Guided discussion is used to assist students to move from an experiential to a reflective mode. Discussion and processing of the activity assists students to develop concepts and language with which to further examine and share their experience and to move to a level of conceptualization and awareness which would be difficult without a concrete or experiential base.

Given the political context of states and territories, a strategic action for the implementation of the pilot and the wider dissemination was a genuine attempt to involve and consult state education and health sectors and systems. For MindMatters to be successful, engagement and ownership needed to occur at different levels – individual, school, principal and other school leaders, state and territory jurisdictions and sectors (Rowling and Hazell, in press). In the pilot an important criterion for inclusion was the commitment of the school to addressing mental health education and promotion, through the identification of a team of staff who would take responsibility for the project, including the school principal.

In terms of health-promotion outcomes (Nutbeam, 2000) the one-year trial demonstrated that intermediate health promotion outcomes of health literacy, social action and influence, healthy public policy, and organizational practice had been achieved. The implementation findings of the intervention trial of MindMatters (Wyn *et al.*, 2000) revealed that:

- the support of the school executive was critical;
- professional development to build the capacity of teachers was essential;
- the trial materials were relevant and easy to use, and supported both classroom and whole-school activity;
- schools were able to form good links with local service providers;
- schools had difficulties implementing a whole-school approach; and
- the health-promoting schools framework matched current practices in schools.

But the success of MindMatters was questioned in that mental health outcomes had not been demonstrated in the 12-month trial. This represents one of the dilemmas for school mental health promotion, "the lack of acceptance that intermediate mental health promotion outcomes such as capacity building, policy development, improved curriculum, better relationships and closer partnerships are legitimate, measurable, and can be linked to more enduring mental health outcomes" (Sheehan *et al.*, 2007: 125).

National dissemination of MindMatters to secondary schools began in 2000. An evaluation survey conducted by the Australian Council of Educational Research (ACER) in 2010 a decade later found that there was significant reach:

- 98% of schools are aware of MindMatters;
- 68% of schools use a core team to implement MindMatters;
- 65% of schools use MindMatters as a curriculum resource;
- 38% of schools use MindMatters as a key organizer for mental health promotion (ACER, 2010).

In terms of efficacy, of 15 trial schools 13 continued to use MindMatters after the study's three years of implementation. Of these, ten have a substantial investment in MindMatters reflected in formal curriculum or policy documents or new structures (www.mindmatters. edu.au/about/evaluation/evaluation_key_findings.html).

Mental health outcomes were measured for cohorts of students. In general, a pattern of improvement was detected across the schools at the three-year assessment relative to baseline on the Healthy Kids Survey domains of "autonomy experience," "school attachment," and "effective help seeking." This meant that the students themselves reported higher levels of connection to school (being cared about and reinforced for positive achievements), higher levels of involvement in decision making (class activities, making a positive difference), and higher levels of knowledge about who to access for help about their problems, than did their counterparts in equivalent year levels prior to the implementation of MindMatters (Rowling and Hazell, in press).

MindMatters continues to reach all school systems and sectors of schooling, with professional learning being accessed by 2678 (83%) schools with secondary enrolments across Australia to date (www.mindmatters.edu.au). A revision of MindMatters based on the evaluation findings (Rowling and Hazell, in press) occurred after about seven years of implementation. The implementation of the whole-school approach was strengthened by representing the way that schools were implementing the materials by the creation of an implementation model (www.mindmatters.edu.au/diagrams/implementation_model/implementationModel-v2.pdf)

An additional strategy to identify pathways of care in school communities, MindMatters+, was implemented from 2002. It focused on the capacity of secondary schools to support students with high needs in the area of mental health. In particular it involved early identification of students with mental health needs, implementation of preventative interventions, policies, and strategies to support students at risk, and encouraging the development of community partnerships to enhance the support of student wellbeing (Anderson, 2005). An index of programs was prepared (see http://mhws.agca.com.au) and professional learning experiences provided for school staff, school-based psychologists, and other support staff (Anderson and Doyle, 2005).

Following the successful uptake by schools of MindMatters and MindMatters+, national funding was made available to develop and trial a resource for primary schools, KidsMatter, followed by materials for Early Childhood, KidsMatter Early Childhood.

KidsMatter

A whole-school implementation framework was utilized during the 2007 and 2008 trial of KidsMatter (KM), a primary school mental health promotion, prevention, and early intervention (PPEI) initiative. A guided process and key resources were used within a four-component framework of: a positive school community; social and emotional learning for students; parenting support and education; and early intervention for students experiencing mental health difficulties (Graetz *et al.*, 2008). A carefully designed implementation process was planned. It included ensuring that staff have a sense of ownership by their participation at all stages of planning and implementation; active support and involvement from school leadership; providing staff with professional learning; follow-up support to develop their skills and confidence in implementing the initiative effectively; and flexibility so that the initiative could be tailored to the specific needs of each school (Graetz *et al.*, 2008).

A variety of resources were available to trial schools: an implementation manual; school audit tools; a programs guide of "programs/packages" that schools can access on each component; state/territory project officers to deliver professional development and provide ongoing support; professional development packages; information sheets for parents and carers; resource packs with additional information and links to support services; and school-based funding, with the amount based on pupil enrolment numbers.

The evaluation involved surveys including teachers and parents/caregivers and assessment of students' mental health using the Strengths and Difficulties Questionnaire (SDQ). It demonstrated positive changes to schools, teachers, parents/caregivers, and children over the two-year trial, using evidence of change related to all four components of the KM framework. A statistically and practically significant improvement in students' mental health (in terms of reduced mental health difficulties and increased mental health strengths) was measured, the impact of KM being more apparent for students who were rated as having higher levels of mental health difficulties at the start of the trial. In particular, students in the abnormal and borderline ranges showed significant improvements over the period of the KM trial with medium-term effect sizes for mental health strengths for students in the abnormal range, and small effect sizes for students in the borderline range (Slee *et al.*, 2009).

In terms of implementation, most progress was made in the area of social and emotional learning for students, and least progress was made in the area of parenting support, education, and early intervention for students. Data on teacher efficacy for school mental health over four time periods were collected. They showed increases in the teachers' ratings of their knowledge, competence, and confidence with respect to teaching students about social and emotional competencies. Data were also collected over four time periods for parents. They showed a small increase in the number of parents who strongly agreed that they had become more involved with the school as a result of KM and had increased their capacity to help their children with social and emotional issues as a result of KM (Slee *et al.*, 2009).

The researchers noted a number of potential limitations, including:

- the challenging role of leadership, particularly transformative leadership, in bringing about change in attitudes, beliefs, and behavior in the school community;
- sustainability of a KM-type intervention was recognized by the school personnel doing the implementing, particularly in the ability of the implementing team to maintain support and provision of resources (Slee *et al.*, 2009).

KidsMatter Early Childhood

KidsMatter Early childhood (KMEC) is a national mental health PPEI initiative specifically designed for early childhood services. It involves the personnel who have a significant influence on young children's lives, and includes families and early childhood professionals, along with a range of community and health professionals, who come together to make a positive difference for young children's mental health during this important developmental period (Slee *et al.*, 2012)

Close attention was paid to monitoring the implementation of KMEC. An Implementation Index was developed for the purpose of this evaluation, based upon the initial work undertaken for the KidsMatter Primary Implementation Index (Dix *et al.*, 2010; Slee *et al.*, 2009). This used the theoretical framework of Domitrovich (2008) and three categories – fidelity, dosage, and quality of delivery (Slee *et al.*, 2012: 18). A range of factors were identified as facilitating the KMEC initiative and were used in the Implementation Index, including leadership, engagement with the initiative, support structures, and links with external agencies. For example, in Quality of Delivery respondents were asked "How effective has the leadership team been in leading the implementation of KMEC at this Early Childhood Service?"

The framework utilized for KMEC involved four components:

1. Creating a sense of community: promoting feelings of belonging, connectedness, and inclusion for all children and families.
2. Developing children's social and emotional skills: children with these skills find it easier to manage themselves, relate to others, resolve conflict, and feel positive about themselves and the world around them.
3. Working with parents and carers: engaging with parents and carers allows early childhood services to act as an access point for information about parenting, child development and mental health, and to share information about the child's experiences and activities.

4. Helping children who are experiencing mental health difficulties: due to the significant contact early childhood services have with children and their families, services are in an effective position to identify problems early, implement strategies to assist the child, and support their family to seek additional help (Slee *et al.*, 2012).

The implementation was guided by facilitators who worked with services to implement the framework delivering professional learning related to each of the four components in KMEC, visiting services to assist and guide early childhood education, and care staff work through the service's action plan. Professional learning was presented to each service, giving them opportunities to identify their service's strengths. In addition, each KMEC pilot service was supplied with a number of evidence-based resources to assist services in promoting early childhood mental health and wellbeing, and to respond to mental health needs of the children within their care.

KMEC facilitators reported three main factors as supporting effective implementation:

1. Leadership: where the leadership was strong and focused on the initiative.
2. Staff engagement: where the staff were engaged and motivated regarding the initiative.
3. Staff commitment: where the staff had a strong belief in and commitment to enhancing the mental health of children.

The use of the implementation index strengthened the researchers' ability to associate significant changes in services over the two years with the impact of the KMEC initiative. Implementation quality was shown to be an important influence on outcomes, with the main factor influencing this implementation quality being the percentage of single-parent families in a service (Slee *et al.*, 2012). Socioeconomic disadvantage can mitigate parent connection to school so additional ways of engaging and working with them may be needed.

This brief review of these interventions demonstrates the building of political support and the evaluation expertise that has occurred as each initiative has been planned and implemented. Evaluators have taken on the challenge of the complexity of school mental health promotion and prevention, and developed designs and tools to assess both quality implementation and mental health and educational outcomes.

Response-Ability

In the implementation of MindMatters in the 1990s it became evident that resources were needed for tertiary institutions who were training teachers. The Australian government funded the Hunter Institute of Mental Health (HIMH [www.himh.org.au/home]) to develop resources – entitled Response-Ability – for pre-service training of school teachers in tertiary institutions regarding mental health issues in children and young people (see more at: www.responseability.org/home/about-response-ability). People who are training to work in schools need to know about the key principles and practices they can adopt to support positive mental health and learning outcomes. Key messages for pre-service teachers included promoting resilience and wellbeing in all students, identifying students experiencing difficulties and helping them to access appropriate counseling or support options, and safeguarding the wellbeing of themselves and colleagues (Kemp *et al.*, 2007). By 1997 innovative Australian-designed multimedia resources were widely available for tertiary educators and their students, with ongoing support from staff of HIMH. Building on this work a recent resource is a six-page teacher's guide to social and emotional wellbeing, which provides frameworks, factual information, and case studies, as well as material that engages the reader in thinking through the situations they encounter. The framework uses the acronym CHILD:

Create safe and supportive environments that promote wellbeing, personal development, and learning.

Help children and young people to develop effective social and emotional skills and manage their behavior.

Identify children, young people, and families who may need additional support for their mental health and wellbeing.

Link children, young people, and families who may need additional support for their mental health and wellbeing.

Develop broader organizational, school community strategies to support wellbeing.

(See www.responseability.org/__data/assets/pdf_file/0009/4878/SEW-A-Teachers-Guide. pdf.)

A flow chart assists readers with problem solving to help children and young people who come to their attention. Teacher wellbeing is also addressed with suggestions for personal and professional strategies for maintaining wellbeing.

A more recent development linked to the KMEC project focuses on the needs of Children's Services Educators. While there are commonalities with the teacher's guide for schools, there are some specific areas focused on the needs of these service providers. For example, areas for their consideration about young children include: failure to reach developmental milestones; poor-quality play that seems limited and repetitive; being anxious, withdrawn, fearful, or upset much of the time; and not talking or communicating appropriately (consider culture and language at home). In this guide greater attention is also paid to family and community contexts such as: parenting styles that are overly controlling, harsh, or critical, or where there is inconsistent supervision; parental/caregiver lack of involvement in children's health, activities, or development; experiences of physical, sexual, or emotional abuse, neglect, or trauma; or unresolved loss and grief and mental illness in a carer (www.responseability.org/__data/assets/pdf_file/0007/4885/Educators-Guide-for-the-website.pdf).

Sustainability

This review of nationally funded initiatives includes the recent KMEC, as well as over a decade of work with MindMatters. The sustainability of MindMatters is a significant achievement. As expertise in schools grows about the importance of school mental health promotion and prevention, new areas for professional development arise. A key strategy by the national government in 2000 was to entrust the dissemination of MindMatters to a national professional principal's association, acknowledging the key role of the school leadership as drivers of sustainability (Fullan and Steigelbauer, 1991).

Sustainability needs to be planned from the start and maintained throughout a minimum of a decade to ensure lasting organizational change (Samdal and Rowling, 2013). The issue of sustainability has arisen within a number of the initiatives reported in this chapter. To contribute to ongoing review, support and action within schools, an awards system has been initiated within MindMatters. The recognition as a "MindMatters School" process is designed to acknowledge schools and school leaders who are working in focused and strategic ways to improve student mental health and learning outcomes using the

MindMatters framework. The recognition process has been in place since 2010. For schools to achieve MindMatters recognition, they have undertaken and evaluated a whole-school approach to mental health and wellbeing over an extended period of time, fulfilling detailed criteria. Some examples of actions that enable a school to fulfill requirements as a MindMatters Schools include the following:

- Leadership builds a framework for maintaining student and staff mental health and wellbeing.
- The school's strategic plan articulates a commitment and intended strategies to build and maintain mental health.
- A core team develops an action plan for a whole-school approach to mental health. Data are collected and continuously used to inform actions, monitor progress, and report to stakeholders.
- Processes are used to select and implement appropriate professional learning for staff, including dissemination of knowledge and skills.
- Communication and relationships across the entire school community are positive, respectful, and health promoting.
- Resources (personnel, time, finances, and physical space) are identified and allocated in ways that build and maintain mentally healthy students.
- Teaching and learning practices engage students in learning to build and maintain mental health and wellbeing as well as improve academic outcomes.
- Student social and emotional needs are considered along with learning, e.g., through pastoral care, mentoring.
- Schools have respectful, active, and visible engagement and partnerships with families and community – in and outside the school.
- Partnerships and pathways with external agencies are established to provide services, referrals and feedback (www.mindmatters.edu.au/whole_school_approach/mindmatters_recognition_and_overview/recognition_as_a_mindmatters_school.html).

These requirements, if they are effectively implemented, create and sustain contexts that are conducive to quality school mental health promotion.

The research to practice dilemma has been recently identified in the KMEC review. The report noted that the sustainability of an effective KMEC initiative in other locations would depend to a substantial extent on the maintenance of the levels of support and resources associated with this pilot (Slee *et al.*, 2012). This concern could be an outcome of the lack of consideration of sustainability of a program at the implementation design stage.

Conclusion

A number of key themes are reiterated through this chapter. Assessing the impact of health interventions has suffered from the lack of quality implementation (Domitrovich and Greenberg, 2000; Durlak and DuPre, 2008; Samdal and Rowling 2013). The links between mental health outcomes and educational outcomes is of growing interest (Slee *et al.*, 2009; Dix *et al.*, 2012). Earlier in this chapter the use of an implementation index in the evaluation of the impact of KidsMatter was noted. It was able to differentiate high- and low-implementing schools with respect to the development of social-emotional competencies (Slee *et al.*, 2009). However as Dix *et al.* (2012) point out, the evaluation did not examine the social and emotional competencies upon academic achievement, nor control for the impact of family socioeconomic status. This gap was addressed in an analysis using results from the Australian National Assessment Program – Literacy and Numeracy (NAPLAN) (ACARA, 2008). The analysis showed that schools that implemented KidsMatter well also had improved learning outcomes for students, equivalent to six months' more schooling by Year 7, over and above any influence of socioeconomic background.

As described at the beginning of this chapter, whole-school approaches in health-promoting schools had been utilized for a number of years as quality health-promotion implementation. A great deal has been learnt in the Australian school mental health promotion described in this chapter. It resonates with a recent framework of eight components for whole-school actions (Samdal and Rowling, 2013). This evidence-based framework for school health implementation was developed from a meta-analysis of health-promoting schools implementation. The framework consists of eight core components identified as (1) preparing and planning for school development; (2) policy and institutional anchoring; (3) professional development and learning; (4) leadership and management practices; (5) relational and organizational support context; (6) student participation; (7) partnership and networking; and (8) sustainability.

Utilizing this work to develop measures on quality implementation holds promise for future research and evaluation. This chapter has described the specific Australian context, although, as can be seen throughout, it is also firmly grounded in global educational and school mental health action.

References

ACARA (2008). *National report: Achievement in reading, writing, language conventions and numeracy*. Canberra; MCEECDYA. Retrieved 16 September 2013 from www.naplan. edu.au/verve/_resources/2ndStageNationalRepor t_18Dec_v2.pdf

ACER (Australian Council for Educational Research) (2010). *MindMatters evaluation report*, Camberwell: ACER. Retrieved 16 September 2013 from: www.mindmatters.edu.au/about/ evaluation/acer_evaluation_2010.html.

AHM (Australian Health Ministers) (1992). *First national mental health plan*, Department of Health. Retrieved 8 March 2014 from: www.health.gov.au/internet/publications

AHM (1998). *Second national mental health plan*, Department of Health and Family Services, Commonwealth of Australia. Retrieved from: www.mhnocc.org/resources/national_out comes_and_casemix_collection/plan2.pdf

Anderson, S. (2005). Key factors in supporting students with high needs in mental health: discussions with the MindMatters Plus demonstration schools. *Australian Journal of Guidance &Counselling*, 15:2, 214–219.

Anderson, S. and Doyle, M. (2005). Intervention and prevention programs to support student mental health: the literature and examples from the MindMatters Plus initiative. *Australian Journal of Guidance & Counselling*, 15:2, 220–227.

Basch, C. E. (2010) *Healthier students are better learners: A missing link in school reforms to close the achievement gap*. Equity Matters: Research Review No. 6. Retrieved 10 November 2011 from: www.equitycampaign.org/i/a/document/ 12557_EquityMattersVol6_Web03082010.pdf

Cumming, J. (1996). *From alienation to engage-ment: Opportunities for reform in the middle years of schooling*. Belconnen, ACT: Australian Curriculum Studies Association.

Department for Education and Employment and Department of Health (1999). *National healthy school standards*, London: Department for Education and Employment.

Dix, K. L., Keeves, J. P., Slee, P. T., *et al.*, (2010). *KidsMatter primary evaluation technical report and user guide*. Adelaide: Shannon Research Press.

Dix, K. L., Slee, P. T., Lawson, M. J., *et al.*, (2012). Implementation quality of whole-school mental health promotion and students' academic performance. *Child and Adolescent Mental Health*, 17: 45–51. doi: 10.1111/j.1475-3588.2011.00608.

Domitrovich, C. E. (2008). Maximizing the implementation quality of evidence-based preventive interventions in schools: a conceptual framework. *Advances in School Mental Health promotion*, 1, 6–28.

Domitrovich, C. E. and Greenberg, M. T. (2000). The study of implementation: current findings from effective programs that prevent mental disorders in school-aged children. *Journal of Educational and Psychological Consultation*, 11, 193–221.

Durlak, J. A. and DuPre, E. P. (2008). Implementation matters: A review of research on the influence of implementation on program outcomes and the factors affecting implementation. *American Journal of Community Psychology*, 41:3–4, 327–350.

Durlak, J. A. and Wells, A. M. (1997). Primary prevention mental health programs for children and adolescents: A meta-analytic review. *American Journal of Community Psychology*, 25:2, 115–152.

Flay, B. R., Biglan, A., Boruch, R. F., *et al.* (2005). Standards of evidence, criteria for efficacy, effectiveness and dissemination. *Prevention Science*, 6:3, 151–258.

Fullan, M. and Steigelbauer, S. (1991). *The new meaning of educational change.* London: Cassell Publishers.

Graetz, B., Littlefield, L., Trinder, M., *et al.* (2008). KidsMatter: A population health model to support student mental health and well-being in primary schools. *International Journal of Mental Health Promotion*, 10:4, 13–20, DOI: 10.1080/14623730.2008.9721772

Greenberg, M. T., Domitrovich, C. E., Graczyk, P., *et al.* (2001). *A conceptual model for implementation of school based preventive interventions: Implications for research, practice and policy.* Report to the Centre for Mental Health Services, Washington.

Hopkins, D., Harris, A., and Jackson, D. (1997). Understanding the school's capacity for development: Growth states and strategies. *School Leadership & Management: Formerly School Organisation*, 17:3, 401–412, DOI:10.1080/13632439769944

Hoyle, T. B., Bartee, R. T., and Allensworth, D. D. (2010). Applying the process of health promotion in schools: A commentary. *Journal of School Health*, 80, 163–166.

Huberman, M. and Miles, M. (1984). *Innovation up close.* New York: Plenum Books.

Ialongo, N. (2002). Wedding the public health and clinical psychological perspectives as prevention scientist. *Prevention and Treatment* 5, article 4. Retrieved 2005, from http://journals.apa.org/pre-vention/volume5/pre0050004a.html.

Jané-Llopis, E. and Anderson, P. (2005). *Mental health promotion and mental disorder prevention: A policy for Europe.* Nijmegen: Radboud University Nijmegen

Kemp, L., Foggett, K., Moore, C., & Stafford, K. (2007). Social and emotional wellbeing in the teacher education curriculum: The Response Ability project. *Proceedings of the Australian Association for Research in Education (AARE) Conference*, Fremantle.

National Crime Prevention (1999). *Pathways to prevention: Developmental and early intervention approaches to crime in Australia. Full report.* Canberra: National Crime Prevention, Attorney-General's Department.

Nutbeam, D. (2000) Health promotion effectiveness: the questions to be answered. In IUHPE, *The evidence of health promotion effectiveness: Shaping new public health in a New Europe*, Chapter 1. Part Two. Evidence Book. Brussels: European Commission.

Olweus, D. (1995). Peer abuse or bullying at school: Basic facts and a school-based intervention programme. *Prospects*, 25:1, 133–139.

Parham, J. (2007). Shifting mental health policy to embrace a positive view of health: A convergence of paradigms. Editorial. *Health Promotion Journal of Australia: Official Journal of Australian Association of Health Promotion Professionals*, 18:3, 173–176. Retrieved 2010 from: http://search.informit.com.au/documentSummary;dn=451763055959214;res=IELHEA

Resnick, M. D., Bearman, P., Blum, R., *et al.* (1997). Protecting adolescents from harm: Findings from the national longitudinal study on adolescent health. *Journal of the American Medical Association*, 278:10, 823–832.

Ross, J. A., Bradley Cousins, J., and Gadalla, T. (1996). Within-teacher predictors of teacher efficacy, *Teaching & Teacher Education*, 12:4, 385–400.

Rowling, L. (2002). Mental health promotion. In L. Rowling, G. Martin, and L. Walker (eds.),

Mental health promotion and young people: Concepts and practice. Sydney, NSW: McGraw Hill.

Rowling, L. (2007). School mental health promotion: MindMatters an example of mental health reform. *Health Promotion Journal of Australia*, 18:3, 229–236.

Rowling, L. and Hazell, T. (in press). Implementing mental health promotion in secondary schools in Australia. In F. A. Huppert and C. L. Cooper (eds.) *Wellbeing: A complete reference guide*, Vol. VI, *Interventions and Policies to Enhance Wellbeing.* London: Wiley Blackwell.

Rowling, L. and Taylor, A. (2005). Intersectoral approaches to mental health promotion. In H. Herman, R. Moodie, and S. Saxena (eds.), *Promoting mental health: Concepts, evidence and practice.* Geneva: World Health Organization.

Samdal, O. and Rowling, L. (2011). Theoretical base for implementation components of health promoting schools. *Health Education*, 111:5, 367–390.

Samdal, O. and Rowling, L. (2013). *The implementation of health promoting schools: Exploring the theories of what, why and how.* London: Routledge.

Sheehan, M., Cahill, H., Rowling, L., *et al.* (2002). Establishing a role for schools in mental health promotion: The MindMatters project. In L. Rowling, G. Martin, and L. Walker (eds.). *Mental health promotion and young people: Concepts and practice.* Sydney, NSW: McGraw Hill.

Slee, P. T., Lawson, M. J., and Russell, A. (2009). *KidsMatter primary evaluation final report.* Centre for Analysis of Educational Futures, Flinders University of South Australia.

Slee, P. T., Murray-Harvey, R., Dix, K. L., *et al.* (2012). *KidsMatter Early Childhood evaluation report.* Adelaide: Shannon Research Press.

Suhrcke, M. and de Paz Nieves, C. (2011). *The impact of health and health behaviours on educational outcomes in high- income countries: A review of the evidence.* Copenhagen: WHO.

Trewin, D. (2001). *Measuring well being: Frameworks for Australian social statistics.* Canberra: Australian Bureau of Statistics.

Valois, R. F., Slade, S., and Ashford, E. (2011) *The healthy school communities model: Aligning health and education in the school setting.* Retrieved 10 November 2011 from: www.ascd. org/ascd/pdf/siteascd/publications/alig ning-health-education.pdf

Walker, L. and Rowling, L. (2007). Mental health takes central role in health promotion activities. Editorial. *Health Promotion Journal of Australia*, 18:3, 171–173. Retrieved 2010, from: http://search.informit.com.au/documentSumm ary;dn=451744422987956;res=IELHEA

Weiner, B. J., Lewis, M. A., and Linnan, L. A. (2009). Using organization theory to understand the determinants of effective implementation of worksite health promotion programs. *Health Education Research,* 24:2, 292–305. doi: 10.1093/ her/cyn019

WHO (World Health Organization). (1998). *WHO's global school initiative: Health promoting schools.* Geneva: World Health Organization.

WHO (2004) *Prevention of mental disorders: Effective interventions and policy options.* Geneva: World Health Organization. Retrieved 2012, from: www.who.int/mental_health/evi dence/en/Prevention_of_Mental_Disorders.pdf

Wyn, J., Cahill, H., Holdsworth, R., *et al.* (2000). MindMatters, a whole-school approach promoting mental health and well being. *Australian and New Zealand Journal of Psychiatry*, 34:4, 594–601.

Zubrick, S. R., Silburn, S. R., Teoh, H. J., *et al.*, (1997). *Western Australian child health survey: Education, health and competence.* Perth: Australian Bureau of Statistics and the Institute for Child Health Research.

Chapter

3

The *"Cool Mind"* Program (*"Programa Cuca Legal"*)
Mental health literacy for middle- and high-school teachers of the public system in Brazil

Gustavo M. Estanislau, Marlene A. Vieira, Taís S. Moriyama, Ary G. Araripe Neto, Isabel A. S. Bordin, and Rodrigo A. Bressan

Introduction

The last decades of research have raised concerns about mental health problems in childhood and adolescence and have exposed the lack of availability of appropriate care for young people in need of mental health assistance (Belfer, 2008), especially in developing countries (Patel *et al.*, 2008). These concerns are justified, since mental health has been continuously considered as crucial to the general wellbeing of any individual. Besides that, psychiatric illnesses are no longer considered only as major causes of specific disability and suffering, but are also linked to general health problems and huge healthcare-related costs (Duarte *et al.*, 2003; Kieling *et al.*, 2011; Patel, 2007). In this context, children and adolescents require particular attention, since many mental health problems identified in adult life begin in childhood and adolescence and can be effectively identified, diagnosed, and treated then.

Unfortunately, mental health needs of children and adolescents continue to be neglected worldwide, since there are few child and youth mental health experts, resources, and centers for the care of these individuals, especially in low- and middle-income countries (Kieling *et al.*, 2011). A careful analysis of the literature suggests that 10–20% of children and adolescents in South America require professional care from specialty mental health services (Collins *et al.*, 2011). The situation in Brazil is particularly alarming, considering the continental proportions of the country and the great cultural differences among regions. According to the Brazilian Institute of Geography and Statistics, 30% of the total population (nearly 56 million individuals) are children and adolescents in the age group between 0 and 17 years old (Instituto Brasileiro de Geografia e Estatillion, 2010). Hence, in an "optimistic" scenario, six million young people would need, at least, one mental health evaluation over the course of the teenage years.

In face of this huge need for mental healthcare, the number of child and adolescent psychiatrists in Brazil is clearly insufficient, with some reports revealing that there are only about 500 such specialized professionals in the whole country. Most of them are

School Mental Health: Global Challenges and Opportunities, ed. Stan Kutcher, Yifeng Wei and Marc D. Weist. Published by Cambridge University Press. © Cambridge University Press 2015.

concentrated in the more developed states in the south and southeastern regions, with an almost complete lack of child and youth mental health professionals in disadvantaged regions. Furthermore, these already scarce resources are frequently not used to meet the most pressing mental healthcare needs of young people and their families. Available data show that up to 86% of the referrals to mental health services are not serious or significant psychiatric disorders, and could be managed in school settings or in primary care units (Bordini, 2012). Consequently, these referrals have been overloading the system and lead to the inaccessibility of mental health professionals to those who really need that level of care.

Recognizing that youth mental health represents a public health problem, the Brazilian government decided to implement a series of interventions to help address this need. For example, the establishment of new services such as the child and adolescent psychosocial attention centers (known as "CAPSi") and the development of strategies for intersectoral cooperation to better meet mental healthcare needs of youth and their families. Nevertheless, such initiatives frequently fall short for reasons such as the general lack of information about mental health and mental illness, the difficulties in communication among various community agencies, mental health professionals and education professionals, and stigma.

This picture of scarcity of resources, inappropriate use of the specialized child and youth mental health specialty services available, and the large number of children and adolescents in need of mental healthcare makes alternative interventions with potential wide-range benefits, using already available resources, particularly strategic and urgent (Patel, 2007).

Our group believe that, in a developing country such as Brazil, the publicly funded educational system could provide a number of favorable conditions to improve mental healthcare for students:

1. In Brazil, since 2009, all children and adolescents from 4 to 17 years old must be enrolled at schools by law. Since this came into effect, school attendance increased to 92% in this age group. Therefore, schools are the place where almost all children and adolescents (with and without emotional and behavioral problems) are.

2. The school years are determinative of long-term vocational and interpersonal success for individuals who are experiencing developmentally appropriate biological, social, and emotional changes.

3. Educators are notably sensitive to behavioral and emotional problems among students as they have both a longitudinal perspective of each student (including the use of performance tests, e.g., math, physical education, music) and an enriched comparative sample of subjects of the same age, educational level, and cultural background (Hinshaw, 2005; Mohit and El Din, 1998; Patel and Thara, 2003).

4. Schools are environments full of potential mental health protective factors (such as development of friendships, good habits, etc.) which may play a decisive and positive role in the life of millions of students.

In line with these considerations, mental health researchers all over the world have been signaling that the partnership with schools could improve public mental health literacy and increase early detection and appropriate referral of cases to child and youth mental healthcare providers (Paternite, 2005; Weist, 2005). However, to achieve this the role of schools needs to be highlighted through actions that effectively assist in facilitating the access to health services, combat stigma, increase opportunities for promotion and main-tenance of treatments, and the ability to promote mental health and prevent problems (Weist, 2005). Training educators to appropriately refer children to health services could favor not only the reduction of the burden of the diseases, but also to positively impact both short- and long-term treatment outcomes with early identification and interventions using treatments that could be less intrusive and more cost-effective. Such opportunities resonate well with the Brazilian population, as evidenced by a survey conducted in nine countries, including Brazil, that demonstrated the impact of a public awareness campaign based on these concepts (Hoven *et al.*, 2008).

In Brazil, public policies addressing the mental health of children and adolescents are in a very preliminary phase of development (Couto *et al.*, 2008), being largely based on ideological initiatives not fully supported by scientific evidence. The delivery of mental healthcare at public schools is extremely rare and there are no specific training programs for teachers, designed either to enhance their mental health literacy or to improve their ability to identify young people at high risk of a mental disorder. The *"Cool Mind"* Program is an initiative affiliated with the Department of Psychiatry of the Federal University of Sao Paulo (UNIFESP) in Brazil, and develops and tests the effectiveness of interventions in school settings, aiming at self-health creation/maintenance skill development and mental health literacy for educators and students alike, looking forward to reduce the stigma related to mental health problems, to help empower educators and students to identify early symptoms of the most frequent psychiatric disorders of childhood and adolescence and to assist in the access to specialized mental health treatment when necessary. We are just now in the early stages of developing this program, and we expect some of the interventions we apply and evaluate could be adopted in the regular curriculum of schools nationwide and in the training of all teachers in the public education system.

In this chapter we will describe an empowering intervention for teachers designed to enhance their ability for mental health case identification by increasing their capacity to identify signs and symptoms of significant mental health problems and mental disorders in students of the public education system and to then make effective referrals to the most appropriate mental health services.

Main objectives of the program

- To develop a mental health training program designed to enhance knowledge of mental disorders, decrease stigma, and enhance case identification and effective referrals for teachers in the public education system.
- To evaluate the effectiveness of the intervention.
- To assess the impressions teachers and students have about general health and mental health; investigate the way they receive information on this topic and their thoughts about the use of educational material about mental health as a supportive tool.

Description of the project

Teacher selection and mental health training

All teachers from the fifth to the last year of high-school from a public school in Sao Paulo City were invited to attend a six-hour training program composed of two three-hour sessions delivered in two consecutive weeks. In the first week, after a brief introduction, a standardized lecture was delivered by a trained child psychiatrist, focusing on: (1) types of mental health problems and mental disorders that affect adolescents; (2) the impact of mental health problems and mental disorders on cognition, thoughts, behavior, feelings, and social skills of adolescents; (3) the differences between normal adolescent behaviors and those behaviors that may represent signs of psychopathological conditions or risk for the development of mental disorders. In the second week, the psychoeducational intervention started with a brief review of the first meeting, with emphasis on the potential behavioral changes and the variations in school performance resulting from mental health problems and mental disorders. Information about when and where to refer students with signs of mental health problems/disorders were also provided at this second meeting.

Training evaluation plan

To evaluate the effectiveness of the mental health training strategy we designed one main longitudinal cohort study with a before and after analysis (pre- and post-tests) without a control group. For this, three questionnaires developed by our team were applied. The first one collected teachers' characteristics (demographics, professional training and experience, professional satisfaction, and self-assessment of vocational skills). The second questionnaire included six vignettes, describing six different adolescents seen in a school context, corresponding to five psychopathological conditions (high risk for: psychosis; depression; conduct disorder; ADHD; mania) and normal adolescent distress. This questionnaire was applied before and after the training to evaluate the acquisition of knowledge concerning the identification of the five psychopathological conditions and to where and when to provide appropriate referral to the individuals affected. Teachers were asked to: (1) identify whether the adolescents described were likely to have a mental health problem/disorder or not; (2) if so, decide if they required a particular type of referral (specialty mental health service, after-school help for academic support, other, or none). An increase in correct answers in the post-test would be consistent with success of the intervention. The third questionnaire was a self-administered tool used after the intervention for a qualitative evaluation of the training strategy aiming to improve the model applied.

Student mental healthcare needs identification

Teachers enrolled in the intervention were asked, before the beginning of the training, to develop an hypothetical list of all students requiring mental healthcare referrals for emotional and/or behavioral problems from their existing class lists. The underlying principle was that if teachers were able to correctly identify mental health problems in their students, those with problems would be on the hypothetical referral list (the potential cases list) and those without problems would not (the control list). Potential cases, randomly selected from the lists created by the teachers as students with emotional/behavioral problems, were selected (grades 5 to 12) and matched by grade, gender, and age to students on the control list.

Cases and controls were invited to attend a one-hour basic mental health lecture, in which students were oriented with respect to the major modifiable risk factors for the development of mental disorders, the benefits of early intervention in mental health and where, how, and when to seek help. Concurrently, participants were asked to fill out the Youth Self-Report (YSR), a screening questionnaire for the identification of emotional and/or behavioral problems in adolescents aged 11–18 years (Bordin, 2013). The YSR provides a behavioral profile of adolescents on scales for both internalizing and externalizing problems. Cut-off points (T-scores) in these scales classify adolescents in three categories: clinical cases (>63), borderline cases (60–63), and within normal range (<60). In this study we considered as YSR positive those students with scores in the clinical or borderline range (T-score >60). These were further classified as having: (1) internalizing problems only (anxiety and/or depression symptoms); (2) externalizing problems only (aggressive behavior and/or rule-breaking behavior); (3) both types of problems; or (4) no problems. Students did not know which of them had been selected by teachers as potential cases and which ones were selected by randomization to be controls. Including controls in the sample allowed us to better estimate the number of students not identified by teachers.

Finally, all individuals who were deemed to be potential cases (YSR scores of 60 and above) were referred to the public health service for assessment and treatment, if necessary. When this was not possible, students were provided mental healthcare in our own service.

In summary, this initiative evaluated teachers' regular ability to identify students with mental health problems (through the list of referrals and the vignettes) and compared questionnaires applied before and after the training to evaluate the effectiveness of the psychoeducational strategy.

Results

In total, 93.5% of the teachers trained reported their experience of the intervention as positive, and 74.2% self-reported to have gained knowledge about mental health.

Before the training, a great number of teachers already knew how to recognize and appropriately refer adolescents with the mental health problems described in the vignettes. The highest rate of correct answers before the training was related to conduct problems (96.7%) and the lowest rates were linked to normal adolescence (66.7%). When analyzing only the teachers who before the training could not identify and/or refer the cases that were described in the vignettes, results showed that the training was partially effective, since at least 50% of these teachers learned to identify and to make the appropriate referral of the adolescents suffering from the five psychopathological conditions described in the vignettes. Of the teachers who before training could not discriminate normal adolescent distress from adolescents with mental health problems/disorders, the psychoeducational strategy was helpful to 60%.

From the 26 students in the lists of referrals (possible cases) requested from the teachers before the beginning of the training and their 26 respective controls (matched for gender, grade, and age), 80.8% were male adolescents.

Some important findings were that teachers could identify correctly students with a greater load of symptoms (having both internalizing and externalizing symptoms) as being in need of mental healthcare, placing them on their referral list, while no students with this profile were found among controls ($p = 0.01$). On the other hand, they showed difficulty in realizing pure internalizing and externalizing behaviors as signs that justified a referral to mental healthcare. According to the YSR, when comparing cases and controls with internalizing problems exclusively to cases and controls with none, teachers presented a tendency to exclude students with only internalizing problems from the referral list, demonstrating that these problems were frequently not recognized ($p = 0.09$).

Finally, the prevalence of mental health problems identified with the YSR among the controls (57.7%) was similar to the teacher-nominated group (53.8%), making it clear that teachers also demonstrated misinterpretation of normal adolescent distress as adolescence with mental health problems/disorders, meaning that teachers may be confusing normal adolescent distress with mental disorders. From this perspective, educational interventions should be emphatic on the differentiation between normal adolescence from adolescence with mental health problems.

By the end of the training, teachers had some suggestions for improvement. These included:

- discussions about real students;
- extending the duration of the training period (increasing the number of sessions);
- more interaction between teachers and presenters;
- shortening the number of questionnaires that they had to complete (some teachers mentioned that they felt like they were working more for the project than for their personal interest);
- addressing practical classroom strategies to be used in helping youth with mental disorders and not just theoretical knowledge about mental health and mental disorders;
- the development of a resource (such as a booklet) with the course material and supporting information) to allow for further self-study.

Assessment of teachers' understanding of mental health and mental disorders within a public school of the South Central Region of Sao Paulo

As part of our quality improvement we performed a qualitative study to: (1) help determine what teachers and students understood about general health and mental health/mental disorders; (2) investigate the way they received information on these topics; (3) seek their opinion about what kind of educational material about mental health/mental disorders would they like to receive.

In this study teachers and students were invited to complete a self-administered questionnaire two months after their participation in the mental health training activities. This consisted of ten questions regarding knowledge and interests about mental health, as well as the methods used by these individuals to obtain mental health information.

The questionnaire consisted of the following questions:

1. What does the word health mean to you?
2. In your opinion what is mental health?
3. How would you like to receive information and orientations on mental health?
4. In your opinion, is the use of informative material important for learning about mental health? Why?
5. Have you already received any information about mental health? Where?
6. Have you heard any TV debate or radio program that addressed mental health? What was the issue discussed?
7. Have you researched or read something on the internet related to mental health?
8. Do you believe the information conveyed in the media about mental health is sufficient? Explain.
9. Have you read stories about mental health in magazines or newspapers? What did these stories address?
10. Do you believe the information conveyed in the media about mental health is sufficient? Explain.

For the data analysis, we used the methodology of the discourse of the collective subject (DCS) which was developed for social opinion surveys in order to determine the collective concepts established in a given community derived from individual reports. Therefore, the use of the DCS usually provides relevant information concerning thoughts, values, and beliefs individually internalized (Lefèvre and Lefèvre, 2005), transforming them into collective statements which are processed using the software Qualiquantisoft.

Results

For the majority of teachers, mental health was linked to the balance between mind and body and was considered as a requirement for happiness. However, for a minority it was correlated to illnesses. Most of the teachers showed great interest in increasing knowledge about mental health, and reported that they would like to receive educational materials on the subject and believed that such information could be useful in informing their day-to-day interaction with students. Most teachers received their mental health information through the television.

Students described general health as fundamental to life. For the majority, mental health is the same as having a healthy mind, while a minority associated mental health with mental illnesses. Despite the potential stigma permeating such an initiative, all students agreed to participate in the *"Cuca Legal"* Project and the majority reported that they were satisfied with the educational activity they experienced.

Conclusion

Recently, child and adolescent mental health has been considered a major public health concern. In Brazil, prevalence of mental illnesses in this population has been found to be higher than formerly expected and the available resources for treatment are scarce, so the development of alternative strategic interventions is urgent. In this context, we addressed the potential role of schools in addressing mental healthcare, especially in the domains of mental health literacy, case identification, and appropriate referral.

From our work and evaluations, we conclude that schools and teachers can play an increased role in addressing mental health needs for young people and that it is feasible to develop various types of school-based interventions to meet these needs. In particular, both mental health literacy and enhancing capacity of in-school case identification of youth with mental disorders can be achieved. The training of educators to refer children to the most appropriate mental health services as soon as needed could favor not only the reduction of the burden of the diseases, but also the prevention of further psychopathology in the long run, leading to treatments that could be less intrusive and more cost-effective. From our perspective, educators are ready and willing to receive good information about mental health which will help them to identify students with mental health problems and disorders, to develop skills to manage these problems and to refer these individuals when necessary.

The *"Cuca Legal"* Program helped teachers in early identification of those in need of mental healthcare. Taking into consideration the fact that health is a far more frequent condition than disorders, this program has proven to be empowering for teachers by increasing their mental health literacy. The intervention was feasible and widely welcome. Further improvements in the intervention have been made and are currently being tested on a larger scale with public school teachers in collaboration with the Sao Paulo State government.

Final considerations

In our experience, conducting a qualitative study helped our group to become familiar with and develop a better understanding of teachers' and students' beliefs, and self-identified needs pertinent to mental health, allowing us to better tailor subsequent interventions. At the same time, our quantitative exploratory pilot study allowed us to identify the weakest areas in terms of teachers' literacy and to evaluate the possible effectiveness of our intervention strategy in that audience before applying it on a larger scale. This improved model will now be further evaluated by our team in a new study we are developing. Should that prove successful, we hope to be able to distribute it widely across Brazil and even have it incorporated into policy to help direct mental health activities in public education nationally.

References

Belfer, M. L. (2008). Child and adolescent mental disorders: the magnitude of the problem across the globe. *Journal of Child Psychology and Psychiatry*, 49(3), 226–236.

Bordin, I. A., Rocha, M. M., Paula, C. S., *et al.* (2013). Child Behavior Checklist/CBCL, Youth Self-Report/YSR and Teacher's Report Form/TRF: An overview of the development of original and Brazilian versions. *Cadernos de Saúde Pública*, 29(1), 13–28.

Bordini, D., Gadelha, A., Paula, C. S., and Bressan, R. A. (2012). School referrals of children and adolescents to CAPSi: The burden of incorrect referrals. *Revista Brasileira. Psiquiatria*, 34(4), 493–494.

Collins, P. Y., Patel, V., Joestl, S. S., *et al.* (2011). Grand challenges in global mental health. *Nature*, 475, 27–30.

Couto, M. C., Duarte, C., and Delgado, P. (2008). Child mental health and public health in Brazil: Current situation and challenges. *Revista Brasileira. Psiquiatria*, 30(4), 384–389.

Duarte, C., Hoven, C., Berganza, C., *et al.* (2003). Child mental health in Latin America: present and future epidemiologic research. *The International Journal of Psychiatry in Medicine*, 33(3), 203–222.

Hinshaw, S. (2005). The stigmatization of mental illness in children and parents: Developmental issues, family concerns, and research needs. *Journal of Child Psychology and Psychiatry*, 46, 714–734.

Hoven, C. W., Doan, T., Musa, G. J., *et al.* (2008). Worldwide child and adolescent mental health begins with awareness: A preliminary assessment in nine countries. *International Review of Psychiatry*, 20(3), 261–270.

Instituto Brasileiro de Geografia e Estatística. (2010). *Census 2010: Brazilian resident population, according to type of residence, sex and age groups.* Available online at: ftp://ftp.ibge.gov.br/Censos/Censo_Demografic o_2010/Caracteristicas_Gerais_Religiao_Defi ciencia/tab1_1.pdf (accessed 10 December 2013).

Kieling, C., Baker-Henningham, H., and Belfer, M., *et al.* (2011). Child and adolescent mental health worldwide: Evidence for action. *The Lancet*, 378, 1515–1525.

Lefèvre, F. and Lefèvre, A. M. (2005). *Depoimentos e Discursos: uma proposta de análise em pesquisa social.* Brasília: Liber Livro Editora.

Mohit, A. and Seif El Din, A. (1998). *Mental health promotion for school children: A manual for school teachers and school mental health workers.* Alexandria, Egypt: World Health Organization, Regional Office for the Eastern Mediterranean.

Patel, V. (2007). Mental health of young people: A global public health challenge. *The Lancet*, 369, 1302–1313.

Patel, V., Flisher, A. J., Nikapota, A., and Malhotra, S. (2008). Promoting child and adolescent mental health in low and middle income countries. *Journal of Child Psychology and Psychiatry*, 49(3), 313–334.

Patel, V. and Thara, R. (2003). *Meeting the mental health needs of developing countries: NGO innovations in India.* New Delhi: Sage (India).

Paternite, C. E. (2005). School-based mental health programs and services: Overview and introduction to the special issue. *Journal of Abnormal Child Psychology*, 33(6), 657–663.

Weist, M. D. (2005). Fulfilling the promise of school-based mental health: Moving toward a public mental health promotion approach. *Journal of Abnormal Child Psychology*, 33(6), 735–741.

A collaborative and sustainable approach to address mental health promotion and early identification in schools in the Canadian province of Nova Scotia and beyond

Yifeng Wei, Stan Kutcher, Ann Blackwood, Don Glover, Cynthia Weaver, Amy MacKay, Vanessa Bruce, Ardath Whynacht, Faten Alshazly, and Mitchell Shea

Background

The adolescent years (here, ages 12 to 24) are a critical period for the onset of mental disorders, when approximately 70% of all lifetime mental disorders can be diagnosed (O'Connell, Boat, Warner, et al., 2009; Kessler, Berglund, Demler, Jin, Merikangas, & Walters, 2005). Mental health problems or mental disorders, if unrecognized and untreated, can lead to substantial negative personal, social, and civil consequences, including school drop-out/incompletion (Breslau, Miller, Joanie Chung, & Schweitzer, 2011; Kessler, Foster, Saunders, & Stang, 1995), poor social relationships (Bhatia, 2007; Shochet, Dadds, Ham, & Montague, 2006), less robust vocational success, justice system contact, early mortality (including suicide), and a high burden of disability (O'Connell et al., 2009; World Health Organization, 2004). While severe mental disorders (such as psychosis) do onset in adolescence (American Psychiatric Association, 2013) most, especially emotional/mood disturbances, are mild or moderate in intensity (Kessler et al. 2012). Substantial evidence for successful treatment of mental disorders in young people exists and positive outcomes may be enhanced if evidence-based treatment is provided early in the course of illness (Rutter et al., 2008). Thus, early identification and early effective interventions, support, and ongoing care for youth developing a mental disorder is needed. This may not only advance positive treatment outcomes, but also may help facilitate healthy psychosocial development (Kutcher, 2011; Waddell, Offord, Shepherd, Hua, & McEwan, 2002).

Since most youth attend school, schools are an obvious venue through which to address their health and mental health needs. Promoting physical health and applying public health interventions, such as vaccinations, in schools has long been supported by international organizations, such as the World Health Organization (WHO), United Nations Educational,

School Mental Health: Global Challenges and Opportunities, ed. Stan Kutcher, Yifeng Wei and Marc D. Weist. Published by Cambridge University Press. © Cambridge University Press 2015.

Scientific, and Cultural Organization (UNESCO), and United Nations International Children's Emergency Fund (UNICEF) (WHO Regional Office for Europe, 1996). More recently, school mental health has received international attention. This has resulted in a plethora of interventions and standalone programs created to address mental health promotion (including social and emotional wellbeing), the prevention of negative mental health outcomes or mental disorders, and early identification of and interventions for mental disorders (on-site or linked to health services) (Calear & Christensen, 2010; Faggiano, Vigna-Taglianti, Versino, Zambon, Borraccino, & Lemma, 2008; Hahn *et al.*, 2007; Lister-Sharp, Chapman, Stewart-Brown, & Sowden, 1999; Neil & Christensen, 2009; Robinson, Hetrick, & Martin, 2011; School-Based Mental Health and Substance Abuse Consortium Knowledge Translation and Review Team, 2012; Waddell, Hua, Garland, Peters, & McEwan, 2007).

While the proliferation and enthusiastic application of programs and interventions have been observed in schools in recent years, numerous challenges in effectively addressing school mental health have been identified (Weare & Nind 2011). Many interventions are only available during research protocols or are subject to the vagaries of funding decisions outside the individual school. School administrators may be inundated with slickly marketed programs that demonstrate little or no substantial research evidence of effectiveness, safety, or cost-effectiveness; or administrators may not have the skills needed to critically evaluate and separate interventions of potential benefit from those without. Educators may not have the competencies or resources needed to implement programs of demonstrated effectiveness. Programs depending on fidelity of delivery may not be easily implemented and applying programs outside existing operational and infrastructural domains may be difficult. Overall, many of these challenges are examples of components overlaid or added to existing school frameworks instead of being seamlessly incorporated into existing school-based structures and activities.

A recent systematic review on the effectiveness of school mental health programs noted that most lacked substantive evidence and were historically applied extramural to existent school capacities. It suggested that future interventions be integrated into existing systems, focus on teacher education, engage parents/families and related community services, and address youth mental health in a whole-school approach (Weare & Nind 2011). Similarly, another comprehensive review of systematic reviews (Wei & Kutcher 2012) noted that these programs often lack long-term evidence of effectiveness, and suggested that youth mental health improvements may be achieved through an integrated pathway to care model that builds a continuum of care involving schools, families, health providers, and the wider community, instead of parachuting standalone programs into schools.

In this chapter we introduce a comprehensive, participatory, and evidence-based approach that was developed, field-tested, implemented, and researched in Canada. It was designed to avoid the challenges of standalone programs and aims to develop a consistent and sustainable collaboration among mental health experts, students, educators, and educational jurisdictions at the policy, practice and research level through the School-Based Integrated Pathway to Care Model (Pathway to Care Model) (Wei, Kutcher, & Szumilas, 2011).

The Sun Life Financial Chair in Adolescent Mental Health team

This innovative approach was created and implemented by an interdisciplinary knowledge translation team, the Sun Life Financial Chair in Adolescent Mental Health (Chair

Team) (www.teenmentalhealth.org), established in 2006 and affiliated with Dalhousie University/IWK Health Centre, Halifax, Nova Scotia, Canada. The vision of the Chair Team is to help improve youth mental health through the effective translation and transfer of best evidence-based scientific knowledge applied in schools and other related settings. The Chair Team is composed of professionals in psychiatry, psychology, education, social work, youth engagement, and communications/media, and is supported by two advisory groups, the Youth Advisory Council (YAC) and the Educator Advisory Committee (EAC). The YAC meets regularly to advise on the work of the Chair Team and create and implement youth engagement activities promoting mental health awareness and reducing stigma in the community. The EAC includes teachers, school administrators, senior government officers from the Nova Scotia provincial Department of Education and Early Childhood Development (DOE), and representatives from the Nova Scotia provincial Department of Health and Wellness and advises on the Chair's educational initiatives. Materials and programs pertaining to school mental health are freely available at the website: www.teenmentalhealth.org.

The School-Based Integrated Pathway to Care Model

The Chair Team has focused its work on youth in junior high and secondary school as this is the age span during which the incidence of mental disorder rises steeply (American Psychiatric Association, 2013), guided by the Pathway to Care Model (Figure 4.1) (Wei, Kutcher, & Szumilas, 2011). The Pathway to Care Model integrates mental health

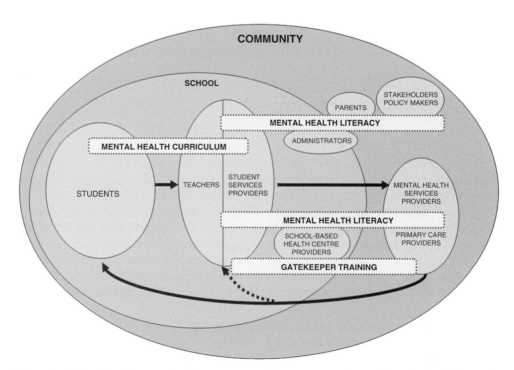

Figure 4.1 School-Based Integrated Pathway to Care Model. From Wei, Kutcher, and Szumilas (2011). Copyright by *McGill Journal of Education*. Reprinted with permission.

promotion, early identification, triage and referral, and continuing care into one framework that engages students, teachers, school support staff, families, health providers, and decision makers to participate in and benefit from various components embedded within. These are: enhancement of mental health literacy for students and classroom teachers, as well as in the wider community; enhancement of early identification of youth with mental disorders, triage, referral, and support through "go-to" educator training; parent/family engagement; mental health training for primary healthcare teams; and enhancement of the pathway through care and referral system linking schools to the most appropriate healthcare providers (Kutcher & Wei 2013; Wei, Kutcher, & Szumilas, 2011).

The model is not prescriptive, but rather molded by community circumstance, informed and supported by best evidence-based resources, and grounded in health and human services provider collaboration. Integral to this approach is a constant feedback loop of consultation, evaluation, and modification of activities and resources that allows for sustainable flexibility that can meet evolving community needs. Model components can be implemented as a whole or individually as parts to serve various school ecologies. The following sections describe how this iterative process developed and evolved through the Pathway to Care Model that entails various projects we conducted in collaboration with multidisciplinary partners.

The foundation is enhancement of mental health literacy among students, teachers, families, and other related stakeholders. The Chair Team defines mental health literacy as: the capacity to understand what constitutes positive mental health and strategies to achieve and maintain positive mental health; understanding and knowledge of mental disorders and their treatment based on best evidence-based research; appropriate attitudes toward mental illness and people living with mental illness (reduction of stigma); and enhancement of help-seeking efficacy, which is the individual capacity and willingness to seek help from appropriate healthcare providers and other related sources for a mental health problem or mental disorder (Kutcher, Wei, McLuckie, & Bullock, 2013).

This model was first piloted in a rural high-school in the province of Nova Scotia in 2009, with the participation of all Grade 10 students ($n = 74$) and teachers ($n = 6$), two local community human services providers, eight primary care health providers, four representatives from specialty child and youth mental healthcare services, and two representatives from the Students Services Section and English Program Service Divisions of the provincial DOE. The Chair Team delivered a one-day training session to all participating teachers on how to teach the Mental Health & High School Curriculum Guide in the Grade 10 classroom. Following the training, teachers studied the material in groups and taught the curriculum within a ten-class duration to the students in order to promote mental health knowledge, reduce stigma, and enhance students' help-seeking efficacy. Meanwhile, "go-to" educator training was co-designed by the Chair Team and representatives from local community services to help school support staff enhance their capacity of early identification and strengthen the link between the school and the community. This training was delivered to five school support staff identified by the principal as staff students naturally go to for help. Following the training, three discussion panels were held between the school support staff and local mental health services to clarify the referral process and confidentiality issues among schools, mental health services, and families. Further discussions were initiated between the provincial DOE and Department of Health (DOH) to clarify issues around access to care and confidentiality. This pilot was completed within the school academic year. Findings demonstrated that participants' mental health literacy level was substantially improved; the quality of referral from the school to health services was improved; and collaboration between the health and education sectors was enhanced (Kutcher & Wei, 2013).

Development and implementation of the Nova Scotia school mental health framework

The successful implementation of the model was reported to the EAC with the intent of furthering discussion on future directions for school mental health in the province. At this time no provincial school mental health policy existed. This resulted in the decision for the Chair Team to host a provincial school mental health summit to bring together educators, bureaucrats, health, and other related stakeholders to create a blueprint for school mental health. This was a novel approach to the creation of provincial education/health policy and was the first time in Nova Scotia that such a policy development process had occurred.

In 2009 the Chair Team hosted the summit, engaging representatives from all five provincial government departments directly serving youth (Education, Health, Health Promotion, Justice, and Community Services), as well as participants from school boards, regional health authorities, youth organizations, the Royal Canadian Mounted Police regional offices, African and First Nations communities, and others. There was unanimous agreement that the province should develop a school mental health framework. This recommendation was accepted by the deputy minister of Health Promotion, who represented the deputy ministers of all departments involved.

Following the summit, a process led by the Chair Team and involving summit participants was developed and applied to create a framework that could then be used by the DOE to create a provincial school mental health strategy. This resulted in "Well-Beings: The Nova Scotia School Mental Health Framework." It identified five themes and related strategies and evaluations: mental health literacy; mental health resources; inter-sector communication and collaboration; care access; and strategies for development, distribution, and dissemination. The full report can be found at: http://teenmentalhealth.org. This framework further endorsed the development of an ongoing collaboration between the Chair Team and the DOE to advance the school mental health agenda in the province. This collaboration led directly to the inclusion of numerous aspects of the school mental health framework into the policy document "Kids and Learning First" (http://novascotia.ca/kidsandlearning/pub/KL-en.pdf) in 2012 (Nova Scotia Department of Education, 2012).

Promotion of mental health literacy through the Mental Health & High School Curriculum Guide

Nova Scotia case

Directed by Kids and Learning First (Nova Scotia Department of Education, 2012) and in partnership with the DOE, the Chair Team implemented a mental health literacy curriculum: Mental Health & High School Curriculum Guide (The Guide) for Grade 9 students in Nova Scotia. This resource provides the foundational component to the Pathway to Care Model. The Guide was designed to increase knowledge about mental health and mental disorders, improve attitudes toward mental health and mental disorders, and promote help-seeking behaviors through six modules, complete with lesson plans and teaching resources.

These are: stigma of mental illness; understanding mental health and mental illness; information on specific mental illness; experiences of mental illness; seeking help and finding support; and the importance of positive mental health. Its latest version, which includes teacher self-study and student evaluation materials, is available online at: http://teenmentalhealth.org/curriculum.

Prior to its application in the province, an earlier version of The Guide was field tested in schools from four provinces in Canada. These field tests led to a number of modifications which were reflected in the version of The Guide used in Nova Scotia. As a first step The Guide was piloted with a rural high-school in the province. Both qualitative and quantitative methods were used to evaluate the pilot. Mental health knowledge was assessed with 30 questions derived from the material in The Guide, and attitudes toward mental illness with eight questions developed by the Chair Team. These were applied immediately after the curriculum had been presented in class and at two months later. The results demonstrated a positive result in short-term knowledge improvement among students, but this was not sustained in the longer term. Both short-term and long-term knowledge improvement were found among teachers (Kutcher & Wei, 2013). Interviews conducted with students and teachers following the second testing revealed that students did not study the content because it was not part of the mandatory curriculum. Student and teacher interviews indicated they very much enjoyed learning about mental health and mental disorders and they felt more confident in seeking help if necessary. They advised the Chair Team to have The Guide integrated into the regular school curriculum.

An additional implementation was applied in two schools of the Tri-County Regional School Board in Nova Scotia. This had the added component of including a francophone school and the local mental health community organization. As well, different approaches to embedding The Guide were studied: spreading out the modules across different subject areas versus keeping the modules together as one block. Results and recommendations obtained were similar to those received in the first pilot (www.teenmentalhealth.org) and the advice provided to the DOE was to present The Guide resource as a single teaching block embedded into the usual school curriculum. This advice was followed by the DOE, who decided that The Guide would be embedded into the provincial school curriculum as part of the Grade 9 Healthy Living course.

With the positive outcomes of and lessons learned from the pilot, the Chair Team obtained approval to embed The Guide within the largest school board in the province, the Halifax Regional School Board (HRSB). This occurred with the active support of the HRSB governing members (www.hrsb.ns.ca) and senior leadership in the DOE. In collaboration with the Student Services and teacher support leadership of the HRSB, in 2012 The Guide training was delivered to all Grade 9 Healthy Living course teachers ($n = 89$), who were expected to teach the content in their classroom across the HRSB. The training addressed the context of adolescent mental health, presented the six embedded modules and supplementary materials, and discussed teaching strategies. The Guide was then embedded in the Grade 9 Healthy Living course. The pre- and post-training evaluation of the teacher training demonstrated significant improvements in teachers' knowledge. Similar results were found for teachers' attitudes toward mental illness (Kutcher et al., 2013). Participants reported that they appreciated this resource and were more confident in teaching the curriculum in the classroom. At the follow-up meeting with HRSB, educators recommended that due to teacher turnover there should be consistent training provided for new teachers who will be teaching the curriculum every academic year.

The Chair Team shared these results with the English Program Services Division of the Department of Education and all seven English-language school boards in Nova Scotia. Encouraged by the results and informed by HRSB teachers' feedback, the Chair Team and the DOE discussed potential strategies to scale up The Guide across all Grade 9 classes in Nova Scotia. Consequently, the train-the-trainer model was developed by the Chair Team with direction from the Department of Education and the decision was made to deliver the training to all teachers who would be teaching the Healthy Living curriculum, as well as to training teams within each school board in the province. The DOE supported the concept that each school board-based training team should include classroom teachers and school support staff (e.g., school counselors), and should include a mental health professional from the local health authority who could additionally function as an expert resource person. The training of school board training teams was linked to the training of Grade 9 Healthy Living teachers in each school board and was conducted across the province in 2012–2013 (further details below). Each school board now has a training team that is expected to support all Grade 9 Healthy Living teachers teaching the curriculum annually. The DOE also modified the learning outcomes of the Grade 9 Healthy Living curriculum to better integrate The Guide into the existing provincial curriculum. Furthermore, the DOE, the Nova Scotia Teachers Plus Credit Union, and the Dalhousie Medical Research Foundation provided financial support to facilitate the roll-out of this province-wide training.

The Chair Team trained 228 teachers and support staff (including 43 trainers). The 43 trainers further took part in an extra half-day of in-depth training. Although the first day of training was consistent with the previous curriculum training model, the extra half-day training for trainers provided opportunities to explore evidence-based research findings, to support greater understanding of mental health and mental disorders, to facilitate discussions on how to integrate The Guide into the provincial curriculum expectations, and to develop practical strategies to support the application of The Guide in the classroom. Program evaluation of the training sessions demonstrated that teachers showed significant improvement of mental health knowledge following the training compared to the pre-training knowledge base ($d = 1.85$). The effect size of the training on knowledge improvement substantially exceeds Cohen's convention for large effect size ($d = 0.8$). Although teachers' attitudes toward mental health were positive before the training, their attitudes were further significantly enhanced following the training. The effect size of the training on teachers' attitudes exceeds Cohen's convention for medium effect size. Similar results were found among trainer participants with regards to knowledge improvement ($d = 2.0$), as well as significant attitude change ($d = 0.53$). The full report of the program evaluation can be found at: http://teenmentalhealth.org.

Ontario Shores case

The success of The Guide in Nova Scotia is attributed in part to its preliminary evidence of effectiveness through program evaluations, and collaboration among the Chair Team, the DOE, and other agencies, and all school boards at every stage of the project. However, due to the reality in Canada that education is a provincial responsibility, the process by which this program developed in Nova Scotia cannot be replicated elsewhere. Considering the goal for The Guide to be nationally implemented, similar results need to be demonstrated elsewhere, regardless of the process used. That is, the universal applicability of The Guide to improve mental health literacy needed to be independent of the method of its delivery. The Ontario

Shores case described below shows how The Guide was delivered using an outcome-based and pragmatically driven approach, but achieved similar results as the Nova Scotia case.

Concurrently with the application of the Nova Scotia process an opportunity arose to assist in the implementation of The Guide in Ontario, Canada's largest province. Here, unlike in Nova Scotia, The Guide was introduced by a mental health tertiary care center, the Ontario Shores Centre for Mental Health Sciences (Ontario Shores) working in collaboration with the Chair Team. Ontario Shores launched their Adolescent Mental Health Literacy Program in October 2011, partnering with the Chair Team to train teachers to apply The Guide initially in four school boards. Ontario Shores functioned as the training and evaluation hub and reached out to partner with schools and school boards through its Adolescent Services section.

Teachers and students from the four school boards received the training on The Guide provided by the Chair Team trainers. Findings on knowledge and attitudes for teachers ($n = 31$) were consistent with Nova Scotia findings (www.teenmentalhealth.org). Teachers' mental health literacy level increased substantially after the training ($d = 1.2$). Teachers' attitudes toward mental health were positive before the training, and were further enhanced after the training ($d = 0.44$) (McLuckie et al., pers. comm.).

Following that training, 409 students were enrolled in a cross-sectional research study that investigated participants' knowledge and attitudes at baseline, immediately after the training, and at two-month (students) follow-up (McLuckie et al., pers. comm.). Compared to baseline, students' knowledge improved substantially (strong effect size) immediately after the training ($d = 0.9$), and was maintained after two months ($d = 0.7$). Students' attitudes also improved significantly after the training, and again was maintained at two-month follow-up ($d = 0.18$).

The availability of training sessions promoted by Ontario Shores and the positive findings from this initiative sparked intense interest from school boards across the province of Ontario. As a result, four more school boards and two private schools joined this project and training was delivered to them in 2012. The Adolescent Mental Health Literacy Program led by Ontario Shores has now created a spontaneous provincial snowball model that engages more school boards over time as boards and educators share positive experiences with each other. Unlike in Nova Scotia, the Ministry of Education in Ontario has not mandated the use of The Guide in the Ontario curriculum, but a great number of schools are already implementing it in accordance with their interpretation of the existing provincial curriculum guidelines. In Ontario a school-/school board-driven process has directed the application of The Guide, but the mental health literacy outcomes achieved by this process have been similarly positive to those found in Nova Scotia, demonstrating that The Guide can be effectively applied with significant and substantial positive results regardless of the structure, infrastructure, or process considerations of any particular jurisdiction.

Ottawa case

Concurrently but independently of the Ontario Shores initiative, a randomized controlled trial (RCT) on the effectiveness of The Guide took place, led by the University of Ottawa (UO) and the Royal Ottawa Mental Health Care and Research Center (the UO study), involving 26 secondary schools in the city of Ottawa, Ontario between 2010 and 2013 (Milin, Kutcher, Lewis, Walker, & Ferrill, 2013). This study measured three outcomes among 534 Grades 11 and 12 students: knowledge uptake and retention; stigma reduction;

and help-seeking efficacy. All participant schools were randomized to one of three groups: curriculum group; curriculum plus additional mental health E-learning group; and control group. The study assessed change in measures for knowledge and attitudes, and further investigated whether The Guide promoted help-seeking efficacy of students. This additional variable had not been previously addressed in either the Nova Scotia or Ontario Shores evaluations. The preliminary data analysis combined the curriculum group and the curriculum plus E-learning group as one group at this stage of the project to compare against findings from the control group. Data show that the control group did not demonstrate statistically significant changes in any of the three outcomes measured. However, the combined curriculum group demonstrated significant improvements in all three outcomes: knowledge, attitudes, and help-seeking efficacy.

While this was purely a research study, and conducted independently of the Ontario Shores initiatives, its findings may buttress the ongoing activities of the Ontario Shores group to further support their rollout of The Guide to interested schools and school boards in Ontario. Their future activities may additionally include disseminating these research findings to the most appropriate senior leadership in the Ministry of Education in Ontario and other potential stakeholders such as youth mental health serving agencies in that province, to try and bring together the grassroots, institutional and government domains.

Overview of the mental health literacy component

These above examples have showcased how The Guide can be differently implemented and evaluated in various settings, with similar and consistently positive results in improving the mental health literacy of students and teachers. While the Nova Scotia model went through a bottom-up (starting from an individual school) and then an integrated top-down (making the program mandatory through the DOE) process, the Ontario process applied diverse and different approaches. There, Ontario Shores, a mental healthcare setting, functions as a central hub to reach out to school boards directly while the UO project reached out to schools through a research project and may continue to disseminate the program through collaboration with Ontario Shores when the research project is finished. As The Guide is rolling out across Canada, other provinces are trying out different approaches to determine the most appropriate manner by which to deliver this resource.

The success of this approach is founded not only on the quality of The Guide materials and training, but also in the manner in which it is applied. First, The Guide is not prescriptive. How it is applied, who is responsible for its application and evaluation, and all process details are determined by the participants and not the developers of The Guide. Thus, The Guide can be applied in any jurisdiction as it can be adapted to how the jurisdiction functions and does not require any substantial changes to be made in the jurisdiction itself. Second, The Guide builds on the existing strengths of all schools, thus utilizing historically validated educational pedagogy as its delivery method. Teachers teach the material and as they prepare to teach the material they significantly and substantively enhance their own mental health literacy without being subjected to special education experiences or programs focused on mental health. Then teachers use their own professional skills to teach the material to students, as they do with all other subjects. Thus, no new human resources or extramural activities are needed to obtain these positive results. Third, because the materials are embedded in existing school curriculum, there are no substantive additional program costs needed to deliver the mental health literacy exposure. This means that expensive and piecemeal interventions (which may or may not have been proven to be effective in increasing knowledge, decreasing stigma, or enhancing help-seeking efficacy) are not required. Furthermore, once the materials are embedded into the existing curriculum and school board-based training teams are put into place, the intervention becomes self-sustaining and likely to be cost-effective and thus, also less likely to be sacrificed when funding is in short supply. All of these components offer substantial value when added to the use of The Guide as a mental health literacy resource for teachers and students alike. Although research demonstrating the impact of The Guide on the school culture or teachers' peer mental health literacy diffusion has not yet been done, it is possible that simple integration of The Guide into school curriculum may have wider benefits on whole-school mental health components.

Enhancement of early identification of youth with mental disorders through the "Go-to" Educator Training

As The Guide was being disseminated to promote mental health literacy among students and teachers, another component of the Pathway to Care Model, the "Go-to" Educator Training program has also been promoted to address the continuum of care along the pathway to care and to supplement The Guide applications in schools (Wei, Kutcher, & Szumilas, 2011). The concept of "go-to" educators is inspired by the fact that in each school there are always educators whom students naturally go to for help. These are what we refer to as "go-to" educators. These individuals can be classroom teachers, guidance counselors, administrators, or other school support staff. By training these on-site individuals to be able to identify students at higher risk of developing mental health problems and mental disorders, and then linking those students with appropriate services (both within and outside the school), youth mental healthcare needs may be addressed more quickly and effectively. These "go-to" individuals are then joined in their training sessions by within-school student services providers (such as psychologists, counselors, social workers, etc.) and community human service, health, and mental health providers. The exact makeup of the groups being trained depends on the unique circumstances within each community. The training model is molded to fit the community, not the community to fit the training model.

This training is considered by the authors to be a strong back-up for The Guide intervention as students and teachers who now have increased their mental health literacy may ask for help when they self-identify or identify others with potential mental health problems or mental disorders. At the system level, "Go-to" Educator Training addresses both early identification and enhanced access to care needs. It does not require additional resources to be added to schools, uses feasibility rather than fidelity approaches and links existing community resources together as part of the training program. At the person level, the training focuses on upgrading individuals' competencies in mental health knowledge, case identification strategies, tools and resources, the navigation of local mental healthcare systems, referral processes, and communication strategies with parents and families.

To be tested together with The Guide program, the Chair Team first conducted a trial of "Go-to" Educator Training in a rural high-school in Nova Scotia involving six "go-to" educators identified by the school principal. Training results showed significantly improved and sustained knowledge (three-month follow-up) in the identification of mental disorders and support of youth at high risk for mental disorder (Kutcher & Wei 2013). Following this, the "Go-to" Educator Training was modified and then delivered to the HRSB, with 134 participants taking part in the training. The findings were consistently significantly and substantively positive with regards to knowledge up-take (d = 2.3) and attitudinal change (d = 0.36) (Wei & Kutcher, 2013).

With the demonstrated success of the "Go-to" Educator Training in these evaluations, the Nova Scotia Department of Education decided to disseminate the "Go-to" Educator Training program in all junior high and secondary schools throughout the province and applied through the SchoolsPlus initiative under the authority of the Student Services Division of the DOE. The SchoolsPlus initiative is a collaborative interagency approach supporting the whole child and their family, with school as the center of human services delivery components.

In this intervention the train-the-trainer model was also applied, and SchoolsPlus took the administrative leadership role to recruit SchoolsPlus coordinators from each school board and link them to the "Go-to" Educator Training program. These coordinators were responsible for embedding the "Go-to" Educator Training into each of their respective school boards. Each coordinator identified a training team and helped principals of individual schools in choosing on-site personnel who would then receive the training program. They also participated in the training delivered by the Chair Team, and acted as logistical supports to the trainer teams once they had been established.

These sessions took place between November 2012 and June 2013 and engaged 169 participants, significantly upgrading participants' knowledge (d = 2.4) and promoting positive attitudes toward mental health (d = 0.3). More information about this train-the-trainer model can be found at: http://teenmentalhealth.org. The training of "go-to" educators delivered by trainers in each school board is continuing and further assessments on how schools are being linked with health providers along the care continuum is being developed.

The Nova Scotia approach to packaging two separate but complementary programs together has created the initial and essential steps for students toward the pathway to mental healthcare. The success of this approach has encouraged other jurisdictions to follow suit. It provides an exemplary case on how a mental health literacy program can be embedded in the school's existing curriculum to sustain its impacts, and how early identification of mental disorders can be achieved through the "Go-to" Educator Training program. It is recommended that these two programs are packaged to deliver to schools together.

Promoting mental health literacy and facilitating smooth transition to post-secondary schools through Transitions

While The Guide functions as the foundational mental health literacy program for the pathway to mental healthcare, the Chair Team has also created other programs that can be applied within the Pathway to Care Model. One of these is Transitions, a comprehensive life-skills resource embedding mental health, targeting students in their final year of secondary school and students who are enrolled in their first year of post-secondary education. Transitions was first created in 2007 to help students address common life challenges when moving into post-secondary school life, improve mental health literacy, de-stigmatize mental illness, increase help-seeking behaviors, and thus help to facilitate smooth transitions from high school to post-secondary institutions. It has been shown to be positively accepted and to enhance both discussion about mental health and help-seeking behaviors in post-secondary school students (Boucher, Szumilas, Sheikh, & Kutcher, 2010).

Transitions is unique in how it presents mental health information to youth in a manner that is de-stigmatizing and readily accessible. In Transitions, mental health information and mental health resource identification are blended together with information about how to deal with the everyday life challenges associated with beginning university or college. Therefore, Transitions not only addresses mental health literacy, but also typical student life. It provides a holistic approach to health and wellbeing that helps empower students with the information they need to make informed choices about multiple aspects of both their physical and mental health.

Transitions has evolved through two stages of development. The first version covered numerous topics, including relationships, finances, time management, study strategies, stress management, sexual health, substance use/abuse, and common mental disorders. It further provided resources and tips for help-seeking. It included two booklets, one passport-sized condensed booklet for students, and one full version for student service staff. This version reached approximately 8000 university students across Canada. An online survey of 112 students reported that over 95% of respondents liked the material, over 40% discussed the material with peers, and 16% had or planned to seek help from counseling services because of what they had read (Boucher *et al.*, 2010).

The second version of Transitions was developed and launched in 2013 to accommodate increasing advances in research findings and an increasingly electronically sophisticated student body. The new version keeps a number of topics that were previously addressed, but organizes them in a more systematic manner and adds new research findings and a harm-reduction approach. It has more detailed description of mental health and mental disorders and focuses on using youth-friendly language, and contextually relevant visual cues. It adds more practical strategies to teach students how to deal with the challenges of their increased independence when entering into post-secondary institutions. Furthermore, in addition to paper copies, the larger booklet can be viewed online as a PDF or downloaded as an eBook, and the passport booklet can be downloaded as a free iPhone app (enhanced by interactive and immediate help-linking features), which makes it accessible to a wider audience. Since the launch of this new version of Transitions in September 2013, it has reached more than 6000 university students in Nova Scotia and it is expected to be delivered to all Grade 12 students in the province with the support of the DOE in late spring 2014. In addition, within the first month, the resource has been shared and viewed across social networks over 13 500 times. Other provinces and national organizations are following Nova Scotia to promote this new material across the country. The Mental Health Commission of Canada, along with The Kids Help Phone and The Jack Project, have provided their endorsement for the inclusion of this resource across Canada at both the final years of school as well as the early years of university or college.

The success of Transitions in both versions is attributed in part to the participatory strategies that have characterized its application. Although written by mental health professionals, the process also engaged local university faculty, counselors, administrators, youth, and parents to provide ongoing feedback during the process of material development. Similarly, the dissemination of Transitions has been carried out through the engagement of a comprehensive network of related stakeholder organizations throughout the province. A similar model is being developed across the country in support of its national roll-out, which will begin in 2014.

Discussions and conclusions

Youth mental health can be effectively addressed (promotion, prevention, intervention) if mental health literacy is embedded in everyday school curriculum in order to promote understanding of mental health and mental disorders, to reduce stigma toward mental disorders, and to enhance help-seeking behaviors of youth in need of care. When this enhanced mental health literacy coincides with linkages between schools and primary care, it creates a better opportunity for early identification and increased access to best evidence-based interventions – both important aspects for good intervention prognosis.

This chapter has provided evidence-based examples of how these goals might be achieved through the Pathway to Care Model. A number of factors have contributed to the success of this model and to the utility of this model for broad national and global dissemination.

First, it is the flexibilities of the Pathway to Care Model that allow the establishment of approaches that best fit local needs and realities. Examples presented in this chapter have shown that different approaches in Nova Scotia and Ontario can have similar significantly positive and substantive results, but that the approaches and applications differ. The model is not prescriptive but facilitatory, and it can be applied to various settings easily and without significant additional investments. Second, regardless of the setting in which the model has been applied, evaluations have indicated that multi-sector collaboration is an important component in its success. For example, the training of teachers on the implementation of The Guide in their classrooms is done by training teams that include teachers, school-based student services providers (e.g., school counselors, psychologists), local healthcare providers, and mental health and addictions care providers. By training such a community representative multidisciplinary group simultaneously, the training process facilitates the network connections that help create and cement the Pathway to Care Model in the community, even in the absence of formal cross-sector linkages or specific health or educational sector policies. Third, the model builds upon the existing strengths and educational social ecology already inherent in the school system and does not require a significant amount of new investment (infrastructure or human resources). It is easily sustainable and likely to be cost-effective. Also, it has been eagerly embraced and naturally championed by teachers, administrators, and other frontline personnel who have seen the positive impacts resulting from The Guide's application.

Furthermore, this work has been accompanied by substantial program evaluation and research as it has developed. Rigorous program evaluation has been used to help develop the interventions and to demonstrate the promising results that the interventions can have. Independent and rigorous research studies have then further been conducted to confirm the significant and substantial positive impact of this approach for students and teachers. This praxis approach has the strength of building each next step of its dissemination on the foundation of solid data regarding its success. This is an important component to the development and widespread dissemination of the model.

It is essential that evidence-based approaches to school mental health be used, and that those approaches can be widely utilized easily and reasonably to maximize their positive impacts. We have been able to demonstrate this within the Canadian context and are now expanding to other countries, some of which have considerably fewer resources than Canada. This combination of evidence and feasibility is essential for the future development of any school mental health initiative. Although school mental health has received increasing attention in recent years and numerous programs have been created for application in schools, it is noticeable that, to-date, limited evidence has been found for the effectiveness of many programs and some may even cause harm (Weare & Nind 2011; Wei & Kutcher, 2012). Therefore, educators need to be careful in selecting best evidence-based programs for use in their institutions and with their students.

This chapter has provided some robustly evaluated examples to show how school mental health evaluation and research can be conducted in the school setting in collaboration with various stakeholders and in support of the ongoing development of effective interventions.

Challenges to the application of these approaches have included: the cost, time, and effort to develop and evaluate the programs; the existing political drive to purchase and apply school external standalone programs instead of using approaches that build on existing strengths (pedagogic, administrative, ecologic); the need to involve a large number of diverse stakeholders (e.g., provincial government bureaucrats, teacher organizations, school administrators, health providers); and the need to find and work with champions at the government, community, and school levels. Solutions to these challenges must be determined at each location and with each level of stakeholders because the nature, scope, and variety of issues that need to be addressed, while sharing some commonalities, are locally unique. The development of strong partnerships with other related organizations operating in different jurisdictions can help address many of these challenges.

In conclusion, this chapter has described a comprehensive model with diverse examples to address youth mental health needs in the school setting, integrated into and with the support of the community into which the school is embedded. The examples of the Pathways to Care Model implementation and related research evidence show it may be a useful framework that can be adopted by other educators and researchers in various locations to promote school mental health literacy and early identification of mental disorders in their school settings, both nationally and internationally. Currently, a number of other Canadian provinces are actively engaged in applying and evaluating these programs and this approach. Other countries such as Brazil and Malawi have also translated, adapted, implemented, and evaluated The Guide in their school settings. All of these national and international initiatives have demonstrated similar positive results as we presented in this chapter. This suggests that addressing numerous aspects of school mental health through a pragmatic mental health literacy approach, built on existing and commonly applied pedagogic process, molded to existing school realities and implemented collaboratively, may offer a useful, effective, successful, and sustainable framework for school mental health globally.

References

American Psychiatric Association 2013, *Diagnostic and statistical manual of mental disorders*, 5th ed., American Psychiatric Association, Washington, DC.

Bhatia, S. 2007, Childhood and Adolescent Depression, *American Family Physician*, vol. 75, no. 1, p. 73.

Boucher, J., Szumilas, M., Sheikh, T., & Kutcher, S. 2010, Transitions: A mental health literacy program for postsecondary students, *Journal of College Student Development*, vol. 51, no. 6, pp. 723–727.

Breslau, J., Miller, E., Joanie Chung, W. J. & Schweitzer, J. B. 2011, Childhood and adolescent onset psychiatric disorders, substance use, and failure to graduate high school on time, *Journal of Psychiatric Research*, vol. 45, no. 3, pp. 295–301.

Calear, A. L. & Christensen, H. 2010, Systematic review of school-based prevention and early intervention programs for depression, *Journal of Adolescence*, vol. 33, no. 3, pp. 429–438.

Faggiano, F., Vigna-Taglianti, F. D., Versino, E., Zambon, A., Borraccino, A., & Lemma, P. 2008, School-based prevention for illicit drugs use: A systematic review, *Preventive Medicine*, vol. 46, no. 5, pp. 385–396.

Hahn, R., Fuqua-Whitley, D., Wethington, H., *et al.*, 2007, Effectiveness of universal school-based programs to prevent violent and aggressive behavior: A systematic review, *American Journal of Preventive Medicine*, vol. 33, no. 2, Suppl, S114–S129.

Kessler, R. C., Avenevoli, S., Costello, J., *et al.* 2012, Severity of 12-month DSM-IV disorders in the National Comorbidity Survey Replication Adolescent Supplement, *Archives of General Psychiatry*, vol. 69, no. 4, pp. 381–389.

Kessler, R. C., Berglund, P., Demler, O., Jin, R., Merikangas, K. R., & Walters, E. E. 2005, Lifetime prevalence and age-of-onset distributions of DSM-IV disorders in the National Comorbidity Survey Replication, *Archives of General Psychiatry*, vol. 62, no. 6, pp. 593–602.

Kessler, R. C., Foster, C. L., Saunders, W. B., & Stang, P. E. 1995, Social consequences of psychiatric disorders I: Educational attainment, *The American Journal of Psychiatry*, vol. 152, no. 7, pp. 1026–1032.

Kutcher, S. 2011, Facing the challenge of care for child and youth mental health in Canada: A critical commentary, five suggestions for change and a call to action, *Health Care Quarterly*, vol. 14, pp. 15–21.

Kutcher, S. & Wei, Y. 2013, Challenges and solutions in the implementation of the School-Based Pathway to Care Model: The lessons from Nova Scotia and beyond, *Canadian Journal of School Psychology*, vol. 28, no. 1, pp. 90–102.

Kutcher, S., Wei, Y., McLuckie, A., & Bullock, L. 2013, Educator mental health literacy: a program evaluation of the teacher training education on the mental health & high school curriculum guide, *Advances in School Mental Health Promotion*, vol. 6, no. 2, pp. 83–93.

Lister-Sharp, D., Chapman, S., Stewart-Brown, S., & Sowden, A. 1999. Health promoting schools and health promotion in schools: Two systematic reviews, *Health Technology Assessment*, vol. 3, no. 22, pp 1–207.

Milin, R., Kutcher, S., Lewis, S., Walker, S., & Ferrill, N. 2013, Randomized controlled trial of a school-based mental health literacy intervention for youth: Impact on knowledge, attitudes, and help-seeking efficacy. Poster presentation at the 60th AACAP Annual Meeting, Orlando, USA.

Neil, A. L. & Christensen, H. 2009, Efficacy and effectiveness of school-based prevention and early intervention programs for anxiety, *Clinical Psychology Review*, vol. 29, no. 3, pp. 208–215.

Nova Scotia Department of Education. 2012, *Kids & learning first: A plan to help every student succeed*, Nova Scotia Department of Education: Halifax, NS.

O'Connell, M. E., Boat, T., & Warner, K. E. (eds.). 2009, *Preventing mental, emotional, and behavioral disorders among young people: Progress and possibilities*, National Academy of Sciences, Washington, DC.

Robinson, J., Hetrick, S. E., & Martin, C. 2011, Preventing suicide in young people: Systematic review, *Australian and New Zealand Journal of Psychiatry*, vol. 45, no. 1, pp. 3–26.

Rutter, M., Bishop, D. V. M., Pine, D. S., *et al.* (eds.). 2008, *Rutter's child and adolescent psychiatry*, 5th ed., Blackwell Publishing Ltd., Oxford.

School-Based Mental Health and Substance Abuse Consortium Knowledge Translation and Review Team. 2012, *Survey on school-based mental health and addictions services in Canada*, Mental Health Commission of Canada: Calgary, AB.

Shochet, I. M., Dadds, M. R., Ham, D., & Montague, R. 2006, School connectedness is an underemphasized parameter in adolescent mental health: Results of a community prediction study, *Journal of Clinical Child and Adolescent Psychology: The Official Journal for the Society of Clinical Child and Adolescent Psychology*, vol. 35, no. 2, pp. 170–179.

Waddell, C., Hua, J. M., Garland, O. M., Peters, R. D., & McEwan, K. 2007, Preventing mental disorders in children: a systematic review to inform policy-making, *Canadian Journal of Public Health*, vol. 98, no. 3, pp. 166–173.

Waddell, C., Offord, D. R., Shepherd, C. A., Hua, J. M., & McEwan, K. 2002, Child psychiatric epidemiology and Canadian public policy-making: The state of the science and the art of the possible, *The Canadian Journal of Psychiatry/La Revue canadienne de psychiatrie*, vol. 47, no. 9, pp. 825–832.

Weare, K. & Nind, M. 2011, Mental health promotion and problem prevention in schools: What does the evidence say?, *Health Promotion International*, vol. 26, Suppl 1, pp. 29–69.

Wei, Y. & Kutcher, S. 2012, International school mental health: Global approaches, global challenges and global opportunities, in *Evidence-based school psychiatry: Child and adolescent psychiatric clinics of North America*, eds. J. Bostic & A. Bagnell, Elsevier, Netherlands, pp. 11–28.

Wei, Y. & Kutcher, S. 2013, "Go-to" educator training on the mental health competencies of educators in the secondary school setting: a program evaluation, *Child and Adolescent Mental Health*, DOI: 10.1111/camh.12056.

Wei, Y., Kutcher, S., & Szumilas, M. 2011, Comprehensive school mental health: An integrated "School-Based Pathway to Care" model for Canadian secondary schools, *McGill Journal of Education*, vol. 46, no. 2, pp. 213–229.

WHO Regional Office for Europe. 1996, *Regional guidelines: Development of health-promoting schools. A framework for action*, WHO Regional Office for the Western Pacific, Manila.

World Health Organization. 2004, *The global burden of disease*, WHO, Geneva.

The future of teaching mental health literacy in schools

Alexa Bagnell and Darcy Santor

Introduction

Health literacy has been recognized as a key factor in determining health outcomes across the lifespan [1,2]. Young people are making choices every day that impact their health outcomes in both the short and long term, and require the information and skills to make these decisions [3]. With the majority of mental illnesses having onset in adolescence and young adulthood, youth are an obvious focus for health promotion and prevention initiatives targeting mental health literacy [4]. From the perspective of health promotion and prevention, improving mental health literacy could have significant impact in terms of empowering individuals and communities in caring for their health. Beyond knowledge acquisition and following health instructions, health literacy is viewed as a personal asset in developing the skills required to make complex decisions about health [5,6]. The fundamental assumption of most health and mental health programs, irrespective of their intended outcome or delivery mechanism, is that knowledge, skills, and awareness can be acquired and that their acquisition can lead to better health choices and positive health improvement [7,8].

Schools are where most young people spend the majority of their waking hours, and where mental health problems can have a significant negative impact on the trajectory of students if they do not receive help for mental health challenges when needed. Although schools have the potential to implement programs that reach the most numbers of youth, educators rarely have expertise in mental health. Yet due to the increasing prevalence of mental health disorders impacting school success in our youth and the poor health outcomes associated, there is growing demand for both mental health education and prevention and intervention strategies provided for youth within schools. This chapter will examine the evolving concept of health literacy and research in the need for and interventions targeting mental health literacy. The rationale for school- and youth-based approaches, as well as the utilization of technology integration and concepts of twenty-first-century learning in reaching youth and educators in and out of the classroom will be discussed. Novel approaches through media to reach youth that both improve mental health knowledge and attitudes, and develop skills in accessing and assessing health information with the goal of better health choices are being developed globally. An interactive web-based program, MyHealth Magazine, illustrates an information technology approach to teaching mental health literacy in and out of schools and developing mental health literacy as an individual asset by establishing a daily presence in the lives of young people [9]. The MyHealth Magazine program is composed of a variety of free (e.g., phone apps) and paid

School Mental Health: Global Challenges and Opportunities, ed. Stan Kutcher, Yifeng Wei and Marc D. Weist. Published by Cambridge University Press. © Cambridge University Press 2015.

subscription-based (e.g., classroom materials and online magazines) resources that are available to young people, educators, and parents.

Health literacy

Health literacy has evolved over the past decade, and is conceptualized as both clinical risk and personal asset [5]. Early definitions emphasized "the ability to read and comprehend prescriptions bottles, appointment slips and other essential health-related materials required to successfully function as a patient" [10]. This definition referred to clinical risk, and specifically literacy skills, and the ability to understand health-related information and materials related to level of education as a determining factor in health literacy. However, health decisions are not based on solely reading information, they also require cognitive and social skills in making a choice around health. Health literacy is "the degree to which individuals have the capacity to obtain, process, and understand basic health information and services to make appropriate health decisions" [11]. This expanded concept has led to health literacy being viewed as a personal asset (Figure 5.1) [5], underscoring the importance of health education and communication skills in providing young people with the tools for making health choices.

Critical health literacy focuses on building relevant developmentally specific health knowledge and skills in a population to help individuals have more control in their health and

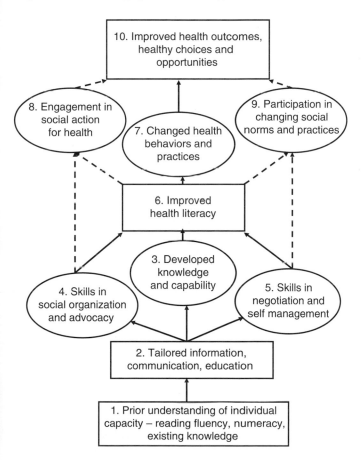

Figure 5.1 Concept of health literacy as an asset. Copied with permission from D. Nutbeam, *Social Science & Medicine* 67 (2008) 2072–2078.

health-related decisions, incorporating both learning and health promotion concepts [5]. At the level of the individual, the World Health Organization (WHO) defines health literacy as obtaining a level of knowledge, personal skills, and confidence to take action to improve personal and community health by changing personal lifestyle choices and living conditions [12]. By improving people's access to health information, ensuring it is relevant to the individual and developing skills to use it effectively, health literacy provides empowerment to individuals and communities in caring for their health [5]. Health decision making is influenced by a range of educational, cognitive, cultural, and ethical issues, including levels of literacy in general [13,14]. Knowledge acquisition theory supports that the method of information delivery has an impact on knowledge uptake and skills, and that learning is shaped by what is already known and how information is obtained and learned [15]. In a review of 38 studies looking at interventions to target low health literacy, there were several discrete design features that improved participant comprehension, including prioritizing information, using tables to display information, and adding video to narrative [8]. These components are important to recognize and address in developing a health literacy program and are determined by the target population characteristics.

The importance of health literacy

Low health literacy is associated with poorer health outcome and decreased use of health services [1]. A recent systematic review of evidence on literacy and health outcomes concluded that "low literacy is associated with several adverse health outcomes, including low health knowledge, increased incidence of chronic illness, and less than optimal use of preventive health services" [14]. In a systematic review of 24 studies by DeWalt, health literacy in children and parents was positively correlated to improved health outcomes [16]. A study of over 5000 Dutch adults found that improving health literacy had the potential to mediate the differences found with lower levels of education and low self-reported poor health [17].

Health literacy skills are an important personal asset for maintaining or improving one's health. From this perspective, low health literacy skills may be a barrier in access to health information and healthcare, medication use, and the prevention of disease [5]. One of the most important factors affecting knowledge uptake is the level of literacy, in general, and health literacy, in particular, of young people. Other studies have shown that although young people believe that accurate health information is available, they do not necessarily have the skills to determine the accuracy of the information in order to make an informed decision about their health [18]. Given the enormous burden of poor health without adequate health literacy, and the potential to reduce negative outcomes with intervention, the US Department of Health and Human Services recently released a national action plan on health literacy [19]. This action plan calls for increased research, development, implementation, and evaluation of interventions to improve health literacy. Accurate health information and decision-making skills need to be accessible in relation to both the individual and their context in order to impact on the decisions made about health every day [12]. Improving mental health literacy in this context of overall health literacy is viewed as a key health promotion initiative to advance the mental health of individuals and communities [12].

Mental health literacy

Mental health literacy has received attention in terms of reducing stigma, promoting resilience, and providing education about mental health and mental illness. In a WHO study looking at barriers to mental health treatment worldwide, low perceived need and attitudinal barriers (e.g., stigma, negative view of treatment) were the most significant barriers in terms of help-seeking and staying in treatment [20]. Addressing knowledge and attitudes through literacy programs can help bridge the gap between what people believe and the science of mental illnesses and their treatment [20]. Measurement of specific knowledge in common mental illnesses (depression, schizophrenia, social anxiety, and post-traumatic stress disorder) in a community population survey of 1000 people revealed that those with personal experience or close to someone with mental illness and female gender scored higher on recognition and awareness of treatment [21]. Higher mental health literacy scores predicted greater belief of these disorders as illnesses, and not perceived weakness, in support of improved mental health literacy reduced stigma [21]. Mental health literacy can dispel myths and help individuals recognize, manage, and prevent illness [22].

Jorm [23] defines the key components of mental health literacy as recognition of mental disorders, knowledge, and belief about risk factors and availability of appropriate help and treatment, attitudes that facilitate recognition and help-seeking, and knowledge about how to seek mental health information. Kelly, Jorm, and Wright recently highlighted the grow-ing body of literature documenting the mental health literacy deficits in adolescents and young adults and reviewed a number of health literacy programs [24].

The objective of mental health literacy programs is to build a knowledge base and provide capacity-building tools for identifying and helping youth with mental illness by targeting health literacy tools for both youth and the adults in their world. In interventions targeting health literacy, proxy measures of improved health behaviors (e.g., knowledge and self-efficacy) are frequently measured, but very few – if any – studies measure behaviors [25]. For most programs, the core element of health literacy is decision-making. Some research suggests that young people begin making decisions about their own health from about age 15 [26]. Given the strong link between general levels of literacy and health literacy, and the evidence that young people begin making decisions about their health during their middle school years, there is a credible argument that health decision-making skills should be an integral part of the school curriculum even before health decisions are being made. [27] Long-term health and well-being of all individuals is inextricably linked with the level of education and literacy that individuals attain over the course of their lifetime, including education around health and mental health [1].

Mental health in schools

Schools today face great demands to teach curriculum, to prepare students with vocational skills, to socialize children to interact with others appropriately, and to meet their health, emotional, and behavioral needs that impact their learning. According to the Canadian Coalition for Children and Youth Mental Health, the mental health of students is the "number one issue facing schools today" [28]. The demands far exceed the supply and capacity of schools. As many as 1 in 5 young people have a mental disorder of some kind, and most psychiatric illnesses begin in adolescence [29,30,31]. Mental health difficulties in youth are one of the strongest predictors of academic failure [4] and absenteeism [32]. Despite the high prevalence of mental illness in children and adolescents, 80% of young people with mental illness do not seek help or receive adequate treatment [33,34,35]. Barriers to help-seeking in a systematic review of 22 qualitative and quantitative studies indicate that perceived stigma, problems recognizing symptoms as warranting help, and wishing to be self-reliant are all obstacles [36].

Schools are a place where youth at risk can be identified and seek help; these barriers are key targets in mental health literacy interventions for youth. It also speaks to the importance of having educators trained in mental health literacy to support and encourage appropriate identification and help-seeking. Since most youth attend school, schools have become an important arena for addressing the growing mental health needs of children and adolescents. Youth spend close to half of their waking hours each day in school. For most children, school is the one natural setting where professionals are consistently available to monitor how they are functioning and learning, and to intervene and support in almost aspects of their lives when necessary.

Teaching mental health literacy to youth

Educators are in a key position to identify and support students with mental health problems and to promote mental health literacy. However, most do not have core knowledge in mental health and do not feel confident they have the skills to identify and support youth with mental health problems. In a large Canadian study surveying 3900 teachers, the majority of teachers reported mental health issues such as anxiety, stress, depression, and ADHD were significant concerns within the school setting, and 87% reported there was a lack of educator training about mental illness, thus creating a barrier for supporting students in their schools [37]. Approximately two-thirds of teachers reported that they had received no training in mental health literacy, and among newer teachers, three-quarters reported never having had any training. Almost all educators sampled expressed a desire to increase their skills and knowledge in the domain of mental health [38]. Ongoing professional learning for teachers and all school staff is clearly warranted.

It is important to include within the many mental health promotion initiatives currently being developed, researching the most effective ways to prepare teachers and provide ongoing information and supports beyond the in-service settings. It is no longer sufficient to provide "one-off" workshops to teachers with facts about mental illnesses and bullying and expect practices to change substantially in school systems. Although many teachers have received some kind of training, studies continue to document the lack of efficacy on the part of teachers with respect to mental health literacy. Evidence supports that along with education there needs to be some practical skills and strategies implemented, and that integrated programs are more successful than standalone education opportunities [39,40].

In Canada there are several initiatives targeting educators in schools to help improve mental health literacy for youth. Two of these programs are Mental Health First Aid (developed by Jorm and colleagues in Australia) [41] and the Mental Health High School Curriculum Guide (developed by Kutcher and colleagues in Canada) [42], which are based on a mental health education curriculum. Both programs have been evaluated and show improvement in knowledge and attitudes about mental health and illness after delivery of the program [37,41,42,43]. Research in mental health outcomes in health promotion studies is lacking, although interventions promoting and increasing mental health literacy appear to be good starting points for future initiatives with focus on changing knowledge and attitudes [42]. Health-promoting school initiatives addressing overall health and integrating this within the school curriculum have shown positive results in health behaviors [44].

Stigma and preconceived beliefs about mental illness impact recognition [43] and help-seeking, and needs to be addressed in any mental health literacy program. Stigma does not appear to be impacted by one-off interventions [43,45], and it is inconclusive in school interventions [46,47]. Teacher beliefs and perceptions regarding mental health issues need to be considered within any training program in order for any change in behavior [37]. This speaks to the need for mental health literacy to be embedded in schools, integrated, and led by educators in creating an environment of acceptance and normalization of mental illnesses in order to improve recognition, decision making, and help-seeking in young people.

Twenty-first-century learning

Information changes daily, and what was fact a decade ago may be different from today based on scientific discoveries and advances in technology. The pace of change over the next several decades due to advances in technology will require different skills than rote learning. Learning for the future requires greater emphasis on the learning of skills over the learning of content, which is the focus of twenty-first-century learning [48]. The content relevant to a student's interests is constantly changing and growing, and instruction should more consistently focus on the skills required to find and use relevant content rather than on the delivery of pre-determined content.

Initiatives in mental health literacy should incorporate these concepts in order to best prepare youth to cope with an ever-changing and progressing healthcare landscape, and to be able to apply these skills to choices and decisions they are making. The core concepts of twenty-first-century learning are moving from static information to discovery of information, tailoring learning to the needs of the individual to make material more relevant, assessing progress in developing skills, and not just memorizing content, and creating lifelong learners beyond the classroom. Some suggestions for implementing these concepts include blending in-class teaching with online learning so learning takes place outside the classroom, and having technology utilized for learning and teaching tools to help customize learning needs and provide ongoing access to information with appropriate guidance and feedback [48].

Use of media

Adolescents utilize media for entertainment, social networking, communication, and education. Youth in the United States now spend an average 7.5 hours per day using some form of media [49], in some cases more hours than they sleep at night and more hours than in school. Internet access has increased dramatically in the past decade, with 95% of Canadians under the age of 55 now having internet access, almost 50% with mobile access; 86% of teens use a search engine at least every week to find out information [50], with similar usage in other developed countries [51]. Tapping into this media usage for access to young people with the opportunity to reach more youth with health information and critical health literacy skills has been the focus of initiatives across the globe.

The impact of the media on health, and the large amount of time adolescents spend with media, make it critical to integrate it in mental health literacy [52]. In keeping with concepts of twenty-first century learning, successful health-promoting media literacy education results not so much from what is taught, as to how it is taught and the skills obtained [53]. To date, studies have measured and shown knowledge uptake, but not measured attitudes and behavior changes [53]. Applications that are interactive and involve peer-led components have been shown to be the most effective with youth in promoting help-seeking [54,55,56].

Research in mental health literacy internet-based programs

Access to health information allows people to take an active role in their healthcare, and developing skills in utilizing this knowledge in health decision making is important in developing mental health literacy as a personal asset. The internet is an increasingly popular way for people to obtain health information, but there are a number of barriers that prevent people making full use of such information. In particular, people may not be motivated to use the internet, or they may not have the skills they need to determine what information is relevant and accurate in making a health decision [57,58,59]. Teaching people to find, evaluate, and use online health information (online health literacy) can improve these skills, but research in this area is limited, and the data in adults are not sufficient, to date, to allow conclusions as to what works in terms of online health literacy [60].

Apart from leisure use, some studies have indicated that the internet has become an instrumental information-searching tool for people with health concerns [61], especially for adolescents [62]. Web-based interventions have improved outcomes in health-related behavioral changes compared to non-web-based interventions delivering similar materials [63]. Informative educational websites containing physical and mental health information, such as the National Institutes of Health, Go Ask Alice!, and beyondblue are examples, commonly termed eHealth initiatives [64]. The dissemination of resources on websites represents one of the most rapidly growing uses of the internet in both an attempt to increase knowledge transfer as well as knowledge uptake. Internet-based mental health resources offer a unique opportunity to link young people and those working with youth with health-expert information and tools to help them with health decision making, identifying needs, and accessing resources [61,65]. Youth have grown up in a rapidly evolving technology culture and are more comfortable in this media.

Previous literature suggested that internet-based intervention on health education for adolescents was more effective than for adults. In a review of help-seeking interventions for young people and effectiveness in improving knowledge, attitudes, and behaviors, the majority of the interventions were via the internet (6/8), and mental health literacy programs showed positive significant changes in knowledge and attitudes toward help-seeking for mental health problems [66]. However, no study has effectively measured a difference in help-seeking behaviors as a result of these studies, mostly related to the difficulty in measuring behavior change in studies [56], although there is some preliminary evidence that these interventions promote help-seeking [54,57]. Those interventions engage young people through interactive forums, games, and websites to enhance their mental health literacy [67,68].

Modern media provide an ideal platform to individually tailor materials and skills as needed in making health decisions. *Inspire Australia* utilizes these resources to promote mental health targeting to reach youth at risk of mental health problems [51]. This program is based around individualizing delivery in facilitating positive mental health in groups of young people at increased risk of mental health difficulties, and with diverse literacy and skill needs. Research supports that interventions that directed the participant to relevant, individually tailored materials reported increased time and frequency spent utilizing the resource [63]. Media also provide the opportunity to translate "one-off" sessions into a daily presence with resources available as relevant in impacting health decisions and help-seeking. A single classroom session for adolescents with ongoing online resources in smoking cessation/prevention

(Spiral Technology Action Research) has shown improvements in outcomes [18]. Classroom-based learning supplemented by web-based learning is effective in increasing knowledge and decision-making skills when there is flexibility and feedback through the web-based materials [69].

Education research shows that learning takes place best in an environment that allows exploration and self-direction [70]. In looking at the challenges of health literacy, it has been recommended that health curricula integrate the usage of internet delivery of information to teach the skills necessary for youth to acquire and evaluate health information [17,40,57]. By engaging youth in the process of health learning in an interactive, immediate and individual way, knowledge is more relevant and can be utilized and integrated in context, thus promoting health literacy as a personal asset and skill.

MyHealth Magazine health literacy program

MyHealth Magazine (www.myhealthmagazine.net) is an online health and wellness program for students and educators developed around these core principles of mental health literacy and effective delivery. The program provides interactive online resources covering health and mental health topics in youth. It is composed of a series of online and classroom-based activities and workshops that can be used independently or be highly integrated. Educators report needing more training around mental health literacy, and how to help young people struggling with mental health issues [37]. Through this resource, educators, students, and parents have access to high-quality, relevant, engaging health and mental health information and tools that are updated every week.

The program was initiated approximately ten years ago, following the suicides of three youth, and was designed to (1) increase mental health literacy and (2) foster help-seeking in young people. The scientific integrity of the magazine content is overseen by the program co-directors, working with experts in the field, while the format and layout of the magazine and all of its components (e.g., Mental Health Minutes) is overseen by an independent creative director. The various components of the program have been formally evaluated over the past ten years and the program has continuously evolved to address the ongoing challenges faced in realizing these goals [54].

There have been significant challenges and opportunities faced at different times during the development of the program, from utilizing online resources to ensuring the sustainability of the program. The magazine has provided a direct opportunity to develop, test, and implement many of the recommendations, ideas and core objectives that have been anticipated by others [9,37,48,57], namely (1) that learning be always accessible; (2) that learning be modular and brief, allowing the learner to focus on specific topics; (3) that learning be interactive, providing immediate feedback; and (4) that learning be very practical and skills based.

1. Always accessible

Utilization data have shown that more people have access to the internet using a variety of devices every year. The benefits and advantages of the internet with respect to standardizing the delivery of information and programming, in a cost-effective manner, is widely acknowledged. Our own research examining the manner in which young people access mental health information demonstrated the need to be able to access information in a confidential manner outside of regular school hours [54]. MyHealth Magazine was developed as an online resource to meet this demand with a site providing accurate and accessible health and mental health information for students and educators.

However, the ease with which information can be posted online now constitutes one of the major threats to any internet program, namely the vast number of websites offering similar information that compete for users' attention. Internet-based health and mental health resources delivered through webpages now face the additional challenge of competing with applications that are deployed to "smartphones." Utilization data suggest that the amount of time that individuals spend on phones has now surpassed the amount of time spent on desktops [71]. Research examining the uptake of internet capable phones, relative to the uptake of broadband-connected computers, suggests that the so-called "digital divide" among high- and low-income earners is less apparent with respect to phone apps than with broadband computers. To increase accessibility, a phone app version of MyHealth Magazine, using both the smartphone and desktop/tablet versions of the program to promote and enhance one another, was developed.

2. Delivery is modular and brief

Effective knowledge uptake requires a strategy that is ever changing to meet the varied and unique demands and wishes of the end-user. Health information that is relevant and tailored is more likely to have uptake and be incorporated in health decisions. Our experience over the past decade has resulted in a two-front strategy of adapting the format of the information to the end user, while pursuing a marketing strategy that seeks to create and drive demand and ensures sustainability [9].

At present, the vast majority of school-based mental health programs fall into one of two groups, namely (1) fixed curricula that will be delivered to students during a fixed period in elementary or secondary school, often by a dedicated or trained educator; or (2) brief, single activity, which most often takes the form of an awareness-raising activity such as a workshop or event. This highlights an untapped need for materials that are brief and structured enough that any educator could deliver relevant mental health programming in any classroom on any given day. Virtually every university in North America already is or will be offering online learning opportunities. They are cheap, accessible to large numbers of people, and at the same time offer outstanding content and pedagogy, which is at least as good as, if not superior to, the average lecture or class. This format provides the opportunity for ongoing learning beyond the classroom and past the end of any school year, incorporating twenty-first-century learning strategies in training youth how to access mental health information that is relevant and timely. The goal is to create a sustained interest or "daily presence" in learning about mental health over the course of an entire lifetime.

This approach runs counter to the traditional learning structure, whereby a student works systematically through a curriculum, and learns and retains information until it is needed. In contrast, the premise behind the current model is (1) that learning is ongoing and information is changing, and (2) that learning can and should happen at any time and in any place. The educator materials are also designed in the same format, to promote mental health literacy and practical skills in helping with mental health problems in students, in brief modular packets. In many ways, brief ongoing learning better approximates the manner in which most individuals will acquire health information. Indeed, after completing formal education, most information will be received in small units, through media. Given that this may be the manner in which health information is predominantly acquired post formal schooling, there is good reason to optimize and promote this approach in mental health literacy [72].

Finding ways to deliver mental health knowledge and programming in small amounts continuously throughout the school year is important – it recognizes the premium on schools that have limited ability to free-up time for a dedicated curriculum while acknowledging the needs of students and educators to have ongoing health learning throughout the school years. Practically, this means packaging learning materials into short activities, which have been marketed to educators as Mental Health Minutes™. Even within multi-week curricula, there is the widely held view that effective instruction will be designed and delivered in 15-minute blocks. This emphasizes the importance of developing brief learning materials that can be delivered as standalone exercises or sequenced within lengthier learning activities, embedded in the daily life of students in learning something about mental health each and every day, week, or month throughout the year.

3. Engaging and interactive

Developing engaging learning materials has been a long-standing objective and priority for educators. Traditionally, this meant developing content that sustained a student's attention through the presentation of interesting materials and engagement techniques. Students are expected to acquire and retain information that will be utilized at some later date. However, we now live in an era where information is delivered, understood, and retained not only in brief sound-bites, but in a manner where feedback is expected to be immediate [73]. The traditional learning model is far less responsive.

Internet-based learning activities offer the possibility of offering every student immediate feedback on learning, through the use of brief knowledge tests that are scored immediately. By implementing smartphone applications, learning activities and interactive knowledge quizzes can render immediate feedback, and can also be facilitated by an instructor in the classroom. This capitalizes on the abilities of skilled instructors to inspire and motivate students, and the benefits of integrating technology to provide immediate feedback on knowledge acquisition.

The internet-based program has the capacity to continuously stream new interactive learning materials (e.g., pop-quizzes, Q&As, tips, did-you-knows) to students while maintaining the presence of certain materials (e.g., how-to sheets, articles, help-seeking resources) that are always available. Accordingly, the phone app contains a number of static, dynamic, and interactive resources that were developed with the dual goals of providing individuals with access to information that is always available (e.g., helplines, screening tools, and resources for promoting help-seeking), as well as access to information that is new and changing (e.g., mental health topic pop-quiz each week, new tips, and did-you-knows about a variety of health and mental health problems).

4. Practical

From a health-promotion perspective, the vast amount of information in a mental health literacy program should be action-oriented and practical (e.g., how to ask for help or decide if you have a mental health problem) as opposed to scientific (e.g., prevalence of depression) or technical (e.g., diagnosis of mental illness). In developing health literacy skills as a personal asset for each student, the goal is to have individuals making better health decisions, sooner. However, health decisions require some knowledge and understanding, and information needs to be balanced to include practical, scientific, and technical content.

Scientific knowledge is engaging (e.g., misuse of stimulants) and quite often more interesting than action-oriented, practical knowledge (e.g., effective studying tips). Both are important, although practical knowledge (e.g., how to talk to a parent about a mental health problem) may be more effective in improving health outcomes, but only with some knowledge that a problem or concern exists and that help is available. Education research shows learning is inherently interactive and works best when student interest can be mobilized and efforts fostered toward goals and outcomes. Technology can help mobilize knowledge, apply skills, and sustain interest to extend learning beyond the classroom.

In addressing the issue of practical delivery of mental health skills, MyHealth developed how-to sheets outlining five or six steps that one might take in dealing with a problem (e.g., for students, how to ask for help from a teacher; or for educators, how to talk to a student about self-harm). The classroom-based smartphone activities are oriented toward useful, skill-based outcomes: (1) where to locate important health information (e.g., where to get help) that is always available; (2) how to deal with specific mental health issues relevant to that individual; and (3) how to go about asking for help when the required information is not available or the proper course of action is not clear. In a climate of ever-changing information and materials available literally at your fingertips, the practical application of how, when, and where to look for information when needed are the health literacy skills for the future.

Conclusion

Given the significant influence that educators have on the development of children and the numerous documented links between academic and psychosocial development, a sustained, research-based focus on effective ways of promoting mental health literacy among educators within schools will help youth to reach their potential. Interventions need to be embedded within the daily life of young people and teach skills to make informed health decisions with the tools they use. Brief "one-off" interventions will be insufficient to produce meaningful changes in mental illness stigma and mental health literacy. Including technology and media in mental health literacy increases the interactivity, relevance, and accessibility of the material for youth, and engages educators in the lives of young people. Educators need to have easy-to-access and -utilize mental health information that improves their knowledge and skills as well. In viewing mental health literacy as a personal asset that requires training and practice in specific health knowledge and skills to help individuals make better health-related decisions, this framework provides the tools to teach these life skills to youth, embedded within the culture and world in which they live.

The expectation is that youth will make health choices, but they do not come ready equipped with the skills to understand and make sense of the barrage of health information available on a search engine and accurately apply it to themselves. The parts of the brain responsible for more "top-down" control (e.g., managing impulses, planning ahead, and making good health choices) are among the last to mature.

Programs incorporating twenty-first-century learning strategies and providing an interactive daily presence embedded in the culture of educators and youth in a school, such as MyHealth Magazine, are in keeping with what we know from health and education research in developing sustainable mental health literacy tools for youth. However, research continues to be needed as to the positive impact this could have on improving health outcomes in youth, and what the key components are in making this change.

References

(1) Berkman, N. D., Sheridan, S. L., Donahue, K. E., Halpern, D. J., & Crotty, K., Low health literacy and health outcomes: An updated systematic review. *Annals of Internal Medicine* 2011;155(2):97–107.

(2) Berkman, N. D., Dewalt, D. A., Pignone, M. P., *et al.*, Literacy and health outcomes. *Evidence Report/Technology Assessment* (Summ) 2004; 87:1–8.

(3) Skinner, H., Biscope, S., Poland, B., & Goldberg, E., How adolescents use technology for health information: Implications for health professionals from focus group studies. *Journal of Medical Internet Research* 2003;5(4):e32.

(4) Kessler, R. C., Foster, C. L., Saunders, W. B., & Stang, P. E., Social consequences of psychiatric disorders, I: Educational attainment. *American Journal of Psychiatry* 1995;152(7):1026.

(5) Nutbeam, D., The evolving concept of health literacy. *Social Science & Medicine* 2008;67(12):2072–2078.

(6) Chiarelli, L. & Edwards, P., Building healthy public policy. *Canadian Journal of Public Health* 2006;97:37–42.

(7) US Department of Health and Human Services. *Healthy people 2000: Understanding and improving health.* Washington, DC, US Department of Health and Human Services, 2000.

(8) Sheridan, S. L., Halpern, D. J., Viera, A. J., Berkman, N. D., Donahue, K. E., & Crotty, K., Interventions for individuals with low health literacy: A systematic review. *Journal of Health Communication* 2011;16:30–54.

(9) Santor, D. A. & Bagnell, A. L., Maximizing the uptake and sustainability of school-based mental health programs: Commercializing knowledge. *Child and Adolescent Psychiatric Clinics of North America* 2012;21(1):81–92.

(10) Ad Hoc Committee on Health Literacy for the Council on Scientific Affairs, American Medical Association. Health literacy: Report of the council on scientific affairs. *JAMA* 1999;281(6):552–557.

(11) Institute of Medicine. Health literacy: A prescription to end confusion. Washington, DC, National Academies Press, 2004.

(12) Chinn, D. Critical health literacy: A review and critical analysis. *Social Science & Medicine* 2011;73(1):60–67.

(13) Broner, N., Franczak, M., Dye, C., & McAllister, W., Knowledge transfer, policy making and community empowerment: A consensus model approach for providing public mental health and substance abuse services. *Psychiatric Quarterly* 2001;72:79–102.

(14) Rootman, I. & Ronson, B., Literacy and health research in Canada: Where have we been and where should we go? *Canadian Journal of Public Health* 2005;96:62–77.

(15) Corrigan, P. W., Kerr, A., & Knudsen, L. The stigma of mental illness: Explanatory models and methods for change. *Applied and Preventive Psychology* 2005;11(3):179–190.

(16) DeWalt, D. A. & Hink, A. Health literacy and child health outcomes: a systematic review of the literature. *Pediatrics* 2009;124: S265–274.

(17) Van der Heide, I., Wang, J., Droomers, M., Spreeuwenberg, P., Rademakers, J., & Uiters, E., The relationship between health, education, and health literacy: Results From the Dutch Adult Literacy and Life Skills Survey. *Journal of Health Communication* 2013;18:172–184.

(18) Skinner, H. A., Maley, O., & Norman, C. D., Developing internet-based eHealth promotion programs: The Spiral Technology Action Research (STAR) model. *Health Promotion Practice* 2006;7(4):406.

(19) US Department of Health and Human Services. Office of Disease Prevention and Health Promotion. *National action plan to improve health literacy.* US Department of Health and Human Services. Office of Disease Prevention and Health Promotion, Washington, DC, 2010.

(20) Andrade, L. H., Alonso, J., Mneimneh, Z., *et al.*, Barriers to mental health treatment: results from the WHO World Mental

Health surveys. *Psychological Medicine* 2013;44:1–15.

(21) Reavley, N. J., Morgan, A. J., & Jorm, A. F. Development of scales to assess mental health literacy relating to recognition of and interventions for depression, anxiety disorders and schizophrenia/psychosis. *Australian and New Zealand Journal of Psychiatry* 2013, DOI: 10.1177/0004867413491157.

(22) Jorm, A. F., Korten, A. E., Jacomb, P. A., Christensen, H., Rodgers, B., & Pollitt, P., "Mental health literacy": A survey of the public's ability to recognise mental disorders and their beliefs about the effectiveness of treatment. *Medical Journal of Australia* 1997;166(4):182–186.

(23) Jorm, A. F., Mental health literacy: Empowering the community to take action for better mental health. *American Psychologist* 2012;67(3):231.

(24) Kelly, C. M., Jorm, A. F., & Wright, A., Improving mental health literacy as a strategy to facilitate early intervention for mental disorders. *Medical Journal of Australia* 2007;187(7 Suppl):S26–30

(25) Clement, S., Ibrahim, S., Crichton, N., Wolf, M., & Rowlands, G., Complex interventions to improve the health of people with limited literacy: A systematic review. *Patient Education & Counseling* 2009;75(3):340–351.

(26) Taylor, L., Adelman, H. S., & Kaser-Boyd, N., Attitudes toward involving minors in decisions. *Professional Psychology: Research and Practice* 1984;15(3):436–449.

(27) Gray, N. J., Klein, J. D., Noyce, P. R., Sesselberg, T. S., & Cantrill, J. A., Health information-seeking behaviour in adolescents. *Social Science & Medicine* 2005;60(7):1467–1478.

(28) Brown, L., Mental health top issue facing schools, coalition says. 2011; Available at: www.thestar.com/news/canada/article/1001024–mental-health-topissue-. Accessed December 9, 2013.

(29) Esser, G., Schmidt, M. H., & Woerner, W., Epidemiology and course of psychiatric disorders in school-age children: Results of a longitudinal study. *Child*

Psychology & Psychiatry & Allied Disciplines 1990;31(2):243–263.

(30) Offord, D. R., Boyle, M. H., Szatmari, P., *et al.*, Ontario Child Health Study: II. Six-month prevalence of disorder and rates of service utilization. *Archives of General Psychiatry* 1987;44(9):832–836.

(31) Roberts, R. E., Attkisson, C. C., & Rosenblatt, A., Prevalence of psycho-pathology among children and adolescents. *American Journal of Psychiatry* 1998;155(6):715–725.

(32) DeSocio, J. & Hootman, J., Children's mental health and school success. *Journal of School Nursing* 2004;20(4):189–196.

(33) Langner, T. S., Gersten, J. C., Greene, E. L., Eisenberg, J. G., Herson, J. H., & McCarthy, E. D., Treatment of psychological disorders among urban children. *Journal of Consulting and Clinical Psychology* 1974;42 (2):170–179.

(34) Leaf, P. J., Alegria, M., Cohen, P., *et al.*, Mental health service use in the community and schools: Results from the four-community MECA study. *Journal of the American Academy of Child & Adolescent Psychiatry* 1996;35(7):889–897.

(35) National Plan for Research on Child and Adolescent Mental Disorders: A report requested by the US Congress submitted by the National Advisory Mental Health Council, 1990.

(36) Gulliver, A., Griffiths, K. M., & Christensen, H. Perceived barriers and facilitators to mental health help-seeking in young people: A systematic review. *BMC Psychiatry* 2010;10:113.

(37) Whitley, J., Smith, J. D., & Vaillancourt, T. Promoting mental health literacy among educators: Critical in school-based prevention and intervention. *Canadian Journal of School Psychology* 2013;28(1):56.

(38) Canadian Teachers Federation. *Understanding teachers' perspectives on student mental health: Findings from a National Survey.* Canadian Teachers Federation, Ottawa, Ontario, 2012; available at: www.ctf-fce.ca/Research-Library/StudentMentalHealthReport.pdf. Accessed February 3, 2014.

(39) Grimshaw, J. M., Shirran, L., Thomas, R., et al., Changing provider behavior: An overview of systematic reviews of interventions. *Medical Care* 2001;39(S2):2–45.

(40) Browne, G., Gafni, A., Roberts, J., Byrne, C., & Majumdar, B., Effective/efficient mental health programs for school-age children: A synthesis of reviews. *Social Science & Medicine* 2004;58(7):1367–1384.

(41) Jorm, A. F., Kitchener, B. A., Sawyer, M. G., Scales, H., & Cvetkovski, S., Mental health first aid training for high school teachers: A cluster randomized trial. *BMC Psychiatry* 2010;10(51):10–12.

(42) Kutcher, S. & Wei, Y., Mental health and the school environment: Secondary schools, promotion and pathways to care. *Current Opinion in Psychiatry* 2012;25(4):311–316.

(43) Skre, I., Friborg, O., Breivik, C., Johnsen, L. I., Arnesen, Y., & Arfwedson Wang, C. E., A school intervention for mental health literacy in adolescents: Effects of a non-randomized cluster controlled trial. *BMC Public Health*;13(1):1–15.

(44) Lee, A., Health-promoting schools: Evidence for a holistic approach to promoting health and improving health literacy. *Applied Health Economics and Health Policy* 2009;7(1):11–17.

(45) Wang, J. & Lai, D., The relationship between mental health literacy, personal contacts and personal stigma against depression. *Journal of Affective Disorders* 2008;110(1–2):191–196.

(46) Schachter, H. M., Girardi, A., Ly, M., et al., Effects of school-based interventions on mental health stigmatization: A systematic review. *Child and Adolescent Psychiatry and Mental Health* 2008;2:2–18.

(47) Pinto-Foltz, M., Logsdon, M. C., & Myers, J. A., Feasibility, acceptability, and initial efficacy of a knowledge-contact program to reduce mental illness stigma and improve mental health literacy in adolescents. *Social Science & Medicine* 2011;72(12):2011–2019.

(48) Premier's Technology Council, A vision for 21st century education. 2010; Available at: www.gov.bc.ca/premier/technology_council/index.html. Accessed November3, 2013.

(49) Henry, J., Kaiser Family Foundation: Daily media use among children and teens up dramatically from five years ago. 2010. Available at: http://kff.org/disparities-policy/press-release/daily-media-use-among-children-and-teens-up-dramatically-from-five-years-ago. Accessed February 3, 2014.

(50) *The Ipsos Canadian Interactive Reid report 2012 fact guide: The definitive resource on Canadians and the internet.* 2012. Available at: www.ipsos.ca/common/dl/pdf/Ipsos_InteractiveReidReport_FactGuide_2012.pdf. Accessed November 3, 2013.

(51) Stephens-Reicher, J., Metcalf, A., Blanchard, M., Mangan, C., & Burns, J., Reaching the hard-to-reach: How information communication technologies can reach young people at greater risk of mental health difficulties. *Australasian Psychiatry: Bulletin of the Royal Australian and New Zealand College of Psychiatrists* 2011;19; S58–61.

(52) Bergsma, L., Media literacy and health promotion for adolescents. *Journal of Media Literacy Education* 2011;3(1):25–28.

(53) Bergsma, L. J. & Carney, M. E., Effectiveness of health-promoting media literacy education: A systematic review. *Health Education Research* 2008;23(3):522–542.

(54) Santor, D., Poulin, C., LeBlanc, J., & Kusumakar, V., Facilitating help seeking behavior and referrals for mental health difficulties in school aged boys and girls: A school-based intervention. *Journal of Youth and Adolescence* 2007;36(6):741–752.

(55) Greenberg, M. T., Weissberg, R. P., O'Brien, M. U., et al., Enhancing school-based prevention and youth development through coordinated social, emotional, and academic learning. *American Psychologist* 2003;58(6–7):466–474.

(56) Gulliver, A., Griffiths, K. M., Christensen, H., & Brewer, J. L., A systematic review of help-seeking interventions for depression, anxiety and general psychological distress. *BMC Psychiatry* 2012;12(81), doi:10.1186/1471-244X-12-81.

(57) Santor, D. A. & Bagnell, A., Enhancing the effectiveness and sustainability of school-based mental health programs: Maximizing program participation, knowledge uptake and ongoing evaluation using internet-based resources. *Advances in School Mental Health Promotion* 2008;1(2):17–28.

(58) Gray, N. J., Klein, J. D., Noyce, P. R., Sesselberg, T. S., & Cantrill, J. A., The internet: A window on adolescent health literacy. *Journal of Adolescent Health* 2005 37(3):243.e1–243.e7.

(59) Benigeri, M. & Pluye, P., Shortcomings of health information on the Internet. *Health Promotion International* 2003;18(4):381–386.

(60) Car, J., Lang, B., Colledge, A., Ung, C., & Majeed, A., Interventions for enhancing consumers' online health literacy. *Cochrane Database of Systematic Reviews* 2011;6, doi: 10.1002/14651858.CD007092.pub2.

(61) Baker, L., Wagner, T. H., & Singer, S., Use of the Internet and e-mail for health care information: Results from a national survey. *JAMA* 2003;289:2400–2406.

(62) Rideout, V. & Henry, J., *Generation Rx.com: How young people use the Internet for health information.* Henry J. Kaiser Family Foundation; 2001. Available at: http://kai serfamilyfoundation.files.wordpress.com/ 2001/11/3202-genrx-report.pdf. Accessed February 3, 2014.

(63) Wantland, D. J., Portillo, C. J., Holzemer, W. L., Slaughter, R., & McGhee, E. M., The effectiveness of web-based vs. non-web-based interventions: A meta-analysis of behavioral change outcomes. *Journal of Medical Internet Research* 2004;6(4):e40.

(64) Bagnell, A. & Santor, D. Building mental health literacy: Opportunities and resources for clinicians. *Child and Adolescent Psychiatric Clinics of North America* 2012;21(1):1–9.

(65) Barak, A. & Grohol, J. M., Current and future trends in Internet-supported mental health interventions. *Journal of Technology in Human Services* 2011;29(3):155–196.

(66) Siemer, C. P., Fogel, J., & Voorhees, B. W. V. Telemental health and web-based applications in children and adolescents. *Child and Adolescent Psychiatric Clinics of North America* 2011;20(1):135–153.

(67) Li, T., Chau, M., Wong, P., Lai, E. S. Y., & Yip, P., Evaluation of a web-based social network electronic game in enhancing mental health literacy for young people. *Journal of Medical Internet Research* 2013;15(5):112–123.

(68) Primack, B. A., Wickett, D. J., Kraemer, K. L., & Zickmund, S., Teaching health literacy using popular television programming: A qualitative pilot study. *American Journal of Health Education* 2010;41(3):147–154.

(69) Sitzmann, T., Kraiger, K., Stewart, D., & Wisher, R., The comparative effectiveness of web-based and classroom instruction: A meta-analysis. *Personnel Psychology* 2006;59(3):623–664.

(70) Partnership for 21st Century Skills. Framework for 21st century learning. 2009; Available at: www.p21.org/storage/docu ments/P21_Framework.pdf. Accessed November 3, 2013.

(71) Reyburn, S., Flurry: Mobile app usage grows 35%. 2012; Available at: www.insidemobi leapps.com/2012/12/05/flurry-mobile-app-usage-grows-35/. Accessed December 9, 2013.

(72) Holstein, R. C., Lundberg, G. D., Donelan, K., *et al.*, Use of the Internet for health information and communication. *JAMA* 2003;290(17):2255–2258.

(73) Rideout, V. J., Foehr, U. G., & Roberts, D. F., Generation M2: Media in the lives of 8- to 18-year-olds. 2010. Available at: http://kff.org/other/poll-finding/report-gen eration-m2-media-in-the-lives-/. Accessed February 3, 2014.

Chapter

6

School-centered mental health
Creating school connectedness that fosters the mental wellness of its community's children, youth, and families

Connie Coniglio, Charlene King, Keli Anderson,
Steve Cairns, Deborah Garrity, Michelle Cianfrone,
and Jeff Stewart

The British Columbia School Centred Mental Health Coalition (the Coalition) is a vibrant, engaged, and diverse stakeholder group who share a vision for British Columbia (BC) schools, namely: *Ensuring that BC schools are safe and caring learning environments that foster the mental wellness of its community's children, youth, and families.* The Coalition was formed in the fall of 2010 when child and youth mental health champions came together, representing educators, researchers, community mental health service providers, tertiary mental health service providers, government policy makers, professionals, and public associations and advocacy groups. Today, the Coalition continues to grow, with over 40 members (see Appendix A), including prominent scholars and researchers in the field of social emotional learning, and highly acclaimed professionals in the fields of mental health and substance use, youth and family engagement, and nutrition and physical development. Expertise is shared in order to enhance our collective understanding of the whole child and impress the importance of attending to child and youth development. A value is placed on connectedness and reaching out broadly to communities where children, youth and families congregate, such as recreation centers, libraries, and cultural centers. The Coalition also provides opportunities for youth and family leaders to offer insights on the conditions they desire in their homes, schools and communities. These insights inform Coalition actions and initiatives taking place across the province.

The Coalition is supported by the considerable expertise and resources of its members, including volunteer co-chairs, steering committee members, and in-kind project management and meeting support. The Coalition meets quarterly to advance its vision and associated goals and objectives.

School Connectedness as an organizing principle

In the spring of 2012, Coalition members coalesced around establishing and promoting an overarching focus on "School Connectedness," including advancing key concepts, strategies, and research. This has become the key organizing principle of the Coalition. "School Connectedness" is about creating a school community where everyone feels safe, seen, heard, supported, significant, and cared for.

School Mental Health: Global Challenges and Opportunities, ed. Stan Kutcher, Yifeng Wei and Marc D. Weist. Published by Cambridge University Press. © Cambridge University Press 2015.

A core component of "School Connectedness" is the notion that schools are the defining center of a community. As such, the potential associated with school/community relationships needs to be fully realized to facilitate the mental wellness of children, youth, and families. Historically, families have entrusted schools to assist them with child and youth development, and local, regional, and provincial services frequently utilize schools as a conduit to support children, youth, and their families. The Coalition recognizes that schools are an underutilized hub for connections that can foster mental wellness in the community.

To further enrich the collaborative process, the Coalition works at the provincial level to facilitate linkages between members of the community to schools through a shared language that defines the values, beliefs, and practices of connectedness. The primary goal of these school–community connections is to nurture the mental health of children, youth, and families through partnerships among members of the community. Partnerships are achieved in a safe and effective manner that fosters a feeling of *belonging* for all. A fundamental tenant of the Coalition is that children, youth, and families must be included as valued members in the planning, implementation, and evaluation of all health-promoting activities.

How does the Coalition nurture the process of connectedness?

The Coalition acts as a *repository* for best practices and emerging innovations and as a hub for activity. A repository generally brings to mind a collection of resources; however, the Coalition's repository is housed in the "home base" of each of the members. Each member holds knowledge about historical and current work underway in their particular domain. Each coalition member brings a unique lens to the development of shared documents, activities and initiatives. This cross-pollination provides an ongoing opportunity to learn from each other while helping achieve consensus on how the vision of school connectedness and community development will be realized. Regular meetings provide an opportunity for *knowledge exchange* between members. Information on current activities and new initiatives across the province are shared. Respectful exchange of ideas and constructive critical feedback from member to member ultimately helps influence the design and implementation of initiatives that come to the table. A particular example of this concept in British Columbia is the work of the McCreary Centre Society, an active Coalition partner with specialized expertise in surveying and reporting on adolescent mental and physical health. The results of the provincial adolescent health survey are utilized to inform the work of the Coalition and its partners. This collaborative environment has contributed to the sustainability of the Coalition as a respected resource for school-centered mental health promotion within the province of BC and has recently garnered national and international recognition, including from the Mental Health Commission of Canada, the National Institute of Families for Child & Youth Mental Health, the Child Welfare League, and, most recently, the World Conference on the Promotion of Mental Health and the Prevention of Mental and Behavioural Disorders.

Coalition members are actively engaged through cross-organizational meetings, list serves, wiki links, and a shared Coalition website. A significant impact of multi-stakeholder collaboration occurring within the Coalition is the alignment of core values and shared goals. Inventories of resources, programs, services, contacts, and success stories and challenges are efficiently shared among members.

Coalition goals

The goals of the Coalition were established from the priorities and values identified by its members. As such, the Coalition represents a wide range of interests and perspectives. It is also represents the diverse sociocultural, geographic, and socioeconomic fabric of the province. The Coalition's goals are focused on improving the mental health of children, youth, and families through the power of aligned commitments and interest in creating connectedness. As such, members work collaboratively to achieve these goals, given the constraints and realities of their own unique settings.

Short-term goals and objectives

1. *Coalition members have*:
   - greater awareness of provincial initiatives – this includes, but is not limited to, child, youth and school professional mental health events, provincial frameworks, connectedness initiatives, school mental health resources, and cross-sector initiatives to improve access to mental health services;
   - increased access to resources; and
   - an opportunity to develop and maintain collaborative partnerships.
2. *BC school professionals, parents/caregivers, students, and policy makers*:
   - access reliable mental health and substance use information and supports; and
   - know how to foster a connected school culture that promotes positive mental health.
3. *BC parents, children, and youth* have opportunities for authentic engagement in the area of school-centered mental health. Authentic engagement can be characterized as a process that is both meaningful and worthwhile for all parties involved. One that is inclusive and open to learning, resulting in collaboration toward a shared purpose built on a foundation of transparency and trust.

Mid-term goals and objectives

1. *BC school staff* support student mental health and wellbeing and foster connectedness in classrooms and school communities.
2. *BC students and parents/caregivers* are authentically engaged in their school communities. Authentic engagement means that the voice of those with lived experience is respected and equally valued in discussion and planning.
3. *Policies* are in place to create a supportive environment for enhancing school connectedness and supporting child and youth mental health. Our goal is to have these policies clearly aligned and embedded in all levels of government and system support.
4. *Mental health services and resources* are integrated seamlessly into school communities[1] (e.g., family health centers in every school and/or community) with connections to schools.

---

[1] School communities include school staff, students, parents, families, and other local residents and organizations that have a stake in the school's success.

Strategies and practices

Similar to the creation of goals, the strategies and practices developed by the Coalition arose from consensus discussions among the members. The Coalition's discussions around strategies and practices focused on four broad areas:

1. parent, student, and community engagement;
2. school staff capacity building;
3. policy environment;
4. service integration.

To guide the design and implementation of strategies and practices in these areas and to promote sustainable, systemic growth, the Coalition identified the following key components:

1. Decision making must be based in valid research and informed by those impacted.
2. Meaningful and timely evaluation of strategies and practices is essential.
3. Broad adoption of practices is most readily achieved when it is felt to be correct by all relevant stakeholders.
4. Strategies and practices must be consistently aligned with systemic support from all levels.
5. Strategies and practices should be embedded in environments that are supportive, developmental, and non-judgmental.
6. It is critical that parents/care providers feel empowered as valued members of the communities that create and deliver mental health strategies and practices.

Ongoing actions and initiatives

To facilitate implementation of these key strategies and actions Coalition members generously contribute resources, enthusiasm, and expertise to support the following activities. All members of the Coalition contribute their time and their organization's resources (e.g., photocopying, space, time to participate on event-planning calls, and support with speaking engagements and workshops on school mental health).

The Summer Institute For the past five years, the Summer Institute has brought together teachers, school counselors, principals, district staff, parents, students, mental health professionals, and school community partners to exchange ideas about how to foster resiliency and connectedness and promote mental wellness in BC schools. It has helped raise awareness of the critical role of educators, schools, and their communities in influencing student mental health and wellbeing. This event is organized with BC Mental Health and Substance Use Services as the lead, with the majority of the planning committee consisting of Coalition members. Other members include government representatives, youth, and past attendees. The planning committee meets monthly over teleconference and is integral in developing ideas, providing feedback and securing speakers. The topics and themes have evolved over time as a result of the feedback provided by those attending year to year. In addition, the event began as a one day event and expanded to two days as a result of increasing demand and popularity. Most recently, the focus on day 1 of the event has been on building strong, resilient and connected school communities, while day 2 has been about addressing mental health and substance use challenges. The format of the day consists of keynote speakers, panel discussions, breakout sessions and a resource fair. There have also been efforts made to include options for parents/caregivers and youth to attend through an evening community event. Previous topics for keynote speakers or panel discussions have included resilience and relationship, self-regulation, social emotional learning, journey of school connectedness, parent and student experiences, systemic sustainability, mental health treatment, and the adolescent brain. Breakout session topics have included ADHD, anxiety, youth concurrent disorder, immigrant youth, weight and body image, LGBTQ youth, substance use and parent engagement. Evaluation of the Summer Institute has consistently indicated high-quality speakers, low cost, opportunities for networking, and appreciation of the resource fair. Feedback from the Summer Institutes show an over-whelmingly positive response to the event and an increasing demand for this type of professional development for educators during the summer and throughout the school year. The 2013 evaluation results showed that over 90% of participants agreed that the Summer Institute achieved its goals of increasing awareness and understanding of mental health issues and increasing knowledge about how to foster resiliency and connectedness in classrooms and schools.

Family Mental Health Alignment Family Mental Health Alignment connects to schools with children, youth, and families on proclaimed days like Family Day and National Child & Youth Mental Health Day (May 7), led by the National Institute of Families for Child & Youth Mental Health. For National Child & Youth Mental Health Day in 2012, the Coalition formed a sub-committee and helped create the new campaign *I care about you*. Schools and communities across BC and Canada asked kids to make statements about what adults do that demonstrate they care about kids. The Coalition continues to inform and support future Child & Youth Mental Health Day activities. Every year, the National Institute of Families for Child & Youth Mental Health (www.familysmart.ca) reviews the results from the previous Child & Youth Mental Health Day activities with the Coalition to give them the opportunity to provide input and support with planning, engagement and implementation through schools for upcoming events. The number of participating schools and communities has doubled over the last two years. In 2013, 130 sites participated in activities to connect kids to caring adults in schools and communities across Canada.

Provincial Professional Development Day This promotes and provides information on the Coalition and ideas for workshops on connectedness at Provincial School Professional Development days. The Coalition continues to present at conferences that engage youth, parents, and school personnel. An example is the BC Parent Confederation of Parent Advisory Councils (BCCPAC). Over 1000 parents are involved in the School Parent Advisory Councils and their annual conference provides an opportunity for them to gain knowledge and skills that can promote their input and engagement in schools across BC.

Student Voice & Focus Student Voice & Focus support youth action and involvement through youth-directed initiatives such as the Youth Summit. This event is organized by BC Mental Health and Substance Use Services in partnership with the Vancouver Canucks of the National Hockey League. It is a free, one-day workshop for high-school age youth in BC to learn about mental health and engage in fun activities and thoughtful dialogue. The event is planned in collaboration with youth organizations that work in the area of mental health, and with youth who are passionate about breaking down barriers and creating connections. The event has grown in the past two years, with the 2013 event having 200 in attendance, increasing to over 1000 youth, teachers, and parents in 2014 from across BC at Rogers arena. The theme of the 2014 event was tools for youth wellness. In addition, the event featured youth with lived experience, provided interactive activities and resources from a variety of youth mental health and substance use organizations. The goals and objectives of the event include:

1. building awareness of mental health and substance use issues;
2. learning about the range of mental health challenges and mental wellness;
3. connecting youth to tools, resources, and services to promote and support mental health; and
4. decreasing stigma associated with mental health challenges.

Evaluation of the event has indicated that the majority of attendees enjoyed learning about mental health and would like to see more events and presentations similar to the youth summit. In addition, most agreed that more class time should be spent on learning from people with mental illness. A highlight for the youth was the sharing of personal stories and the interactive breakout sessions and panel discussions. In the post event survey youth began to think of mental illness in a new and different way; words associated with mental illness became more positive (e.g., strength, courage, support, awareness, misunderstood). Furthermore, youth reported understanding that everyone struggles with mental health at times; there is a difference between mental illness and mental health; and that one can learn skills to develop positive mental health in self and others.

Provincial Engagement Provincial Engagement welcome the inclusion of those with similar objectives and vision for children, youth, and families. The Coalition strives to enhance the link between child, youth, family, and community needs with those who make and implement policy. In addition, the Coalition believes in assertively leveraging every opportunity available to help inform policy that impacts the mental health of children, youth, and families. The Coalition is closely linked with pan-Canadian activities and organizations. For example, The National Child & Youth Mental Health day has excellent uptake in schools across BC and connects adults to children and youth and homes to schools. Another example is the School Connectedness Capacity Building Initiative, jointly sponsored by the Coalition and the Directorate of Agencies for School Health (DASH BC), exploring existing strong practices in BC school communities to enhance school connectedness. The initiative is identifying BC school communities that have demonstrated success in improving school connectedness, and working with them to share their story and learning with others. The focus is to gain a deeper understanding of what good connectedness practice entails and to share it broadly with schools across the province.

Enhanced shared understanding

One of the greatest strengths of the Coalition comes from the ongoing collaboration of its members. For example, quarterly meetings and the Summer Institute are designed to facilitate a rich exchange of local, provincial, national and international trends, research, actions and initiatives in child, youth, and family mental health. These activities and others (see Appendix B) reveal the ongoing collaborative activities that are taking place between members and their respective organizations. The spirit of collaboration is safe and inviting. Ideas, suggestions, and broader alliances reflect the deep belief that "connectedness" starts with the Coalition. When this belief is modeled by the Coalition and translated into school-centered action, systemic silos are destroyed, increasing the potential for enhancing the mental health of children, youth, families and whole communities. The School Connectedness Capacity Building Initiative, mentioned earlier, is a good example of the collaboration that has been fostered by the Coalition. The initiative is guided by a cross-sector steering committee that includes representatives of government, a health promotion NGO, and Coalition members from the research community and education sector organizations for families, educators, trustees, and superintendents. The steering committee members work collaboratively across the silos, bringing their individual and their organizations' expertise to the table to strengthen the overall initiative.

Building sustainability

As a growing Coalition, the intent and value for connectedness requires strategic alignment to other provincial initiatives if it is to be sustainable and successful. This does not mean the Coalition loses its mandate or vision, but rather connectedness also applies to connecting with systems in order to collaborate and have greater potential to influence actions that can promote schools as the center for the mental health of children, youth, and their families in communities. Since its inception, members of the Coalition have intuitively understood the value of this approach, and have encouraged a growing diversity of affiliation and perspective in the membership. It is understood that each new Coalition member, regardless of their background or the system they work in, adds a unique and important dimension to the network of connections around the Coalition table. In an effort to formalize and support this intuitive but non-traditional way of working together, the Coalition has started exploring a structural approach to collaborative work known as "Collective Impact." The Collective Impact approach advances structural principles such as a common agenda, shared indicators of success, mutually reinforcing activities, and continuous communication – all key components of successful multi-stakeholders collaboration to address challenging issues. At the same time, the Collective Impact approach also discourages the simple, pre-determined solutions, acknowledging that meaningful change occurs as a result of the exchange of ideas and experiences, and that the most effective solutions emerge from that collaborative dialogue. By moving more explicitly and intentionally toward a Collective Impact-based approach to collaboration, the Coalition intends to strengthen the foundational approaches that have supported its collaborative work to date – benefiting from a growing global body of literature and experience related to Collective Impact – and at the same time evolve the collective understanding of how this work is done from intuitive to intentional and explicit.

Appendix A: Current member organizations (January 2013)

- Ministry of Children and Family Development
- Ministry of Health
- Ministry of Education
- Institute of Families for Child & Youth Mental Health
- BC Pediatric Society
- BC Mental Health & Addiction Services
- BC Children's Hospital
- BC Provincial Family Council
- BC Confederation of Parent Advisory Councils
- BC School Trustees Association
- BC School Superintendents Association
- BC School Principals & Vice-Principals Association
- BC Teachers Federation
- BC School Counsellors Association
- Learning Assistance Teachers Association
- Special Education Association
- The F.O.R.C.E. Society for Kids' Mental Health
- McCreary Centre Society
- UBC School of Nursing
- UBC Faculty of Education
- Centre for Addiction Research, UVIC
- WITS Program, UVIC
- FRIENDS For Life Program, MCFD
- Kelty Mental Health Resource Centre
- Directorate of Agencies for School Health (DASH BC)
- Dalai Lama Centre of BC
- School District 78 (Fraser Cascade)
- School District 71 (Comox Valley)
- School District 60 (Peace River North)
- School District 57 (Prince George)
- School District 43 (Coquitlam)
- School District 41 (Burnaby)
- Villages of Attachment

Appendix B: BC School-Centered Mental Health Coalition Logic Model, 2013–2016

Inputs	Activities What is the Coalition doing?	Outputs What is the Coalition producing?	Outcomes - What is the Coalition achieving?		
			Short	Medium	Long

Inputs

- Expertise/ Resources from 42 Coalition Members (list member organizations)
- 2 Co-chairs
- 6 Steering Committee Members
- Meeting space – in kind
- Secretariat
- Funding partners

Activities — What is the Coalition doing?

- Meet regularly to exchange information on mental health events, projects and opportunities
- Build capacity by assisting and promoting knowledge exchange and educational opportunities (e.g. webinars/events)
- Invite service providers, students and families to be part of events promoted through Coalition
- Bridge information and people around school mental health initiatives provincially and nationally (act as the trusted source of *school-centred mental health* in BC)
- Link to new curriculum/ assessment frameworks (e.g., social emotional competency)
- Compile, translate and share research-based knowledge and resources on school connectedness

BCSCMHC definition of **School Connectedness** to be defined by the end of 2013

Outputs — What is the Coalition producing?

- Bi-monthly meetings
- List serve
- Wiki
- Information forwarded to member networks through emails, wiki and website
- Participation in Sub-Committees:
  - ✓ Annual Summer Institute
  - ✓ Annual Youth Summit
  - ✓ May 7th – Child /Youth Mental Health Day
  - Opportunities to collaborate w/coalition members (e.g.,Joint Presentations/supports)
- Input provided on local, provincial and national school centred mental health initiatives (e.g., letter to Minister of Education)
- Active representation at provincial meetings involving child, youth and family mental health
- Knowledge exchange events – future(e.g. ProD for parents, educators, students)
- Landscape analysis/scan
- Affirmed statements – branding, core values, definitions/common language, elevator speech
- Inventory of resources, programs, services, contacts to support enhancing school connectedness (research → practice)
- Grassroots stories widely disseminated

Outcomes — Short

Representatives from a range of organizations are engaged in a network and community of practice

Coalition members have
- greater awareness of provincial initiatives;
- increased access to resources; and
- sustain more collaborative partnerships

BC school professionals, parents/caregivers, students and policymakers…
- access reliable mental health and substance use information & supports;
- know how to foster a connected school culture that promotes positive mental health

BC parents, children and youth have opportunities for authentic engagement in the area of school-centered mental health

Outcomes — Medium

BC school staff support student mental health and well-being and foster connectedness in classrooms and school communities

BC students and parents/caregivers are authentically engaged in their school communities

Policies are in place to create a supportive environment for enhancing school connectedness and supporting child and youth mental health

Mental health services and resources are integrated seamlessly into school communities (e.g. Family Health Centres in every school and/or community) with connections to schools

Outcomes — Long

Vision: British Columbia schools are safe and caring learning environments that foster the mental wellness of its community's children, youth and families

Figure 6.1 BC School-Centered Mental Health Coalition Logic Model, 2013–2016. *The British Columbia School-Centered Mental Health Coalition was originally formed in the fall of 2010. In meetings in the fall of 2011, and into the spring of 2012, the growing number of Coalition partners agreed that advancing the concept, body of research and strategies that enhance "School Connectedness" was the most important rallying point of our collective work.*

Chapter

7

Components of mental healthcare in schools in China
An overview

Yasong Du

Mental health awareness in schools

Definition of child mental health

In 1948, around the time of the definition of health by the World Health Organization (WHO), child mental health in China came on the scene as the result of serious social concerns about the wellbeing of young people. In Chinese culture, a child's good mental health is a state of their psyche and their behavior which shows the existence of three aspects that are "good enough": (1) The absence of any diagnosed psychopathological problem or psychiatric illness; (2) the coexistence of a reasonable ability to adjust and an ability to rebel against anything which, in the child's soul and consciousness, makes no sense or is unfair; (3) the existence of a "positive self-image," the self as a unique and precious individual, with its own aspirations and identity.

The child who works hard and succeeds at school is a child who is in good mental health. The progressive elaboration of this health partly depends on the quality of the child's equipment; it is thus a constitutional aspect of his or her being resulting from the embodiments of individual genetic inheritance. A child's mental health is also influenced by his or her environment; it means that positive or adverse stimuli arising from a rapidly changing material, family, and social environment, and the relationship that he or she may cement with other humans and with which he or she becomes imbued in order to construct his or her personality.

In China there have been two models that gained general acceptance to define and discuss what is meant by mental health of children and youth. One is a medical model – the traditional medical model in China. The other is a psychosocial model which the WHO advocated. These two models have been seen as being in conflict during certain periods, but have been regarded as complementary in others.

Mental health status in schools

In China there are only a few child psychiatrists and they are generally located in psychiatric hospitals, mental health centers, and general hospitals. The reality is that for about 40 million children and adolescents in China, there are fewer than 200 child psychiatrists in total. The ratio of children to psychiatrists is 1:500 000 in China (compared to 1:4000 in developed countries such as the United States). From the 1990s, pediatricians, teachers, and doctors in child mental healthcare have demonstrated an increasing interest in the field of child and

School Mental Health: Global Challenges and Opportunities, ed. Stan Kutcher, Yifeng Wei and Marc D. Weist. Published by Cambridge University Press. © Cambridge University Press 2015.

youth mental health services. Training courses and seminars have been offered from a variety of professional fields to introduce and teach skills and strategies for identification and intervention of child mental health problems, such as the Chinese–Canadian ADHD program with Professor Stan Kutcher in Canada, and the BANANA project about ADHD with Professor David Coghill of the United Kingdom. These collaborations were sited in Shanghai from 2005 to 2013. Related to these initiatives, regional and national continuing mental health educational programs were being offered for teachers in schools by Chinese teams.

Compared to 15 years ago, there is now in China a greater awareness of the need for child mental health services among professional health workers, educators, and the general population. In 2007 Yu and Du (2007) published a study that explored and compared students' awareness and knowledge about mental health problems in junior and senior high-school students in Shanghai. In this sample, 737 middle-school students completed a children's mental health knowledge questionnaire and the Strengths and Difficulties Questionnaire (SDQ). The results showed that junior high-school students had higher scores in the peer problems factor and pro-social behavior factor of the SDQ and scored lower in the emotional symptoms factor and the hyperactivity-inattention factor of the SDQ. Compared to junior high-school students, senior high-school students could better recognize mental health problems. Neither the junior nor the senior high-school students considered that treating mental health problems with medicine or with talking with somebody were likely to be effective interventions. All the students regarded family factors as an important cause of mental health problems. The junior high-school students preferred talking with their parents to solve mental health problems, while the senior ones did not.

There is also a very large deficit of professional health workers in child mental health services all over China. The current organization of child mental health services is not enough to meet the needs of the population, and most trained mental health providers work in the large cities (e.g., Shanghai, Beijing, Changsha).

Since 1970, China has been the most populous developing country in the world. To address concerns about potential overpopulation, the Chinese government created a one-child policy for each family. A society which had always had a large-family culture found itself caught off-guard and rather at a loss when the first generation of the one-child and a historically foreign 4:2:1 family structure came into being. Research (Du, 2013) addressing the impact of this policy on the child has reported that children growing up in one-child families are characterized by excessive dependence on parents and personality traits of self-centeredness, petulance, and poor socialization skills.

Strategies and procedures to identify mental disorders in young people

Developmental strategies in children and adolescents

Assessment of children and adolescents for the identification of mental disorders in China usually takes place in direct interviews with the child and family, and addresses emotions, cognition and behavior from a developmental perspective. The developmental psychopathologist is concerned with identifying the dynamic processes that underlie the course of development. In this paradigm, psychopathology is conceptualized as developmental deviation, which is defined in relation to non-disordered development. Following from that consideration, treatments or interventions are best informed by an understanding of underlying neuro-developmental processes and their trajectory over time. A mental disorder is not something that one "has," that is, a pathogenic entity; rather, disordered behavior, cognition, and/or emotion are seen as developing over time as a result of complex transactions among genetic, biological, and psychosocial processes that influence adaptation at particular developmental transition points. It is very important to take into account the demands and definition of context in interpreting and evaluating children's patterns of adaptation and mal-adaptation, as well as any types of mental disorders. Disorders have developmental histories that almost always predate their identification and emergence as serious problems. From a developmental psychopathology perspective, it is not optimal to wait until mental disorders become sufficiently severe and ingrained to merit a diagnosis before intervening. Based on this understanding, much of what a mental health provider does in a school setting is to try to identify the earliest expressions of disturbances in behavior, cognition, or emotions that can be the target for effective intervention.

The instruments to screen mental disorders in schools

The relationship between schools and the diagnosis of mental disorders in China has considered two parallel tracks: screening and gatekeeper approaches. In one, mental disorders that manifest themselves in the school setting have not been identified by standardized screening or assessment tools that are universally applied. Neither, however, have there been effective applications of gatekeeper approaches where in-school professionals have demonstrated the competencies needed to identify and refer young people with a mental disorder. Furthermore, mental health providers, until very recently, did not routinely involve the school in helping to evaluate or assist in the treatment of young people with a mental disorder once the child had begun assessment or treatment. These traditional practices have begun to change in the past decade as greater public awareness about the high prevalence and morbidity of mental disorders in young people in China has emerged.

The growing appreciation of the magnitude of this problem has led to calls for routine and standardized screening instruments to be applied in the clinical setting during the evaluation of children and adolescents who may be suffering from a mental disorder, and to involve schools in the data gathering necessary for this to be successfully completed. There is also a greater willingness to apply a variety of screening tools in school settings to identify young people at high risk for a mental disorder. In general, instruments such as the Child Behavior Checklist (CBCL), SDQ, the Child Depression Inventory, and the Conners Scale for ADHD are now more commonly used. The CBCL and SDQ are the most popular and widely used psychopathology evaluation instruments in China, and both of them have been normalized for in Chinese populations. These rating scales are not only used for screening, but also may be used clinically for confirming symptoms or monitoring treatment in some school settings.

Regardless of which of these tools might be applied in the school setting, a young person identified by a screening instrument must undergo further and more detailed assessment to determine "caseness" (which refers here to a person with a mental health disorder). In our experience, with supervision from a number of child psychiatrists, some professionals in schools are able to use screening measures to appropriately identify youth with common mental disorders such as ADHD and anxiety disorders; however, their competencies to work with mental health professionals for further detailed assessments and management are lacking.

Mental disorders in children and adolescents

Mental disorders in children and adolescents were a relatively new concept introduced to the general public and to Chinese educational and health professionals only a few decades ago. Before the 1980s the predominant focus on health for young people in schools was on physical dimensions, but this gradually expanded to become a wider construct and began to include a focus on addressing psychological development as well. This increasing attention paid to mental health for children and adolescents was encouraged in part by epidemiological research demonstrating the extent of this issue across China.

Common mental disorders in Chinese children and adolescents: epidemiologic studies

A nationwide survey conducted in 1987 by Chinese government agencies of 460 613 children aged 0–14 showed that 12 242 children were mentally disabled, yielding a prevalence of mental retardation of 2.66%. In 1992 Xin screened 24 013 primary-school students aged 4–16 using the Chinese version of Achenbach's CBCL in 22 provinces in China. The results showed the total prevalence of mental health problems to be 12.96%. In the same sample, the teacher questionnaire for school behavioral problems showed a rate of 6.95%.

Li et al. (1993), using the CBCL on 8644 children aged 4–16 in Hunan Province, showed that: (1) the prevalence of behavioral problems is quite high at a rate of 14.89%; (2) mental health problems were positively related to age – older children had a higher prevalence than younger children; (3) the prevalence of mental health problems was lower in cities (14.18%) than in rural areas (16.13%), suggesting that children's mental health problems were positively related to economic level; (4) generally, there was a higher prevalence for boys (18.49%) than girls (10.80%), except for emotional disorders where girls had a higher prevalence; (5) for young children of 4–6 years, the most frequent problems were developmental disorders; for 6–11-year-olds, both developmental and behavioral problems become frequent; while for 12–16-year-olds, behavioral and emotional problems become prominent.

Kou et al. (2005) completed a survey using the SDQ for 2128 students from 12 primary and middle schools in Shanghai. Full parent and teacher data were available for 1965 subjects and self-report data for only 690 subjects. The results showed that the scores of pro-social behavior, hyperactivity, inattention, and emotional symptoms subscales had different profiles in different mental health problems. Du (2012) conducted a study on mental health problems in boarding high-schools and demonstrated that the prevalence of behavioral problems was 11.2% in males and 10.2% in females; the prevalence of emotional problems was 16% in males and 10.5% in females; and learning disabilities were about 10% for the entire group.

Jiang et al. (2013) addressed changes in mental health problems over time from 2000 to 2011, focusing on the characteristics and treatment of children with ADHD in the specialty psychiatric hospital in Shanghai. Eighty percent of the ADHD patients (2000 sample) were male and the majority of them met criteria for the diagnosis prior to the age of seven years. The mean age at the time of first clinic attendance was ten years and the mean duration of illness at the time of the initial visit was 2.9 years. Both of these findings changed over time, showing earlier age at presentation and shorter duration of untreated illness. In these samples, 20% of respondents were non-residents of Shanghai and 11% had comorbid psychiatric diagnoses (primary depression and tic disorder). Among the 576 youths (58%) who visited the hospital more than once, 77% were treated with central nervous stimulants and the proportion of children who were administered behavioral therapy increased significantly over time.

Education challenges for children and adolescents in China

In China, now, each city has a limited number of prestigious key secondary schools with experienced teachers and high levels of success on national academic testing. There are also a limited number of state controlled key universities which admit students with the best academic scores through nationwide competition. If a student is enrolled into a prestigious key university they can usually be assured of lifelong vocational success, and most of them will attain good government positions and high-income jobs. As a result, there is intense pressure on students (from their families and from themselves) to be admitted to the best secondary schools and to do very well on the state examinations. The schools themselves inculcate a culture of competition and academic success. The impact of these extreme stressors for some students can be extensive. Research by Quian has demonstrated significant examination- and success-related behavioral and emotional problems, including but not limited to: feeling overburdened by school work; examination anxiety; lack of motivation; compulsive behaviors; problems in interpersonal relationships; anxiety; and pessimism. Zhou *et al.* (2012) demonstrated in a cross-sectional study of 1818 secondary-school students who completed the SDQ and Adolescent Self-rating Life Events Checklist (ASLEC), that academic stress (74%), criticism from others (66%), family conflict (29%), peer bullying, and interpersonal conflict (26%) were the most frequently reported mental health problems and contributed substantially to perceived stress and lower levels of pro-social behaviors.

Emotional symptoms that are considered to be school setting-related are also common in younger children, where they may have a significant impact on the quality of life and function of the children. Gu *et al.* (2011) conducted a cross-sectional study on anxiety symptoms and quality of life among students in primary school. They found that a high proportion of primary school students reported clinically significant symptoms of anxiety. Along with age, gender, and level of parental education, the severity of self-reported anxiety symptoms was closely associated with children's self-reported quality of life.

These negative events were one of many factors associated with perceived stress and lower levels of pro-social behavior in secondary-school students.

Mental health interventions in schools

National appreciation of the tremendous burden placed in China on individuals, families, and societies as a result of mental health problems has increased greatly in the last two decades. The appreciation extends to the heavy burden that pediatric emotional disorders comprise as well. Unfortunately, specialty mental health services will never be adequate to address the high prevalence of pediatric mental health disorders. As a result of these realizations a number of initiatives have been undertaken to help address some of these mental health concerns in the school setting.

Counseling, support groups, or psychotherapy are now often provided for students in the school setting. Counseling is the most commonly employed strategy and can focus on individual students, a student plus parents, or groups of students. Insufficient work has been done to assess the impact of these school-based interventions on student outcomes or on their impact in addressing mental health care needs of students.

Who are the professionals providing assistance for mental disorders in schools?

Recently there have been changes in focus on what schools are addressing in China. There has been a movement from mostly academic interventions to an approach that is more holistic, addressing intellectual, moral, physical, aesthetic, mental health, and labor education. In the last decade, school counselors or psychotherapists have been placed in some schools with the primary purpose of providing mental health services to students in schools. Most were trained by psychologists or psychiatrists and have developed skills in screening for mental health problems, intervening to improve behaviors and address emotional problems. For youth identified with a mental health problem, the school counselor conducts an interview and considers the magnitude and scope of the problems and their potential relationship to the school environment. For students who have more significant and persistent difficulties the counselor provides on-site interventions and will refer to a psychiatrist in a local health clinic or general hospital for additional care. If the student demonstrates a severe mental disorder, a referral is made directly to a psychiatrist in a general hospital or a specialty psychiatric hospital. When this process is proceeding smoothly it provides a good collaborative system of care for the student with a mental disorder.

Where are additional mental health resources available for students?

Peer relationship and interventions

Peer interventions and friends provide an important context for the development of emotional, social, and cognitive competencies. The development of positive peer relations and friendships is an ongoing and increasingly complex task that begins in infancy and continues through adolescence and early adulthood. In general, children and adolescents with positive peer relations are able to engage in self-perspective taking, empathy, collaboration in activities and tasks, and initiation and reciprocation of interaction in both primary and secondary schools. Some children and adolescents who have difficulty initiating or sustaining peer interactions may be actively rejected by others. The impact of peers on behaviors of young people is well known, but little research in China has been conducted on the use of peer education or peer support models of interventions in schools. One increasing concern in China is that of internet addiction, which takes young people away from the peer and social development needed to learn the pro-social skills that will be necessary for positive adult life. Studies of interventions for internet addiction in China have demonstrated a positive impact of cognitive behavior therapy (Du *et al.*, 2010).

Family

Chinese culture stresses material and emotional dependence on the family. High values are accorded to close knit interpersonal ties and interdependence among family members. The interdependence takes two forms – children's dependence on parents and aged parents' dependence on grown offspring – so the family environment fosters the familial values of mutual support and intergenerational relationships. The most important family correlates of mental health problems in school-aged children include scolding and beating of children by their parents, hostile relationships between parents, divorce, and poor home support for academic work. Given these problems, however, it is considered that divorce of parents has the most significant negative effect on children's emotional wellbeing, peer relationships, parent–child relationship, and academic success, and is strongly related to behavioral problems.

Community

From 1980, China had begun to open itself to Western values, beliefs, and habits, and a variety of cultural inputs such as the internet, mobile phones, and other electronic devices. These influences spread very quickly and are now found in every part of China. Along with these sociocultural changes, juvenile delinquency and crime have increased as a result of the increasing number of students with internet addiction and school refusal. The rapid urbanization policies of the Chinese government have also had a major impact on the health and wellbeing of children, particularly those in rural areas whose parent (often the father) or parents have left to find work in the city, leaving their child behind to be raised by a single parent or by grandparents. The rural migrant workers have been the backbone of the labor force that provides the muscle for rapid urban growth and development in the cities of China. However, the children are not best served when their parents migrate to the cities in search of work. There are many social and psychological issues facing children that will influence their future because of what is happening to them, as they are often without the guidance, love and nurturing of their parents. They are the children who are bearing the high psycho-social burdens of growing up without their parents. The literature (Schuller, 1994) on migration and its impact on young people has mostly showed that this process is highly stressful for all concerned and may present with potentially negative impacts on the mental health of all family members. Some children move from rural areas to cities with their parents, and they often experience a series of losses, including loss of home, separation from other family members and friends in schools, loss of a sense belonging, loss of identity, and loss of social support networks while in the process of settling in the new city.

Who can help children in the school setting?

In China, mental health professionals who work with children in schools can include child psychiatrists, clinical psychologists, social workers, occupational therapists, and mental health nurses. Care can be provided through a team approach, and the team can include a mixture of the above professionals. Parents often consider taking their children to see a psychiatrist only as a last resort. The child psychiatrist is only one part of a team of mental health professionals who can help children deal with stress and symptoms, and prescribe medication if needed. Other team mental health professionals have an important role in helping children maintain mental health wellness as well as treating behavioral and emotional disturbances.

School counselors, psychologists, or psychotherapists who have been trained in psychology and psychotherapy can also provide help in the form of counseling and psychotherapy, and they are more readily available for students as they are often sited in schools.

Also in the school setting, social workers can help children to improve their social development, relationships and social skills in the children's family, community, and school environment. They can also help children and their family with family therapy and parent counseling.

Occupational therapists are concerned about the planning and evaluation of therapeutic interventions with regards to personal life skills, as well as vocational and educational rehabilitation. They provide children and adolescents with skills to help them overcome their problems in their family and in school.

Mental health nurses are trained in teams on individual therapy, group therapy, general counseling, and psycho-education. Not all schools have all these potential providers available to them, but increasingly there are opportunities to link some of these resources to schools, opportunities which did not previously exist.

Collaborative work inside the school

School counselor

Parents whose children have been referred for psychiatric treatment often ask if they have been bringing up their children in the right manner. It is natural for parents to be anxious and wonder if they have done something wrong when their children face distress. Because of the important roles that schools play in Chinese society, parents often approach a school counselor with these concerns. The school counselor can help parents with the following: advice on how to handle or bring up children; arranging interviews with a psychiatrist during which parents can work through their feelings; clarify issues pertaining to their child's treatment and its impact on his/her academic life; and learn behavior change methods, and how to access community resources such as a family service center.

Primary care professionals

Primary care of child and adolescent mental health disorders is not popular and is not developed in China. Many primary care health providers (community healthcare doctors and pediatricians) have insufficient skills for diagnosis and treatment of child and adolescent mental disorders, and the need to enhance primary care capacity across China in this area is immense. Primary care physician training programs in child and adolescent mental healthcare are just beginning. Liu et al. (2013) compared the differences in understanding of ADHD in pediatricians who had taken a continuing education training program on this subject. Results showed there were significant improvements in general knowledge about, and treatment of ADHD before and after the training course. Physicians who worked in urban settings had a better baseline knowledge of medication treatments than those outside urban areas. Recognizing the potential for psychological interventions for treatment of child and adolescent mental disorders, in recent years more and more primary care professionals are being provided with access to counseling and psychological treatment training opportunities.

Child psychiatrist

The role of the child psychiatrist is one of consultation with other mental healthcare providers and direct care for the most severely ill children and adolescents. Usually they practice in a hospital setting and oversee inpatient treatments for a variety of conditions, including but not limited to: suicidal behavior, psychosis, conduct disorder, anorexia nervosa, persistent school refusal, internet addiction, and aggressive and violent behavior.

Training courses offered by foreign experts

In recent years there have been more and more training courses and seminars offered by foreign experts for numerous mental health-related professional fields to introduce a range of identification and intervention for child mental health problems.

An important example of such a program is the Chinese–Canadian ADHD program with Professor Stan Kutcher from Canada in collaboration with Dr. Y. Du of Shanghai. This program originally began to help train health and education professionals such as child psychiatrists, primary healthcare doctors, pediatricians, counselors, teachers, and education administrators. The results showed that the awareness of and the intervention skills about ADHD increased substantially. Furthermore, the results showed that teachers in schools can successfully use the SNAP-IV to screen ADHD children in the school setting and then refer those who screen positive for ADHD to primary healthcare doctors supported by child psychiatrists who can diagnose and treat ADHD in their clinics. This program has produced the ADHD community intervention model, a horizontally integrated training course–awareness–referral–intervention approach now being applied in Shanghai.

The BANANA project is another ADHD-focused program with Professor David Coghill of the United Kingdom. This collaborative research program was sited in Shanghai and Hunan Province from 2005 to 2013. The first part of the research identified the prevalence of ADHD in Shanghai and Hunan Province, where no previous data about epidemiology had been collected. Another result was that teachers from rural primary schools in Hunan province learned how to successfully screen and identify children with ADHD. Further work using similar approaches is being planned, and the hope is to use the lessons learned from these international collaborations to build further strengths and approaches to school-based mental health in China.

Conclusions

Addressing child and adolescent mental health in schools in China is a relatively new initiative for both the government and the community. While the past decade has seen substantial interest and some promising changes in this field, there is yet much to improve in order to benefit children and adolescents in China in the long run. The previous promising work – such as actively engaging collaborative mental health professional teams in schools, the support from the government and the community, and the national and international collaborations – has set the strong foundation for the future development and implementation of child and youth mental health programs in schools in China.

References

Du, Y. S., *Mental health disorders in children*, People's Medical Publishing House Co. Ltd., 2013.

Du, Y. S., *Attention deficit hyperactivity disorder*, People's Medical Publishing House Co. Ltd., 2012.

Du, Y. S., Jiang, W. Q., Vance, A., Longer term effect of randomized, controlled group cognitive behavioral therapy for Internet Addiction in adolescent students in Shanghai, *Australian and New Zealand Journal of Psychiatry*, 2010;44(2): 129–134.

Gu, H. L., Fan, J., Yang, H. L., *et al*. Anxiety symptoms and quality of life among children living in the Pudong District of Shanghai: A cross-sectional study, *Shanghai Archives of Psychiatry*, 2011;23(3): 154–160.

Jiang, L. X., Li, Y., Zhang, X. Y., *et al.*, Twelve-year retrospective analysis of outpatients with Attention Deficit Hyperactivity Disorder in Shanghai, *Shanghai Archives of Psychiatry*, 2013;25(4): 236–242.

Kou, J. H., Du, Y. S., & Xia, L. M., Reliability and validity of Strengths and Difficulties Questionnaire in Shanghai Norm, *Shanghai Archives of Psychiatry*, 2005;17(1): 25–28.

Li, X. R., Wan, G. B., Su, L. Y., *et al.*, Epidemic survey of mental health in children aged 4–16 in Hunan Province, *Bulletin of Hunan Medical University*, 1993;18:43–46.

Liu, Y., Zhao, Z. M., Liu, Y., *et al.* Study on awareness rates of attention hyperactivity disorder in child health care doctors, *Chinese Journal of Child Health Care*, 2013;21(6): 636–639.

Schuller, S., Load and stress in school: Their success and possibility of coping with them. *Studia Psychologica*, 1994;26: 41–54.

Yu, Y. M. & Du, Y. S., An investigation on awareness of mental health problems in middle school students in Shanghai, *Shanghai Archives of Psychiatry*, 2007;19(2): 75–78.

Zhou, L. L., Fan, J., & Du, Y. S., Cross-sectional study on the relationship between life events and mental health of secondary school: Students in Shanghai, China, *Shanghai Archives of Psychiatry*, 2012;24(3): 162–171.

Chapter 8

Mental health education for children and adolescents in China

Linyuan Deng and Xiaoyi Fang

In China, mental health education for children and adolescents refers to any function related to the mental health of children and adolescents, including mental health classes offered in elementary through high-school, on-campus activities related to mental health, and psychological counseling and guidance. There are two goals of mental health education: first, to promote healthy mental development in children and adolescents and prevent mental and behavioral problems and, second, to help children and adolescents solve mental and behavioral problems throughout their development as well as reduce the related adverse effects of these problems. Over a long period and based on influences from traditional psychology, mental health education for children and adolescents in China was aimed at solving problems during child and adolescent development. In recent years, China has increasingly emphasized healthy development in children and adolescents as well as preventing mental and behavioral problems.

This chapter will focus on four aspects of mental health education for children and adolescents in China: (1) the history of child and adolescent mental health education development in China; (2) the current mental health status and preventive interventions for mental and behavioral problems in children and adolescents in China; (3) current mental health education for children and adolescents in China; and (4) the major issues and future prospects for child and adolescent mental health education in China.

Developmental history of mental health education for children and adolescents in China

In the 1980s mental health education for children and adolescents began to receive attention in China; this area has 30 years of developmental history thus far. Based on a historically informed literature analysis, we divided the developmental progress of mental health education for children and adolescents in China into four stages: emulation, start-up, development, and prosperity.

The emulation stage (early 1980s)

In the 1980s developed countries and regions improved the psycho-educational system in schools in part through the creation of significant numbers of professional education faculties in universities, which greatly inspired the development of mental health education in China. In China, mental health education began by introducing related theories

School Mental Health: Global Challenges and Opportunities, ed. Stan Kutcher, Yifeng Wei and Marc D. Weist. Published by Cambridge University Press. © Cambridge University Press 2015.

and research results from foreign countries. Certain articles that introduced child and adolescent mental health education from the United States, Germany, the former Soviet Union, and other countries became available in newspapers and magazines. Publishing such articles initially stimulated interest in mental health education among Chinese people.

Since 1981 various Chinese scholars and institutions have begun to follow school mental health models derived from developed countries, and successfully conducted surveys on student mental health in Beijing, Shanghai, and other cities, yielding a series of published survey reports. For example, in a survey of 473 elementary school students in 1981 for Beijing, the proportion of children with mental health problems was 17.3%; a survey in 1982 for 487 elementary school students by Shanghai Mental Health Center showed that the proportion of the children with mental health problems was 21.1%. These findings generated extensive interest from psychologists and educators within China (Ye, 1997). Since that time, scholars' enthusiasm for research on mental health education in elementary through high-school has increased, and articles are frequently published that call attention to the importance of addressing student mental health. Scholars and educators alike began to increasingly introduce school-based interventions such as counseling derived from programs ongoing in other countries.

The main achievements from this stage were to identify the extent of mental health problems for Chinese children and adolescents for the first time and raise general social awareness on mental health in elementary through high-school, especially for educators. Based on the work at this stage, the education sector began to realize the importance of mental health in students, which not only laid a foundation for the future in mental health education, but it also encouraged the creation of policy measures to initiate such development.

The start-up stage (middle and late 1980s)

In 1986 Professor Ban (Ban Hua, a professor in the School of Education Science, Nanjing Normal University) first proposed the concept of "psychological education," which defines psychological education as education in psychological diathesis or mental health and distinguishes "moral, intellectual, physical, and aesthetic" education (Ban & Cui, 2003). Since this time, mental health education for children and adolescents has attracted much attention from educators. In December 1988, the central government promulgated "The notice about the reform and strengthening of moral education in elementary through high school by the Central Committee of the Communist Party of China," which proposed "a comprehensive training in moral and mental quality should be conducted to students." This was the first document issued by the Chinese government on mental health education for children and adolescents.

Since that time, the importance of mental health education has gradually been realized in elementary through high-school. Certain schools in the large- and medium-sized cities have begun to engage in mental health work, including: head teacher-guided courses, mental health activities, lectures, and psychological mailboxes (i.e., providing suggestions through replying to written letters from chidren asking for help about their mental distress). Within a few years, many schools delivering mental health education activities appeared in Beijing, Tianjin, Shanghai, Nanjing, Zhejiang, and other places.

The work that composed this stage was primarily due to spontaneous exploratory behavior by the schools and teachers, without sufficient theoretical guidance, policy support, or rigorous evaluation. These attempts were not large in scale, but they were important for demonstrating possible approaches to mental health education and promoting the concept to educators nationally.

The development stage (1990s)

In 1990 the State Council (the State Council of the People's Republic of China, namely the Central People's Government, is the highest executive organ of state power, as well as the highest organ of state administration) approved and promulgated the "Working Regulations on the Health in School," which provided that "health education should be included in the teaching plan in school." In 1992 the State Education Commission, which is now named the Ministry of Education, formulated and issued the "Basic Requirements on the Mental Health Education in Elementary through High Schools," wherein mental health education was included as one of the eight main requirements for teaching in schools. Thereafter, new national policies and documents were continuously issued with an emphasis on strengthening mental health education, reducing students' burdens, and providing quality-oriented education for students. In 1999, to better regulate and guide mental health education for children and adolescents in China, the Ministry of Education constructed an expert advisory committee for mental health education in schools, later known as the Steering Committee of Experts in School Mental Health Education of the Ministry of Education.

In 1991, Professor Ban published an article "Psychological Education Discussion" in the Chinese journal *Educational Research*, which systematically described mental education-related issues for the first time and laid a theoretical foundation for developing mental health education during this stage. In the same year, Zheng Richang and Chen Yongsheng edited and published the first edition of *Psychological Consultation in School* in China.

Compared with the previous two stages, a large number of studies on child and adolescent mental health education were performed with an increasingly widespread range of research topics. In sum, the work at this stage included the following four aspects: (1) investigating the mental health status of students in elementary through high-school; (2) identifying mental health problems for children and adolescents in special groups; (3) preventive intervention for children and adolescents' mental health; and (4) discussions on ethnic and cultural differences related to mental health.

The survey reports released at this stage deepened our understanding of mental health education for students in elementary through high-school in each sector of society. In addition, research in this area also rapidly increased. Many key projects for the State Education Commission at this stage were related to student mental health problems and educational countermeasures. Due to attention from the Chinese government and researchers for each sector in society, in 1994 an academic conference on mental health education was convened for the first time at the First High School in Yueyang, Hunan (the "National Academic Conference on the Psychological Consultation and Education in Elementary through High Schools").

In practice, classroom teachers or leaders in charge of moral education in schools, local professionals in teaching and research institutions, and a small number of psychologists became the pioneers of practice-based research in the mental health education field in China. Many "featured schools" (model schools) for mental health education gradually emerged across the country. Certain schools provided experimental courses in cooperation with research institutes, which had a great, nationwide impact. Further, many books in mental health education were published, such as *Psychological Education*, which was edited by Ban Hua (1994), and *Introduction to School Psychological Counseling* by Zhang Shengyuan (1998).

In addition, the wider society became increasing attentive to mental health for students in schools. On March 2, 1988, the *China Teenagers News* established a "confidential phone" hotline, which was the first psychological counseling hotline offered to children by a news organization in China. In 1989, Beijing Normal University opened the first psychological hotline for pupils, which became the current "Edelweiss psychological hotline for students." In 1991 the *China Youth Daily* also founded the "Youth Hotline" to provide psychological consultation and crisis assistance specifically for young people.

The prosperity stage (late 1990s to the present)

This stage was marked by the issuance of "Several Suggestions on Strengthening the Mental Health Education in Schools," which was released by the Ministry of Education in 1999. At this stage, the Chinese government was becoming increasingly attentive to mental health education in schools. In March 2001, mental health education for adolescents was included in "The Tenth Five-Year Plan for National Economic and Social Development of the People's Republic of China," which was approved by the Fourth Session of the Ninth National People's Congress. In September 2002, the Ministry of Education issued the "Guidelines of Mental Health Education in Schools," which was revised in 2012. The guidelines proposed that schools should continuously implement mental health education throughout the entire education and teaching process, and educational administrative departments at each level should include mental health education in the evaluation index system for school supervision. In December of the same year, the Ministry of Education held the first National School Mental Health Education Conference in Xiamen. At this conference, the "Guidelines of Mental Health Education in Schools (2012 revision)" were generated.

Over the past decade, mental health education activities in schools have improved and increased substantially, and research on mental health education in schools has deepened and become more systematic. Such research not only includes theoretical discussions on operating models for mental health education in schools and other aspects, but it also includes investigations on the current conditions for specific issues, such as learning difficulties and the processes and challenges on implementation of mental health education in schools. Such research also includes discussions on practical application and various delivery methods. At this stage, textbooks and certain reading materials on mental health education that have been highly influential in China were also published, such as *Mental Health Education* (Huang & Xia, 2001); *Growth Navigation for Elementary School Students* (Shen & Fang, 2003) and *Growth Navigation for Middle School Students* (Shen & Fang, 2002); and *Students' Psychological Health Education and Guidance* (Lin, 2008).

During this stage, teacher training for mental health education and establishment of psychological counseling services were strengthened in elementary through high-schools in China. From the perspective of professional training, certain colleges and universities have actively constructed new specialties or adjusted their subjects and curricula to focus on training specialized, skilled personnel in mental health education for schools. Further, teacher pre-service training and certification in mental health education has been actively organized in many areas. For example, since 1999, Shanghai has required that mental health teachers in schools receive mental health training for one year and pass an examination following such training. After a certificate is issued, the teachers are then permitted to teach mental health curriculum in schools. In addition, many schools have also established psychological counseling rooms to provide counseling and other forms of psychosocial intervention for the individuals and student groups.

Mental health problems and preventive intervention for children and adolescents in China

Child and adolescent mental health problems in China

Over the past 30 years, Chinese investigators have extensively researched the level of mental health and primary mental health problems for children and adolescents in China. Certain researchers have summarized the mental health problems for Chinese children and adolescents during different periods. For example, Ye (1996) indicated that, in the 1990s, children and adolescents in China had five major categories of mental health problems: emotion, self-control, personality, rebelliousness, and sexual troubles. Zhang (2008) believed that, during China's social transformation period, children and adolescents demonstrated eight main types of mental health problems, including social development, psychological pressure, learning adaptation, interpersonal relationships, emotional distress, marriage and sex such as adolescent dating, cohabitation, and sex offending, and career exploration and planning, and internet-related problems.

The following conclusions are based on analyses from over 20 large-scale surveys in this field, reported since 2000.

1. Mental health problems for Chinese children and adolescents are primarily focused on learning, interpersonal relationships, and emotional regulation/negative emotions, which account for a large proportion of mental health problems in Chinese children and adolescents (Lin & Wei, 2001).
2. The mental health status of boys and girls differed. Most studies showed that girls have lower mental health levels than boys, which is primarily manifested as significantly higher scores for interpersonal and emotion problems (e.g., depression and anxiety), somatization, and learning stresses compared with boys (Deng et al., 2009; Deng, Guo, & Ma, 2007; Gu & Lu, 2006; Hou et al., 2006; Jiang et al., 2008; Jin, Wei, & Sun, 2010; Liu & Zhang, 2005; Niu & Zhang, 2007; Wang, 2007; Xu & Lu, 2009; Xue et al., 2012; Yan et al., 2010; Zheng & Wang, 2008). Studies have also found that paranoia scores for boys are significantly greater than for girls (Gu & Lu, 2006; Niu & Zhang, 2007).
3. The mental health levels for students in different grades also differed. Several studies have shown that the mental health levels for students in high-school are lower than for junior middle-school students (Deng et al., 2007; 2009; Fang et al., 2008; Sun, 2012; Xu & Lu, 2009; Yan et al., 2010). The mental health levels for high-school students in Grade 10 were lower, while the mental health levels for students in Grade 7 were higher (Fang et al., 2008; Sun, 2012). Among such students, scores for somatization and terror factors in junior middle-school students were significantly higher than for high-school students (Hou et al., 2006; Zhang & Wang, 2001; Zheng & Wang, 2008). The scores for learning and emotional factors in high-school students were significantly higher than for

junior high-school students (Deng *et al.*, 2009; Hou *et al.*, 2006; Xu & Lu, 2009; Yan *et al.*, 2010). The mental health problems for high-school students may be related to increasing pressure from their studies, interpersonal relationships, and social adaptation (Jiang *et al.*, 2008; Lian & Meng, 2002; Sun, 2012). Compared with other grades, students in Grade 10 are those that have just entered a new school. In addition to the pressure from studies, they are adapting to the new environment and it is the students in Grade 10 that overall report more extensive mental health challenges (Lian & Meng, 2002).

4. The mental health levels for students from rural areas were worse than for urban students, which was primarily reflected in the factors for interpersonal relationships (Gu & Lu, 2006; Liu, W., 2005; Liu, K., 2006; Xue *et al.*, 2012) and may be related to the poor financial background of rural students (Gu & Lu, 2006).

5. The incidences for mental health problems differed greatly because of different scales used. In general, the incidence of mental health problems demonstrated in studies using the Chinese Middle School Student Mental Health Scale (MSSMHS) (e.g., Sun, 2012; Xu & Lu, 2009; Yan *et al.*, 2010) was much greater than for studies using the Symptom Checklist (SCL-90) (e.g., Xue *et al.*, 2012). The difference may be related to the different evaluation and item endorsement and scoring criteria used for the different scales. Currently, no study has compared the two different measures nor evaluated either against a gold standard such as diagnostic "caseness."

Development of other mental health problems in children and adolescents in China

In addition to the mental health problems described above, new problems in Chinese children and adolescents have been identified in recent years, such as child and adolescent suicide, internet addiction, and campus bullying. Studies have shown that the incidence of reported suicidal ideation was relatively high for high-school students in different regions (Yuan *et al.*, 2008), and this number has been increasing (Tao & Gao, 2005). Suicide has become the leading cause of death for the 15–34-year-old population in China (Wang, 2006; Ji & Chen, 2009). Moreover, some surveys using questionnaires revised from YRBSS (Youth Risk Behavior Surveillance System) showed that smoking, drinking, and other addictive drug abuse (Luo *et al.*, 2003; Sun *et al.*, 2006; Xie *et al.*, 2007) have begun to appear in children and adolescents. Among such concerns, due to the rapid development of the internet, internet addiction in children and adolescents has become increasingly prominent (Deng *et al.*, 2012; Zhang *et al.*, 2011). A study showed that the rate of internet addiction in middle-school students was 11.2% (Zhang *et al.*, 2011), using Lei and Yang's APIUS (Adolescent Pathological Internet Use Scale) (Lei & Yang, 2007). Studies related to school bullying found that bullying was frequent in elementary and junior middle schools (Hu & Sang, 2011; Kong *et al.*, 2013). The rate of bullying in older elementary school children was as high as 25.6%, and the incidence for often bullying others was 10.5% (Hu & Sang, 2011), while 13.9% of students in junior high-school were bullied, and 2.3% bullied others (Kong *et al.*, 2013). The bullying behavior negatively impacts mental health development in children and adolescents (Li, 2007).

Over this time, the overall description of mental health status in children and adolescents has changed. Using the approach from a "cross-sectional study of history," Xin and Zhang (2009) systematically analyzed the trajectory for mental health levels in adolescents against the background of social change. The results show that, in 1992–2005, the mental health levels for Chinese children and adolescents followed a declining trend; negative psychological characteristics, such as psychological problems, anxiety level, and depression level, gradually increased, while positive psychological characteristics, such as self-esteem, gradually decreased, albeit at a slower rate. During this period, the level of variation (gap between high and low scores on measures of psychological health) in child and adolescent mental health significantly increased, which indicates that certain children and adolescents may have serious psychological problems or mental disorders.

Current mental health education for children and adolescents in China

Mental health education in children and adolescents is emphasized by the Chinese government

Since Professor Ban Hua first proposed the "psychological education" concept in 1986, mental health education for children and adolescents has attracted widespread attention in the education sector. The Chinese national government and relevant government departments have issued multiple documents and policies to guide and regulate mental health education in elementary through high-school. We compiled the relevant evidence and found that, from 1988 through the end of 2012, the Chinese national government and relevant departments have produced more than 20 documents and policies related to mental health education in elementary through high-school. Initially, such documents and policies called attention to mental health education for children and adolescents; later, such documents clarified various components related to child and adolescent mental health education, such as curriculum, class hours, and teacher training. These documents demonstrate that the Chinese national government was greatly interested in mental health education for children and adolescents. The "Guidelines of Mental Health Education in Schools (2012 revision)," which was revised and issued at the end of 2012, was important for guiding mental health education in China's elementary through high-schools. Such policy documents not only increasingly provide a clear policy basis for implementing mental health education in schools (Ye, 2008), but also strongly promote mental health education development in elementary through high-school. However, it was just the beginning, with little funding support following those policies.

Current mental health education for children and adolescents

School facilities

Currently, mental health education in Chinese elementary through high-school is primarily implemented in the following ways: mental health courses; publicizing mental health knowledge; individual psychological counseling; establishing psychological files for students; and organizing mental health lectures (Liao, 2008).

The research results from a 2005 survey that included 1767 schools from 28 sample provinces in the eastern, central, and western regions showed that mental health courses within existing school curriculum were offered in the eastern, central, and western regions in 49.6%, 56.8%, and 38.1% of schools, respectively. In the medium and large cities, as well as small towns and rural areas, such education was offered in 64.0%, 43.3%, and 34.2% of schools, respectively. The central and western regions, as well as small towns and rural areas, lacked textbooks for mental health education. In addition to offering courses and setting up class bulletins, mental health education was primarily implemented by constructing counseling rooms in the eastern region, organizing activities and lectures in the central region, and curriculum inclusion among other subjects in the western region. Of the total number of sample schools, 52.7% have constructed their own counseling room; 68.1% of such rooms were open three hours or less weekly. The schools in the eastern region, as well as large and medium cities, conducted research and discussion on their mental health education courses more frequently (Xu, 2005).

Teaching staff

Statistics show that the number of school teachers for mental health in China is less than 40 000, which is not even 10% of the required number under ideal conditions (Liao, 2008); these data indicate a serious shortage, given the large population of greater than 200 million students. In the urban or developed areas, due to the economic development and enhanced awareness, with increasing emphasis on mental health in school, the lack of teachers qualified to teach mental health has improved considerably in recent years. However, in certain small towns and rural areas the situation is not optimistic. More importantly, the level of specialization for the current mental health teachers in elementary through high-school is far below the standard required. A survey by Wang and Zhang (2003) showed that the professional backgrounds for psychology teachers in schools varied greatly. The mental health teachers with a professional background in psychology or mental health only accounted for 18%, which did not reach 40% even after including teachers with an educational background in pedagogy. The remainders are primarily teachers with backgrounds in Chinese, history, biology, and other liberal arts.

Comprehensively comparing the mental health education facilities and teaching staff in schools from different provinces and cities showed that the level of mental health education in Chinese elementary through high-schools has gradually increased, but the following problems remain.

1. The development for urban areas is much more robust than in rural areas. In rural schools, their concepts for mental health education lag behind, the teachers are not directed to teaching mental health, and the teacher training level in mental health education is low (Ye, 2008).
2. Regional development varies. The eastern region began to develop earlier, with rapid developments and higher rates of teacher preparation, while the western region developed later and more slowly (Ye, 2008; Zhang & Zhang, 2013).
3. Despite the school mental health education initiatives currently in place, certain problems remain, such as confusing mental health education with moral education; teachers with inadequate professional skills in mental health education are providing mental health education; school counseling rooms are not properly staffed and not available to students; the lack of mental health education resources (such as textbooks); poor uptake in many schools in implementation of mental health in existing curriculum and lack of support from families and communities for mental health education (Fu, 2001; Meng, 2006; Piao & Liu, 2007; Song, 2001). Therefore, there is much room for improvement.

The effects of mental health education for children and adolescents

Although many researchers have published articles that suggest the positive effects of mental health education on students' healthy growth in elementary through high-school (Fang & Lin, 2003; Hou et al., 2006; Wang & Yang, 2012), few researchers have empirically studied and discussed the actual effects of mental health education in schools. Only some teams (Bian et al., 2002) have done such experimental education research. Bian's group proposed a new model for "full participation in the development of students' psychological counseling" based on experiences from foreign countries and Hong Kong. The model was implemented in an elementary school in the Jinhua region of Zhejiang province over a three-year period, with nearly 460 students participating. The model was largely based on interventions directed toward encouraging, rewarding, and promoting positive contact between teachers and students, designed to improve teacher–student interaction. The results show that the post-test scores for the experimental group were significantly better than for the control group on seven dimensions: learning attitudes, interpersonal anxiety, loneliness, self-blame, over-sensitivity, phobia, and impulsiveness, with no significant difference between the two groups for somatization symptoms, which demonstrated that the model was conducive to promoting mental health in students.

In addition, a few schools performed some pilot studies on the effects of mental health education in school. For example, the 19th Middle School in Beijing has established a positive mental health center, which focuses on developing students' intrinsic positive qualities and discovering their potentials. Mental health education in this school includes teaching mental health classes, providing a variety of mental health-promoting activities, organizing cultural weeks with psychological characteristics and group mental health development activities, offering regular lectures for both teachers and parents, and independently developing the ten psychological tips of "happy to learn, happy life every day." The preliminary results from the positive mental health education were significant, with a remarkable effect on multiple dimensions of mental health noted (Yu, 2013). Personality development in the students was balanced, their academic performance and capacities for learner autonomy improved. Common psychological problems decreased. The examination anxiety levels for the student declined. The students' concentration in class significantly improved. The guidance from the positive mental health education enabled the students to face difficulties in preparing for examinations with positive attitudes and behaviors, which significantly improved the pass rate for the high-school and college entrance examinations.

Studies on preventive interventions for child and adolescent mental health problems

In addition to school-based mental health education activities, different preventive intervention programs were also developed by various researchers, and generally all have demonstrated some positive effects on child and adolescent mental health dimensions. Following are some examples. (1) Zhou and Ye (2002) used participatory teaching to test the effects of life-skills education. They found that, after intervention, children and adolescents in the intervention group scored significantly higher in six out of the ten aspects investigated, including the relationship between students, caring for others, self-confidence, stress relief, independent problem-solving, and decision-making. (2) Zhang and

Zheng (2013) provided relationship education through interpersonal communication courses and individual counseling for students and found that the experimental group significantly improved in interpersonal sensitivity, hostility, and general mental wellbeing after the intervention. (3) Xu (2005) conducted a ten-week emotional education and counseling intervention with two lessons per week. After the intervention, scores from the experimental group on the Eysenck emotional stability test showed significant improvement in each dimension ($p < 0.05$), while the pre-test and post-test scores for the control group were not significantly different. (4) Deng *et al.* (2013) developed a mental health education program for internet addiction based on cognitive behavior theory. After three weeks of intervention the experimental group showed a downward trend in internet addiction, while an increase was observed for the control group. The average weekly time spent online decreased by 1.9 hours for the experimental group, while the control group time increased by 3.46 hours. (5) Fang and Lin (2003) developed a preventive intervention program for youth smoking, "Stay Away from Tobacco" (SAFT), based on cognitive behavior theory. Students in Grades 7, 8, 10, and 11 were selected for a six-week experiment, which included a preventive intervention for smoking once per week. After the intervention, the proportion of smokers in the intervention group decreased from 12.7% before the intervention to 7.5%, while the proportion of smokers in the control group increased from 7.3% to 9.6%. These studies suggest that a variety of mental health and wellbeing enhancement interventions delivered in the school setting may generate positive results. Further research in this area is rapidly developing.

The primary problems and future development of child and adolescent mental health education in China

Although attention on mental health education for children and adolescents in China has increased and yielded many achievements, the following problems remain.

Duplicating and confusing mental health and moral education

Currently, in China, from the national Ministry of Education to the elementary through high-schools, mental health education in school is supervised by the Moral Education Department of the National Ministry, and many full-time and part-time school teachers in mental health were originally engaged in moral education instruction. The goal for moral education is to shape students as objects with a clear political direction and value orientation, and the primary objective is to improve ideological and moral qualities in students through the key methods of indoctrination, imitation, and norms. Mental health education is more person-oriented and student-centered, and focused on enhancement of mental wellbeing. In creating mental health education, the age-appropriate developmental needs of students were respected to promote better social development and enhance problem-solving capacities. Thus, moral and mental health educations are different in their nature, function and working models. Allocating mental health education to the department of moral education may affect normal development and impede normal development in mental health education. Therefore, in the future, mental health education functions must be clearly separated from moral education.

Professional development for teachers in mental health education should be improved

Although mental health education in elementary through high-school in China has received more attention and many regions and schools have invested substantial effort in addressing this, professional development for teachers in mental health education needs to be improved, and the certification and training system also requires improvement.

Currently, only a small portion of mental health education teachers have a professional background in psychology or mental health education. From the Ministry of Education to the local education authorities and departments, clearly articulated teacher qualifications and curriculum requirements for school mental health education have not been defined, and a standard authentication mechanism is not available. Many schools require that mental health teachers have a counselor certification (level two counselor certificate) issued by Ministry of Human Resources and Social Security of the People's Republic of China. However, the requirements for a counselor certification issued by the Ministry of Human Resources and Social Security of the People's Republic of China were not specifically designed for student mental health work in elementary through high-school. Moreover, the course is not sufficient to guarantee that the certificate holder has the necessary knowledge and skills for psychological counseling.

Further, for professional training in colleges and universities, despite nearly 350 universities in China having a psychology college/department/specialty, almost no universities have established a full training course for school psychologists. Professional training for students in psychology includes more academic research and less applied training. Fortunately, in recent years, a few colleges and universities in education or psychology, such as the Faculty of Education and the School of Psychology in Beijing Normal University (the employer for these authors), began to establish graduate training programs for elementary through high-school mental health education. However, such programs are in the early stages and exploration processes.

Mental health education lacks empirical research

Currently, most schools provide mental health education based on foreign models or their own experiences, which lacks strong support from empirical investigation data of the effectiveness of the approaches they have chosen. Although many schools have established student growth or mental health records, few schools have systematically collected or used such data for evaluating the impact of student mental health education. Moreover, almost no school has supported or performed independent empirical research on the effectiveness of mental health education in their setting; thus, it is difficult to understand the specific effects of mental health education in schools on students, teachers, or school functioning. Therefore, there is no currently available scientific information that could be used by policy makers or administrators to enhance or improve school mental health education. In the future, a national evaluation system must be developed, addressing both the processes and results of interventions so that we can develop more evidence-based mental health education.

Lack of an appropriate mental health measurement for school children and the Chinese culture

The mental health surveys for school children currently used by Chinese scholars were primarily translated or revised from foreign countries, such as the Self-Reporting Inventory (SCL-90) and Mental Health Test (MHT). Approximately 60% of the studies used the Self-Reporting Inventory (SCL-90) as a measuring tool. These scales were developed based on Western culture and mental health problems of Western children and adolescents. We know that the Western and Chinese cultures differ greatly, which may produce different opinions on emotional, cognitive, and behavioral dimensions for children and adolescents. For example, Western culture emphasizes individualism, while Chinese culture emphasizes collectivism. Certain behaviors that are acceptable in Western culture, such as self-determination, are less acceptable in Chinese culture. If a child is too self-determining in his/her own affairs, he/she may be considered non-compliant by parents, teachers, or authorities in Chinese culture. Therefore, an appropriate mental health scale for school children that is suitable for the Chinese culture must be developed, tested, and validated.

Such development is not balanced with large regional differences

Overall, mental health education for elementary through high-school in China was initiated and developed without taking into consideration the large regional differences that exist. The eastern, developed regions, as well as the large and medium cities, began earlier and rapidly developed, while the western and rural areas began to develop later and slower, with a large gap compared to the east. Therefore, more interaction and mutual education between different regions, as well as urban and rural areas, are necessary. Structures to support such cross-national integration have yet to be developed.

Further, some impetus is developing to shift educational interventions from primarily problem-centered to prevention-centered

In the past, most research addressed the problems or difficulties that children and adolescents had, and then developed programs to solve those problems. However, research has shown that preventive intervention may, for some outcomes, be more effective than problem solving. Therefore, we should pay much more attention to how to positively promote the wellbeing of students as well as preventing negative developments.

Further challenges

Addressing the stigma around mental disorders and enhancing capacity of schools and mental health teachers to identify, refer, and support youth with mental health problems and mental disorders are areas for further research and development in China. Although some advances in this have been made in work with migrant children, further universally applied emphasis reaching all students and all schools may yet have to be developed. The role of schools in addressing mental health needs of young people may grow and evolve over the next decade. As a recent study by Xin and Zhang (2009) demonstrated, over the period

1992–2005, the mental health status of young people in China decreased. This and other findings again challenge China to further invest in addressing the mental wellbeing of its youth. As it does that, it can be expected that schools will play important and substantial roles.

References

Ban, H. (1991). Psychological education discussion. *Educational Science Research*, 5.

Ban, H. (1994). *Psychological Education*. Anhui Education Press.

Ban, H., & Cui, J. (2003). Overview of the research on psychological education and moral education relationships. *Forum on Contemporary Education*, 7, 38–41.

Bian, Y., Li, S., & Zhu, X. (2002). A research on students' developmental mental guidance with all people involved. *Psychological Science*, 25(6), 697–701.

Deng, S., Guo, R., & Ma, Y. (2007). A survey of the mental health status of Baise middle school students. *Journal of Youjiang Medical College for Nationalities*, 29(2), 157–159.

Deng, H., Yang, J., Deng, B., *et al.* (2009). A cross-sectional survey of mental health among middle school students in Guiyang City. *Chinese Journal of School Health*, 30(8), 715–716.

Deng, L., Zhang, J., Fang, X., Liu, Q., Yang, H., & Lan, J. (2012). Perceived parental conflict and adolescents' internet addiction: the mediating effect of adolescents' conflict appraisal and emotional management. *Psychological Development and Education*, 28(5), 539–544.

Fang, S., Jing, J., & Wang, L. (2008). Mental health status of middle or high school students in Nanning. *Chinese Journal of Child Health Care*, 16(5), 565–567.

Fang, X. & Lin, D. (2003). Prevention and intervention of adolescents' smoking behavior. *Acta Psychologica Sinica*, 35(3), 379–386.

Fu, W. (2001). Problems & countermeasure of psychological-health education in primary & middle schools. *Theory and Practice of Education*, 21(8), 42–44.

Gu, J. & Lu, H. (2006). Research of the mental health of high school students in Zhang Jiagang. *Occupation and Health*, 22(1), 52–53.

Hou, Z., Jia, H., & Guo, J. (2006). A cross-sectional investigation of mental health level of 1397 middle school students. *Medical Journal of Chinese People's Health*, 18(9), 788–789.

Hu, F. & Sang, Q. (2011). Relations between self-concept and bullying in school among seniors in primary school. *Chinese Journal of School Health*, 32(8), 938–938.

Huang, X. & Xia, L.(2001). *Mental health education*. Higher Education Press.

Ji, C. & Chen, T. (2009). Prevalence of suicide behavior in middle school students and its correlations with mental emotional disorders. *Chinese Journal of School Health*, 30(2), 112–115.

Jiang, Y., You, C., & Ding, H. (2008). Study on the influential factors on mental health of secondary school students in Beijing. *Maternal and Child Health Care of China*, 23(24), 3374–3376.

Jin, Y., Wei, X., & Sun, Y. (2010). Investigation report on mental health of secondary school students in Lanzhou. *Education Exploration*, 1(140), 41.

Kong, Y., Wang, F., An, H., & Cao, H. (2013). Prevalence survey about campus bullying involvement of urban junior high school students. *China Educational Technology & Equipment*, 9, 63–65.

Lei, L. & Yang, Y. (2007). The development and validation of adolescent pathological internet use scale. *Acta Psychologica Sinica*, 39(4), 688–696

Li, J. (2007). Prevention of bullying behavior in school. *Journal of Jiaozuo Teachers College*, 23(2), 69–70.

Lian, R. & Meng, Y. (2002). Mental health status of high school students in Fuzhou. *Chinese Journal of School Health*, 23(2), 165–166.

Liao, Q. (2008). The status quo of the mental health education system in primary and high schools and its problems. *Journal of Yangtze Normal University*, 24(6), 149.

Lin, C. (2008). *Students' Psychological Health Education and Guidance*, Beijing Normal University Press.

Lin, C. & Wei, Y. (2001). Discussion on future trend of school psychology. *Educational Research*, 7, 30–34.

Liu, H., & Zhang, J. (2005). Norm of Symptom Checklist (SCL-90) in Chinese middle school students. *Chinese Mental Health Journal*, 18 (2), 88–90.

Liu, K. (2006). Research and comparison on the mental health situation of middle school students from city and country. *Journal of Hengyang Normal University*, 27(5), 168–171.

Liu, W. (2005). Analysis of the investigation in mental health status of adolescent students in Weifang. *Contemporary Educational Science*, 11, 38–39.

Luo, C., Peng, N., Zhu, W., Zhou, Y., & Gao, G. (2003). Risk behaviors of adolescents in Shanghai: Smoking, drinking and addictive drug use. *Chinese Journal of School Doctors*, 17(2), 104–107.

Meng, N. (2006). Discussion on school mental health education status. *Education Exploration*, 176(2), 88–89.

Niu, X. & Zhang, H. (2007). The investigation of mental health status and its factors among secondary school students in Yinchuan. *Chinese Journal of School Doctors*, 21(3), 265–267.

Piao, T. & Liu, H. (2007). Research on mental health among primary and secondary school students. *Education Exploration*, 9, 62.

Shen, J. & Fang, X. (2002). *Growth navigation for middle school students.* China Light Industry Press.

Shen, J. & Fang, X. (2003). *Growth navigation for elementary school students.* Beijing Education Publishing House.

Song, D. (2001) View the problems of mental health education among primary and secondary school students. *Educational Science Research*, 9, 64–67.

Sun, L. (2012). Study on Mental health status of 1091 middle school students in Changchun area. *China Journal of Health Psychology*, 20(5), 759–761.

Sun, L., Zhu, H., Zhang, C., Li, J., Zhao. P., & Tang, M. (2006). Analysis of health risk behavior of adolescents in Sichuan Province. *Chinese Journal of School Health*, 27(12), 1069–1072.

Tao, F. & Gao, M. (2005). Trends of health-risk behaviors and their risk or protective factors on adolescent students in Hefei, Anhui Province, China, 1998–2003. Study on Public Health in Asia.

Wang, H. & Zhang, X. (2003). Investigation into and analysis of present condition of school psychological soundness teachers. *Shanghai Research on Education*, 5, 28–30.

Wang, J. (2007). The investigation of mental health status among 2180 secondary students in Xiaoyi. *Journal of Shanxi Medical College for Continuing Education*, 17(3), 46–47.

Wang, W. (2006). *Depression, suicide and crisis intervention.* Chongqing Press.

Wang, W. & Yang, J. (2012). Strengthen the mental health education among primary and secondary school: Based on the investigation of present situation on mental health education in primary and secondary school in Chongqing. *China Education News*, 3, 1–5.

Xie, D., Bu, K., Liang, Y., Mai, Z., & Zhao, H. (2007). The investigation of behavior among adolescents' smoking, drinking and abuse on addictive drugs in Foshan. *Chinese Journal of School Doctors*, 21(5), 523–526.

Xin, Z. & Zhang, M. (2009). Changes in Chinese middle school students' mental health (1992–2005): A cross-temporal meta-analysis. *Acta Psychologica Sinica*, 41(1), 69–78.

Xu, G. (2005). Research into the influence of the sentiment education on sentimental stability of grade one students of junior middle schools. *Journal of Xin Yu College*, 6, 28.

Xu, M. (2005). Investigation and analysis of mental health education status among primary and secondary school students. *Exploring Education Development*, 3, 78–83.

Xu, Y. & Du, Y. (2007). An investigation on mental health status of internet addicted middle school students in Shanghai. *Shanghai Archives of Psychiatry*, 19(1), 1–3.

Xu, L. & Lu, W. (2009). Survey and analysis of mental health status among middle school students. *Journal of Guizhou Education Institute*, 25(11), 76–79.

Xue, J., Bi, C., Yang, J., & Wang, Z. (2012). The analysis and research of Kashgar Prefecture Uyghur middle school students' mental health.

Journal of Jilin Institute of Physical Education, 4, 96–98.

Yan, Y., Wang, Y., He, X., Cao, R., & Lu, Y. (2010). Investigation of mental health status among secondary school students. *Zhejiang Journal of Preventive Medicine*, 22(9), 33–34.

Ye, W. (1996). Analysis of contemporary adolescents' mental health status. *Youth Studies*, 1, 16–17.

Ye, Y. (1997). Review and prospect on mental health education in Chinese primary and secondary school. *Journal of the Chinese Society of Education*, 2, 34–37.

Ye, Y. (2008). The past twenty years of mental health education in the mainland of China. *Journal of Fujian Normal University (Philosophy and Social Sciences Edition)*, 5(6), 148–155.

Yu X. (2013). Mental Health Education of Beijing No. 19 high school. Presented at the annual conference of National Mental Health Education, Shandong, November, 22–24.

Yuan, C., Yao, R., Tao, F., *et al.* (2008). Study on the psychosocial factors to suicide ideation and attempts among adolescent students in Bengbu area. *Chinese Journal of School Health*, 29(11), 997–1001.

Zhang, B. & Zheng, L. (2013). An experimental research of junior high school students' mental health intervention. *Health Research*, 33(3), 234–237.

Zhang, D. (2008). Integrated research on the mental health and its education among Chinese adolescents. *Journal of Southwest University (Social Sciences Edition)*, 34(5), 22–28.

Zhang, J., Liu, J., Deng, L., Fang, X., Liu, Z., & Lan, J. (2011). Parent–adolescent relations and adolescents' internet addiction: The mediation effect of loneliness. *Psychological Development and Education*, 6, 641–647.

Zhang, M. & Wang, Z. (2001). Mental health state of middle or high school students. *Chinese Mental Health Journal*, 15(4), 226–228.

Zhang, M. & Zhang, X. (2013). Problems and countermeasures of mental health education in primary and secondary schools. *Journal of Anhui Health Vocational & Technical College*, 12(2), 92–93.

Zhang, S. (1998). *Introduction to School Psychological Counseling*. Shanghai Press and Publication.

Zheng, R. & Chen, Y. (1991). *Psychological Consultation in School*. People's Education Press.

Zheng, Z. & Wang, G. (2008). Mental health status in high school students. *Journal of Psychiatry*, 21(6), 421–422.

Zhou, K. & Ye, G. (2002). The role of life skill education on mental health of middle school students. *Chinese Mental Health Journal*, 16(5), 323–326.

School mental health programs in India
Current status and future directions

Devvarta Kumar, Srikala Bharath, Uma Hirisave,
Sanjay Agarwal, and Hemang Shah

Childhood and adolescence mark significant transitions in physiological, cognitive, emotional, moral, social, and other domains. Though most children sail through these transitions, some become stressed, which can lead to psychological problems. School mental health (SMH) programs have proven efficacy in enhancing psychological well-being of school-going children. As mentioned in other chapters in this book SMH programs have been integrated into the school system in various countries (Teich, Robinson, & Weist, 2007; Weist & Murray, 2007; Weston, Anderson-Butcher, & Burke, 2008). The World Health Organization (WHO) also advocates SMH to be an integral part of school health systems, having components of promotion of psychosocial competence, mental health education, and provision of services for those needing mental health interventions (Hendren, Weisen, & Orley, 1994). In India there is growing realization about the need for implementation of SMH (Agarwal, 2004; Malhotra, 2004). For example, the Central Board of Secondary Education (CBSE) has emphasized the importance of reducing stress in children and inculcating positive attitude through programs in schools (CBSE, 2008). The CBSE recommends that all secondary and senior secondary schools should employ a counselor and engage in exercises toward building student self-concept, self-image, ability to withstand pressures, and sense of enterprise as central aspects of the learning process (CBSE, 2008). In fact, the CBSE has started inclusion of life-skills training in curriculum as it helps the learner to face life with a sense of confidence and conviction (CBSE, 2004).

Escalating child and adolescent mental health problems also underscore the need for SMH programs. Various epidemiological studies implicate a high prevalence rate of mental health problems in children and adolescents in India. In a multi-center epidemiological study of child and adolescent psychiatric disorders in urban and rural areas, the prevalence rate was found to be around 12% (Srinath & Sitholey, 2005). In another study in India, 9.34% of the sample (consisting of 4–12-year-old children) were found to have one or more psychiatric problems, and inclusion of these children in an SMH program showed positive outcomes (Malhotra, 2005). These rates of serious mental health problems in children and youth in India are consistent with findings from other countries (e.g., Costello, Egger, & Angold, 2005).

Given these considerations, both the promotion of mental health broadly for children and youth, and early and effective intervention for more serious problems are in need of significant enhancement in India, and a logical and cogent strategy is to do this work in schools. However, as in other developing nations, efforts are very far from being national in scope. The Government of India launched the National Mental Health Program (NMHP) in

School Mental Health: Global Challenges and Opportunities, ed. Stan Kutcher, Yifeng Wei and Marc D. Weist. Published by Cambridge University Press. © Cambridge University Press 2015.

1982 with the objectives to provide mental healthcare for all, to encourage the application of mental health knowledge in general healthcare, and to promote community participation in the mental health service development (Ministry of Health and Family Welfare, Government of India, 1982). Subsequently, in 2008 a few components of SMH, such as life-skills education and counseling in schools, were integrated in the NMHP. Apart from the NMHP, there are various other policies that address issues related to the wellbeing of children. For example, the Integrated Child Development Services (ICDS), initiated in 1975, has an objective to lay the foundation for proper psychological, physical, and social development of the child (Ministry of Women and Child Development, Government of India, 1975). Likewise, the National Policy for Children (NPC), implemented in 1974, emphasizes the initiation of programs that ensure safety of child rights and create proactive environments to ensure healthy mental and physical growth of children (Ministry of Women and Child Development, Government of India, 1974). Recently, the Ministry of Health and Family Welfare has initiated a program titled "Rashtriya Bal Swasthya Karyakarm" under the National Rural Health Program (Ministry of Health and Family Welfare, Government of India, 2013). The program aims to screen 270 million children and adolescents from 0 to 18 years for defects at birth, diseases, deficiencies, and development delays, including disabilities. It has provision for multiple levels of screening and layers of services. Apart from other health professionals, there is provision for a psychologist at the district level for helping children experiencing developmental delays and disabilities.

These policies are progressive as they target holistic growth of children; however, due to improper implementation the outcomes are not very encouraging (Kapur, 2007). For example, in the ICDS, the services are supposed to be delivered by village-level workers (called the Aanganwadi workers), who are over-burdened, meagerly paid, and not technically well-equipped to handle complex psychological issues. Thus, there is some emphasis on SMH but actual implementation is falling far short of what is being called for. Often, the mental health of school children becomes a hot topic of discussion when something highly undesirable (such as suicides after examination results) occurs. It leads to some transient activities which disappear once the issue in question begins to settle down. However, in order to target mental health of children, as well as to help children with psychological problems at the right juncture (e.g., to avoid losing formative years), a comprehensive multi-layered SMH strategy is required.

In this chapter we elaborate and evaluate the works being done in the field of SMH in India. We then explore the stumbling blocks in the implementation of a comprehensive SMH system and finally propose a model SMH strategy suitable for this country.

SMH in India: current status

As of now, SMH in India is limited to some short- and long-term efforts by a few individuals and centers. As in most countries, there is lack of an integrated and comprehensive SMH strategy for the whole nation. The short-term programs largely consist of sensitization or educational programs with a primary focus to increase awareness in the community about the mental health issues of children and adolescents. The programs are usually conducted in the form of workshops and interactive sessions by mental health professionals (Kumar *et al.*, 2009; Shah & Kumar, 2012). However, these programs focus mostly on teachers and lack in-depth coverage of topics because of the short duration of the programs (usually of 1–2 days' duration). The follow-up assessments show some effectiveness of these programs in terms of teachers' increased concerns about psychological wellbeing of children and referrals of children with psychological problems to psychiatric services (Kumar *et al.*, 2009; Shah & Kumar, 2012). However, in the absence of inclusion of all the stakeholders and lack of repeated interactions with the target groups, the long-term outcomes of such programs are questionable.

There have been a few efforts toward long-term SMH services where institutions working in the field of mental health send teams of experts to schools on a periodic basis to conduct awareness programs for teachers and students, as well as helping children with minor or major psychological problems (Vaidya & Dhavale, 2000; Sinha, Kishore, & Thakur, 2003). Such promotion-and-prevention mental health service by experts is definitely a welcome step. But again, these efforts are limited when considering the broader national landscape. In general, schools are not forthcoming in taking steps to ensure the existence of mental health services for children. In our interactions with schools we have found very few schools showing interest in employing counselors.

At the National Institute of Mental Health and Neurosciences (NIMHANS), Bangalore, some systematic efforts have been made toward development of SMH models. Kapur and her colleagues have been working in the field of SMH for many years, covering both rural and urban areas (Kapur, 1995; 1997; 2011; Kapur & Cariappa, 1978; 1979; Kapur & Hirisave, 2004, 2006; Kapur, Koot, & Lamb, 2012). In the 1970s they started a two-phase program to train school teachers in early detection and management of mental health problems among children (Kapur, 1995). The first phase oriented the teachers toward various psychological problems, and in the second phase some of the motivated teachers were trained in managing those children with minor psychological problems who did not need referral to a specialist and could be managed in the natural setting of a school. Later, they initiated a comprehensive SMH program for rural areas, which included working with both children and teachers. It targeted overall psychosocial and cognitive development of rural school children. Stimulation to children was provided through various activities such as games, artwork, cognitive activities, drama, dance, and so on. A child-friendly approach was used to work with children in small groups for an hour each day of the week. Simultaneously, the teachers were sensitized to the issues related to mental health of children and overall psychosocial development. Systematic pre- and post-assessments were done to evaluate the outcome of the program, which included assessment of cognitive functions as well as scholastic and behavioral problems, with the help of established tools such as Raven's Progressive Matrices (Raven, 1941), Seguin Form Board (Seguin, 1907), and Rutter's Child Behaviour Questionnaire (Rutter, 1967). The results showed significant improvement in children in motor, cognitive, language, emotional, and social skills domains. Later, this program was successfully replicated with tribal children. The program was tailored according to the sociocultural background of tribal children. Pre- and post-assessments indicated positive effects of the program on the scholastic abilities of these children (Kapur, 2007). These efforts are continuing; however, it has not taken a wider state- or national-level shape because of resource constraints.

Based on her experience in the areas of mental health of Indian children, Kapur (1995) has advocated that a comprehensive SMH system should have components targeting primary, secondary, and tertiary preventions. She emphasizes the inclusion of parents, teachers, and mental health professionals in the program and highlights the need for sensitizing the parents and teachers toward the importance of enhancement of the quality of life of young children by underlining the importance of communication, play, and other such positive activities.

Life-skills promotion is an important domain of SMH. The WHO integrated the term "Life Skills" in SMH (WHO, 1997). In India a comprehensive work of "Health promotion using life-skills in adolescents" was initiated at NIMHANS by Bharath and Kumar (Bharath, 2001; Bharath & Kumar, 2008; 2010). Their model started with a focus on psychosocial competence by facilitating behavioral, emotional, and social skills in adolescents. The students participated in a year-long life-skills education (LSE) program focusing on enhancement of critical thinking and problem-solving abilities, improvement of communication skills and interpersonal relations, strengthening stress-coping abilities, and making them self-aware and empathic. The program included a total of 261 schools of four selected districts of a south-Indian state (with approximately 50 000 students and around 1000 teachers). In the first stage, a total of 31 master trainers were trained who later trained the teachers. The teachers then, under the supervision of master trainers and the experts from NIMHANS, carried on the implementation of the LSE program in the selected 261 schools. Some highlights of this program include comprehensive coverage of adolescent developmental themes such as motivation, hygiene, discipline, peer relationship, adolescent turmoil, social responsibility, sexuality, and drug abuse. The teachers were trained as life-skills facilitators in order to ensure integration of the program in the school system. The use of experiential and participative strategies with an emphasis on peer learning was encouraged. Last but not least, there was provision of an inbuilt assessment of outcome of the program. For the outcome assessment a randomly selected group of 605 students were compared with a control group on measures of coping, self-esteem, adjustment, and psychopathology. The results revealed that the groups differed significantly on coping, self-esteem, and adjustment. A total of 100 teachers were randomly selected for their feedback on the program and they felt that the program had positive impact on various things such as classroom behavior and self-confidence. The program is continuing and capacity building (by training the teachers and counselors in this model of the program) is done every three months (Bharath & Kumar 2010). Also, its implementation and outcome assessment in secondary schools is being envisaged. Dr. Bharath has used this model of training teachers as life-skills educators in yet another low- and middle-income country (LAMIC), Cambodia, toward suicide prevention in school-going adolescents (Jegannathan, Dahlblom, & Gullgren, 2014).

An intervention program for preschoolers, titled "Promotion of wellness for preschoolers," has also been attempted (Nithya Poornima, 2007). It is a structured intervention program which involves preschoolers and their mothers as the targets to improve mother–child interaction as well as to enhance pro-social behavior and cognitive skills of children. In a study, 30 mother–child pairs underwent this program (three weekly sessions for mothers and 15 sessions for children) and they were compared with a wait-list control group. Intervention with mothers focused upon introduction to normative child development, effective parenting, shaping positive behavior, healthy communication, pro-social behavior, and pre-academic skills. Intervention for children focused on communication, conflict resolution, pro-social skills, and pre-academic skills. Mothers were compared within and between groups on factors such as parenting and disciplining styles, whereas children were compared on pre-academic skills, developmental quotient, attachment style, and pro-social behavior. The intervention brought about positive changes in parenting, interpersonal relationships, cognitive competence, and pre-academic skills (Nithya Poornima, 2007).

Apart from these, the Zippy's Friends program, which promotes mental health and emotional wellbeing of young children, is currently going on in various countries, including India (Patel *et al.*, 2008). This is a universal program developed for primary-school children, and encourages children to explore and think of solutions for the problems. In India it was launched in 2004 in partnership with a non-governmental organization (NGO), Sangath. More than 12 000 children have been included in this program since its launch (Partnership for Children, 2014). At present, this program is limited to one of the states of India and needs to be expanded to other states.

However, these efforts, especially the relatively comprehensive approaches, are sporadic and there is an urgent need for SMH mandatorily to become a part of the larger school system. Mental health experts are raising this issue and even school boards are expressing concerns (CBSE, 2004; Shastri, 2008). We now move on to identify the obstacles in effective SMH implementation in India and steps to overcome these obstacles.

Obstacles to effective SMH implementation in India

There are various obstacles to the effective implementation of comprehensive SMH. The most important stumbling blocks in implementation are lack of a trained workforce and financial constraints. The Indian mental health system has an acute shortage of trained mental health professionals. Various professionals such as psychiatrists, clinical psychologists, psychiatric social workers and psychiatric nurses are very few in number, making the running of clinical services in mental hospitals a Herculean task. For example, there is not even one psychiatrist and nurse per 100 000 population (Jacob *et al.*, 2007). Limited training avenues, resource limitations, migration of trained professionals, and similar factors can be responsible for such a dearth in the workforce. It creates a genuine difficulty for these clinicians to get into additional services which may require their regular involvement. Limited funding is another problem that hinders SMH activity on a long-term basis.

Schools are also somewhat reluctant to be involved in running these programs. Most often when service providers approach schools for SMH-related activities, the school authorities show apathy and take note of the lack of personnel resources for such activities, or the stigma that the parents might attach to such programs. Teachers also show reluctance and often treat it as an additional responsibility (Shah, 2007). In fact, it would be unwise to say that teachers are completely unaware of "joyful learning" and other related good teaching practices; however, to what extent they really use these techniques is questionable (Kapur, Koot, & Lamb, 2012). Similar to school authorities, parents are antagonistic toward such services as they worry about labeling if their children are seen by mental health professionals. As mentioned, sensitization or training efforts on positive mental health are very limited, contributing to stigma about interaction with mental health experts. Of late, mental health professionals are trying to counter stigma related to mental illnesses by sensitizing people about various myths related to mental illnesses and emphasizing the role of positive mental health in the overall wellbeing of an individual. For example, interactive programs in communities, publication of information brochures, and organization of outreach camps are regularly carried out by various state and central government organizations. However, these efforts need to be more vigorous, and to really emphasize the important role of schools in mental health promotion. We now discuss the practical steps to overcome these obstacles for initiation of large-scale SMH activities.

SMH in the Indian context: issues to be considered

A few issues need to be borne in mind while developing the model SMH system for India. The following reflect our recommendations for principles that should guide SMH development based on review of global literature and our own experiences:

- An integrated program that focuses both on promotion of positive mental health and prevention of psychological problems, applicable to children from varied socioeconomic backgrounds, is required (Durlak & Wells, 1997; Hirisave & Nithya Poorniam, in press; Huang *et al.*, 2005; Kapur, 1995; Patel *et al.*, 2008).
- A better linkage among schools, parents, mental health experts, community service providers, and other such agencies related to school children is required (West, Lowie, Flaherty, & Pruitt, 2001).
- SMH services need to be "health" rather than "illness" oriented (Patel *et al.*, 2008). It should not remain limited to a few with problems. During formative years children with even minor problems may fail to achieve their full potential. In fact, the illness-oriented services not only remain limited to children with problems, but also face resistance (e.g., from parents) as they lead to fear of labeling.
- Ideally, a universal program focusing upon factors such as competence and self-esteem should include all the children in a school, whereas targeted programs with psychological intervention components should cater to those children who are at risk of developing psychological problems (e.g., due to psychosocial adversities) or have psychological problems (Bharath & Kumar, 2010; Bharath, Kumar, & Mukesh, 2007; Hendren *et al.*, 1994).
- There is a huge dearth of mental health professionals in India. The programs should be planned in a manner that empowers the stakeholders and decreases the requirement of the involvement of trained mental health professionals at each stage.
- SMH requires sincere involvement of parents, teachers and other community agencies. However, a large chunk of parents with limited education, limited resources, and other constraints lack motivation (or even if they are motivated find it difficult due to their resource constraints) to get involved in such programs proactively. Therefore, it is imperative that the program is tailored according to the needs of people of various socioeconomic backgrounds.
- An overburdened school system, both in terms of manpower and financial resources, should be assisted in running the SMH in a way that it does not entail an extra burden. The practical solution, as mentioned earlier, is to train and empower some of the teachers to initiate life-skills and other positive mental health activities in their schools.
- Kapur and colleagues (Kapur, Koot, & Lamb, 2012) suggest that issues such as the sustainability of the program, inclusion of rural children, regular evaluation of the program, provision to help teachers to cope with their emotional problems and appropriateness of the program when used on a nationwide scale should be given importance.

What needs to be done?

Keeping the above-mentioned issues and challenges in mind, there should be a concerted effort to develop a comprehensive program. The program should focus on involvement of all stakeholders, personnel development, sustainability, countering obstacles such as stigma and resource crunch, and wider coverage (covering both rural and urban areas across all states of India). We elaborate these steps of the SMH program implementation here.

Involvement of all stakeholders

The program should involve all stakeholders such as teachers, parents, mental health professionals, and governmental and non-governmental organizations related to education and child welfare. Ignorance and stigma related to mental health and illness prevalent in the society can be an obstacle to involving stakeholders in the SMH. We suggest two practical steps that can help in overcoming this obstacle and facilitate the involvement of stakeholders. First, liaising with the media (both print and electronic) to disseminate information about the role of positive mental health in overall growth of children, and second, approaching skills to allow the mental health professionals to interact with parents and teachers in any common forum, for example, parent–teacher meetings will be helpful. Further, apart from face-to-face interactions, the mental health experts can supply brochures and other audio-visual materials on effective parenting, stress reduction, problem solving, resilience, and other such topics to schools, which can be distributed among students, parents, and teachers. These activities will help in disseminating information, breaking the stigma and motivating the stakeholders in getting involved in SMH activities.

A multilayered program

The SMH activity should be multilayered and at the first level there is a need for involvement of those agencies that are at the helm of policy decisions related to mental health, education, and student welfare, both at the center and state levels. The central and state nodal centers should also monitor funding and pay attention to personnel development (such as trained school counselors). At the intermediate level there should be teams that directly monitor the SMH both in terms of direct supervision of the program as well as conducting regular needs assessment to appraise policy makers. Trained school teachers (or, if available, counselors or school psychologists) in conjunction with parents and school administration should implement the SMH program.

Focus on capacity building in schools

It is ideal that all schools should employ trained school psychologists to implement SMH services; however, keeping the available resources in view it looks unlikely to be achievable. Involving existing school resources may make the program fiscally more sustainable (Hann & Weiss, 2005). There should be emphasis on capacity building in schools to ensure continuity. Organizations working in the field of mental health can start short-term courses focused on child guidance and various aspects of SMH so that schools can send some of the inclined teachers to be trained and take the role of student counselors (Bharath & Kumar, 2010; Kapur, 1995). This can help in running the life-skills and other related programs in schools. For example, Zippy's Friend is a successful program worldwide; however, it needs special training for teachers to run this program (Patel et al., 2008). If the primary schools are encouraged to identify and train teachers in running this program, it can be easily implemented. It is imperative to highlight here that for the additional work of SMH, the schools must reward the teachers appropriately (e.g., increased salaries) to keep their interest sustained in the program.

Outcome assessment

Evaluative measures need to be built into the program for ensuring effectiveness and the experience of children receiving services should be an integral part of the evaluation

(Bharath & Kumar, 2010; Hirisave & Nithya Poornima, in press). A reflection of change due to implementation of any SMH program may be a key to garnering active support of stakeholders such as teachers (Han & Weiss, 2005).

International liaison

Seeking international liaison in the forms of conferences and expert interactions can help in initiation of collective efforts. As the cultures, needs, and resources of the South Asian countries are similar, interaction among the experts of this region is important. Centers of excellence in each region can work with a few schools to create empirically tested excellence in SMH, which can be applied to wider SMH services in the regions.

Use of technology

Use of technology such as tele-medicine can help in delivering services to the larger group with limited requirement of resources. For example, the teachers handling the SMH services in school can consult the mental health experts through tele-conferencing if they need to seek guidance for any specific issue or a child.

Conclusions

In India there is realization that SMH should be a national goal; however, far less has been done toward its actual implementation. Though there are some sincere efforts in this direction, a comprehensive SMH system remains elusive. Considering the importance of SMH for psychological wellbeing of children and adolescents, there is an urgent need for the planning and effective implementation of a comprehensive SMH system. Sensitization of stakeholders, utilization of available school resources for capacity building, proactive use of technology and media, establishment of national and international networks, and similar other efforts are some practical steps that can be taken in this direction.

References

Agarwal, S. P. (2004). Child and adolescent mental health: A pragmatic perspective. In S. P. Agarwal, D. S. Goel, R. L. Ichhpujani, R. N. Salhan, & S. Shrivastava (Eds.), *Mental health: An Indian perspective (1946–2003)* (pp. 290–292). New Delhi: Directorate General of Health Services, Ministry of Health & Family Welfare (India).

Bharath, S. (2001). Life skills education initiatives for adolescents in India. In M. Kapur & P. Bhola (Eds.), *Psychological therapies with children and adolescents* (pp. 207–213). Bangalore: NIMHANS.

Bharath, S., & Kumar, K. V. K. (2008). Health promotion using Life Skills Education approach for adolescents in schools: Development of a model. *Journal of Indian Association of Child and Adolescent Mental Health*, 4, 5–11.

Bharath, S., & Kumar, K. V. K. (2010). Empowering adolescents with life skills education in schools: School Mental Health program – Does it work? *Indian Journal of Psychiatry*, 52, 344–349.

Bharath, S., Kumar, K. V. K., & Mukesh, Y. P. (2007). School mental health program: clinical guidelines. In A. Avasthi & S. Gautam (Eds.), *Task Force on Clinical Practice Guidelines for Psychiatrists in India (Child and Geriatric Psychiatry)*. Chandigarh: IPS publication.

Central Board of Secondary Education (CBSE) (2004). Life skills education in class VII. Circular no. 11/04 of 2004 http://cbse.gov.in/circulars/2004/Circulars_11.htm retrieved on January 27, 2014.

Central Board of Secondary Education (CBSE) (2008). Counselling in Schools. Circular no. 08 of 2008. www.cbse.nic.in/welcome/htm retrieved on July 27, 2009.

Costello, E. J., Egger, H., & Angold, A. (2005). The epidemiology of child and adolescent psychiatric disorders: I. Methods and public health burden. *American Academy of Child and Adolescent Psychiatry*, 44, 972–986.

Durlak, J. A., & Wells, A. M. (1997). Primary prevention mental health programs for children and adolescents: a meta-analytic review. *American Journal of Community Psychology*, 25, 115–152.

Hann, S. S., & Weiss, B. (2005). Sustainability of teacher implementation of school-based mental health programs. *Journal of Abnormal Child Psychology*, 33, 665–679.

Hendren, R., Weisen, R. B., & Orley, J. (1994). *Mental health programmes in schools*. Geneva: World Health Organization.

Hirisave, U., & Nithya Poornima, M. (In press). Preventive and promotive interventions for psychological problems in young children. *Trend report on psychological survey in research*. New Delhi: ICSSR.

Huang, L., Stroul, B., Friedman, R., *et al.* (2005). Transforming mental health care for children and their families. *American Psychologist*, 60, 615–627.

Jacob, K. S., Sharan, P., Mirza, I., *et al.* (2007). Mental health systems in countries: Where are we now? *Lancet*, 370, 1061–1077.

Jegannathan, B., Dahlblom, K., & Gullgren, G. (2014). Out-come of a school-based intervention to promote life skills among young people in Cambodia. *Asian Journal of Psychiatry*, http://dx. doi.org/10.1016/j.ajp.2014.01.011

Kapur, M (1995). *Mental health of Indian children*. New Delhi: Sage.

Kapur, M. (1997). *Mental health in Indian schools*. New Delhi: Sage.

Kapur, M. (2007). *Learning from children: What to teach them*. New Delhi: Sage.

Kapur, M. (2011). *Counselling children with psychological problems*. Bangalore: Pearson Education.

Kapur, M., & Cariappa, I. (1978). Evaluation of training programme for school teachers in student counselling. *Indian Journal of Psychiatry*, 20, 289–291.

Kapur, M., & Cariappa, I. (1979). Training in counselling for school teachers. *International Journal for the Advancement of Counselling*, 2, 109–115.

Kapur, M., & Hirisave, U. (2004). Promotion of psychosocial development of rural school children. Project funded by NCRI-Human Resource Development Ministry, Govt of India.

Kapur, M., & Hirisave, U. (2006). *Manual for pre-school teachers*. Bangalore: NIMHANS.

Kapur, M., Koot, H. M., & Lamb, M. E. (2012). *Developmental psychology and education: Bridging the gap*. New Delhi: Manak Publications.

Kumar, D., Dubey, I., Bhattacharjee, D., *et al.* (2009). Beginning steps of school mental health in India: A teacher workshop. *Advances in School Mental Health Promotion*, 2, 29–34.

Malhotra, S. (2004). Child and adolescent psychiatry in India: Slow beginnings and rapid growth. In S. P. Agarwal, D. S. Goel, R. L. Ichhpujani, R. N. Salhan, & S. Shrivastava (Eds.), *Mental health: An Indian perspective (1946–2003)* (pp. 227–232). New Delhi: Directorate General of Health Services, Ministry of Health & Family Welfare (India).

Malhotra, S. (2005). Study of psychosocial determinants of developmental psychopathology in school children. In B. Shah, R. Parhee, N. Kumar, T. Khanna, & R. Singh (Eds.), *Mental health research in India: Technical monograph on ICMR Mental Health Studies* (pp. 91–97). New Delhi: Indian Council of Medical Research.

Ministry of Health and Family Welfare, Government of India. (1982). National Mental Health Program. http://mohfw.nic.in/WriteReadData/ . . . /9903463892NMHP%20detail.pdf, retrieved on May 28, 2014.

Ministry of Health and Family Welfare, Government of India. (2013). Rashtriya Bal Swasthya Karyakram. http://nrhm.gov.in/nrhm-components/rmnch-a/child-health-immuniza tion/rashtriya-bal-swasthya-karyakram-rbsk/background.html, retrieved on May 28, 2014.

Ministry of Women and Child Development, Government of India. (1974). National Policy for Children. http://wcd.nic.in/icds.htm, retrieved on May 28, 2014.

Ministry of Women and Child Development, Government of India. (1975). Integrated Child Development Services Scheme. http://wcd.nic.in/icds.htm, retrieved on May 28, 2014.

Nithya Poornima, M. (2007). Efficacy of promotive intervention with lesser privileged pre-schoolers. PhD thesis submitted to NIMHANS, Bangalore.

Partnership for Children (2014). Zippy's friends in India. www.partnershipforchildren. org.uk/teachers/zippy-s-friends-teachers/ where-is-the-programme-running/india-2.html, retrieved on May 28, 2014.

Patel, V., Flisher, A. J., Nikapota, A., & Mahotra, S. (2008). Promoting child and adolescent mental health in low and middle income countries. *Journal of Child Psychology and Psychiatry*, 49, 313–334.

Raven, J. C. (1941). Standardisation of progressive matrices. *British Journal of Medical Psychology*, 14, 137–150.

Rutter, M. (1967). A children's behaviour questionnaire for completion by teachers: Preliminary findings. *Journal of Child Psychology and Psychiatry*, 8, 1–11.

Seguin, E. (1907). *Idiocy: Its treatment by the psychological method*. New York: Columbia University.

Shah, H. (2007). *Pilot project on developing guidelines for learning disorder in Gujarati language*. Gujarat: The Gujarat Mental Health and Allied Sciences Foundation.

Shah, H. M., & Kumar, D. (2012). Sensitizing the teachers towards school mental health issues: An Indian experience. *Community Mental Health Journal*, 48, 522–526.

Shastri, P. S. (2008). Future perspective of planning child guidance services in India. *Indian Journal of Psychiatry*, 50, 241–243.

Sinha, V. K., Kishore, M. T., & Thakur, A. (2003). A school mental health program in

India. *Journal of Academy of Child and Adolescent Psychiatry*, 42, 624.

Srinath, S., & Sitholey, P. (2005). Epidemiological study of child and adolescent psychiatric disorders in urban and rural areas. In B. Shah, R. Parhee, N. Kumar, T. Khanna, & R. Singh (Eds.), *Mental health research in India: Technical monograph on ICMR Mental Health Studies* (pp. 86–90). New Delhi: Indian Council of Medical Research.

Teich, J. L., Robinson, G., & Weist, M. D. (2007). What kind of mental health services do public schools in the United States provide? *Advances in School Mental Health Promotion*, 1, 13–22.

Vaidya, G., & Dhavale, H. S. (2000). Child psychiatry in Bombay: The school mental health clinic. *British Journal of Hospital Medicine*, 61, 400–401.

Weist, M. D., & Murray, M. (2007). Advancing school mental health promotion globally. *Advances in School Mental Health Promotion*, 1, 2–12.

West, M. D., Lowie, J. A., Flaherty, L. T., & Pruitt, D. (2001). Collaboration among the education, mental health, and public health systems to promote youth mental health. *Psychiatric Services*, 52, 1348–1351.

Weston, K., Anderson-Butcher, D., & Burke, R. (2008) Developing a comprehensive curriculum framework for teacher preparation in expanded school mental health. *Advances in School Mental Health Promotion*, 1, 25–41.

World Health Organization (1997). Program in Mental Health: Life Skills in Schools WHO/MNH/PSF/93.7A Rev.2, Geneva: World Health Organization.

School mental health
A perspective from Iraq

AbdulKareem AlObaidi

Background

Iraq is a country located in the Middle East and is part of the Arab world. It borders Turkey, Syria, Jordan, Iran, Kuwait, and Saudi Arabia. The city of Baghdad is its capital. The region is known as "The Cradle of Civilization"; once known as Mesopotamia, "the land between two rivers," referring to the Tigris and Euphrates. For millennia it has been of profound historical and political significance as the site of ancient civilizations. The earliest city-state known to human beings was found here (Ur). Historically, Iraq's great creativity and inventions contributed significantly to human development; however, Iraq has been the focus of political and military conflict in modern times. In the 1960s–1970s the country flourished, with its health and education systems being regarded as the most advanced in the region. However, the Iraq–Iran War between 1980 and 1988, followed by the first Gulf War (1990–1991) after the Iraqi invasion of Kuwait has resulted in significant and substantial negative impacts on the country. This was followed by international sanctions and isolation of Iraq from the rest of the world for 13 years. In 2003 Iraq experienced a military invasion and occupation by a multinational coalition led by America and Britain. An insurgency and sectarian violence emerged after the invasion. As a consequence, millions of Iraqis, particularly young people, were killed or injured. More than four million Iraqis were forced to leave their homes, either internally displaced, or become refugees in neighboring countries.

The already fragile infrastructures were destroyed by large-scale looting and civil disorder which occurred directly after the invasion. Moreover, Iraq had experienced a high level of international displacement of academics, and medical and science professionals, particularly after the persecution of intellectuals during the 2003 US-led war and invasion of the country (Gustafsson, 2006). This has had a significantly negative impact on education and health services in the country. The attrition of academics and the collapse of research activities due to instability and violence have subsequently contributed to the loss of the scientific base for social sciences in the country, in particular, services involving children in health and education systems (AlObaidi and Piachaud, 2007; AlObaidi et al., 2013a).

Child and adolescent mental health problems/disorders in Iraq

Iraq is an example of the challenging mental health needs of children in low-income and conflict-affected countries. Children and adolescents constitute half of Iraq's population of 33 million (COS, 2011). Mental health problems experienced by Iraqi children and

School Mental Health: Global Challenges and Opportunities, ed. Stan Kutcher, Yifeng Wei and Marc D. Weist. Published by Cambridge University Press. © Cambridge University Press 2015.

adolescents are substantial and a number of published studies have showed increased rates of mental health problems among Iraqi children and adolescents. For example, 20–30% of children and adolescents have been suggested to have post-traumatic stress disorder (PTSD) due to high exposure to traumatic experience (Ahmad *et al.*, 1998; Lafta *et al.*, 2014; Razokhi *et al.*, 2006). A study by Al-Jawadi and Abdul-Rhman (2007) in Mosul city in the north of Iraq suggested that 37% of children between 1 and 15 years who were patients at primary health clinics presented with mental health problems (Al-Jawadi and Abdul-Rhman, 2007). In Baghdad, PTSD was reported among 14% of respondents in a survey of 600 primary school children, and also among 30% of respondents on a sample of 1090 adolescents living in Mosul (Razokhi *et al.*, 2006) and among 20% of children of Iraqi Kurds in the north (Ahmad *et al.*, 1998). A recent survey on the prevalence of PTSD conducted during 2010 among male adolescents from secondary schools in Baghdad suggested that 55% of boys aged 13–19 years have experienced trauma, and 17.1% have symptoms of PTSD (Lafta *et al.*, 2014). In a clinical sample study conducted in Baghdad during 2005, anxiety disorders were diagnosed in 22% of children studied and behavioral problems were identified in 18% of children (AlObaidi *et al.*, 2010b). The prevalence of attention deficit hyperactivity disorder (ADHD) among primary-school children in Baghdad is approximately 10% according to a recent survey (AlObaidi and Ali, 2009). Another survey applied DSM-IV criteria to diagnose social phobia among a sample of secondary school children in Baghdad during 2003 and suggested prevalence rate of 1.6% (Hummadi and AlObaidi, 2014).

Despite the above-mentioned data, major national epidemiological surveys investigating child and adolescent psychosocial and mental health have not been conducted. There is some interest in scientific exploration; however, its scope is still limited. As data show, there is unsystematic coverage in the literature and research mostly focuses on the impact of war and violence on the psychosocial wellbeing of Iraqi children (AlObaidi, 2011; AlObaidi *et al.*, 2013a).

Many factors, both personal and environmental, contribute to the mental health problems of young Iraqis. Many children and youth are victims and witnesses to violence and traumatic events, seeing family members become victims, being displaced from their homes, and experiencing ongoing chronic instability. Furthermore, Iraqis have experienced severe deprivation, economic embargoes, and civil unrest as a result of the war. The wellbeing of people in Iraq, especially children, has been severely undermined by the continuous state of violence and poverty, and the failure of the education and health systems (AlObaidi, 2011; AlObaidi *et al.*, 2009). For example, 20–25% of Iraqis live below the poverty line (IRIN, 2009). Such circumstances have raised concerns about the long-term effects of trauma and stress on the mental health of the country's youth (AlObaidi, 2011). In spite of all this, the majority of children and adolescents in Iraq do not develop mental disorders and among factors behind that may be family and local community support to build "resilience" further, it also may be that most children and youth were successful in adapting to the negative environment and therefore survived.

Child and adolescent mental health services in Iraq

Mental health service development in Iraq is relatively new. Around 60 years ago, medical care for adults with mental illnesses was established in government-operated psychiatric hospitals in the capital city, Baghdad. Just three decades ago psychiatric services became part of general hospital care across Iraq (Sadik and AlJadiry, 2006). However, there is no formal child and adolescent mental health system; mental healthcare for children is commonly provided in out-patient mental healthcare clinics for adults. In addition, a number of institutes for children with special needs and residential homes for orphans are run by governmental and non-governmental agencies. Multidisciplinary work and various forms of psychotherapies, such as behavioral and play therapies, are not part of standard medical practice. School-based child and adolescent mental health services (CAMHS) are not available. The psychosocial services of the juvenile justice system are almost non-existent. The shortage of human resources in the field of child psychosocial care presents a challenge to the development of child mental health service delivery and development in Iraq (AlObaidi et al., 2010a). The contribution of national and international non-governmental organizations (INGOs), such as the United Nations Children's Fund (UNICEF), has been hindered by the current instability and violence, causing many to quit Iraq due to the high risk exposure to staff (AlObaidi, 2011).

These circumstances generated large national and international concerns about and demand for services, particularly for children's health, including mental health and education (AlObaidi, 2010; AlObaidi and Attalah, 2009). However, a great number of factors have prevented the development and advancement of CAMHS in Iraq, such as the intense and turbulent political, social, and economic conflicts and crises mentioned above. In addition, although public education about mental health is considered to be essential to promote CAMHS, increasing mental health knowledge and raising awareness of children's mental health in Iraq has been difficult due to unsystematic coverage of the topic in the literature. Furthermore, stigma associated with mental illness is high within the Iraqi community and contributes negatively to mental health services development (AlObaidi et al., 2010a). A survey with a random sample of 500 adults in Baghdad showed that 50–70% thought that people with mental health problems are largely to blame for their conditions, should not get married, should not have children, and should not be contacted by other people (Sadik et al., 2010). Some preliminary promising work has been done to push forward the agenda to change this negative scenario. For example, children's rights and needs for services and therapeutic/educational interventions have been examined in some research studies, and show that child protection should be the priority of the community and national agenda (AlObaidi et al., 2009; 2013b; AlObaidi and Budosan, 2011).

School mental health programs in Iraq and suggestions for development

It has been widely addressed that school is a usefully venue to help develop and promote child emotional wellbeing and it is regarded as an important site for mental health promotion and prevention to ameliorate child and adolescent mental health problems with the least stigmatization (Durlak et al., 2011; Greenberg, 2010; Seif-El Din, 2004; Vostanis et al., 2013; Weare, 2013: Weare and Markham, 2005; Weare and Nind, 2011). Globally, the magnitude of child and adolescent mental health problems challenges resources for care even among developed countries (Belfer, 2008). Despite a clear development of school mental health services in developed countries, there are many challenges facing their appropriate implementation (Vostanis et al., 2012) due to many factors, including stigma. In general, raising awareness about child and adolescent mental health needs within a community and among policy makers and stakeholders is often challenging in peaceful times, let alone in times of wars and disasters, where children's needs are likely to be more complex and closely linked to basic needs of security, food, shelter, education, and family connections (Fayyad *et al.*, 2008; Jones, 2008).

For any initiative in Iraq, it is important to acknowledge the unique context of this country and the difficulty that people confront in dealing with everyday life in a country that has persisted in a state of violence and political instability and extreme levels of suffering and poverty. The devastation of Iraq's education and health infrastructures and the assassination and forced exile of a large number of Iraqi professionals, including teachers, doctors, nurses, and academics, indicate that it is more appropriate to describe the task as rebuilding rather than reforming the education and health system.

According to the Central Organization for Statistics, in the 2011 academic year, the total number of schools in Iraq was 20 462 with 6 890 922 students (age 4–18 years) enrolled who were served by 417 797 teachers and other staff members (COS, 2011). However, the Iraqi school system currently lacks a mental health strategy; there are no school-based CAMHS; and Iraqi educators are not trained to understand and identify children with learning and emotional problems (AlObaidi *et al.*, 2013b). As mentioned in the previous section, Iraq is facing challenges such as a general shortage of mental health professionals and paraprofessionals, and the lack of multidisciplinary approaches and childcare providers in health. Furthermore, mental health and education operate under extremely difficult circumstances and with fragmented infrastructures, and are under-prioritized by the state and the community. Thus, it is not surprising that promoting CAMH and establishing CAMHS in Iraq present a great challenge (AlObaidi *et al.*, 2010a). We propose a model of how the school-based mental health services can be established in Iraq based on its current contexts and realities.

The essential first step in developing school-based mental health services is to define the major school-based mental health needs and practical paths to satisfy those needs, with attention to mechanisms (e.g., teacher-training processes) that can affect program implementation and sustainability. Teachers play a major role in school-based mental health promotion. Teachers' confidence and skills are fundamental in this area (Lendrum *et al.*, 2013). Teachers in Iraq need training to be able to help foster the social and emotional development of students, to use effective classroom management strategies, and to identify emotional and behavioral problems requiring referral to specialty clinical assessment and treatment (AlObaidi *et al.*, 2013b). Teachers may also benefit from a wide range of developments in technology and communications to access information, and receive training and support. Training for teachers should focus on understanding social and emotional wellbeing of children, enhancing emotional literacy and skills to identify early signs of child mental health problems, and realizing that a complex interaction of factors are operating in the school, family, and community (Jorm *et al.*, 2010). School-based mental health programs should target multiple health issues in the context of a whole-school approach (Jané-Llopis *et al.*, 2005). In addition, Weare (2013) presents us with some characteristics of effective school mental health programs that can be implemented, including pre-service and ongoing professional education and training about child mental health issues for teachers. Weare (2013) argues that school mental health programs should focus on positive mental health and students' strengths, not solely on the problems. She recommends developing universal targeted plans and starting early with long-term goals. The whole-school approach and links with academic learning and liaison with families and communities are essential for effective and successful school mental health programs (Weare, 2013).

Experts in child and adolescent mental health need to explore ways in which they can collaborate with schools to develop and implement teacher education programs to enhance student mental health (AlObaidi *et al.*, 2013b). The collaboration of different systems (e.g., education, welfare, and health) is essential to ensure the establishment and implementation of mental health services for children and adolescents and to place schools as the major site to address child and adolescent needs in the CAMH system. It is also crucial to develop policies, plans, and guidelines to support the development of school mental health programs and to prevent the system from becoming fragmented, ineffective, expensive, or inaccessible. These policies and plans should present the values, principles, and objectives of improving the mental health of children and adolescents, and reducing the burden of illness caused by child and adolescent mental disorders in the population. This approach should be part of the national health plan in Iraq.

Meanwhile, other important steps need to be taken in Iraq to develop the whole system for child and adolescent mental health, with a major focus on school mental health. This includes population needs assessment such as interviews with health workers, educators, clergy, law enforcement officials, children, adolescents, and their parents. Second, it is important to gather best evidence available for effective and successful strategies to develop CAMH and school programs. Third, it is fundamental to set up the vision, values, principles, and objectives prior to the commencement of school mental health initiatives. Grand negotiations among stakeholders at the education, health, and NGO levels are crucial to initiate cooperation and establish guidelines for responsibilities and related legislation.

In addition, the magnitude of child mental health needs in Iraq and the limited availability of health and mental health services require a community-based approach, focusing on empowering families, teachers, religious, and cultural leaders, and community health workers. School mental health programs priorities may start with focusing on mental health education through mental health literacy programs to improve the understanding of mental health and mental illness, reduce stigma toward mental illness and encourage help-seeking behaviors if needed in both students and teachers. Programs may be developed to address issues like school dropout and bullying, and promote resilience as preventive measures. Programs should be culturally appropriate and focusing on understanding mental health and reducing stigma associated with mental health problems. The needs of children with physical and mental disabilities should be addressed in national education plans and legislation to enforce mainstream education to be inclusive of those children (AlObaidi and Budosan, 2011). Furthermore, resources for service monitoring and outcome effectiveness research are needed, as the present lack of statistical data and research findings make it difficult to plan, implement, and evaluate child and adolescent mental health programs (AlObaidi *et al.*, 2013a).

Conclusions

There is a substantial amount of work that needs to be pushed forward to improve the mental health of children and adolescents in Iraq, which will bring both challenges and opportunities. The mental wellbeing of Iraqi children and adolescents is the crucial element in the recovery of Iraq. Addressing the basic health and mental health needs of children and adolescents will bring hopes for the country to recover, survive, and bloom in the future.

References

Ahmad, A., Mohamed, H. T., and Ameen, N. M. (1998). A 26-month follow-up of posttraumatic stress symptoms in children after the mass escape tragedy in Iraqi Kurdistan. *Nordic Journal of Psychiatry*, 52, 357–366.

Al-Jawadi, A. A. and Abdul-Rhman, S. (2007). Prevalence of childhood and early adolescence mental disorders among children attending primary health care centers in Mosul, Iraq: A cross sectional study. *BMC Public Health*, 7, 274. www.biomedcentral.com/1471-2458/7/274 (accessed September 16, 2013).

AlObaidi, A. K. (2010). Iraqi psychiatrist in exile helping distressed Iraqi refugee children in Egypt in non-clinical settings. *Journal of the Canadian Academy of Child and Adolescent Psychiatry*, 19(2), 72–73.

AlObaidi, A. K. (2011). Iraq: Children and adolescents' mental health under continuous turmoil. *International Psychiatry*, 8(1), 5–6.

AlObaidi, A. K. and Ali, N. S. (2009). Attention deficit/hyperactivity disorder among schoolchildren in Baghdad. *Journal of Canadian Academy for Child & Adolescent Psychiatry*, 18(1), 4–5.

AlObaidi, A. K. and Attalah, S. F. (2009). Iraqi refugees in Egypt: An exploration of their mental health and psychosocial status. *Intervention*, 7(2), 145–151.

AlObaidi, A. K. and Budosan, B. (2011). Mainstreaming educational opportunities for physically and mentally disabled children youth in Iraq. *Advances in School Mental Health Promotion*, 4(1), 35–43.

AlObaidi, A. K., Budosan, B., and Jeffery, L. (2010a). Child and adolescent mental health in Iraq: current situation and scope for promotion of child and adolescent mental health policy. *Intervention*, 8(1), 40–51.

AlObaidi, A. K., Corcoran, T., and Scarth, L. (2013a). Psychosocial research with children in Iraq: current health practice and policy in a context of armed conflict. *International Psychiatry*, 10(3), 72–74.

AlObaidi, A. K., Jeffrey, L., Scarth, L., and Albadawi, G. (2009). Iraqi children rights: Building a system under fire. *Medicine, Conflict & Survival*, 25(2), 145–162.

AlObaidi, A. K., Nelson, B. D., AlBadawi, G., Hicks M. H. R., and Guarine, A. J. (2013b). Child mental health and service needs in Iraq: Beliefs and attitudes of primary school teachers. *Child and Adolescent Mental Health*, 18(3), 171–179.

AlObaidi, A. K. and Piachaud, J. (2007). While adults battle, children suffer: Future problems for Iraq. *Journal of the Royal Society of Medicine*, 100, 394–395.

AlObaidi, A. K., Scarth, L., and Dwivedi, K. N. (2010b). Mental disorder in children attending child psychiatric clinic at the general paediatric hospital in Baghdad. *International Journal of Mental Health Promotion*, 12(3), 24–30.

Belfer, M. L. (2008). Child and adolescent mental disorders: The magnitude of the problem across the globe. *Journal of child Psychology and Psychiatry*, 49, 226–236.

Central Organization for Statistics (COS) (2011). Annual abstract of statistics 2010–2011. http://cosit.gov.iq/english (accessed August 29, 2013).

Durlak, J. A., Weissberg, R. P., Dymnicki, A. B., Taylor, R. D., and Schellinger, K. (2011). The impact of enhancing students' social and emotional learning: A meta-analysis of school based universal interventions. *Child Development*, 82, 474–501.

Fayyad, J., Salamoun, M. M., Karam, E. G., Karam, A. N., Mueimneh, Z., and Tabet, C. C. (2008). Child mental health services in war and peace. In: M. E. Garralda and J. P. Raynaud (eds.), *Culture and conflict in child and adolescent mental health*. Lanham, MD: Jason Aronson.

Greenberg, M. (2010). School-based prevention: Current status and future challenges. *Effective Education*, 2, 27–52.

Gustafsson, B. (2006). The community must unite over Iraq. *Nature*, 444(7118), 422.

Hummadi, B. F. and AlObaidi, A. K. (2014). Social phobia among secondary school students in Baghdad/Iraq. *Journal of Canadian Academy for Child & Adolescent Psychiatry*, 23(1), 70–71.

IRIN. (2009). Iraq: Over 20 percent of Iraqis live below the poverty line. www.irinnews.org/report/84526/iraq-over-20-percent-of-iraqis-live-below-the-poverty-line (accessed February 20, 2014).

Jané-Llopis, E, Barry, M. M., Hosman, C., and Patel, V. (2005). Mental health promotion works: A review. *Promotion and Education*, 2 (suppl), 9–25.

Jones, L. (2008). Responding to the needs of children in crisis. *International Review of Psychiatry*, 20(3), 291–303.

Jorm, A. F., Kitchener, B. A., Sawyer, M. G., and Cvetkovski, S. (2010). Mental health first aid training for high school teachers: A cluster randomized trial. *BMC Psychiatry*, 10:51 www.biomedcentral.com/1471–244X/10/51 (accessed December 15, 2013).

Lafta, R., AlObaidi, A. K., and Aziz, Z. S. (2014). Post-traumatic stress disorder among male students in secondary schools in Baghdad. *Journal of Abnormal Child Psychology* 3, 121.

Lendrum, A., Humphrey, N., and Wigelsworth, M. (2013). Social and emotional aspects of learning (SEAL) for secondary schools: Implementation difficulties and their implications for school-based mental health promotion. *Child and Adolescent Mental Health* 18(3), 158–164.

Razokhi, A. H., Taha, I. K., Taib, N. I., Sadik, S., and Al Gasseer, N. (2006). Mental health of Iraqi children. *Lancet*, 368, 838–839.

Sadik, S. and AlJadiry, A. M. (2006). Mental health services in Iraq: Past, present and future. *International Psychiatry*, 3(4), 11–13.

Sadik, S., Bradley, M., Al-Hasoon, S., and Jenkins, R. (2010). Public perception of mental health in Iraq. *International Journal of Mental Health Systems*, 4, 26.

Seif-El Din, A. (2004). Prevention and intervention in school settings. In: H. Remschmidt, M. L. Belfer, and I. Goodyer (eds.), *Facilitating pathways, care, treatment and prevention in child and adolescent mental health*, Berlin: Springer-Verlag, pp. 326–334.

Vostanis, P., Humphrey, N., Fitzgerald, N., Deighton, J., and Wolpert, M. (2013). How do schools promote emotional well-being among their pupils? Findings from a national scoping survey of mental health provision in English schools. *Child and Adolescent Mental Health*, 18(3), 151–157.

Vostanis, P., O'Reilly, M., Taylor, H., *et al.* (2012). What can schools teach child mental health services? Practitioners' perceptions of training and joint working. *Emotional and Behavioural Difficulties*, 17(2), 109–124.

Weare, K. (2013). Child and adolescent mental health in schools. *Child and Adolescent Mental Health*, 18(3), 129–130.

Weare, K. and Markham, W. (2005). What do we know about promoting mental health through schools? *Promotion and Education*, 12, 4–8.

Weare, K. and Nind, M. (2011). Mental health promotion and problem prevention in schools: What does the evidence say? *Health Promotion International*, 26(S1), 29–69.

Supporting a whole-school approach to mental health promotion and wellbeing in post-primary schools in Ireland

Aleisha M. Clarke and Margaret M. Barry

Introduction

This chapter addresses curriculum innovation in Ireland regarding the promotion of positive mental health and wellbeing of adolescents in post-primary schools. The adoption of the Health Promoting Schools Framework in combination with the introduction of Social, Personal and Health Education (SPHE) as a mandatory subject in post-primary schools is examined. The implementation of SPHE is based on a partnership approach between the Department of Education and Skills, the Department of Health, and the Health Service Executive in establishing a national-level support system for implementation on a whole-school basis.

Since the 1970s an array of approaches to addressing school-based mental health promotion has been employed in Irish post-primary schools. In 2002 a broad-based health education program, SPHE, was introduced as a mandatory subject in the Junior Cycle (age 12–15 years) of post-primary schools. It has since been expanded to the Senior Cycle (16–19 years). The formal establishment of SPHE within the school system gave structure and coherence to that which was often informally in place in schools in Ireland. SPHE, as part of the school curriculum, supports the personal development, health, and wellbeing of young people and helps them create and maintain supportive relationships. SPHE adopts a whole-school approach to promoting positive mental health and wellbeing. Its key components include: (1) curriculum teaching and learning; (2) organization, ethos, and environment; and (3) partnership and services. The nationwide delivery of this subject is facilitated by a multi-sectoral support system which provides regular in-service training for teachers, supplies support and resources, and ensures quality control.

In this chapter we review key components of the SPHE curriculum with particular relevance to promoting adolescents' mental health, and explore the challenges in implementing a whole-school approach. The potential of online school-based mental health promotion interventions is considered. Findings from a systematic review of online mental health promotion and prevention interventions for young people aged 12–25 are presented and the potential use of evidence-based online interventions within the school context is considered. Given the important role teachers, parents, and community stakeholders play in the implementation of a whole-school approach to mental health promotion, this chapter further presents findings from ongoing work on the development of online resources to

School Mental Health: Global Challenges and Opportunities, ed. Stan Kutcher, Yifeng Wei and Marc D. Weist. Published by Cambridge University Press. © Cambridge University Press 2015.

assist adults in supporting youth mental health in Ireland. This research, which is being conducted by the authors in collaboration with the Inspire Ireland Foundation and Young and Well Cooperative Research Centre in Australia, is examining the needs of parents, teachers, health, and mental health professionals in relation to youth mental health and bridging the disconnect between adults and young people in terms of both digital and mental health literacy. The implications of the research findings for supporting schools in promoting adolescents' mental health and wellbeing in the context of current policy and practice are discussed.

Policies and practices in promoting the mental health and wellbeing of adolescents in schools

It is estimated that 10–20% of young people worldwide experience mental health problems [2]. Several large-scale studies conducted in Ireland indicate that about one in five young people in Ireland experience serious emotional distress at any one time [3–7]. Of these young people, it is reported that only a small minority are in contact with any form of helping agency [3–6]. The mortality rate from suicide in the 15–24 age group in Ireland is the fourth highest in the EU [7] and the third highest among young men aged 15–19 [8]. Changing economic, social, and cultural conditions increase young people's vulnerability to negative life outcomes. Results from the My World Study [9] conducted with 14 306 young people age 12–25 years in Ireland found that over one-fifth of young adults indicated that they had engaged in self-harm and 7% reported a suicide attempt. Excessive drinking and experience of financial distress were found to be significantly related to poor mental health. The presence of "one good adult" was significantly associated with lower mental health distress and higher positive adjustment.

The promotion of mental health and wellbeing during adolescence is critical to the cognitive, emotional, social, and academic development of young people. Poor mental health during adolescence is associated with health and social problems such as school failure, delinquency, and substance misuse, and increases the risk of poverty and other adverse outcomes in adulthood [1]. Interventions that promote positive mental health equip young people with the necessary life skills, supports, and resources to fulfill their potential and overcome adversity. The importance of the school setting for promoting young people's mental health and the opportunities it provides for effective mental health promotion, prevention, and early intervention have been evident for some time. For instance, the World Health Organization (WHO) Health Promoting Schools initiative [10] has emphasized the role of schools in promoting generic life skills and providing supportive environments that foster positive youth development and a sense of connectedness with the family, community, and broader context of young people's lives. The last two decades have seen a considerable growth in the international evidence base for mental health promotion in schools. A number of systematic reviews have shown that comprehensive mental health promotion interventions carried out in collaboration with families, schools, and communities lead to improvements not only in mental health but also improved social functioning, academic and work performance, and general health behaviors [11–19].

National policies on mental health and suicide prevention in Ireland have also endorsed the important role schools play in promoting young people's mental health [20]. A Framework for Junior Cycle [21], which outlines plans by the Department of Education and Skills to reform the Junior Cycle (12–15 years) in post-primary schools, places a strong emphasis on the development of young people's mental health and wellbeing. The framework provides broad scope for schools to develop and reinforce a young person's mental health and wellbeing, stating that "learning should take place in a climate founded on the collective well-being of school, community and society" (p. 4). National guidelines for mental health promotion and suicide prevention have also been produced for post-primary schools based on national and international evidence and best practice [22]. These guidelines aim to support schools in developing a whole-school approach to mental health promotion and suicide prevention, which focuses on the entire school community, not just individual students or those with identified needs. Essential components of the whole-school approach are outlined in the guidelines and include: positive staff–pupil relationships, staff development and education, strong leadership and clear disciplinary policies, teamwork, focus on skills, attitudes and values rather than facts and information, active involvement of parents, local community, and key local agencies. The guidelines recommend that schools should adopt the National Educational Psychological Service (NEPS) support model for the promotion of mental health. This model, which is based on the WHO's model for school mental health promotion, comprises a three-tiered continuum of support:

1. *School Support for All* – promoting positive mental health for all members of the school community.
2. *School Support for Some* – identifying young people at risk of developing unhealthy patterns of behaviors or those already showing early signs of mental health difficulties, and providing additional supports.
3. *School Support for a Few* – implementing interventions for young people with more complex and enduring mental health and emotional needs with the support of external agencies.

The implementation of the three-tiered continuum of support requires the whole-school coordination of support and resources in providing the spectrum of needed interventions at each level. Engagement with key stakeholders including students, teachers, parents, and curriculum support staff, together with health promotion and psychological services, such as the Health Promotion Service, NEPS, and Child and Adolescent Mental Health Services (CAMHS), is essential to the successful implementation of this model. The Health Promoting School Framework (HPSF) is recommended as a guide for schools in reviewing, devising, and adopting a whole-school support plan.

Health Promoting Schools Framework

Ireland was an early adopter of the HPSF, which was developed in Europe in the 1980s through the European Network of Health Promoting Schools (now referred to as Schools for Health in Europe). A health-promoting school is characterized as a school which is constantly strengthening its capacity to be a healthy setting for living, learning, and working by focusing on all the conditions that affect health [10]. The health-promoting school aims to:

• provide a framework for developing health-promoting initiatives in a way that supports and enhances the implementation of the curriculum;
• support the planning, implementation, and evaluation of health-related activities; and
• enhance the links between a school and its community.

As part of the HPSF, schools are encouraged to focus on four key areas for action: (1) physical and social environment; (2) curriculum and learning; (3) family and community partnerships;

and (4) policies and planning. The HPS model is considered a process that develops and evolves in line with the ever-changing life of the school. It is a dynamic concept underpinned by reflective planning and a learning cycle that supports ongoing development and growth. From the outset, the health-promoting school concept was supported by both Health and Education Departments in Ireland. To date, however, the promotion of positive mental health has not received widespread attention as part of the HPSF approach. Weare and Markham [23] state that effective work to promote mental health will not happen by chance. There is a need for explicit training and coordinated strategies and programs, based on sound research evidence and assessment of their effectiveness. The introduction of the SPHE curriculum as a mandatory subject in the Junior Cycle of post-primary schools in 2002 was an important step in strengthening the implementation of mental health promotion within the school system in Ireland.

Social, Personal and Health Education curriculum

SPHE employs a broad definition of youth health, encompassing physical, personal, emotional, and social aspects. SPHE is designed to reflect and facilitate the application of principles that underpin post-primary education in Ireland. Building on SPHE in primary schools, SPHE at post-primary level aims to enable students to develop personal and social skills, promote self-esteem and self-confidence, develop a framework for responsible decision-making, and promote physical, mental, and emotional health and wellbeing. SPHE comprises a spiral curriculum with ten strands offered in each of the three years of the Junior Cycle [24] and five strands offered in the two years of the Senior Cycle [25]. For each strand, there is a rationale and a list of learning outcomes which identify what students should understand and be able to do on completion of the strand. The curriculum framework is designed to be an enabling curriculum. Individual schools are encouraged to use the flexible nature of the framework to plan SPHE in their unique setting, choosing resources that support the rationale and learning outcomes prescribed by the curriculum.

The nationwide delivery of the subject is facilitated by a multi-sectoral support system which takes the form of a partnership between the Departments of Education and Skills (DES), the Health Service Executive (HSE), and the National Council for Curriculum and Assessment (NCCA). The service comprises a national office and four regional support teams. Each team consists of a partnership between a Health Promotion Officer from the local HSE region and a Regional Development Officer from the Department of Education and Skills. The regional support service teams provide regular in-service training opportunities to schools, including whole-school training and courses for teachers, school coordinators, and school management on a range of modular topics, teaching approaches, and specific resources. Assistance with health-related policy developments and other in-school supports, such as program planning and help with identifying locally appropriate resources, are also offered by a team of Regional Development Officers working in partnership with Health Promotion Officers throughout the country (see www.sphe.ie).

Mental health promotion within SPHE

Several strands within the Junior Cycle have a mental health component. For example: Belonging and Integrating; Self-Management; Communication Skills; Friendships; Relationships and Sexuality; Emotional Health; and Influences and Decisions. One of the five strands in the Senior Cycle is devoted specifically to mental health. Teachers can exercise their own discretion in their choice of resources for the delivery of the mental health strands. Some of these are standalone resources for general application, while others form part of a broader whole-school mental health initiative.

Working Things Out through SPHE [26] is an example of a mental health resource used by teachers for the Junior Cycle. Its theoretical rationale stems both from narrative psychological [27] and social and emotional learning [28]. Presented in a CD format, the resource consists of 12 youth mental health narratives supported by training and a teacher's pack. The nine SPHE lessons cover a range of mental health topics such as school transition (lesson 1), bullying and family conflict (lessons 2 and 3), managing anxiety (4), eating disorders (5), dynamics of school socialization (6), suicide and bereavement (7), obsessive compulsive disorder (8), and a wrapping-up lesson. An evaluation of the *Working Things Out through SPHE* program was carried out using a randomized controlled trial with 782 students assigned to participate in either the standard program (SPHE) or the intervention. While both groups showed improvement over time in terms of emotional and behavioral difficulties, male students identified as "at risk" in the intervention group showed significantly greater improvements than males "at risk" in the standard program [29].

MindOut is an example of another mental health promotion curriculum-based program. The program was designed as a resource for transition-year students (aged 16–17 years). The program is founded on theoretical literature related to a competence enhancement approach and protective factors for mental health [30]. The program aims to promote positive mental health through the exploration of stress and coping, sources of support, emotions (anger, conflict, rejection, depression), relationships, understanding of mental health, and the importance of supporting others. The program is composed of 13 sessions which include activity-based exercises followed by time for reflection and discussion. Byrne *et al.* [31] conducted a randomized controlled evaluation of the *MindOut* program with 1850 students aged 15–18 years from schools in Ireland and Northern Ireland. The program was found to have a significant positive impact on students' knowledge, attitudes, and skills.

Implementing a whole-school approach to mental health promotion

The HPSF combined with the SPHE curriculum offers a useful structure for strengthening the school's capacity as a mental health promoting setting for living, learning, and working. Central to this is the implementation of a comprehensive approach with the use of coordinated strategies aiming to bring about change at the level of the individual, the classroom, and the school in the context of the wider community. Weare and Nind [12] contend that the health-promoting schools approach is generally seen as providing essential supportive structures, positive climates, empowered communities, and end-user involvement. However, they also point out that this approach makes it more difficult to evaluate and demonstrate measurable change. In their review of the evidence on mental health promotion and prevention in schools, Weare and Nind highlight the lack of robust evaluations generating "hard outcomes" from whole-school programs. This contrasts with the bulk of the international evidence on school-based mental health promotion interventions, which is drawn from highly structured programs delivered in a systematic way, lending themselves to outcome research based on traditional randomized controlled trial designs. It is argued that the lack of specific implementation guidelines makes it difficult for schools to identify how to achieve a health-promoting schools approach and results in a wide array of practices across schools and countries [12,32,33]. Samdal and Rowling [33] call for greater attention to creating a science base for the implementation of a health-promoting schools approach. As part of this, greater clarity around the operationalization of what is to be implemented and how it should be implemented is recommended in order to achieve optimum results.

A meta-analysis of the literature conducted by Samdal and Rowling [34] sought to identify implementation components critical to health-promoting school practice. Eight key components were identified, which were grouped into three categories: (1) *School Leadership* – leadership and management practices; policy and institutional change; (2) *Establishing Readiness for Change* – preparing and planning for school development; professional development and learning; student participation; (3) *Organizational Context* – relational and organizational support context; partnership and networking; sustainability. Samdal and Rowling state that the eight theory-driven implementation components identified are relevant for all types of health-promoting school initiatives. The components have particular relevance for mental health promotion as they identify the range of factors operating at the level of the intervention, providers, communities, delivery system, and support system which are specific to the local context. These components, thus, provide a critical framework or "science of delivery" to guide the whole-school implementation of mental health promotion in Irish post-primary schools.

Adopting these components as part of a whole-school approach to mental health promotion brings a shift away from delivering discrete interventions and measuring their "linear" impact on individual students. A case study of a mental health promotion intervention implemented within the context of disadvantaged primary schools in Ireland revealed the reality of program implementation and exemplified how the local contexts for program implementation can differ across schools and the impact this can have on program implementation [35]. This case study, which was conducted alongside a clustered RCT design [36,37], revealed that many of the factors which affected the implementation of the Zippy's Friends emotional wellbeing program for primary schools were whole-school practices. Factors such as community engagement, parental involvement, organizational practices, school ethos and environment, and characteristics of program implementers were found to differ significantly across the schools [35]. The case study findings are in keeping with the implementation research to date, which indicates the need for evaluation approaches to include assessment and monitoring of the complex interaction of factors operating at the classroom, school and wider community level that impact on implementation [32,38–41].

Evaluations on the implementation of SPHE in Irish secondary schools have reflected several of the whole-school implementation issues highlighted in the literature [42–46]. An evaluation carried out with pupils, parents and teachers across 12 schools in Ireland revealed a number of issues at the level of the school that hindered the implementation of SPHE within a whole-school context [46]. These included resource availability to support teachers in delivering the program; timetabling within an already overcrowded "academic" curriculum; the absence of a critical mass of teachers who are trained and committed to change; engaging the interest and commitment of the school principals in bringing about a supportive school ethos and organizational practices; and partnership between stakeholders within the school and the school community. The remainder of this chapter will explore the potential of online resources in addressing two of the most frequently reported barriers to implementation in Ireland, namely resource availability and capacity building among teachers, principals, and the wider community in the promotion of positive youth mental health [46,63].

Potential of online resources in addressing gaps in mental health promotion curriculum

For most young people, online technologies are a part of their everyday lives. In Ireland, young people aged 16–24 years are the most frequent users of the internet. Data from the European Commission highlights the steady increase in young people's use of the internet over the past seven years, with 34% of young people reporting they had accessed the internet in 2005. In 2011, 92% of 16–24-year-olds reported having accessed the internet. Of this group, 78% of young people accessed the internet on a daily basis [47].

Results from the My World Survey carried out with young people in Ireland highlight the importance of the internet as a source of support for young people's mental health and wellbeing. For young people aged 12–19 years in post-primary school, the internet was the third most frequently reported source of support after friends and parents. For young adults aged 17–25 years (post-secondary level), the internet was the most frequently reported source of support for mental health and wellbeing, followed by friends and parents [9]. The findings from this study provide evidence that for young people the internet can be seen as a "tool and a setting for action" [48] in improving their mental health and wellbeing. With the extraordinary uptake of new technologies by young people, online and mobile phone applications provide an ever-increasing range of options in the delivery of school-based mental health promotion and prevention interventions.

The evidence regarding internet-delivered mental health interventions has been accumulating. A systematic review of online mental health promotion and prevention interventions available for young people aged 12–25 highlights the potential role of the internet for the delivery of mental health interventions for young people [49]. A total of 28 studies evaluating 21 web-based interventions were identified. Interventions included structured online modules, mental health information resources, online gaming interventions, blogging, and online therapy. Findings from the mental health promotion interventions indicated that there is some evidence that skills-based interventions presented in module format can have a significant impact on young people's mental health literacy skills, support-seeking behavior, and wellbeing. In terms of online mental health prevention interventions, there is evidence across multiple studies that computerized cognitive behavioral therapy (cCBT) interventions can have a significant and lasting impact on anxiety and depression among young people identified as at risk of developing a disorder.

Several of the interventions with good-quality evidence identified in this review were implemented with young people in the school setting. An important finding was that the implementation of online interventions within the school setting, with the provision of teacher support, helped in reducing the relatively high rates of program drop-out reported in many of the studies. Program drop-out was found to be highest among those young people most "at risk" [50]. Evidence to support this was shown in one study which reported a 98% program completion rate when implemented as part of the curriculum at school in comparison to 30% completion rate at home [51].

One intervention that consistently showed positive findings across multiple school studies is the online cognitive behavioral program *MoodGym* [50,52,53]. Moodgym is an internet-based program which consists of five interactive modules and is designed to prevent or decrease symptoms of anxiety and depression in young people. Another promising intervention, *The Managing Stress* course, is an Australian-based stress management internet-based program which is designed for secondary-level students aged 13 years [54].

This six-week mental health promotion course aims to develop participants' knowledge about stress and effective coping strategies, to increase participants' use of effective coping strategies, and produce improved perceptions of competence to cope with stress. In addition to the online course, related classroom learning activities are provided to reinforce knowledge and skills taught online.

Other web-based promotion and prevention programs identified in this review include: *ReachOut Central*, an online gaming intervention [55]; a mobile phone self-monitoring mood application for use in consultation with the young person's general practitioner [56]; *Master Your Mood Online*, a cCBT intervention combined with a "chat box" where participants with depressive symptoms interact with a trained professional [57]. These interventions are examples of the range of promising online interventions which can be used to support positive youth mental health in the school setting. Many of the challenges faced in trying to improve mental health promotion in schools – such as increasing availability and accessibility of resources, increasing interactivity across the school community, and fostering timely and ongoing evaluation – may be achieved or facilitated, in part, by supplementing school interventions with interactive, internet-based tools. Interactive learning modules have the advantage of presenting information at a manageable pace and facilitating acquisition of decision-making skills by use of interactive, choice-based learning modules. Additionally, the impact of school programs may be enhanced by offering young people the opportunity to participate in online modules designed to address their unique needs, to extend learning beyond the classroom or to provide participants with the opportunity to ask follow-up questions or seek help anonymously [58]. Today's young people do not see the distinction between online and face-to-face communication that older generations still perceive. Consequently, the school mental health field must capitalize on this new reality. As argued by Rickwood [59], school mental health has to adapt to and embrace the opportunity to enter the e-spectrum of interventions for mental health, whereby we can substantially increase our ability to reach young people and support their mental health and wellbeing.

Bridging the digital disconnect: using technology to develop resources for parents and teachers in supporting young people's mental health

The growing demand and expansion of online mental health resources has significant implications for key stakeholders within the school community and the role they play in supporting young people. Building the capacity of the school workforce and parents through awareness raising, training in the promotion of mental health, and skill development is fundamental to mainstreaming and sustaining action in the area of youth mental health. The use of an online platform has several advantages, including efficient and effective delivery of education materials, convenience and portability, flexibility, higher retention, greater collaboration, cost savings, and global opportunities [60,61].

Bridging the Digital Disconnect is a three-year program of research conducted in Ireland that aims to develop online mental health and digital literacy resources for parents, education, health, and mental health professionals who wish to support the mental health of young people aged 12–25 years. This program of research is being carried out by the Health Promotion Research Centre at the National University of Ireland Galway and the Inspire Ireland Foundation in collaboration with the Young and Well Cooperative Research Centre in Melbourne, Australia (www.yawcrc.org.au). The research aims to assess and address the "digital disconnect" between young people and adults in order to develop effective technology-based mental health supports by exploring adults' willingness to use technology to support their work with young people and their needs in relation to the use of technology to support young people. Based on this research, a series of online resources will be developed and tested paying particular attention to the potential for different needs among: (1) parents; (2) teachers; (3) youth workers; (4) health professionals including general practitioners (GPs), social workers, and health promotion officers; and (5) mental health professionals including psychologists, psychiatrists; and suicide resource officers. The first online resource to be developed is designed to meet the needs of parents and, following this, an online resource for education professionals including SPHE teachers and guidance counselors will be developed.

A series of needs assessments have been carried out nationally with parents and professionals working with young people to inform the development of these resources [62,63]. The results from the needs assessment with parents and education professionals point to the need for support in relation to youth mental health among parents and teachers and the potential of online technologies in providing these supports. Over two-thirds of parents (69.8%) stated they were likely/very likely to look for help on the internet if their child was going through a tough time. One-quarter of parents (24.6%) disagreed that they could help their child through a tough time and a similar figure (22.1%) stated they had used the internet to search for mental health information in the past month. Over 90% of teachers and school guidance counselors reported that they use the internet for professional reasons on a daily basis. Searching for mental health information was the third most frequently reported use of the internet. Of all the professionals that took part in the survey ($N = 900$ youth workers, education, health, and mental health professionals) teachers felt the least confident to (1) promote wellbeing in young people's lives; (2) determine if a young person needs mental health support; and (3) help a young person if they have a mental health problem. In relation to mental health resource needs, teachers requested online mental health promotion resource material, including lesson plans, videos addressing mental health topics, and youth-friendly online activities. Teachers also requested guidelines on how to communicate with parents and suggestions for including parents in youth mental health activities [63].

The development of online resources for parents, education, health, and mental health professionals as part of the *Bridging the Digital Disconnect* research project is about creating a new approach to the way we work with and understand the opportunities of new technologies for better mental health among young people. Rickwood [59] states "Practice, policy and research supporting young people's mental health must prioritize the implementation and integration of new technologies as a way to enhance our current capacity in young people's mental health" (p. 25). The significant rise of internet use, paired with the many recent advances in computer networking and multimedia technology, has created potential new avenues to enhance the implementation of mental health promotion in schools beyond standalone interventions. The potential benefits of integrating emerging technologies with critical components of health-promoting schools, as identified by Samdal and Rowling [34], may be broad and far-reaching for mental health promotion. These technologies present new options to support and enhance existing practices, including the delivery of online mental health promotion in-service training to education professionals in a timely and efficient manner, developing real and meaningful partnerships with parents and the broader community, and engaging students in a manner that is empowering, interactive, and current for young people. These actions combined with the provision of ongoing support and evaluation tools to schools, which can also be delivered with new technologies, will in turn facilitate the long-term anchoring and sustainability of mental health promotion in Irish post-primary schools.

Conclusion

This chapter examined the implementation of a whole-school approach to mental health promotion within post-primary schools in Ireland. The HPSF, in combination with the introduction of the SPHE curriculum as a mandatory subject in the Junior Cycle of post-primary schools, offers a useful structure for strengthening the school's capacity in adopting a whole-school approach to mental health promotion. A major challenge in adopting a whole-school approach is the operationalization of what is to be implemented beyond classroom-based interventions and how this should be done. The lack of specific implementation guidelines makes it difficult for schools to identify concrete actions to achieve a whole-school approach to mental health promotion. This results in a wide array of practices across schools and further increases the challenge of establishing effective mental health promotion implementation in schools. Key components of health-promoting schools identified by Samdal and Rowling [34] provide Irish post-primary schools with a critical framework to guide implementation of mental health promotion at a whole-school level. This chapter reviewed the mental health components of SPHE for Irish post-primary schools and examined the potential of emerging technologies in developing and testing resources to support these identified components within an Irish context. The growth of online interventions provides an ever-increasing range of options in the delivery of school-based mental health promotion and prevention interventions. In addition, the development of online resources in Ireland to build the capacity of the school community, including teachers and parents, through training in the promotion of mental health and skill development presents new options in moving beyond the classroom to fully embrace a whole-school approach. Given the ever increasing role of technology in young people's lives, further development and integration of technology-based resources, to complement and extend the work that is currently being done within Irish post-primary schools, is fundamental to the future of mental health promotion in schools.

References

1. Jenkins, R., Baingana, F., Ahmad, R., McDaid, D., & Atun, R. Social, economic, human rights and political challenges to global mental health. *Mental Health in Family Medicine*. 2011; 8: 87–96.

2. Kieling, C., Baker-Henningham, H., Belfer, M., *et al.* Child and adolescent mental health worldwide: Evidence for action. *Lancet*. 2001; 379: 1515–1525.

3. Cannon, M., Coughlan, H., Clarke, M., & Kelleher, I. *The mental health of young people in Ireland: A report of the Psychiatric Epidemiology Research across the Lifespan (PERL) Group Dublin*: Royal College of Surgeons in Ireland; 2013.

4. Lynch, F., Mills, C., Daly, I., & Fitzpatrick, C. Challenging times: Prevalence of psychiatric disorders and suicidal behaviours in Irish adolescents. *Journal of Adolescence*. 2005; 29(4): 555–573.

5. Martin, M., Carr, A., Burke, L., Carroll, L., & Byrne, S. *The Clonmel Project: Mental Health Service needs of children and adolescents in the south east of Ireland*. Health Service Executive South; 2006.

6. Sullivan, C., Arensman, E., Keeley, S. H., Corcoran, P., Perry, I. J. *Young people's mental health: A report of the findings from the*

lifestyle and coping survey. The National Suicide Research Foundation; 2004.

7. National Office for Suicide Prevention. *Annual Report 2009.* HSE; 2009.

8. Eurostat. Suicide death rate: By age group; 2009. (Online) Available from http://epp.eur ostat.ec.europa.eu/tgm/table.do?tab=table& init=%201&language=en&pcode=tsdph240& plugin=1 (Accessed October 28, 2013).

9. Dooley, B. & Fitzgerald, A. *My World Survey national study of youth mental health.* Headstrong. 2012.

10. World Health Organization. *WHO's Global School Health Initiative: Helping schools to become "Health-Promoting Schools."* World Health Organization; 1998.

11. Barry, M. M., Clarke, A. M., Jenkins, R., & Patel, V. A systematic review of the effectiveness of mental health promotion interventions for young people in low and middle income countries. *BMC Public Health.* 2013; 13: 835.

12. Weare, K. & Nind, M. Mental health promotion and problem prevention in schools: What does the evidence say? *Health Promotion International.* 2011; 26 (suppl 1), i29–i69.

13. Durlak, J. A., Weissberg, R. P., Dymnici, A. B., Taylor, R. D., & Schellinger, K. B. The impact of enhancing students' social and emotional learning: A meta-analysis of school-based universal interventions. *Child Development.* 2011; 82(1): 405–432.

14. Payton, J., Weissberg, R. P., Durlak, J. A., *et al. The positive impact of social and emotional learning for kindergarten to eight-grade students: Findings from three scientific reviews.* Collaborative for Academic, Social, and Emotional Learning; 2008.

15. Barry, M. & Jenkins, R. *Implementing mental health promotion.* Churchill Livingstone/ Elsevier; 2007.

16. Tennant, R., Goens, C., Barlow, J., Day, C., & Stewart-Brown, S. A systematic review of reviews of interventions to promote mental health and prevent mental health problems in children and young people. *Journal of Public Mental Health.* 2007; 6(1): 25–32.

17. Adi, Y., Killoran, A., Janmohamed, K., & Stewart-Brown, S. *Systematic review of the effectiveness of interventions to promote mental wellbeing in primary schools: Universal approaches which do not focus on violence or bullying.* National Institute for Clinical Excellence; 2007.

18. Wells, J., Barlow, J., & Stewart-Brown, S. A systematic review of universal approaches to mental health promotion in schools. *Health Education.* 2003; 103(4): 197–220.

19. Greenberg, M., Domitrovich, C., & Bumbarger, B. The prevention of mental disorders in school-aged children: Current state of the field. *Prevention & Treatment.* 2001; 4(1): 1–52.

20. Health Service Executive. *Reach Out: national strategy for action on suicide prevention 2005–2014.* National Suicide Review Group and Department of Health and Children; 2005.

21. Department of Education and Skills. *A framework for Junior Cycle.* Government Publications; 2012.

22. Department of Education and Skills. *Well-being in post-primary schools: Guidelines for mental health promotion and suicide prevention.* Government Publications; 2013.

23. Weare, K. & Markham, W. What do we know about promoting mental health through schools? *Promotion and Education.* 2005; 12(3–4): 118–122.

24. National Council for Curriculum and Assessment. *Social, personal and health education curriculum.* Government Publications; 2000. (Online) Available at: www.curriculumonline.ie/uploaded files/PDF/jc_sphe_sy.pdf (accessed October 28, 2013).

25. National Council for Curriculum and Assessment. *Social, personal and health education curriculum: Senior Cycle curriculum framework.* Government Publications; 2011. (Online) Available at: www.ncca.ie/en/Curric ulum_and_Assessment/Post-Primary_Educa tion/Senior_Cycle/SPHE_framework/SPHE_ Framework.pdf (accessed October 28, 2013).

26. Fitzpatrick, C., Power, M., Brosnan, E., Cleary, D., Conlon, A., & Guerin, S. Working things out through SPHE: A journey from community to clinic and back. *Advances in School Mental Health Promotion.* 2009; 2(3): 38–45.

27. Sarbin, T. R. *Narrative psychology. The human storied nature of human conduct.* Praeger Publishers/Greenwood Publishing Group; 1986.

28. Elias, M. *Promoting social and emotional learning: Guidelines for educators.* ASCD; 2003.

29. Fitzpatrick, C., Conlon, A., Cleary, D., Power, M., King, F., & Guerin, S. Enhancing the mental health promotion component of a health and personal development programme in Irish schools. *Advances in School Mental Health Promotion.* 2013; 6(2): 122–138.

30. Byrne, M., Barry, M. M., & Sheridan, A. Implementation of a school-based mental health promotion programme in Ireland. *International Journal of Mental Health Promotion.* 2004; 6(2): 17–25.

31. Byrne, M., Barry, M. M., NicGabhainn, S., & Newell, J. The development and evaluation of a mental health promotion programme for post-primary schools in Ireland. In Jensen, B. B. & Clift, S. (eds.), *The health promoting school: International advances in theory, evaluation and practice.* Canterbury Christ Church University College and the Danish University of Education; 2005. pp. 383–408.

32. Dooris, M. & Barry, M. M. Overview of implementation in health promoting settings. In Samdal, O. & Rowling, L. (eds.), *The implementation of health promoting schools: Exploring the theories of what, why and how.* Routledge; 2013. pp. 14–33.

33. Samdal, O. & Rowling, L. *The implementation of health promoting schools: Exploring the theories of what, why and how.* Routledge; 2013.

34. Samdal, O. & Rowling, L. Theoretical and empirical base for implementation components of health-promoting schools. *Health Education.* 2011; 111(5): 367–390.

35. Clarke, A. M., O'Sullivan, M., & Barry, M. M. Context matters in programme implementation. *Health Education.* 2010; 110(4): 273–293.

36. Clarke, A. M. An evaluation of the Zippy's Friends emotional wellbeing programme for primary schools in Ireland. PhD thesis, National University of Ireland Galway; 2011.

37. Clarke, A. M., Bunting, B., & Barry, M. M. (2014) Evaluating the implementation of a school-based emotional wellbeing programme: a cluster randomised trial of Zippy's Friends for children in disadvantaged primary schools. *Health Education Research,* doi:10.1093/her/cyu047.

38. Bumbarger, B., Perkins, D., & Greenberg, M. Taking effective prevention to scale. In Doll, B., Pfohl, W., & Yoon, J. (eds.), *Handbook of youth prevention science.*: Routledge; 2010. p. 433–444.

39. Ringeisen, H., Henderson, K., & Hoagwood, K. Context matters: Schools and the "research to practice gap" in children's mental health. *School Psychology Review.* 2003; 32(2): 153–168.

40. Durlak, J. Why program implementation is important. *Journal of Prevention and Intervention in the Community.* 1998; 17(2): 5–18.

41. Greenberg, M., Domitrovich, C., Graczyk, P., & Zins, J. *The study of implementation in school-based preventive interventions: Theory, research, and practice.* Center for Mental Health Services, Substance Abuse and Mental Health Administration, US Department of Health and Human Services; 2005.

42. Millar, D. *A preliminary review of the SPHE needs analysis survey (2000–2001).* Marino Institute of Education; 2003.

43. Millar, D. *Review of records of in-service training for teachers of SPHE: February 2001 to April 2003.* Marino Institute of Education; 2003.

44. Burtenshaw, R. *Review of social, personal and health education at Junior Cycle.* Marino Institute of Education; 2003.

45. Geary, T. & Mannix-McNamara, P. *Implementation of social, personal and health education at Junior Cycle.* University of Limerick; 2003.

46. Nic Gabhainn, S., O'Higgins, S., & Barry, M. M. The implementation of social, personal and health education in Irish schools. *Health Education.* 2010; 110(6): 452–470.

47. Eurostat. Internet: level of access, use and activities; 2011. (Online) Available at:

http://epp.eurostat.ec.europa.eu/portal/page/portal/information_society/data/main_tables (accessed October 28, 2013).

48. Blanchard, M. *Navigating the digital disconnect: Understanding the use of information communication technologies by the youth health workforce to improve young people's mental health and wellbeing.* Orygen Youth Health Research Centre, Centre for Youth Mental Health. University of Melbourne; 2011.

49. Clarke, A. M., Kuosmanen, T., & Barry, M. M. *A systematic review of the evidence on the effectiveness of online mental health promotion and prevention interventions for young people.* Health Promotion Research Centre, National University of Ireland Galway; 2013.

50. O'Kearney, R., Kang, K., Christensen, H., & Griffiths, K. A controlled trial of a school-based internet program for reducing depressive symptoms in adolescent girls. *Depression and Anxiety.* 2009; 26(1): 65–72.

51. Fridrici, M. & Lohaus, A. Stress-prevention in secondary schools: Online- versus face-to-face-training. *Health Education.* 2009; 109(4): 299–313.

52. Calear, A. L., Christensen, H., Mackinnon, A., Griffiths, K. M., & O'Kearney, R. The YouthMood Project: A cluster randomized controlled trial of an online cognitive behavioral program with adolescents. *Journal of Consulting and Clinical Psychology.* 2009; 77 (6): 1021–1032.

53. O'Kearney, R., Gibson, M., Christensen, H., & Griffiths, K. M. Effects of a cognitive-behavioural Internet program on depression, vulnerability to depression and stigma in adolescent males: A school-based controlled trial. *Cognitive Behaviour Therapy.* 2006; 35(1): 43–54.

54. Van Vliet, H. & Andrews, G. Internet-based course for the management of stress for junior high schools. *Australian and New Zealand Journal of Psychiatry.* 2009: 43(4): 305–309.

55. Shandley, K., Austin, D., Klein, B., & Kyrios, M. An evaluation of "Reach Out Central": An online gaming program for supporting the mental health of young people. *Health Education Research.* 2010; 25(4): 563–574.

56. Kauer, S. D., Reid, S. C., Crooke, A. H. D., *et al.* Self-monitoring using mobile phones in the early stages of adolescent depression: Randomized controlled trial. *Journal of Medical Internet Research.* 2012; 14: e67.

57. van der Zanden, R., Kramer, J., Gerritis, R., & Cuijpers, P. Effectiveness of an online group course for depression in adolescents and young adults: A randomized trial. *Journal of Medical Internet Research.* 2013; 14: e86.

58. Santor, D. A. & Bagnell, A. Enhancing the effectiveness and sustainability of school-based mental health programs: Maximising program participation, knowledge uptake and ongoing evaluation using internet-based resources. *Advances in School Mental Health Promotion.* 2008; 1(2): 17–28.

59. Rickwood, D. Entering the e-spectrum: An examination of new interventions for youth mental health. *Youth Studies Australia.* 2012; 31(4): 18–27.

60. Murray, E. Web-based interventions for behaviour change and self-management: Potential, pitfalls, and progress. *Medicine 2.0.* 2012; 1(2): 1–12.

61. Barak, A. & Grohol, J. M. Current and future trends in internet supported mental health interventions. *Journal of Technology in Human Services.* 2011; 29: 155–196.

62. Clarke, A. M., Kuosmanen, T., Chambers, D., & Barry, M. M. *Bridging the digital disconnect: Exploring parents' views on using technology to promote young people's mental health.* Health Promotion Research Centre, National University of Ireland Galway and Inspire Ireland Foundation in collaboration with the Young and Well Cooperative Research Centre; 2013.

63. Clarke, A. M., Kuosmanen, T., Chambers, D., Barry, M. M. *Bridging the digital disconnect: Exploring youth, education, and mental health professionals' views on using technology to promote young people's mental health.* Health Promotion Research Centre, National University of Ireland Galway and Inspire Ireland Foundation in collaboration with the Young and Well Cooperative Research Centre; 2014. www.youngandwellcrc.org.au/knowledge-hub/publications/bridging-the-digital-disconnect-professionals/

School mental health in Israel

Background, services, and challenges

Moshe Israelashvili

Israel is a small country, yet it is very diverse. In its northern territories there is a popular ski area during the winter while the southern territories, approximately one-third of Israeli territory, are a desert. Due to relatively high birthrates, the massive post-World War II's Jewish immigration from European and Arab countries to Israel, followed by continuous waves of Jewish immigrants who continue to arrive, to this day, from, literally, all parts of the world, Israel's population has grown from about 800 000 citizens, on the day of its establishment (1948), to almost 8 000 000 (2013). In addition to diversity in the cultural backgrounds of the ex-immigrant Jews, who became Israeli citizens, as well as in their skin color and mentality, the Israeli population comprises various religions, with 76% Jews, 20% non-Jews, mostly Arabs of various religions (e.g., Muslims, Christians, Druze, Bahá'í), and 4% unclassified. Compared to other Western countries, the population is considered relatively young (28% are aged 0–14, compared with an average of 17% in other Western countries) (WHO, 2013). The country's population is growing at a rate of 1.8% and with this growth there is a relatively high population density (overall, 310 people per square kilometer), especially in the center of the country (ICBS – Israel Central Bureau of Statistics, 2007). A very typical characteristic of many Israelis would be their direct and intensive interpersonal interaction with neighbors, colleagues, and even strangers, with no inhibitions about asking others about their political, financial, and personal tendencies. Finally, another aspect of diversity in Israeli reality is the mixture of ancient past, daily present, and the fascinating future; i.e., the Past – walking in the footsteps of King David or Jesus, exactly where they and other "figures" used to live; the Present – being exposed to urban ecological troubles, such as air pollution, condensed and tall buildings; and the Future – uncovering Israel's ultra-developed hi-tech industry, which gave it the label of being a "Start-up Nation" (Senor & Singer, 2009). All of these aspects of diversity and intensiveness lead many tourists, after they've taken a stroll along Israel's streets and landscapes, to feel surprised and astonished (especially for those who knew Israel 50 or more years ago).

Hence, for many people, exposure to Israel, and especially living in Israel, is a very vivid and significant experience. Yet, speaking about mental health, several additional aspects of the reality in Israel should be further highlighted.

Several background notes regarding Israel

While it is beyond the scope of the current chapter to characterize and discuss all features of Israeli society, several characteristics are especially relevant for better understanding of

School Mental Health: Global Challenges and Opportunities, ed. Stan Kutcher, Yifeng Wei and Marc D. Weist. Published by Cambridge University Press. © Cambridge University Press 2015.

issues related to school mental health. Here are four such issues: stress and happiness; early education; minority–majority feelings; and Jewish history.

Stress and happiness

Living in Israel is a stressful experience. This is due to both security reasons, as well as ecological reasons. From the security point of view, since its establishment in 1948, the Israeli population (both Jews and non-Jews) has been repeatedly exposed to life-threatening events. Almost every 6–10 years there is a major war between Israel and one, or several, of the Arab countries surrounding it. In between these wars, there are security events almost on a daily basis that cannot be ignored, such as repeated events of terrorist attacks carried out against Israeli citizens and/or the kidnapping of Israeli soldiers. Hence, the large-scale wars, the relatively small-scale terrorist acts, and the exposure to daily security checks in every public building (e.g., malls, banks, school, and government offices) and public transportation might lead most people to feel insecure and stressed. Moreover, stressful feelings among Israeli citizens might reflect not only the security problems, but also ecological problems. Namely, it should be noted that Israel is a very small country, and almost half of it is a desert, with very limited periods of rain during the year. As a result of the steady growth of the Israeli population, major ecological problems have emerged – a growing number of skyscrapers as the land is extremely limited in territory; heavy traffic in the more populated areas, almost throughout the day; increasing air pollution, leading more people to suffer from health problems (e.g., a dramatic increase in children's asthma); hot and humid weather at least six months of the year, leading people to "isolate themselves" in air-conditioned offices and cars (that might also lead to health problems); and a lack of awareness regarding the importance of keeping public areas clean.

Nevertheless, everyone who travels across Israel, lives in Israel for a while, or explores the comprehensive picture (e.g., data regarding wellbeing in Israel) will realize that this is not the case; i.e., most Israelis live normal lives in spite of the security situation. One indication of this would be the relatively low rates of mental health problems among the Israeli population. In a study conducted by Tal, Eoe, & Corrign (2007) it was found that about 3% of the entire population suffers from anxiety disorders and about 7% from affective disorders, with no statistically significant differences between Israeli-Arabs and Israeli-Jews (see also Levav et al., 2007). Similarly, in a cross-national comparison of depression, it was found that when taking into account the country's socioeconomic status, the prevalence of depression (about 4%) among the Israeli population is relatively low in comparison to most other countries in the world (Rai, Zitko, Jones, Lynch, & Araya, 2013).

This does not mean to say that the security situation is not dangerous, but rather these points are brought to emphasize the significant positive aspects of living in Israel, such as frequent and open social interactions, more meaning to life, intensive familial bonds, and an unexplainable sense of hope (for more elaboration on these issues see Israelashvili, 2005; Israelashvili & Benjamin, 2009).

Early education

Early education is well developed in Israel, with about 95% of Jewish children and about 80% of non-Jewish children already enrolled in pre-kindergarten education at the age of three. Hence, children reach elementary school after they have already: (1) been exposed to moral and social education; (2) have already experienced some small-scale home separation, social pressure, and transitions; and (3) been observed within a group of their age-cohort.

The last point is especially important, since such observation enables young children who suffer from mental health problems to be identified and provided appropriate treatment. Moreover, one of the major tasks of Israeli kindergarten teachers (i.e., who teach children who are age five years) is to observe the kindergarten children during the first six months and then to send those who seem to be at risk for "lack of school readiness" to psycho-educational screening, conducted by trained educational psychologists (Raviv,1989).

Minority–majority feelings

The State of Israel was established as a State for the Jews; accordingly, the majority (80%) of the Israeli population is Jewish. Yet, the remaining 20% of non-Jewish Israeli people are very prominent within Israeli society. Practically speaking, most of the Arab population lives in Arab villages and cities, has its own religious, cultural, and sociological rituals, and speaks Arabic in school and the home. Nevertheless, there are extensive daily contacts between Jews and Arabs, especially after graduation from high-school. One implication of this is the growing resemblance between these two populations, in terms of increasing (yet, independent) adoption of Western values, such as pursuing higher education, intensive consumerism, and a search for individualistic wellbeing.

With regards to mental health, the co-existence of Jews and non-Jews together, alongside the unavoidable exposure to Jewish symbols (see below), leads some adolescents – especially, but not only, Arabs – to debate their national, cultural, and sometimes even personal identity. Such an identity conflict is especially prominent among Arab adolescents who live in mixed Israeli cities (e.g., Haifa) and among Christian Arab adolescents (in comparison to Muslim Arab adolescents) (Kakunda-Mualem & Israelashvili, 2012). Such feelings of identity confusion during adolescence might have a significant impact on students' mental health, especially if it leads them to "passing" (Ginsberg, 1996) – i.e., ignoring their roots and trying to be identified as related to the majority, as witnessed among a number of Arab emerging adults (see Goren, 2006). This and related phenomenon are relevant not only to the Arab population living in Israel, but rather to all other sub-populations that altogether compose the mosaic of the Israeli society; for example, the ultra-orthodox population, comprising about 20% of Israel's population.

Jewish history

Being a state for the Jews, from early childhood on, all citizens (including the Arab population) are exposed to Jewish – even more than global – values and rituals. One example would be the prominent references to the World War II Holocaust, in which six million Jews were murdered by the Nazis. Except for the National Memorial Day for Holocaust victims and repeated references to it in the media, most Israeli high-schools organize a trip for their senior students to visit the major sites in Europe where the Holocaust took place (Lazar, Chaitin, Gross, & Bar-On, 2004). It should be noted that participation (or lack of participation) in such a trip might trigger a large scope of psychological and motivational phenomenon, such as a re-assessment of one's personal and social values (Lazar, Chaitin, Gross, & Bar-On, 2004) and/or the thriving of one's level of resilience (Goroshit, Kimhi, & Eshel, 2013). Interestingly, in recent years several Arab high-schools have made the decision to organize such a tour for their students as a way of helping the (Arab) students better understand the mentality of the Jewish population, within which they are supposed to function after graduating from high-school.

As mentioned above, these four issues are only examples of what should be taken into account when trying to comprehend the role and need for school mental health services in Israel.

The Israeli school system

Since the establishment of the State of Israel in 1948, several major reforms have taken place within the Israeli school system; some of them have had a major impact on the students', as well as the school staff's, daily lives. Below is a list of the four major reforms that took place in the Israeli educational system and can be seen as the basis for some of the major mental health problems among school students, as will be elaborated later in this chapter.

The inclusion of most schools – i.e., Jewish and non-Jewish, religious and secular, etc. – under the supervision of the Israel Ministry of Education (1953). This act had, and still has, major implications in terms of daily life in schools, as most of the school roles and activities are governed by the ministry (e.g., unified curriculum), with relatively limited freedom on how to conduct such top-down duties. However, it should be noted that the ultra-orthodox (Jewish) schools are still independent in most of their pedagogical, educational, and financial decisions. Taking into account that the birth rate among the ultra-orthodox population is twice as high compared to all other segments of Israeli society, this means that a growing number of children are only partially following the Ministry of Education guidelines. One major example of these children's different school experience is the different curriculum they study as a result of their leader's decision not to allow their students to be enrolled in the matriculation examinations (see below).

The Act toward School Reform that was adopted by the Israeli government in the early 1970s. According to this Act, municipalities were encouraged to shift from a two age-cohort educational development – i.e., eight years of elementary school followed by four years of high-school – to a three age-cohort educational development – i.e., six years of elementary school, followed by three years of junior high-school, and then another transition to a three-year high-school (Chen & Fresko, 1978). Due to the monetary initiatives suggested by the Ministry of Education, most of the municipalities followed this Act, with currently about 80% of Israeli students obliged to experience three transitions during their educational development (i.e., from kindergarten to Grade 1; from Grades 6 to 7; and from Grades 9 to 10). In light of the vast literature on the possibly negative implications of the transition to junior high-school (e.g., Eccles & Roeser, 2011), it is interesting that almost no extensive study has yet been performed in pursuit of evaluating the wellbeing, academic achievements, and personal development of Israeli students who've been exposed to those three transitions, in comparison to those who only experience two school transitions.

Expansion of the matriculation examinations. The plan to conduct matriculation examinations at the end of high-school can be traced back to the pre-state period (1935), as an indication of the knowledge which students have gained during their time at school. However, a major reform in the matriculation examination format was made in 1977, according to which decisions regarding the content and the level of each examination were taken from the school staff and given to the student, except for several issues (e.g., a mandatory basic-level examination in English). This reform had four major implications: (1) students', and their parents', expectations to successfully pass the matriculations increased; (2) schools are obliged to teach, and enable testing, on a much larger scope of learning levels; (3) the ability to compare the achievements of different students within the same school has been seriously limited; (4) schools started to compare and fight each other on how many students will undergo the more prestigious matriculation examinations (e.g., level 5 in mathematics). All these implications have gradually led to a situation, in which the whole school system in Israel (not including the ultra-orthodox population) is intensely busy with preparation for the matriculation examinations (e.g., Dovrat Committee, 2003). Practically speaking, the academic demands and teachers' pressure on the school students dramatically increases when they enter junior high-school. Unsurprisingly, in a recent study, conducted by a subdivision of the Israeli Ministry of Education, it was found that the percentage of students who feel that their teachers really care about them (i.e., apart from their academic achievements) drops from 65% in Grades 5–6 to 45% in Grades 7–8, and to only 37% in Grades 10–12; in addition, it was found that only 46% of all high-school students feel that the materials learned in school are important for their future occupational life and career (RAMA, 2013). Finally, it should be noted that recent data indicate that within the Israeli school system, approximately 20% do not study in Grade 12; approximately 9% of those studying in Grade 12 do not take the matriculation exams; and approximately 23% of those who take the matriculation exams are not eligible for a Matriculation Certificate (Beller, 2013).

The currently occurring change in the Ministry of Education's attitude toward parental involvement in schools. Despite most school principals' opposing feelings, last year the Israeli Ministry of Education began to give higher priority to parental involvement in schools and to pursue the best ways to encourage it. The decision to change the traditional – and well-accepted by many teachers and school principals – attitude of "it's better to keep them away from the school yard" into "it's important to bring them in" was triggered by the accumulating evidence regarding the importance of parents' inclusion within schools, in order to promote students' achievements and to decrease students' involvement in problem behavior within the school setting (e.g., Greenbaum & Fried, 2011).

Each one of the above-mentioned reforms has its either positive or negative implications on daily life within the school setting. However, together they have led to a sense of alienation among the students, with a dramatic drop in students' reports of feeling free to talk with their teachers about personal matters (from 59% in Grades 5–6, to 36% in Grades 7–8, and to 27% in Grades 10–12; RAMA, 2013).

School mental health services

At the end of World War II (1945) and as a result of the Holocaust, the stream of orphans who emigrated from Europe to Palestine was very significant. These immigrants and orphan children had a lot of adjustment problems, some due to the problematic separation from their parents (some of whom saw their parents being murdered by the Nazis), while for others, due to the problem of relocation. As a result, mental health services for youth and children began to emerge in various parts of Israel. Many of the mental health staff were, themselves, Holocaust survivors who studied psychology and psychiatry before the Holocaust began. Hence, when the State of Israel was established (1948), individuals and organizations already had some experience with providing mental health services to those children who were in need. However, only about 12 years later the Israel Ministry of Education, in collaboration with the Ministry of Labor, made the decision to establish the Psycho-Educational Service (PES). The mission of the PES was to better identify and support children who are dealing with educational and occupational issues, such as the transition from elementary school to either a vocational school or a school that would enable them to learn for the matriculation examinations (and as a result, continue on to higher education). In addition, the PES was responsible for helping school students with mental health problems, either within the school or by directing them to mental health hospitals (Benyamini & Klein, 1970). Shortly after the PES was established, it became evident that the demand for mental health services exceeded their capacity. As a result, the Ministry of Education made the decision in 1965 to train some of the teachers – in the beginning only within elementary schools – to serve as teacher-counselors who would support children who needed help in dealing with problems related to the transition into the school (i.e., school adjustment) and problems related to the transition from the school (i.e., to either vocational or regular high-school). The teacher-counselor was not meant to replace the school psychologist, but, rather, to support the student on-site, within the school environment, until, if needed, the psychologist invited the student to therapy. Two lessons were quickly learned: (1) students should be counseled by professionals; (2) training a person (e.g., a teacher) to serve as a school counselor takes time. A third (quantitative) lesson emerged during the same period of time, with the inclusion of junior high-schools into the educational system (see above). This reform highlighted the extensive need for supporting junior high-school students, especially in terms of better managing their social relationships, as well as in better dealing with the academic demands that were suddenly imposed upon them – i.e., by teachers who were already worried about the approaching matriculation examinations (see above). It was in 1971 that a new profession was announced within the Israeli educational system – a school counselor. Unlike the situation in those days in other states in the world (e.g., the United States; Buckner, 1975; Freeman & Thompson, 1975), the role of the school counselor was not limited to academic or vocational problems, but rather to the school students' entire life, including a variety of issues such as health-related problems including oral health, smoking prevention, substance abuse, obesity, sexual activity, stress reduction, nutrition, and hospitalization (Klingman, 1984). However, as mentioned above, the school counselor was neither meant to nor trained to do intensive psychotherapy, but rather, counseling alone; therapy was (and is still) offered by school psychologists, who work in collaboration with school counselors. A major difference between the school counselor and the school psychologist is the framework of employment. The school counselor is a member of the school staff, and hence she or he is present in the school on a daily basis, but is also obliged to teach a school subject as part of his or her job. In contrast, the school psychologist is a member of the county (municipality) psychological service, receives a salary from the municipality, and usually visits the school one day per week. Another difference in the school counselor's versus the school psychologist's work is the administration of educational and psychological tests, which are only administered by school psychologists, although the results are jointly discussed with the school counselor and other relevant professionals (Raviv, 1989).

Currently, the PES of the Ministry of Education has three major wings: (1) *the psychology wing*, which supervises the school psychologists, who are in charge of educational screening, mental health diagnosis, and individual therapy for those students who do not require hospitalization; (2) *the counseling wing*, which supervises the school counselors, who are in charge of conducting organizational screening, consultation with teachers, individual counseling for students who need it to improve their academic or social functioning within the school environment, and the inclusion of children with special needs; (3) *the prevention wing*, which is responsible for the development and implementation of prevention programs (e.g., substance abuse; HIV; bullying; sexual harassment) and positive development programs (e.g., life skills; family relationships; the school-to-army [or -life] transition) within the relevant school environments.

In addition, there are several sub-units within the PES that are relatively independent and work across the three major wings. These are the units dealing with issues related to special education, learning disabilities, early education, and emergency and trauma. Altogether there are 2100 school psychologists working in 270 county stations across the entire State of Israel, alongside 3500 school counselors who are working at all levels and segments of the Israeli K-12 educational system. It should be noted that, at least with respect to school psychologists, the number of mental health professionals per school student in Israel is considered to be the highest in the world, with the ratio of 583 school-age children per school psychologist in Israel, compared to 773 children in Denmark, 1224 in Canada, 1506 in the United States, and 10 272 in Germany (Jimerson, Stewart, Skokut, Cardenas, & Malone, 2009).

Needless to mention that sometimes the school principal or the school board prefer not to have a school psychologist or counselor, usually under the premise that "our students don't have mental health problems"; sometimes students are afraid of sharing their problems with the school counselor or psychologist, as it might have negative implications for their image among the school staff or their peers (Al-Krenawi, 2002; Israelashvili, 1999; Tal, Eoe, & Corrign, 2007); and many times the students' parents are reluctant to admit that their child needs support from a mental health professional as it might threaten their own self-esteem. Nevertheless, generally speaking, unlike the situation in the United States or other nations (e.g., Splett, Fowler, Weist, McDaniel, & Dvorsky, 2013), there is no need to justify the role of school psychologists in Israel, nor to address major barriers to enable a role for school psychologists. Rather, school psychologists and school counselors are well embedded in the Israeli school system and every K-12 student who is in need of mental health support can apply and receive at least preliminary help within the educational system she or he belongs to.

Practitioners who work in these services undergo intensive and prolonged professional training, which goes well beyond their university training. This is true especially for issues related to counseling and psychotherapy during times of war and disaster. Due to Israel's security problems and repeated exposure to war, the PES has acquired a lot of knowledge about how to help children and adults (i.e., the parents and school staff) be prepared for coming crises, as well as better management during times of war (Raviv, Zeira, & Sharvit, 2007). Ironically, with many retired volunteers and additional resources that are available during times of war, it sometimes seems that during times of national emergency mental health professionals are reaching out for the client (rather than vice versa), especially in communities with higher socio-economic status (SES) (Raviv & Weiner, 1995).

Mental health problems among Israeli students

In the last survey conducted by the PES (Erhard, 2008), most of the school counselors, across populations and school levels, reported that approximately 20% of their time in school is devoted to individual counseling with students who suffer from problems related to mental health. Interestingly, the most prominent problems were not those related to academic achievements (which 30–50% of their time in individual counseling was devoted to), but rather to problems related to students' emotional state (50–70%), personal crisis (50–70%), relationships with peers (45–65%), and behavioral problems, such as behavior management (40–60%). Below are case reports representing three typical mental health problems that school staff (including the school counselor) tend to encounter on a daily basis.

Social isolation

David's parents were immigrants from Ethiopia who came to Israel about 20 years ago. Even though he was one of the few dark-skinned children in his elementary school, internally he felt like everybody else. David remembers his (Caucasian) elementary school principal who called him when he was in Grade 2 and said to him: "In our school, the color of clothing makes no significant difference, nor does the color of skin – if you won't succeed in school, it would be your fault, not anybody else's." David was really a very good student, and even though his parents were illiterate, and couldn't help him with homework, he didn't need any help. Whenever he did have a problem he approached one of the excellent elementary school teachers and felt very comfortable asking for and receiving their help. It was the school principal's idea to take advantage of the compulsory transition from elementary to junior high-school and sent David to a much better school than most of his classmates were meant to join. "You'll show them how clever you are; your high grades are rightly your own." On the evening before the academic year started, a very honorable person came to visit David's parents. It was the community Kase (a traditional Ethiopian religious-spiritual leader). "I came here to bless your talented child," said the Kase, "His success in the new school will be a success for the entire ex-Ethiopian community . . . we need him as a stigma-breaking pioneer." The excitement was well noticed in David's parents' faces,

The first math teacher entered David's new junior high-school class on time. Interestingly, the teacher forgot to say "good morning." His first words were as follows: "Junior high school is not elementary school . . . you have to start working much harder . . . you have to be prepared for the matriculation examinations awaiting you in 4 years from now . . . I won't stand for any disturbances during class time, nor will I stand for failure in one of the coming examinations." These words were followed by a list of dates of examinations, starting in a few days. Strangely, all the following teachers who entered the class later repeated almost the same words as the math teacher. However, it was the last teacher, who was the main teacher of the class, who made David really worried; "This is not a synagogue or a church and I am not God; don't come to me to cry and ask for my help; rather, try harder and show me that you deserve to be sitting on your chair." The amount of homework was huge, yet in the first days David worked hard and did it well. However, the amount and difficulty of academic demands was increasing; David especially had difficulty with English classes. When David inquired how other children managed with the English class and homework, he discovered that almost all of the children in his class had a private teacher who assisted them at home; David knew his parents had no money for that. To prevent himself from making mistakes, David gradually became silent; not only during the English lessons, but in all of the classes. It was his choice to spend the recesses alone as well; nevertheless, when he realized that he was the only student in his class who had not been invited to a Saturday night party at one of the student's homes, it was too much for him. The following day David's math teacher thought that David was sleeping during class time, and when he approached him with the intention of waking him up, the teacher smelled alcohol;

David was completely drunk. Later, David told the school counselor that he stole money to buy the alcohol ... but "I don't care about anything ... just leave me alone."

Helping David was not limited to personal counseling and family intervention. Rather, a major organizational change was needed in order to reduce the newcomers' shock. A part of that organizational change was to teach the school teachers *not* to transfer *their own* tension regarding the students' success rates in the future matriculation examinations to the students in the first moment the students began junior high-school.

Death encounter

Joseph's teacher was really worried. Joseph's eyes were red and he looked very tired. Unlike other days, Joseph argued with almost every sentence she said, no matter what the subject was. She knew him as a talented and easy-going student; however, his behavior today was completely different. At the end of the class the teacher asked him to stay and inquired what was going on with him. Joseph didn't cooperate, "Nothing ... simply nothing." It was Joseph mother's call later that afternoon that clarified the situation: "Did you hear about the poor soldier who was murdered yesterday by a terrorist? ... that was our neighbor's son." When the teacher asked the mother what she wanted her to do, the mother answered: "Joseph didn't sleep the whole night, I saw the light in his room ... when I asked him what happened and why he didn't sleep, he said something about life being meaningless ... you know [continued the mother] this is not the first time Joseph has mentioned something like this; he talked this way about a year ago, when me and my ex-husband told him that we were going to get divorced."

The school psychologist had to work hard in order to persuade Joseph to talk. Once he did, a mixture of death wishes emerged, some relating to his parents' divorce and others relating to the soldier-neighbor's death. "I really don't enjoy living ... and as it is only a matter of time, why should I wait and not kill myself right now?" In response to the school psychologist's question, Joseph reported that he had once asked a friend to give him his brother's gun and for a moment thought of doing it, but then he made the decision to wait. "You know," he said, "all my friends have some relative in the army and most of them carry guns, so whenever I wish to kill myself I can do it very easily."

The school psychologist was familiar with this type of statement. As early as her first days as a school psychologist she had heard a lot of children speaking about the ease of accessing guns "from a brother of a friend of mine who is in the army." She was also actually a little bit surprised (though happy) that none of the many children she had met over the years had ever put their thoughts into actions. Referring to Joseph, her main fear was that he might be the first one to do it; the sad look in his eyes was a little bit terrifying.

Finally, the school psychologist, together with the school counselor, conducted a workshop for Joseph's class, on stress, coping, and the meaningfulness of life. Parallel to this, she referred Joseph's mother to family counseling, warning her that Joseph had some unresolved issues regarding the divorce.

Management of the student–parent relationship

Fatma is an 18-year-old girl, living in an Arab village in the northern part of Israel. Her father is a wealthy person and makes his living from a building company he owns. The school counselor knew Fatma by sight only, since they'd never talked before. Yet she knew Fatma was one of the best and more talented students in her grade. It was in the school yard that Fatma asked the counselor if she could talk to her for a minute. When they met, Fatma asked for help in dealing with her father. "I enjoy learning and I want to continue learning ... I know I can become a medical doctor or something like this, and this is what I want to be ... however, my father says that as a woman, I should get married and have children ... moreover, he has already talked to a relative of ours and they agreed on having me marry their son ... I know that son, he is 25 years old, he is old and I really don't care about him. Why should I get married to him? Why should I get married? Why is my father so old-fashioned and putting so much pressure on me?" Fatma was crying, saying that her father told her she has no choice but to obey him: "My daughter won't go to university, where you will come into contact with drugs, men and sins everywhere." The school counselor completely understood the situation. Being an Arab herself, she was well familiar with the traditional norms, even though she herself was encouraged by her parents to continue to higher education (yet, now they were complaining that she was still unmarried, at the age of 26). However, the school counselor knew how powerful Fatma's father was in the village and what might happen to the whole school, not to mention herself, when the father realized that it was her, the school counselor, who was making his daughter go against his will.

The meeting that the school counselor organized was well designed. All the parents of Fatma's peers from her grade were invited. The meeting started with the highest religious authority in the area speaking about the importance of learning "as written in the Koran." This was followed by the school principal, who spoke about his, and the whole school staff's, gratitude to the parents "for having such talented children." The school counselor was the third to speak; in her presentation, she spoke about ways to make decisions. The school counselor used many examples to demonstrate the difference between modern versus old-fashioned ways of making decisions. For example, she said, an old-fashioned way of making decisions is ignoring the internet. A well-planned example of this was internet use in the building business. The school counselor's final point referred to the school students' future life. She said: "I know you all want your children's wellness and happiness, so don't be egocentric and only think about your own wellness; remember how much you hated the compulsory tradition you had to conform to when you were young."

The following day Fatma entered the school counselor's room. "I don't know exactly what happened yesterday night, as we – the students – were not invited, but somehow afterwards my father talked to me and said that your examples about the building company were really nice ... could you instruct me on how to elaborate more on this issue to make him listen to my case?"

These three examples are very common in Israel, though not necessarily restricted to life in Israel. Several similarities among them should be mentioned: each of these cases has the potential of becoming (or almost becoming) a major mental health problem; in all of these cases, the school staff served as the only address for these children who were in need; in all of these cases, the boundaries between the students' life circumstances and their academic performance were non-existent; finally, in all of the three cases there was not a clear-cut and easy solution, but rather a need for a mixture of individual, group, and community interventions in order to promote the mental health of the children. These similarities are very challenging to the school system. However, what is more important is that the school system cannot, and should not, ignore their existence.

Israeli teachers' reluctance to implement mental health programs

A major problem in the promotion of school mental health services in Israel is the school teachers' resistance to implementing programs that are related to students' mental health. This is true for both programs that aim to prevent problems related to mental health, as well as programs that foster youth's positive development (Israelashvili, 2002). Existing studies indicate that source of teachers' reluctance can be attributed to multiple reasons, including organizational factors, pedagogical factors, personal factors, and doubt regarding the program's contribution (e.g., Baker, Kupersmidt, Voegler-Lee, Arnold, & Willoughby, 2010; Han, Weiss, & Weiss, 2005). However, the challenge of gaining teachers' support in programs related to students' mental health is crucial for the future of school mental health (Stauffer, Heath, Coyne, & Ferrin, 2012).

Three studies were conducted among Israeli (Jewish and Arab) teachers in order to find culturally relevant interventions that promote teachers' positive involvement in supplying mental health services: in the first study, we explored the relationships between the teachers' exposure to major life events and their support in conducting prevention interventions in their school (Apelbaum & Israelashvili, 2000). The second study compared the teachers' pedagogical beliefs and theoretical orientation and knowledge and their involvement in the implementation of programs related to mental health issues. In this study a comparison was also made between teachers who teach in regular junior high- and high-schools and those who teach in more open and demo-cratic schools (Karol & Israelashvili, 2002). The third study explored the type of training teachers had in conducting intervention programs (in general) and their readiness to be involved in programs related to mental health (Hadas & Israelashvili, 2004). All of these studies highlighted the factors related to the teachers as individuals, rather than organizational or environmental factors, as the main reasons for teachers' reluctance to be involved in running such programs. Namely, the teachers' personal life experiences (e.g., encounters with major life events), occupational satisfaction (e.g., burnout), and especially personal ideology regarding children's education (i.e., huma-nistic ideology) explained most of the variance in their readiness to collaborate and implement mental health programs. In light of these findings, an intervention to promote teachers' readiness to cooperate with mental health programs was established. The intervention was based on three components: (1) proactive outlining of potential reasons for reluctance, followed by teachers' reflections and discussion; (2) expansion of the length, circumstances, and organization of teachers' preparation for the pro-grams' implementation. These changes are needed in order to enable teachers' personal reflections on the given program based on their own personal life experience; and (3) strengthening the school counselors' ability to conduct discussions with teachers in a way that they (the school counselors) won't threaten the teachers and/or be threat-ened by the teachers' emotional openness and the teachers' personal resistance toward the school counselor following the discussion.

This proposed intervention has been implemented in various contexts, and gained positive feedback from teachers, school counselors, and school psychologists (e.g., Israelashvili, 2008).

Summing-up

Awareness of the general importance of school mental health, and the need to further develop it, is well grounded in the Israeli school system. Moreover, the presence of school mental health professionals, across the various sections of educational systems in Israel, is prominent and well-established. Thus, it can be concluded that decision makers, in the field of education and schooling, do pay attention to this issue. Yet, like in many other aspects of Israeli existence, in times of emergency and trouble, the readiness and the activities that target the provision of mental health services, both in general and especially in the school context, are very evident and highly developed; sometimes even over-developed, with reaching out for students.

Nevertheless, researchers and practitioners in the field of school mental health do face several challenges that are common to other nations in the world. Among them are: (1) the resistance to preventive, preliminary interventions, especially due to their time-consuming nature, and to the teachers' lack of proper training in managing (parts of) them (see Franklin, Kim, Ryan, Kelly, & Montgomery, 2012); (2) barriers to approach a comprehensive school–family–community system agenda and ways to disseminate it (see Weist, Paternite, Wheatley-Rowe, & Gall, 2009); (3) the lack of evidence-based documentation of implementation science in school mental health (see Owens et al., 2013); and (4) research on ways to promote, update, and develop new procedures and tools for the use of people related to school mental health (see Fabiano, Chafouleas, Weist, Carl Sumi, & Humphrey, 2014).

Thus, it seems that the major challenge for school mental health in Israel lies in the need to better manage professional mental health manpower, as well as promoting better models of provision of mental health services in times of peace, and not only in times of war. All of these activities should be conducted in such a way as not to interfere with the natural, community-based, and culturally based mechanisms that enable people in Israel to continue to manage and thrive in spite of the vast number of threats to mental health that living in Israel involves.

References

Al-Krenawi, A. (2002) Mental health service utilization among the Arabs in Israel. *Social Work in Health Care*, 35, 577–89.

Apelbaum, L., & Israelashvili, M. (2000). *Teachers' exposure to stress and attitudes toward prevention programs*. Unpublished MA Thesis, Tel Aviv University.

Baker, C. N., Kupersmidt, J. B., Voegler-Lee, M., Arnold, D. H., & Willoughby, M. T. (2010). Predicting teacher participation in a classroom-based, integrated preventive intervention for preschoolers. *Early Childhood Research Quarterly*, 25, 270–283. doi:10.1016/j.ecresq.2009.09.005

Beller, M. (2013). Assessment and evaluation of the Israeli education system. http://rama.education.gov.il. Retrieved August 29, 2013.

Benyamini, K., & Klein, Z., (1970). The educational system and mental health in children and families in Israel. In A. Jarus, J. Marcus, J. Oren, & C. Rapaport (Eds.), *Children and families in Israel: Some problem areas mental health perspectives* (pp. 209–234). New York: Gordon and Breach.

Buckner, E. T. (1975). Accountable to whom? The counselor's dilemma. *Measurement & Evaluation in Guidance*, 8(3), 187–192.

Chen, M., & Fresko, B. (1978). The interaction of school environment and student traits. *Educational Research*, 20, 114–121.

Dovrat Committee (2003) http://cms.education.gov.il/educationcms/units/ntfe/odot/koahmesi mahodaot.htm. Retrieved August 28, 2013.

Eccles, J. S., & Roeser, R. W. (2011). Schools as developmental contexts during adolescence. *Journal of Research on Adolescence*, 21, 225–241.

Erhard, R. (2008). *"Seker Shefi": school counseling and psychological services within the educational system*. Jerusalem: Ministry of Education, the Psycho-Educational Services Branch.

Fabiano, G. A., Chafouleas, S. M., Weist, M. D., Carl Sumi, W., & Humphrey, N. (2014). Methodology considerations in school mental health research. *School Mental Health.* doi:10.1007/s12310-013-9117-1

Franklin, C. G. S., Kim, J. S., Ryan, T. N., Kelly, M. S., & Montgomery, K. L. (2012). Teacher involvement in school mental health interventions: A systematic review. *Children and Youth Services Review,* 34(5), 973–982.

Freeman, S. W., & Thompson, C. R. (1975). The counselor's role with learning disabled students. *School Counselor,* 23(1), 28–36.

Ginsberg, E. K. (1996). Introduction: The politics of passing. In E. K. Ginsberg (Ed.), *Passing and the fictions of identity* (pp. 1–18). Durham, NC: Duke University Press.

Goren, B. (2006). *Passing among Arab students: A coping strategy with discrimination.* Unpublished MA Thesis, Tel Aviv University.

Goroshit, M., Kimhi, S., & Eshel, Y. (2013). Demographic variables as antecedents of Israeli community and national resilience. *Journal of Community Psychology,* 41, 631–643.

Greenbaum, C., & Fried, D. (2011). Introduction and summary: Relations between the family and the early childhood education system. In C. Greenbaum and D. Fried (Eds.), *Family–preschool (K 3) collaboration: A review and recommendations* (pp. 9–50). Jerusalem: Israel Academy of Science.

Hadas, R., & Israelashvili, M. (2004). Teachers' own perceptions of competence in running prevention programs. Unpublished MA thesis, Tel Aviv University.

Han, S., Weiss, S., & Weiss, B. (2005). Sustainability of teacher implementation of school-based mental health programs. *Journal of Abnormal Child Psychology,* 33, 665–679.

Israelashvili, M. (1999). Adolescents' help-seeking behavior in times of community crisis. *International Journal for the Advancement of Counselling,* 21, 87–96.

Israelashvili, M. (2002). Life skills programs: A threat or a challenge? In N. Maslobati & Y. Eram (Eds.), *Value education in educational context* (pp. 397–412). Tel Aviv: Ramot. (Hebrew)

Israelashvili, M. (2005). Staying normal in an abnormal world: Reflections on mental health counseling from an Israeli point of view. *Journal of Mental Health Counseling,* 27, 238–247.

Israelashvili, M. (2008). From acquaintance to engagement: Support in confronting primary prevention hassles. *Journal of Primary Prevention,* 29, 403–412

Israelashvili, M., & Benjamin, B. A. (2009). Context and diversity in the provision of counseling services in Israel. In P. Heppner, S. Ægisdóttir, A. Leung, K. Norsworthy, & L. Greenstein (Eds.), *Handbook of cross-cultural counseling: Cultural assumptions and practices worldwide.* (pp. 449–464). Thousand Oaks, CA: Sage Publications.

Israel Central Bureau of Statistics (2010). Sources of population growth, by district, population group and religion. Retrieved October 15, 2014, from www1.cbs.gov.il/reader/shnaton/shnatone_new.htm?CYear=2010&Vol=61&CSubject=2.

Jimerson, S. R., Stewart, K., Skokut, M., Cardenas, S., & Malone, H. (2009). How many school psychologists are there in each country of the world? International estimates of school psychologists and school psychologist-to-student ratios. *School Psychology International,* 30, 555–567.

Kakunda-Mualem, H. & Israelashvili, M. (2012). Religion, religiosity and personal characteristics as risk factors for negative life-attitudes. *School Counseling,* 17, 120–146. (Hebrew)

Karol, E. & Israelashvili, M. (2002). Teachers' attitudes toward prevention programs. Unpublished MA Thesis. Tel Aviv university.

Klingman, A. (1984). Health-related school guidance: Practical applications in primary prevention. *Personnel & Guidance Journal,* 62, 576–580.

Lazar, A., Chaitin, J., Gross, T., & Bar-On, D. (2004). A journey to the Holocaust: Modes of understanding among Israeli adolescents who visited Poland. *Educational Review,* 56, 13–31.

Levav, I., Al-Krenawi, A., If rah, A., Geraisy, N., Grinshpoon, A., Khwaled, R., & Levinson, D. (2007). Common mental disorders among Arab-Israelis: Findings from the Israel National Health Survey. *Israel Journal of Psychiatry & Related Sciences,* 44, 104–113.

Owens, J. S., Lyon, A. R., Brandt, N. E., Warner, C. M., Nadeem, E., Spiel, C., & Wagner, M. (2014). Implementation science in school mental health: Key constructs in a developing research agenda. *School Mental Health*, 6(2), 99–111.

Rai, D., Zitko, P., Jones, K., Lynch, J., & Araya, R. (2013). Country- and individual-level socioeconomic determinants of depression: Multilevel cross-national comparison. *British Journal of Psychiatry*, 202, 195–203.

RAMA (2013). Data on school climate and pedagogical environment. http://cms.education.gov.il/EducationCMS/Units/Rama/Meitzav/Aklim_2012.htm. Retrieved August 29, 2013.

Raviv, A. (1989). School psychology research in Israel. *Professional School Psychology*, 4, 147–154.

Raviv, A., & Weiner, I. (1995). Why don't they like us? Psychologists' public image in Israel during the Persian Gulf War. *Professional Psychology: Research and Practice*, 26, 88–94.

Raviv, A., Zeira, M., & Sharvit, K. (2007). Community psychology in Israel. In S. M. Reich, M. Riemer, I. Prilleltensky, & M. Montero (Eds.), *International community psychology: History and theories* (pp. 335–349). New York: Springer.

Senor, D., & Singer, S. (2009). *Start-up nation: The story of Israel's economic miracle.* New York: Twelve

Splett, J. W., Fowler, J., Weist, M. D., McDaniel, H., & Dvorsky, M. (2013). The critical role of school psychology in the school mental health movement. *Psychology in the Schools*, 50(3), 245–258.

Stauffer, S., Heath, M. A., Coyne, S. M., & Ferrin, S. (2012). High school teachers' perceptions of cyberbullying prevention and intervention strategies. *Psychology in the Schools*, 49, 352–367.

Tal, A., Eoe, D., & Corrign, P. W. (2007). Mental illness stigma in the Israeli context: Deliberations and suggestions. *International Journal of Social Psychiatry*, 53, 547–763.

Weist, M. D., Paternite, C. E., Wheatley-Rowe, D., & Gall, G. (2009). From thought to action in school mental health promotion. *International Journal of Mental Health Promotion*, 11(3), 32–41.

WHO (2013). World Health Statistics 2013. www.who.int/gho/publications/world_health_statistics/EN_WHS2013_Full.pdf. Retrieved September 15, 2013.

Chapter 13

Development of a mental health literacy program for secondary school students in Japan

Yasutaka Ojio, Kumiko Ohnuma, Tomiko Miki, and Tsukasa Sasaki

Introduction

Mental health literacy education and prevention of mental illnesses

Adolescence and emerging adulthood are considered the peak periods for the onset of mental illnesses, with approximately 75% of all mental illnesses diagnosed in adults having had an onset before the age of 25 years (Jones, 2013; Kessler *et al.*, 2005). It is therefore crucial for students to have appropriate knowledge and beliefs about mental illnesses that will aid their recognition, management, and prevention. Such knowledge and beliefs are referred to as mental health literacy (MHL) (Jorm *et al.*, 1997; Jorm, 2012). In particular, it is important that students develop the capacity to seek appropriate help for any mental health problems they may suffer. Help-seeking is a multi-step decision that involves an affected individual (1) identifying the problem, (2) acknowledging that they need help and/or treatment for the problem, (3) understanding that mental health problems (or illnesses) are treatable, and (4) being motivated to seek help and/or treatment (Gulliver *et al.*, 2010; Santor *et al.*, 2007). To acquire the knowledge and beliefs necessary for these steps, MHL education is necessary for students during adolescence. Since most adolescents spend much of their time at school, schools may be the best place to provide such education (Hendren *et al.*, 1994; Wei *et al.*, 2011; World Psychiatric Association *et al.*, 2005), and programs for use in schools have been developed in several countries (Wei *et al.*, 2013).

Current status of MHL education in Japan

In Japan, however, mental health education is rarely provided in schools, including elementary, junior, and senior high-schools. It is especially striking that current school health textbooks, which follow the curriculum guidelines of the Japanese government, contain nothing about mental illnesses (Ojio *et al.*, 2013). Before 1982, health textbooks for high-school students included detailed explanations of mental illnesses (the names of diseases were listed along with their major symptoms) and also noted the increasing rate of psychiatric hospitalization at the time. The Eugenic Protection Act of the Japanese Government at the time, which aimed to prevent the genetic reproduction of mental illnesses, was also explained in the textbook (Imamura *et al.*, 1963). This content was,

School Mental Health: Global Challenges and Opportunities, ed. Stan Kutcher, Yifeng Wei and Marc D. Weist. Published by Cambridge University Press. © Cambridge University Press 2015.

however, totally removed in 1982, to reduce the volume of the curriculum in elementary and high-schools (National Institute for Educational Policy Research, n.d.). This policy of curriculum volume reduction on mental health-related topics was adopted to reduce the psychological stress of students who were facing stiff academic competition to enter the more socially respected high-schools and universities, which was considered a tough goal for most Japanese students at the time. As a result, knowledge of mental illnesses is generally poor in Japanese adolescents, although a few studies have investigated the issue, and has been shown to be poor in adults, which may be related to lack of mental health education during their school years (reviewed by Ando et al., 2013). Furthermore, most Japanese people have few opportunities to learn about mental illnesses even after leaving school. In general, Japanese people tend to consider that the major cause of mental illnesses is private psychosocial factors, including weakness of personality, and ignores biological and biosocial factors (Kurumatani et al., 2004; Nakane et al., 2005; Tanaka et al., 2005). In addition, the majority of Japanese people tend to maintain a large social distance from individuals with mental illnesses (Katsuki et al., 2005; Mino et al., 2001).

To improve this situation, we have developed a school-based education program on mental health and illnesses. In the present chapter we explain the content and effects of the first version of the program, which is currently being improved for the next version. In developing the program we tried to make it concise and able to be taught by school staff. The reason for this was to make the program feasible and sustainable in most fields of school education (Han & Weiss, 2005; Santor & Bagnell, 2012). The schedule in Japanese schools is very tight due to the heavy demands of regular curriculum and events such as sports and cultural activities, and preparation for entrance examinations to higher-level schools. If the program was long and required several hours to teach, many schools would not be able to employ it. Further, if the program needed to be taught by health professionals outside the school, that would also likely hinder its application, given that schools may not be able to find an appropriate person to teach the program. We therefore tried to develop a program that could be taught in two 50-minute sessions, by school nurses in the Japanese school health system. The Japanese school health system (or yōgo teacher system) is quite different from the systems in other countries. To aid readers' understanding, we will explain the system in the next section.

The school nurse (yōgo kyōyu) system in Japan

Under the Japanese Government Act on School Health (Ministry of Education, Culture, Sports, Science and Technology, n.d.), all Japanese schools from elementary to junior high-school (from Grade 1 to Grade 9), both public and private, must have a full-time school nurse (yōgo kyōyu) assigned as a member of the school staff. "Yogo" means nursing and "kyoyu" means teacher in Japanese. Senior high-schools are also recommended to have full-time school nurses under the Act, but it is not mandatory. "Full-time" means that one or two school nurses are assigned to each school to stay and take care of the students' health every day. The number of school nurses in each school is usually one, but can be two depending on the number of students in the school. Yōgo kyōyu are usually stationed in the healthcare room of schools and give first aid to students who visit the healthcare room for physical or mental difficulties and injuries. They conduct annual health check-ups of students, with the cooperation of physicians and dentists (usually of private practices) in the school area, which provides good opportunities for yōgo kyōyu to understand the health condition of each student. They are also licensed to give classes or courses of health education to the students, although this is not mandatory.

In recent years, demands to take care of the mental health needs of students have rapidly increased in Japanese schools and, accordingly, the role of *yōgo kyōyu* in mental healthcare has also become more important. A substantial portion of students who are not able to stay in their classrooms due to mental problems, victimization by bullying, and other reasons, spend substantial amounts of time in the healthcare room during their time at school. In the healthcare room they not only receive mental health support but also carry out their regular academic school tasks. This is referred to as "healthcare room schooling" (*hoken-shitsu tōkō*). The number of such students has increased in recent decades. *Yōgo kyōyu* take care of these students, often very intensively, with cooperation from other teachers, school counselors (usually part-time), families, and sometimes medical staff outside the school. Against this background we considered that, in Japan, *yōgo kyōyu* were the best candidates for delivering our mental health education program to students.

Principles and content of the program

The MHL education program we developed for secondary school students is designed to address the current status of mental health education in Japanese schools. The program was developed by a collaborative team consisting of psychiatrists, public health nurses, and *yōgo kyōyu*, to be delivered by *yōgo kyōyu* in secondary schools. The *yōgo kyōyus* were trained for delivery of the program in their schools by one or two of the authors (YO and TS). The objective of the program was to provide an opportunity for students to learn about the symptoms of mental illnesses that are frequent in adolescents, to understand that mental difficulties are not rare in adolescents, and to encourage them to seek help when they are in difficulty.

Table 13.1 summarizes the content of the program. The program consisted of two 50-minute sessions. The sessions, Lesson 1 and 2, were given one week apart. Teaching methods included lectures, e-animation, and group discussion. The e-animation lasted for approximately four minutes per unit, and was taken from the website of the Ministry of Health, Labor, and Welfare of Japan (www.mhlw.go.jp/kokoro/youth/movie/b/index.html), which provides e-animations explaining the symptoms of a number of mental illnesses, including major depression, schizophrenia, and panic disorder and others. In the present program, the e-animations for major depression and schizophrenia were used. The goal of Lesson 1 was for students to learn the signs and symptoms of mental difficulties and illnesses and understand that mental health problems and mental illnesses are not rare in adolescents and may develop in them and their peers. Recognition of the problem is the first step in seeking help from an appropriate professional, and essential to avoid delay in help-seeking (Gulliver *et al.*, 2010). The goal of Lesson 2 was for the students to understand how they should behave when they themselves or their peers are suffering from mental difficulties. The contents of Lesson 1 included general explanations of mental illnesses, including prevalence, onset age, risk factors, treatability and possibility of recovery, and frequent symptoms in adolescence, in lecture style. Frequent misunderstandings about mental illnesses were also explained. Typical adolescent cases of major depression and schizophrenia in their initial phases were shown using the e-animation. The contents of Lesson 2 included descriptions of typical resources of help, such as psychiatric out-patient clinics, by showing pictures. How the diagnoses are made and examinations for the diagnoses were also explained. At the end of the lessons, the students engaged in group discussions for about 15–20 minutes, in which they were asked to think about appropriate solutions that would help them if they were suffering from mental difficulties.

Table 13.1 Instructional modules and major contents

	Lecture	Animation	Group discussion
Lesson 1 (50 minutes)	Explanation of mental illnesses (prevalence, onset age, risk factors, treatability and possibility of recovery, and frequent symptoms in adolescents). Frequent misunderstandings of mental illnesses in general people.	Showing typical cases of major depression and schizophrenia.	–
Lesson 2 (50 minutes)	Showing a picture of a mental clinic to show that the clinics are usually like normal offices, not places giving unusual or frightening impressions.	–	Appropriate solutions that help youth who are suffering from difficulties in mental health.
Goal of Lesson 1	Understanding that mental health problems and mental illnesses are familiar to themselves. Studying symptoms of mental health problems in adolescents.		
Goal of Lesson 2	Understanding how to deal with mental illnesses when they or their peers suffer from them.		

Method

The pilot study and evaluation of the program

The pilot study of the program was conducted from November to December 2012. The participants comprised 118 Grade 9 students (61 males and 57 females, aged 14–15 years) of a secondary school in Tokyo, Japan. The school is affiliated to the Faculty of Education, the University of Tokyo. The school requires an admission examination at the secondary school entry. The two lessons were given once per week over a two-week period at the health education class by the full-time *yōgo kyōyu* (school nurse). Students were allowed to stop participating in the program if they experienced any discomfort.

Evaluation of the effects

We conducted pre-, post-, and three-month follow-up evaluations on the effects of the program, using a self-report questionnaire. Students who participated in the program were requested to complete the questionnaire, which dealt with knowledge and beliefs about mental illnesses and mental healthcare, and intentions to seek help and support others with mental difficulties. The questionnaire consists of 16 true-or-false items (Table 13.2). Two

Table 13.2 Questions on knowledge and beliefs about mental illnesses and their treatment

Statement	True/false	Rate % (n) correct responses		
		Pre-test	Post-test	Follow-up test
Most mental illnesses frequently begin at adolescence.	T	69.1 (65)	100 (94)***	93.6(88)***
Mental illnesses are caused by the weaknesses of or bad personality.	F	75.5 (71)	98.9 (93)***	94.7 (89)***
Mental illnesses are treatable.	T	95.7 (90)	100 (94)	100 (94)
Lifestyle, including sleep habit, has effects on prevention and recovery of mental illnesses.	T	86.2 (81)	90.4 (85)	96.8 (91)
Somatic symptoms including fatigue, abdominal pains and nausea may occur as an early symptom of mental illnesses.	T	86.2 (81)	96.8 (91)*	97.9 (92)**
People who suffer from mental illnesses should endure the symptoms.	F	97.9 (92)	97.9 (92)	98.9 (93)
Most mental illnesses improve without treatment.	F	92.6 (87)	96.8 (91)	100 (94)
Early treatment makes a significant difference in the prognosis of mental illnesses.	T	94.7 (89)	94.7 (89)	96.8 (91)
In order to receive psychiatric treatment, we need to go to general hospital.	F	72.3 (68)	100 (94)***	96.8 (91)***
Medical examinations including blood tests may be necessary for diagnose of mental illnesses.	T	28.7 (27)	86.2 (81)***	52.1 (49)***
Medication improves many mental illnesses.	T	29.8 (28)	91.5 (86)***	76.6 (72)***
People who are on psychiatric treatment cannot go to work and school.	F	89.4 (84)	97.9 (92)**	95.7 (90)
People with a diagnosis of mental illnesses cannot get a general job.	F	96.8 (91)	98.9 (93)	100 (94)
Treatment may be stopped when the condition improves.	F	72.3 (68)	73.4 (69)	62.8 (59)
Most subjects with mental illnesses need to receive in-patient treatment.	F	84 (79)	97.9 (92)**	89.4 (84)
Average length of a hospital stay for mental illnesses is 2–3 years.	F	79.8 (75)	98.9 (93)***	92.6 (87)**

***$p < 0.001$, **$p < 0.01$, *$p < 0.05$ (better at post-test and the follow-up test than pre-test)

vignettes of cases of mental illnesses were used to test whether students could tell the names of the illnesses. These vignettes were similar to those used by Jorm *et al.* (1997), but were made more easy to understand. The vignettes presented cases of secondary school students who met the diagnostic criteria of DSM-IV for major depression (case 1) and schizophrenia (case 2). Major depression and schizophrenia were chosen because they are the frequent and severe mental health disorders which likely have their onset in adolescence (Kessler *et al.*, 2005). The questionnaire was administered during regular school hours.

In the questionnaire, students were asked (1) whether the person in the vignette had any mental illnesses and to select the most appropriate diagnosis from the following options: no problem, depression, schizophrenia, eating disorder, social phobia, and unable to tell (Tables 13.3a and 13.4a); (2) to choose appropriate solutions (or what they would do) from the options in Tables 13.3b and 13.4b for major depression and schizophrenia, respectively, if they had the difficulties described in the vignette; and (3) to choose the

Table 13.3 Answers to the questions on the vignette of a major depression case

	Rate % (*n*) of the correct responses		
	Pre	Post	Follow-up
a. Rate of students who answered with the correct name of the illness	38.3 (36)	94.7 (89)***	91.5 (86)***
b. Question: What will you do if you have the problem described?			
I would do nothing, because it's not a disease.	16.0 (15)	3.2 (3)**	1.1 (1)**
I would wait and see a little more.	27.7 (26)	9.6 (9)**	22.3 (21)
I would talk to someone who can be trusted.	46.8 (44)	87.2 (82)***	74.5 (70)***
I don't know what to do.	9.6 (9)	0 (0)**	2.1 (2)**
c. Question: What will your peers do if you have the problem described?			
I would do nothing, because it's not a disease.	5.3 (5)	0 (0)	1.1 (1)
I would wait and see a little more.	34.0 (32)	18.1 (17)**	18.1 (17)**
I would avoid conversation with him or her.	1.1 (1)	0 (0)	1.1 (1)
I would advise him or her to change the behaviour	10.6 (10)	4.3 (4)*	3.2 (3)
I would talk to someone who can be trusted.	33.0 (31)	74.5 (70)***	72.3 (68)***
I don't know what to do.	16.0 (15)	3.2 (3)**	4.3 (4)*

***$p < 0.001$, **$p < 0.01$, *$p < 0.05$ (compared with pre-test).

Table 13.4 Answers to the questions on the vignette of a schizophrenia case

	Rate % (*n*) of the correct responses		
	Pre	Post	Follow-up
a. Rate of students who answered with the correct name of the illness	19.1 (18)	93.6 (88)***	86.2 (81)***
b. Question: What will you do if you have the problem described?			
I would do nothing, because it's not a disease.	4.3 (4)	2.1 (2)	0 (0)
I would wait and see a little more.	7.4 (7)	4.3 (4)	13.8 (13)
I would talk to someone who can be trusted.	54.3 (51)	88.3 (83)***	76.6 (72)***
I don't know what to do.	34.0 (32)	5.3 (5)***	9.6 (9)***
c. Question: What will your peers do if you have the problem described?			
I would do nothing, because it's not a disease.	2.1 (2)	0 (0)	0 (0)
I would wait and see a little more.	9.6 (9)	9.6 (9)	9.6 (9)
I would avoid conversation with him or her.	8.5 (8)	2.1 (2)*	4.3 (4)
I would advise him or her to change the behavior.	7.4 (7)	0 (0)	3.2 (3)
I would talk to someone who can be trusted.	47.9 (45)	86.2 (81)***	74.5 (70)***
I don't know what to do.	24.5 (23)	2.1 (2)***	8.5 (8)**

***$p < 0.001$, **$p < 0.01$, *$p < 0.05$ (compared with pre-test).

actions they would take if their peers had the difficulties described in the vignette, from the options in Tables 13.3c and 13.4c for major depression and schizophrenia, respectively.

Ethical aspect

This study was approved by the University of Tokyo Human Research Ethics Committee.

Data analysis

Wilcoxon signed rank test was used to compare the rate of the students who gave correct answers for each question between pre vs. post and pre vs. follow-up tests. Because the distribution of the data were significantly skewed, McNemar's test was used to compare the knowledge and the students' attitude (or selection of appropriate behaviors) between pre vs. post and pre vs. follow-up tests. The level of significance was set at $p < 0.05$. SPSS version 21.0 for Mac (2012) was used in the statistical analysis.

Results of the pilot study

Participants
Of the 118 Grade 9 students, 102 students (86.4%; 52 males and 50 females) participated in the lessons. None of the students withdrew during the lessons. Out of the 102, 94 students (92.1%; 47 males and 47 females) completed the pre, post, and follow-up tests for the evaluation.

Effects on knowledge and beliefs
Table 13.2 shows the proportion of students who correctly responded to each of the 16 questions dealing with knowledge of mental illnesses and treatment, at pre, post, and follow-up tests. Prior to the lessons, most of the students knew that mental illnesses were treatable (95.7%), that early treatment made a significant difference in the prognosis (94.7%), that people who were undergoing psychiatric treatment could go to work and school (89.4%), and that people with a diagnosis of mental illnesses could get a general job (96.8%). However, few students knew that medical examinations were often required for the diagnosis of mental illnesses (28.7%) and that medication improved many mental illnesses (29.8%). The rates of the correct answers for these two questions were significantly higher at the post-test and the follow-up tests compared with the pre-test. The total score (the number of correct answers) for the knowledge improved significantly from a mean/median of 12.1/13.0 at pre-test to 15.2/15.0 at post-test ($r = 0.81$, $p < 0.001$). At the follow-up (after three months) the total score was significantly higher than the score at the pre-test ($r = 0.72$, $p < 0.001$), although the mean/median of the score fell to 14.5/14.5.

Recognition of mental difficulties and selection of appropriate solutions
Tables 13.3a and 13.4a show the rates of students who selected the appropriate diagnosis of in the two vignette cases and the appropriate solutions for those problems, respectively. At the pre-test 38.3% and 19.1% of students selected the correct diagnosis for the vignette cases of major depression and schizophrenia, respectively. The rate of the correct answers significantly increased at the post-test and the follow-up test (94.7% and 93.6% at the post-test [$p < 0.001$, and $p < 0.001$], and 91.5% and 86.2% at the follow-up test [$p < 0.001$, and $p < 0.001$] for major depression and schizophrenia, respectively). The rate of students who selected the appropriate help-seeking intention ("I would talk to someone who can be trusted") significantly increased at the post- and follow-up tests, compared with the pre-test (Tables 13.3b and 13.4b). For the vignette of major depression, the rate changed from 46.8% at the pre-test to 87.2% at the post-test ($p < 0.001$) and 74.5% at the follow-up test ($p < 0.001$). For the vignette of schizophrenia, the rate changed from 54.3% at the pre-test to 88.3% at the post-test ($p < 0.001$) and 76.6% at the follow-up test ($p = 0.001$).

Intention of helping peers with mental difficulties

Tables 13.3c and 13.4c show the rates of students who selected the appropriate answers for questions about the actions they should take if their friends are suffering from mental difficulties. The rate of the students who selected the appropriate intention to help their peers with mental difficulties ("I would talk to someone who can be trusted") significantly increased after the lessons (Tables 13.3c and 13.4c). For the vignette of major depression, the rate changed from 33.0% at the pre-test to 74.5% at the post-test ($p < 0.001$) and 72.3% at the follow-up test ($p < 0.001$). For the vignette of schizophrenia, the rate changed from 47.9% at the pre-test to 86.2% at the post-test ($p < 0.001$) and 74.5% at the follow-up test ($p < 0.001$).

Discussion

There have been few studies of school-based MHL education programs in Japan. To our knowledge, a couple of investigators have been engaged in this area, but with no publications and therefore with no detailed information available. As a result, we recently developed a school-based MHL program for Japanese secondary school students to bridge the gap in this important but under-addressed area in Japanese secondary schools. Our goal for the development of the program is to make it concise and school staff led, because these may lead to the program being employed in a greater number of schools in Japan. In the present study, we examined the effect of the first version of the program with a self-report questionnaire, administered before, immediately after, and three months following implementation. Our findings showed that the program had a significant effect on students' knowledge about mental illnesses and their treatment, and further their intention to seek appropriate help and to support their peers who are suffering mental difficulties. The significant effect was observed immediately after and also after three months following this concise, school staff-led program. The effect on the help-seeking intention may, however, be interpreted with caution. Although the students better understood the importance of help-seeking than before the program, whether they actually seek help when they have mental health difficulties was not evaluated. The actual behavior may be related to stigma or feeling shy/embarrassed for seeking help for these kind of difficulties. Change of such feelings (or stigma) is an important focus of the MHL education program for adolescents. We are partly revising our program in consideration of this issue. Videos of the patients who have experienced mental illnesses may be used as a potential approach to address stigma.

To our knowledge, there have been a very limited number of school-based MHL education programs of this short length for adolescents. Pinfold et al. (2003) developed a concise school-based MHL program of two 60-minute sessions, and examined its effect. The program dealt with knowledge about mental illnesses and psychiatric care and the stigma toward mental illnesses. Their program employed a short video, lecture, and information leaflets. A short talk with people with mental illnesses was also included in the program. The program had a significant positive effect on knowledge about and attitude toward mental illnesses in the adolescents, which may be similar to the present study. What was different between their program and the present program, however, was the person who taught the program. Their program was delivered by mental health professionals from outside the school.

Most school-based MHL programs developed thus far have been professional-led (Wei *et al.*, 2013). A small number of school staff-led programs have been developed (Kutcher *et al.*, 2013; Naylor *et al.*, 2009; Petchers *et al.*, 1988; Rahman *et al.*, 1998). Naylor *et al.* (2009) developed a school staff-led MHL program on knowledge and beliefs about mental illnesses and stigma toward them. The program was administrated by teachers responsible for pastoral care. The program consisted of six 50-minute sessions on mental health issues common to young people. The effect of the program was examined in a simple non-randomized pre-/post-test control group design, and a significant effect was observed on knowledge and attitudes. Naylor *et al.* (2009) and ours may both show that the programs given by school staff could be as effective as those given by mental health professionals; for this, the school staff may need to be trained to become familiar with mental health issues through training sessions. A difference between the two studies was the length of the program. While the program in the present study consisted of two 50-minute sessions, the program in Naylor *et al.* (2009) comprised six sessions. The MHL program in MindMatters from Australia is also school staff-led, but it is left up to each school and teacher to decide how many hours to spend teaching the program (Wyn *et al.*, 2000, MindMatters, n.d.).

MHL programs that are delivered by school staff, especially by school nurses, may have several advantages compared with programs delivered by health professionals outside the school, such as physicians and public health nurses. Classes implemented by school nurses may encourage students to seek help from school nurses directly for mental difficulties. This may be especially true in the Japanese system, where the school nurses (*yōgo kyōyu*) are full-time, being stationed every day at the same school. Another advantage is that *yōgo kyōyu* are likely to be able to deliver the mental health program with careful consideration for needs of students who have mental health programs because *yōgo kyōyu* observe students' health regularly.

Several limitations may be noted in the present study and the program. The number of participants (students) was small. The effect was examined without a control group, in an uncontrolled trial. To test the effect, we used a brief self-report questionnaire, which was originally developed for this study and not tested using a large number of adolescents. The limitation of pen-and-paper assessments, which suffer from potential social desirability bias, may also be noted. The *yōgo kyōyu* who gave the lessons in the present program were interested in mental health and might have background mental health knowledge. Without training the school staff, the effect of the program may not be generalized.

Conclusions

In summary, we have developed a concise, school staff-led MHL education program for secondary school students. The lessons were given by a full-time *yōgo kyōyu* in the Japanese school health system. The effect was significant on knowledge of mental illnesses and their treatment. Attitudes to seeking help and assisting peers for help-seeking if needed also improved, and the effects maintained three months after the program was given. This suggests that this concise, school staff-led MHL education might be effective. The study is, however, small and preliminary. Further studies of the present program using a larger number of students, with a control group, may be required. Thus far, there have been a limited number of studies on the effect of concise, school staff-led MHL education. In Japan, an important approach may be to incorporate an MHL program like the present one into the normal school curriculum of health. Effective programs in other countries with different school health systems may be introduced to and adapted by Japanese secondary schools to nourish MHL programs in Japan.

References

Ando, S. Yamaguchi, S., Aoki, Y., et al. (2013). Review of mental-health-related stigma in Japan. *Psychiatry and Clinical Neurosciences*, 67(7), 471–482.

Gulliver, A., Griffiths, K. M., and Christensen, H. (2010). Perceived barriers and facilitators to mental health help-seeking in young people: A systematic review. *BMC Psychiatry*, 10, 113.

Han, S. S. and Weiss, B. (2005). Sustainability of teacher implementation of school-based mental health programs. *Journal of Abnormal Child Psychology*, 33(6), 665–679.

Hendren, R., Weisen, R., and Birrell, O. J. (1994). Mental health programmes in schools. Available at: http://whqlibdoc.who.int/hq/1993/WHO_MNH_PSF_93.3_Rev.1.pdf, accessed January 7, 2014.

Imamura, Y., Sugimoto, R., Asakawa, S., et al. (1963). *Kou-Tou Hoken Kyo-iku*. Taishukan Inc. (Japanese)

Jones, P. B. (2013). Adult mental health disorders and their age at onset. *British Journal of Psychiatry*, 202, 5–10.

Jorm, A. F. (2012). Mental health literacy: Empowering the community to take action for better mental health. *American Psychologist*, 67, 231–243.

Jorm, A. F., Korten, A. E., Jacomb, P. A., et al. (1997). "Mental health literacy": A survey of the public's ability to recognise mental disorders and their beliefs about the effectiveness of treatment. *Medical Journal of Australia*, 166, 182–186.

Katsuki, F., Goto, M., and Someya, T. (2005). A study of emotional attitude of psychiatric nurses: Reliability and validity of the Nurse Attitude Scale. *International Journal of Mental Health Nursing*, 14(4), 265–270.

Kessler, R. C., Berglund, P., Demler O., et al. (2005). Lifetime prevalence and age-of-onset distributions of DSM-IV disorders in the National Comorbidity Survey Replication. *Archives of General Psychiatry*, 62, 593–602.

Kurumatani, T., Ukawa, K., Kawaguchi, Y., et al. (2004). Teachers' knowledge, beliefs and attitudes concerning schizophrenia: A cross-cultural approach in Japan and Taiwan. *Social Psychiatry and Psychiatric Epidemiology*, 39(5), 402–409.

Kutcher, S., Wei, Y., McLuckie, A., and Bullock, L. (2013). Educator mental health literacy: A program evaluation of the teacher training education on the mental health & high school curriculum guide. *Advance in School Mental Health Promotion*, 6 (2), 89–93.

MindMatters (n.d.). Available at: www.mindmatters.edu.au/default.asp, accessed January 7, 2014.

Ministry of Education, Culture, Sports, Science and Technology (n.d.). Available at: www.mext.go.jp, accessed December 30, 2013.

Ministry of Health, Labor and Welfare (n.d.). Available at: www.mhlw.go.jp/kokoro/youth/movie/b/index.html, accessed December 30, 2013).

Mino, Y., Yasuda, N., Tsuda, T., et al. (2001). Effects of a one-hour educational program on medical students' attitudes to mental illness. *Psychiatry and Clinical Neuroscience*, 55(5), 501–507.

Nakane, Y., Jorm, A. F., Yoshioka, K., et al. (2005). Public beliefs about causes and risk factors for mental disorders: A comparison of Japan and Australia. *BMC Psychiatry*, 5, 33.

National Institute for Educational Policy Research (n.d.). Curriculum guideline databases. Available at: www.nier.go.jp/guideline/index.htm, accessed January 7, 2014.

Naylor, P. B., Cowie, H. A., Walters, S. J., et al. (2009). Impact of a mental health teaching programme on adolescents. *British Journal of Psychiatry*, 194(4), 365–370.

Ojio, Y., Togo, F., and Sasaki, T. (2013). Literature search of school based mental health literacy education programs. *Japanese Journal of School Health*, 55, 325–333.

Petchers, M. K., Biegel, D. E., and Drescher, R. (1988) A video-based program to educate high school students about serious mental illness. *Hospital and Community Psychiatry*, 39(10), 1102–1103.

Pinfold, V., Toulmin, H., Thornicroft, G., *et al.* (2003). Reducing psychiatric stigma and discrimination: Evaluation of educational interventions in UK secondary schools. *British Journal of Psychiatry*, 182, 342–346.

Rahman, A., Mubbashar, M. H., Gater, R., *et al.* (1998). Randomised trial of impact of school mental-health programme in rural Rawalpindi, Pakistan. *Lancet*, 352(9133), 1022–1025.

Santor, D. A. and Bagnell, A. L. (2012). Maximizing the uptake and sustainability of school-based mental health programs: Commercializing knowledge. *Child and Adolescent Psychiatric Clinics of North America*, 21(1), 81–92

Santor, D. A., Poulin, C., Leblanc, J., *et al.* (2007). Online health promotion, early identification of difficulties, and help seeking in young people. *Journal of the American Academy of Child and Adolescent Psychiatry*, 46, 50–59.

Tanaka, G., Inadomi, H., Kikuchi, Y., *et al.* (2005). Evaluating community attitudes to people with schizophrenia and mental disorders using a case vignette method. *Psychiatry and Clinical Neuroscience*, 59(1), 96–101.

Wei, Y., Hayden, J. A., Kutcher, S., *et al.* (2013). The effectiveness of school mental health literacy programs to address knowledge, attitudes and help seeking among youth. *Early Interventions in Psychiatry*, 7(2), 109–121.

Wei, Y., Kutcher, S., and Szumilas, M. (2011). Comprehensive school mental health: An integrated "school-based pathway to care" model for Canadian secondary schools. *McGill Journal of Education*, 46, 213–230.

World Psychiatric Association, World Health Organization, International Association for Child and Adolescent Psychiatry and Allied Professions. (2005). *Atlas child and adolescent mental health resources: Child mental health atlas.* Available at: www.who.int/mental_health/resources/Child_ado_atlas.pdf, accessed January 7, 2014.

Wyn, J., Cahill, H., Holdsworth, H., *et al.* (2000). MindMatters, a whole-school approach promoting mental health and wellbeing. *Australian and New Zealand Journal of Psychiatry*, 34(4), 594–601.

A peer mental health educator model in African schools
Untapped potential

Kenneth Hamwaka

"There is no health without mental health" goes an adage that supports the assumption that access to mental health literacy and services is vital and a backbone to all forms of human growth. Oftentimes, access to information and services to the youth in the school setup is provided by elderly individuals, such as teachers and counselors. There is generally little confidence that young people can support one another through peer-to-peer intervention, commonly referred to as peer mental health education, where learners share information through clubs administered by a group of peers called peer mental health educators. The purpose of this chapter is to present an overview of a practical model of peer mental health educators in Malawi, justify the possibilities and gains of peer mental health education in the school systems, and prove that learners can equally play a vital role in enriching the social, educational, personal, and vocational lives of fellow learners both in and out of the school environment. The chapter further provides an opportunity to prove that peer health education plays a pivotal role in facilitating the concept of education for all through improved access to quality education.

Current global perception on mental health and the role of peer health educators

The World Health Organization (WHO) has boldly singled out mental health as the issue of the moment and that everyone and every organization should take keen interest in ensuring that people, especially the young, are provided with literacy, interactive strategies, and increased access to mental health services such as medical and psychotherapy. Peer health educators are well positioned to provide such services at the school level, where issues of mental health have not been taken seriously and at times completely misunderstood or ignored. Kutcher et al. (2013) acknowledged the fact that mental health literacy through peer health educators provides the foundation for schools to actively promote mental health literacy, including messages that seeking help is a sensible and supportive act rather than a sign of weakness. Kutcher further urged that through peer health educators, the youth can easily be empowered to actively participate and be involved in discussions about when, how, and where to seek help whenever they need it.

According to Hamwaka (2013), peer health educators are a key to the holistic development of learners, and in supporting learning and management of an educational institution.

School Mental Health: Global Challenges and Opportunities, ed. Stan Kutcher, Yifeng Wei and Marc D. Weist. Published by Cambridge University Press. © Cambridge University Press 2015.

He notes that a peer health educator is likened to a model in society whose personality profile should include assertiveness, patience, empathy, and pragmatism. These are values that best govern societies and individuals, and if schools manage to impact and achieve these values in the learners then there is a likelihood that learners' personal, educational, vocational, and social growth could be improved.

UNESCO's (2012) report on youth development identified schools as centers of teaching and learning, and that most youth initiatives need to start and expand into communities from there. UNESCO appreciates that a school is a complex society that brings together learners and teachers of different backgrounds and experiences into one environment, where they need to socialize and get along with each other well. This is based on the understanding that learners spend more hours at school than in their respective homes, and as such there are bound to be conflicts and misunderstanding between learners themselves and between learners and teachers. Peer health education fits perfectly in schools because learners are empowered to support each other rather than waiting for teachers to resolve their differences.

In response to the UNESCO call to promote youth development through schools, a school-based peer health education program has proved to be an effective interaction strategy by many organizations in Africa, such as in The Gambia (1990–2006) and Sierra Leone (2002–2006) by the Nova Scotia–Gambia Association (NSGA). The aims of the initiatives are to improve the health and wellbeing of youth through equipping them with the knowledge, skills, and confidence to take responsibility for their own health. This is accomplished through the development of well-informed, well-trained teams of school-based peer health educators who are motivated to share their knowledge and training with their fellow students and the communities around them.

According to The Gambia and Sierra Leone reports noted above, notable key points of a peer health education program are follows:

1. The peer health educators were able to develop and conduct an ongoing series of presentations, classroom by classroom, in their schools on the whole range of health-related issues confronting young people, including STIs and HIV/AIDS.
2. The peer health educators were trained in a variety of strategies to engage their peers and encourage healthy behavior and attitudes.
3. Where possible, the peer health educators also developed community outreach programs targeting neighboring schools, out-of-school youth, and the general public.

Peer health educators model in Malawi

Selection criteria

Potential peer health educators (youth aged 12–20 years) were identified by school administrators and youth club leaders. The school administrators and youth club leaders used the following criteria to identify the participants: must have a positive influence over fellow youth; patience; team building; tolerance; understanding; self-control; role model; ability to keep abreast on new information and knowledge on health issues; ability to deal with emotions and difficult situations; non-judgmental attitude; adaptive and flexible; ability to encourage and provide support; ability to maintain confidentiality and foster trust; ability to make decisions; and ability to look at things from various perspectives.

Youth chosen to be peer health educators were offered the opportunity to become peer mental health educators. They were informed that their participation would include a period of training in peer mental health education followed by supported application of their peer mental health education activities through the GCYDCA (Guidance, Counselling and Youth Development Centre for Africa). All youth who chose to be peer mental health educators agreed to participate in the training sessions that were conducted by GCYDC staff.

Description and statistics

The training sessions had 141 participants drawn from 35 schools in three districts of Malawi. The participants comprised 105 youth peer health educators and 35 teachers from three different regions of Malawi. Each training session lasted one day. Youth and educators were trained together.

In-school youth (n = 105) *were drawn as follows:*

Salima   15 schools × 3 = 45
Lilongwe   10 schools × 3 = 30
Mchinji   10 schools × 3 = 30

Teachers (n = 36) *were drawn as follows:*

Salima   15 schools × 1 teacher per school = 15 teachers
Lilongwe   10 school × 1 teacher per school = 10
Mchinji   11 schools × 1 teacher per school = 11 teachers

Materials used during training

The materials used in the training sessions included: (1) *Training Manual for Peer Mental Health Education in African Schools and Communities*, which was also translated into Chichewa, a local language; (2) *Guide to Peer Mental Health Educators in Africa*, which was available for the trainers and only in English.

Assessment during backstopping

After training of the peer educators there is a need to check on them regularly to see how they are managing. Such visits are referred to as backstopping. A post-training assessment was made to document the impact of the peer mental health education training in Malawi through application of backstopping activities. A total number of 50 learners were selected as volunteers and were involved in the assessment. Table 14.1 summarizes the results of the responses provided by the learners, which were classified into nine thematic areas and presented in descending order of frequency of positive responses. The "frequency of response" column indicates the raw number of respondents who positively endorsed each theme/description category. The results are also graphically presented as shown in Figure 14.1.

Overall, this evaluation of the peer mental health educator training experience demonstrated positive benefits. The percentage of respondents who endorsed positive impacts across all theme/description categories ranged from 92% (for improved learner performance) to a low of 64% (for improved time management). To our knowledge, this is the first development, delivery, and evaluation of a peer mental health training program in Africa. While this evaluation does not meet the standards of a prospective cohort study or a randomized control trial, its results suggest that this approach may have substantial benefits

Table 14.1 Impact of peer mental health education training on individuals and communities

Theme/description	Frequency of response
Improved learner performance	46
Improved access to mental health information	45
Improved teacher–learner relationship	44
Improved literacy levels in mental health	40
Reduced stigma and discrimination	39
Improved learner–learner relationship	36
Improved school–community relationships	35
Improved access to mental health services	32
Improved time management	32

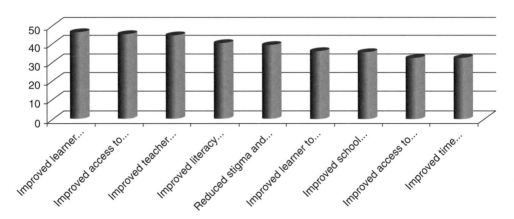

Figure 14.1 Impact of peer mental health education training on individuals and communities.

and that it is feasible in implementation. The resources created for and used in this peer mental health training program will be made available to all sub-Saharan African countries upon completion of the larger project.

Potential general benefits of the peer mental health educator approach

In addition to the outcomes of the peer mental health training described above, post-training group discussions with all youth and educator participants revealed a number of themes that were considered to be important in addressing the larger context of potential impacts or general benefits of this approach for young people in schools and communities.

Respondents identified the following possible benefits that should be considered for evaluation in the further roll-out of the program. These were:

1. Peer mental health education may be able to improve youth mental health through increased access to mental health education and through a variety of peer health activities that encourage wider community–school–stakeholder relationships.

2. Mental health in young people and increased willingness to seek care when needed may be enhanced with increased youth access to peer-provided mental health education and increased application of peer mental health education activities delivered through youth clubs and other school and community interactive strategies.

3. Peer mental health education may positively impact overall community mental health literacy by increased linking between schools and communities through peer mental health educator-led activities such as drama.

4. The education system needs to improve the quality of teacher knowledge and attitudes about youth mental health and mental disorders. This could be achieved by programs training teachers on mental health literacy or by embedding mental health curriculum in schools that teachers would then be trained to use.

5. Involvement in peer mental health education may result in improvement in the general wellbeing of the learners and other school stakeholders.

Conclusion

Although this peer mental health educator process is just at its beginning in Malawi, the results obtained to date and the theory and data underlying the success of peer health education suggest that this approach may be useful and effective in increasing mental health literacy, mental wellbeing, and acceptance of the importance of mental health among young people in sub-Saharan Africa. Young people who have successfully completed this training program are beginning their field experiences and further information about those will be forthcoming.

Our experience in the development and early stages of application of this process has further suggested that it is important to link or even embed peer mental health education activities within existing institutions and organizations, such as schools or well-established community-based youth clubs. In this way we may be able to determine if there are additional benefits to this process, such as improvements in the learning environment of schools, changes in mental health literacy/stigma in communities, or enhancement of learning outcomes in participants such as grades or school completion. Further research into the value of this approach is needed, including measurement of any improvements in mental health knowledge, decreases in stigma, and enhancement of help-seeking behavior in young people exposed to peer mental health education. Additionally, the impact of being a peer mental health educator on the psychological, emotional, and behavioral functioning of young people needs to be examined in future evaluations.

References

Hamwaka, K. (2013). *African peer education model*. Lilongwe: International Publishers.

Kutcher, S., Hamwaka, K., and Chazema, J. (2013). *African school mental health curriculum guide*. Lilongwe: International Publishers.

UNESCO (2012). Youth Development Report. Paris: UNESCO.

The current state of school mental health approaches and initiatives in Mexico and Chile

Julia Gallegos-Guajardo, Norma Ruvalcaba-Romero, and Muriel Halpern

The promotion of school mental health is crucial as a growing number of students experience or are at risk of psychological problems such as anxiety, depression, disruptive behavior, and ADHD (Gladstone & Beardslee, 2009; Neil & Christensen, 2009; World Health Organization, 2004). Particularly in developing countries, these problems are compounded with constraints such as high poverty, effects of globalization, violence and neglect, high unemployment rates, and a struggling education system. There is an urgent need for scientific knowledge related to the promotion of school mental health in developing countries; as Patel and Sumathipala (2001) reported, this research is barely conducted and published in comparison to other parts of the world. The purpose of this chapter is to provide comprehensive information of the current state of school mental health in Mexico and Chile, discuss the efforts that have been made, and provide suggestions to enhance current practices and to guide further research.

School mental health in Mexico

Mental health problems of adolescents in Mexico

At present we are experiencing a national context in which unfavorable life conditions prevail for most parts of the country. According to data provided from the United Nations Children's Fund (UNICEF), 53.8% of the child population lives in poverty conditions, 2.2 million adolescents between 15 and 17 years of age are not in school, and approximately 1300 of those under 18 years old have died due to violent reasons linked to organized crime (UNICEF México, 2011). The Organization for Economic Cooperation and Development (Organización para la Cooperación y el Desarrollo Económico, OCDE, 2013) estimates that 18.9% of youngsters between 15 and 19 years of age are not involved in any educational or labor activities. All of these factors are considered as risk factors that can have a negative impact on both mental health and social adjustment of Mexican children and adolescents.

Surveys conducted nationally revealed alarming data about the mental health situation of adolescents in Mexico; we highlight studies carried out by the National Institute of Public Health and the Juan Ramon de la Fuente National Institute of Psychiatry. Data presented in Table 15.1 were collected from the report of the Secretary of Public Education (SEP) related to the first National Survey of Exclusion, Intolerance and Violence in Public Middle Schools and High Schools (2008). The data collection was the responsibility of the National Institute of

School Mental Health: Global Challenges and Opportunities, ed. Stan Kutcher, Yifeng Wei and Marc D. Weist. Published by Cambridge University Press. © Cambridge University Press 2015.

Table 15.1 Signs of depressive symptomatology

Sign	% Men	% Women
Over the last month students experienced:		
Desire to cry	46	74.5
I couldn't stop feeling sad	47	61.5
I felt lonely	44	60
I felt that people didn't like me	43	54
I felt fearful	44	56
I thought my life had been a failure	36	45
I lost appetite	46	62
I felt sad	62	80
Students that have felt, thought, or done:		
Their life feels meaningless	29	43
They have been in situations for which they want not to live anymore	29	46
They have thought that dying was worth more than being alive	19	30.5
They were about to commit suicide	8.5	17
They have injured themselves with the purpose of committing suicide	5	12

Source: (SEP, 2008).

Public Health and corresponds to feelings of failure, difficulty regulating sadness, and both conception and intention to commit suicide; the data matches that presented by Borges, Medina-Mora, Zambrano and Garrido (2006). Their study pointed out that in 2002 suicide was the ninth cause of death for 5–14-year-olds, and the third cause for 15–29-year-olds.

The study conducted by the Ramon de la Fuente National Institute of Psychiatry is part of an international initiative coordinated by the World Health Organization, that in co-financing with the National Council of Science and Technology (CONACYT) and the SEP, started data collection for the National Survey of Mental Health in Adolescents (Benjet *et al.*, 2009).

This study revealed that nearly half of the adolescents met criteria for a mental disorder at some time in their lives; phobias, impulsiveness, anxiety and affective disorders, and substance abuse prevailed. It is worth mentioning that phobias in particular were highly prevalent, with about 15% of the adolescents meeting the criteria within the last 12-months. It should also be noted that average age for onset was 12 years of age, for both generalized anxiety disorders and affective disorders. As a possible explanation to the phenomenon of a greater prevalence in adolescents rather than in adults, the study concludes that it may have to do with this generation's exposure to fast-paced social change and to greater stress and adverse events (Benjet *et al.*, 2009).

With respect to the treatment adolescents get, relevant data were found that derived from this same study. Less than 1 in 7 adolescents that presented symptomatology of mental disorders had received some kind of mental health service the previous year; and among those who made used of it, only half of them received a minimally proper treatment. Service use was categorized by sector. The "healthcare sector," which was identified as a proper treatment, consists of having consulted any mental health provider, including psychiatrists, psychologists, counselors, psychotherapists, mental health nurses, and social workers in a mental health specialty setting, or general medical practitioners; the "non-healthcare sector" included consulting in any setting other than a specialty mental health setting or consulting a religious advisor, and the use of complementary/alternative medicine including self-help groups. Finally, "school-based services" consisted of having attended a special-needs school or special classes or therapies in the school (Benjet *et al.*, 2009). The authors concluded that adolescents have very important and urgent needs that health services are not taking care of, a reason why greater priority should be given to implement a public health policy that can expand the availability of mental health services and also reduce the barriers for service utilization.

Social imbalance problems of adolescents in Mexico

In addition to what has been described, interpersonal relations problems as well as the alarming increase of violence and delinquency that have occurred in Mexico, need to be taken into account. According to official data that derive from the National Survey of Victims and Perception about Public Safety (ENVIPE), conducted by the National Institute of Statistics, Geography, and Informatics (INEGI, 2012), 30.6% of Mexican homes had at least one victim of crime. The National Survey of Exclusion, Intolerance, and Violence in Public Middle Schools and High Schools (SEP, 2008) was conducted with a representative sample of youngsters between 15 and 19 years of age; some of the results are presented in Table 15.2. It should be noted that, even when men tend to apply physical

Table 15.2 Percentage of students that have carried out the following actions against their classmates

Action	% men	% women
Insult	44	26
Ignore	40	43.5
Use nicknames	39	18.5
Reject	36.5	35
Hide their belongings	27	16
Gossip	22.5	31
Hit	15	7

Source: (SEP, 2008).

violence more often, women tend to be the source of more actions related to psychological violence, such as gossiping or ignoring.

The same study, which had a national sample of 14 306 high-school students, found that 1710 (11.95%) youngsters had been arrested for one or another reason; 482 (3.3%) confessed to have sold drugs during the last year and 1731 (12.10%) students were said to be gang members.

It is important to highlight that the diversification of activities is a main characteristic of youth gangs, who have gone through common illegal activities such as robbery, and moved on to be associated with organized crime such as drugs, prostitution, and human and gun trafficking, as emphasized in the study conducted by the Secretaría de Seguridad Pública (2010). This study revealed the existence of nearly 9384 gangs throughout the country.

According to Sullivan, it is important to use preventive measures in order to avoid this evolution. Following this same line, we present the results obtained by a study conducted by Ruvalcaba *et al.* (2012), where 18% of the sample studied was at risk of presenting conduct disorders; this percentage increases to 32% in those groups at risk, specifically male adolescents who are members of a gang or live in shelters. Additionally, it was found that male adolescents are the ones who tend mostly to get involved in this type of behavior, specially robbery and vandalism, misdeeds, graffiti, fights, and guns.

One of the purposes of the study by Ruvalcaba *et al.* (2012) was also to identify the influence of socioemotional competence over becoming involved in conduct disorders. Correlational results revealed significant associations among variables. Key variables associated with fewer conduct problems were stress management and interpersonal competence.

All these data point to the need for developing prevention strategies that are based on promoting protective factors among adolescents, toward more positive development and avoiding their involvement in risky behaviors. It is necessary to focus research on studying protective factors; on the implementation of programs that enable adolescents' proper use of internal and external resources, and form their perception with respect to their values and positive perspectives.

Efforts toward prevention and promotion of resilience

Research into universal school-based prevention for anxiety and depression has increased during the last decade, yielding promising results (Gladstone & Beardslee, 2009; Neil & Christensen, 2009). This research has focus on the identification of protective factors that could affect adolescents' mental health, such as social and emotional skills, and on the evaluation of social and emotional learning programs that aimed to increase students' resilience. An example of these programs is the *FRIENDS for Life* program, developed by Barrett and colleagues (Barrett, 2012a; 2012b) to promote children's and adolescents' emotional resilience. The program is being implemented in 22 countries around the world and has strong empirical support.

AMISTAD para Siempre (Barrett, 2008a; 2008b), the culturally adapted Spanish version of the *FRIENDS for Life* program, is a social and emotional program designed to enhance resilience in children and adolescents. It incorporates physiological, cognitive, and behavioral strategies to assist students in coping with stress and worry. The behavioral component includes the monitoring of feelings and thoughts, out-of-session mental imagery, exposure, and relaxation training. The cognitive component teaches students to recognize their feelings and thoughts and the link between them. It also teaches them to identify faulty cognitions and incompatible self-statements, and to elaborate alternative interpretations of difficult situations. Learning techniques include group discussion, hands-on activities, and role-play. The program can be delivered at all levels of prevention, early intervention, and treatment. It can be implemented at the universal, selective, or indicated level of prevention within a school or community setting.

The program consists of ten weekly sessions of 75 minutes, plus two booster sessions usually implemented one and three months after the tenth session. Approximately one session is dedicated to learning each of the seven steps represented by the *FRIENDS* acronym. The Spanish acronym is parallel to the English in terms of the concepts taught. After the introductory session, students start to learn the letter *F*, which stands for "Feeling worried?" followed by the letter *R* for "Relax and feel good," *I* for "Inner helpful thoughts," *E* for "Explore solutions and coping plans," *N* for "Nice work; reward yourself," *D* for "Don't forget to practice," and *S* for "Smile and stay calm." Within each session, the facilitator models the skills, and after the skills are taught, students have opportunities to practice in small groups and debrief with the whole group. The program encourages the building of social support groups and respect for diversity. There are two informational sessions for parents of about 1.5 hours each. In these sessions parents learn about the skills and techniques taught in the program, about the importance of family and peer support, and the practice of problem solving rather than avoidance of anxiety-provoking situations. A healthy family step plan and effective parenting strategies are also provided.

There have been significant revisions in the most recent editions of the *FRIENDS for Life* programs (Barrett, 2012b). In line with new scientific findings, new editions include more content encouraging positive attention and mindfulness practice, community involvement, altruism, and empathy for all living beings and the environment. Furthermore, there has been an increased focus on connecting with extended family and the community, as well as encouraging the recognition of both distant and close connections. Lastly, home activities have been expanded to encourage better sleep, healthy eating, and physical activity (Barrett *et al.*, 2013).

The *FRIENDS for Life* program has been endorsed by the World Health Organization as an effective program for the prevention and treatment of anxiety and depression in children and youth (World Health Organization, 2004). The program is also one of the programs listed in the National Registry of Evidence-Based Programs and Practices (NREPP) of the Substance Abuse and Mental Health Services Administration (SAMHSA) in the United States (NREPP, 2014). Several studies from different parts of the world have evaluated the program effectiveness at the universal level of prevention (e.g., Barrett & Turner, 2001; Essau *et al.*, 2012; Stallard *et al.*, 2005).

A number of studies have evaluated this program with Mexican children and adolescents. To illustrate, Gallegos *et al.* (2013a) evaluated the effectiveness of the *AMISTAD para Siempre* program with 1031 Grade 4 and 5 students (ages 9–11). Eight schools from a northern city in Mexico were randomly selected and assigned to either an intervention or standard curriculum instruction. All schools in the study were categorized as level six, which reflects low SES and accounts for 70% of the population (INEGI, 2006). Fifteen teachers implemented the *AMISTAD para Siempre* program for ten consecutive weeks, and 16 served as control. The impact of the program was evaluated immediately after the intervention and after six months. The program showed a positive effect by reducing symptoms and risk for depression, and increasing the proactive coping skills of the overall sample. Fidelity of implementation was assessed randomly in 17% of the sessions, indicating a mean for treatment structure was 3.05/4.00 and the mean for teachers' skills was 3.18/4.00, indicating that the program was implemented moderately well.

Social validity was also evaluated (Gallegos *et al.*, 2013b). Participants were 498 students, ages 9–11, who received the *AMISTAD para Siempre* program. Upon completion of the program, students, parents, and teachers were surveyed regarding their perceptions on the utility and enjoyability, and their global satisfaction. Results indicated that students, parents, and teachers evaluated the program as helpful and enjoyable. Particularly, teachers reported that most of them learned a lot about enhancing resilience in their students, and that the program was very useful for them. These findings are similar to results that have been reported with Australian, Canadian, and German populations, thus suggesting that the program is likely to be well received in a school setting. Gender differences were found; girls reported the program as more useful and enjoyable than did boys. The skill that students and parents found more useful was changing negative thoughts into positive, and positive correlations were also found between level of satisfaction and outcome measures. The correlations suggested that the higher the level of students' satisfaction with the program, the lower the scores on the depression scale and the higher the scores on the proactive coping skills scale.

Other studies of *FRIENDS* adapted for Mexican youth include one focused on children living in an orphanage (Gallegos *et al.*, 2012), children dealing with cancer (García, 2013), and with preschool children (Zertuche, 2012). The results of the studies conducted with Mexican youth are similar to the findings that have been reported by other investigators, and suggest that providing *FRIENDS for Life* as a universal prevention program is an effective strategy for promoting school mental health. The fact that the intervention can be delivered by classroom teachers is an added benefit that adds to the cost-effectiveness of the prevention strategies since a large number of students can be reached over a relatively short period of time (Gladstone & Beardslee, 2009; Neil & Christensen, 2009). In order to strengthen the benefits of the program, further studies should increase parental involvement and try to include more positive measures that could provide a better picture of students' level of resilience before and after the program.

In conclusion, the key areas of progress on the mental health state of Mexican adolescents are related to the identification of mental health problems in youth using validated instruments from the WHO, and in conducting correlational research to identify risk and protective factors for problems such as anxiety, depression, and conduct disorders. This has been a major step, as most of the studies have been focused on adults. Further studies should include a more representative sample that includes adolescents from other states of the country with a more comprehensive age range. There has been progress as well in the promotion of school mental health in adolescents, through the implementation of evidence-based resilience programs such as *FRIENDS for Life*. However, more research is needed that includes the implementation and evaluation of other programs beyond *FRIENDS for Life*, and that includes also a more representative sample.

In summary, there are major challenges to improving mental health among adolescents in Mexico, including high levels of poverty, increasing violence and gang involvement, and general limitations in systems focused on promoting mental health and treating mental health challenges. There has been some progress, but this has been focused more on implementing and testing specific evidence-based interventions for

Mexican youth, such as the *FRIENDS for Life* program. As of yet, there has been little systemic change toward broader efforts to scale up a full continuum of mental health promotion, prevention, and intervention for youth in schools, and ideas in this book on experiences in doing the same in other countries will be a useful tool for much needed multi-sectoral policy improvement.

School mental health in Chile

Social and educational background in Chile

The National Statistics Institute (INE) and the National Child Service (SENAME) worked together on the design of public policies to improve the living conditions and development of children and adolescents in Chile (SENAME & INE, 2005). By 2002, 30% of 15 million inhabitants were children and adolescents under 18; 14% were between 6 and 13 years. Unfortunately, for the Census of 2012, there were procedural mistakes that have generated technical and political disputes in the country, so it has not been possible to update this information.

Regarding education, since 2003 comprehensive education – primary and secondary – is obligatory in Chile, and the state is the funding guarantor, as stated in Law 19.876 (MINEDUC, 2003). The net rate of children between 0 and 5 years attending preschool education in Chile by 2011 was 43%, with a lower rate for socially disadvantaged groups. The net attendance rate of basic education was 92% by 2011, but this changes in secondary education, with net rate of attendance being 72%; again, within this figure there are differences between poorer and richer populations (68% versus 84%). The reasons for not attending classes in this period are: "pregnancy, maternity or paternity" (12%), "not inter-ested" (12%), "finish school" (18%), "economic difficulties" (14%), and "other reasons" (16%) (Ministry of Social Development, 2011).

Psychosocial risk and prevalence of mental health problems in children and adolescents in Chile

Regarding the psychosocial risk and the prevalence of mental disorders, the psychosocial vulnerability in Chile is higher in rural households (50.8%) and those in the lower socio-economic stratum.

The data are extracted from two main surveys measuring psychosocial vulnerability in Chile: the National Socio-Economic Survey (CASEN) developed by the Ministry of Social Development (Ministerio de Desarrollo Social) and the CENSUS (CENSO) applied by the INE.

CASEN measures poverty through income and determines indicators of poverty and indigence. The same methodology has been used since 1987, with comparable indicators over time, making it possible to assess their developments, and has wide application, allowing comparison of the national situation with that of other countries.

Poverty and extreme poverty are measured in absolute terms, using income as an indicator of the ability to satisfy basic needs, so that these minimums are stated in terms of a certain income level – the poverty line. The poverty line is the minimum stated amount per person to meet food needs.

This survey characterizes households in categories, defining income as the sum of autonomous household income, monetary transfers received by the home from the state, and the imputed rent of the house. The psychosocial vulnerability indicators are the incidence of poverty and extreme poverty.

The Census allows characterization of the population for the implementation of social, health, and education programs.

The Census demonstrates differences in illiteracy, an educational gap in average years of schooling, and access to technologies (Census 1992–2002). Similar results were observed for the years of schooling (Ministry of Social Development, 2011). Recent results from the Longitudinal Survey of Early Childhood (ELPI) reported that from a cohort of 14 000 children between six months and seven years, 57.2% had a normal developmental level and 27.8% were delayed, with an accumulation in lower-income groups.

The "at risk" and "advanced" groups of the same cohort completes the sample (Microdata Center of the University of Chile, 2012). In the same study, 23.8% of children presented socioemotional problems at a clinical range. A higher figure (31.1%) was reported for lower-income groups (Microdata Center of the University of Chile, 2012).

In 2009 the aim of a large epidemiological state-funded study was to determine the prevalence of mental disorders in children and adolescents during a year. A sample of 1558 children and adolescents was evaluated. The prevalence rate for any psychiatric disorder was 22.5% (19.3% for boys and 25.8% for girls). The prevalence rate was higher among the children, aged 4–11, in comparison with adolescents, aged 12–18 (27.8% and 16.5%, respectively). The most prevalent diagnoses were disruptive disorders (14.6%) and anxiety disorders (8.3%), followed by affective disorders (5.1%) and substance abuse (1.2%). Eating disorders and schizophrenia were infrequent (Vicente et al., 2012).

Efforts toward prevention and promotion of resilience

Twenty-three years ago, Chile signed the Convention on the Rights of the Child in 1989, which together with the progress of democratic, social, educational, and health services, laid the foundations for the development of integrated public policies for preschool- and school-aged children. Currently, there are three public preventive programs for children and adolescents: "Chile Grows with You," "Skills for Life," and "Chile Prevents."

"Chile Grows with You" (Chile Crece Contigo), although it is not a school program, represents a milestone in care, promotion, and universal prevention for early childhood. It ranges from pregnancy until the child enters school. It promotes child development in the most vulnerable, protects childhood, and accompanies and supports all children and their families (Sectoral System of Social Protection, 2009; SENDA, 2011).

In Chile, for over ten years, the National Board of Student Aid and Scholarships (Junta Nacional de Auxilio Escolar y Becas), through the School Health Program, developed a universal and targeted intervention program for municipalities that recorded higher rates of psychosocial risk, called "Life Skills Program" (Programa Habilidades para la Vida). It engages in promotional activities with children, parents, and teachers, and detects and intervenes with risk groups for adaptation and learning outcome (George & Hurtley, 2006). This program seeks to "develop a structured educational response at school community" for the academic success of children. This program is a benefit to the biopsychosocial development of children in primary school. The program measures are aimed at reducing risk factors and enhancing protective factors. In the short term, it aims to improve learning levels; in the long-term, it aims to promote psychosocial welfare and decrease damage for mental health in those children involved in the program. The actions are designed to reduce risk factors and enhance protective factors. Schools identify psychosocial risk through the construction of indicators called "risk profiles" in children who attend the preventive workshops implemented by the program. High-risk schools are determined by family income variables. Individual risk includes mother's age at birth, father's presence at home, child's chronic illness, school absenteeism, and mental disorders in the family, with or without impairment, and family involvement in the community (George et al., 2004). About 20% of schools in Chile are at risk, including 181 000 children receiving the program (Guzmán et al., 2011). The familial risk is associated to overall risk of children and is used in working with them.

The program detects the level of severity of mental health problems in childhood through the construction of special indexes in children in Grade 1 and implements a strategy of referral to the local network of healthcare (George et al., 2004). The same program has shown that mental health problems in Grade 1 predict significantly poor academic performance three years later and is an independent risk factor (Guzmán et al., 2011).

Up to the year of 2014, the program has been implemented in 1818 schools, distributed all along the country. The number of students included is 341 635, with an annual budget of US$8.7 million (JUNAEB, 2014).

The interventions of the *"Life Skills Program"* are stepwise, WHO-based (promotion/prevention/intervention), and has the support of the local community; consulting mental health authorities are Sheppard Kellam and Thomas Anders (Guzmán et al., 2011). This program has been evaluated through the years using outcome indicators (Delgado et al., 2006; Guzmán et al., 2011). The results are encouraging: 64.7% of schoolchildren prevention workshop participants leave the psychosocial risk category (George & Hurtley, 2006). In addition, children receiving intervention improved their scores in educational tests (Delgado et al., 2006), assessed by the Evaluation System of Education Quality (Sistema de Evaluación de Calidad de la Educación, SIMCE).

In Chile, the school dropout figures in 2003 reached a value of 0.7% between 7 and 13 years, and 7.2% between 14 and 17 years (Ministry of Social Development, 2011), with high prevalence of drug use in school dropouts, showing an inverse relationship to those who attend school. The National Council for the Control of Narcotics (Corporación Nacional de Control de Estupefacientes, CONACE) developed in 2002 a selective prevention program for children and adolescents at risk for school dropout (repeaters, high absenteeism, and school and conduct problems) to avoid deinstitutionalization (CONACE, 2005). The intervention strategies differed according to the psychosocial engagement areas compromised, with school reintegration being the objective of social integration in the educational field (CONACE, 2005).

Since 2010 the new national institution for the prevention of substance use (National Service for Prevention and Rehabilitation of Drug and Alcohol, or Servicio Nacional para la Prevención y Rehabilitación del Consumo de Drogas y Alcohol, SENDA) developed preventive programs within an integrated prevention and promotion system called *"Chile Prevents"* (Chile Previene), targeting abuse of drugs and alcohol (SENDA, 2011). *"Chile Prevents"* is a comprehensive and continuous program, starting in early childhood education. They are universal prevention programs included as educational projects in each school community, organized according to each school period. For example, the universal prevention program for children of 3–6 years is called "Treasure Hunt." It promotes skills development, attitudes, and habits of self-care and healthy lifestyles, and strengthens resources and competences. It is developed through the review of everyday situations in a participatory and proactive manner. The middle-school selective prevention program is called "In Time" and focuses on vulnerable educational institutions. The main objectives are to increase protective factors and to reduce risk factors, to increase parenting skills of significant adults, to prevent and/or reduce the consumption of drugs and/or alcohol, and to detect students with risk factors and refer those with high-risk drinking. So far there are no published reports on the outcomes of the *"Chile Prevents"* program.

By March 2014 the program had reached every school in the country, including municipal, subsidized, or private paid schools. It is also expected to certify 1500 schools as preventive schools.

Public policies and mental health programs

Since the restoration of democracy in 1990, the Chile government has passed legislation to propel the modernization of the state with a rights-based approach (Ministry of Health, 2011). Chile has developed public policies on child mental health and school prospectively, focusing on the highest risk groups in psychosocial development. The Ministry of Health formulated the National Mental Health Plan and Psychiatry, integrating aspects of mental health policy planning and programming. It recognized people's biological, psychological, and social dimension, and stimulated out-patient care with community-based approaches (Ministry of Health, 1999). At present, the focus is on rights and health equity and states that mental health remains at an unsatisfactory level. A National Mental Health Strategy considers the social determinants of health, cost-effective strategies for promotion, and outcome. It coordinates state, private, and civil society activities and programs. The objectives are the full development of the capacities of people, to improve good mental health in the population, to reduce social health determinants, to increase life skills, and to detect early and effective intervention on mental disorders and high risk factors in order to prevent the emergence of problems and mental disorders, and to improve quality of life of people with mental health problems and illnesses, ensuring the necessary treatments (Ministry of Health, 2011).

Primary mental health facilities

The current level of emotional/behavioral problems among children and adolescents in Chile is disturbing. It is estimated that about one-fifth of the population of children and adolescents in Chile have mental health problems that are serious enough to provoke psychosocial dysfunction (Vicente *et al.*, 2012).

There have been some promising approaches to addressing child and adolescent mental health needs at the national level. For example, at the end of 2010 the public health network attending children and adolescents had psychologists in all primary healthcare facilities, and there were 73 community mental health centers (Ministry of Health, 2011).

However, children under 18 years are mainly treated as out-patients, accounting for 28% of people treated, representing a smaller proportion of what belongs to this group (World Health Organization and Chilean Ministry of Health, 2006). The long-term objectives are to enhance, reinforce, and diversify network coverage for mental health in Chile (Ministry of Health, 2011).

Human resources and register

The distribution of human resources between urban and rural areas is slightly unequal, with a ratio of 1.4:1 for psychiatrists between the capital and regions, and every year the number of new psychiatrists specializing in children and adolescents is still low (World Health Organization and Chilean Ministry of Health, 2006). Additionally, mental health data and its management are limited by undue information systems, poor technological infrastructure, lack of online systems, and insufficient human resources (Ministry of Health, 2011).

Challenges and opportunities for the future

Public policies on child and adolescent mental health are evolving in Chile. There is a growing interest within the state to devote resources for child development. Recently, the National Council for Children was established, and its purpose is to implement the changes necessary to ensure the rights of children. This council will coordinate different institutions and sectors that are related to childhood and adolescence (Secretaria General de Gobierno, 2014). This represents an opportunity to develop programs that consider strategies for mental health promotion and the prevention of mental health problems/disorders in this group.

Schools of Medicine, such as the Graduate School of the University of Chile, are coordinating with the Ministry of Health for more training places for medical specialists in child and adolescent psychiatry in order to improve national coverage. In the last two years, training places increased twice (Specialist Training Program, Graduate School, Faculty of Medicine, University of Chile, 2014).

Moreover, the Secretariat of Crime Prevention, in association with a private foundation named "Paz Cuidadana," are developing a pilot program at schools called "PreVe," which is inspired by the "Positive Behavior Program" from the Institute on Violence and Destructive Behavior, University of Oregon, USA (Ministry of the Interior and Public Security, Secretariat for Crime Prevention, Prevention Area, 2010).

The challenge for the coming years is to establish networks for data collection and exchange of scientific information about evidence in program effectiveness of school mental health in Latin America. Currently, it seems that both Mexico and Chile have sufficient knowledge of the prevalence of mental health problems and mental disorder, and acknowledge the need for universal and targeted programs for at-risk child and adolescent development. Teams that currently perform interventions and research should share their experiences, enhancing the participation of different actors from the various institutions involved in the care of children.

Conclusions

A high number of school-aged population adolescents from Mexico and Chile are experiencing mental health problems. Barriers such as poverty and school dropout are present in both countries, but more pronounced in Mexico. Progress has been made in both countries to identify mental health problems and promote resilience in students, and to identify risks for mental health. However, many things can be done to improve the current work. For example, there is a need to develop and evaluate several prevention programs that could be implemented at different levels of prevention: universal, selected, and indicated. For this, it is crucial to continue studying risk and protective factors in order to identify "high risk" populations and provide them with tailored interventions that could address their particular needs.

Future work could benefit from learning about the effective practices that are being implemented in other countries; always taking into account the important role of culture. It is imperative to evaluate and document all efforts made through systematic assessments of outcome indicators. The major challenge will be to effectively integrate the scientific knowledge obtained into public policies that will promote youth's quality of life. This means developing tailored interventions using the epidemiological and correlational data obtained in previous studies, lessons learned from previous implementations, and international data regarding the theories and models that work for enhancing resilience in the youth population. In order to move toward equity and justice, children's and adolescents' protection should be guaranteed by offering real opportunities to improve their resilience, such as a prompt identification of mental health problems and access to proper treatment through a mental health service provider and/or access to resilience programs. Doing this should help to reduce the high prevalence of mental disorders and the disability associated with them.

The practical next steps for our countries rely on continuing the work that has been done, with more focus. This means conducting more comprehensive studies to understand the role that risk and protective factors play in the resilience of our children and youth, exploring the role of culture in the manifestation of mental health problems in Mexicans and Chileans, and incorporating this knowledge in the design of tailored interventions. Cross-cultural studies are part of our agenda as well. Appropriate measures to evaluate mental health status and resilience are scarce in our countries. We have been working on the validation of scales such as the Resilience Scale of Adolescents, and the validation studies of other related measures are part of our plans. Promoting dialogue between countries is also important; and learning more about what strategies and public policies have worked for us will provide guidelines for further actions. At the moment there are no formal Central/South American coalitions for child and adolescent mental health, and a critical next step will be creating one in order to expand and enrich our current work

References

Barrett, P. (2008a). *AMISTAD para Siempre: Cuaderno de Trabajo para Niños* [FRIENDS for Life: Workbook for children]. Brisbane, Australia: Australian Academic Press.

Barrett, P. (2008b). *AMISTAD para Siempre: Manual para Líderes de Grupo* [FRIENDS for Life: Manual for Group Leaders]. Brisbane, Australia: Australian Academic Press.

Barrett, P. M. (2012a). *FRIENDS for Life: Group leaders' manual for children* (6th edn.). Brisbane, Australia: Pathways Health and Research Centre.

Barrett, P. M. (2012b). *My FRIENDS Youth Resilience Program: Group leaders' manual for youth* (6th edn.). Brisbane, Australia: Pathways Health and Research Centre.

Barrett, P., Cooper, M., & Gallegos, J. (2013). Using the FRIENDS programs to promote resilience in cross-cultural populations (pp. 85–108). In Prince-Embury, S. & Saklofske, D.H. (eds.), *Resilience interventions for youth in diverse populations*. New York: Springer.

Barrett, P., & Turner, C. (2001). Prevention of anxiety symptoms in primary school children: Preliminary results from a universal school-based trial. *The British Journal of Clinical Psychology*, 40, 399–410.

Benjet, C., Borges, G., Mora, M., *et al.*, (2009). La Encuesta de Salud Mental en Adolescentes de México (pp.90–98). In Rodríguez, J., Kohn, R., & Aguilar-Gaxiola, S. (eds.), *Epidemiología de los trastornos mentales en América Latina y el Caribe*. Washington, DC: Organización Panamericana de la Salud.

Borges, G., Medina-Mora, M., Zambrano, J., & Garrido, G. (2006). Epidemiología de la conducta suicida en México, in Secretaría de Salud (pp. 205–236). *Informe Nacional sobre Violencia y Salud*. México: Secretaría de Salud:.

CONACE (2005). *Technical area for prevention, marginality program, psychosocial intervention, selective prevention of drug use for children and adolescents in social vulnerability*. Santiago, Chile: CONACE.

Convention on the Rights of the Child (1989). *Adopted and opened for signature, ratification and accession by General Assembly resolution 44/25 of 20 November 1989 entry into force 2 September 1990, in accordance with article 49*. Viewed September 24, 2013, www.ohchr.org/en/professionalinterest/pages/crc.aspx

Delgado, I., Zuñiga, V., & Jadue, L. (2006). Final consulting: A comparative study of students who participated in the life skills program and SIMCE 4th grade 2005. Internal document, JUNAEB.

Essau, C. A., Conradt, J., Sasagawa, S., & Ollendick, T. H. (2012). Prevention of anxiety symptoms in children: Results from a universal school trial. *Behavior Therapy*, 43, 450–464.

Gallegos, J. Linan-Thompson, S., Stark, K., *et al.* (2013a). Preventing childhood anxiety and depression: Testing the effectiveness of a school-based program in Mexico. *Psicología Educativa*, 19, 37–44.

Gallegos, J., Rodríguez, A., Gómez, G., Rabelo, M., & Gutierrez, M. (2012). The FRIENDS for Life program for girls living in an orphanage: A pilot study. *Behaviour Change*, 29, 1–14.

Gallegos, J., Ruvalcaba, N., Garza-Tamez, M., & Villegas-Guinea, D. (2013b). Social validity evaluation of the FRIENDS for Life Program with Mexican Children. *Journal of Education and Training Studies*, 1, 158–169.

García, J. (2013). Efecto de un programa cognitivo-conductual en la resiliencia de niños con cáncer. Master thesis in Health Psychology. Universidad Autónoma de Nuevo León.

George, M. & Hurtley, M. (2006). JUNAEB, Health School Department, Life Skills Program. Viewed September 24, 2013, www.junaeb.cl.

George, M., Squicciarini, A. M., Zapata, R., Guzmán, M. P., Hartley, M., & Silva C. (2004).

Early detection of risk factors for mental health in schools. *Revista de Psicología de la Universidad de Chile*, 13, 9–20.

Gladstone, T. & Beardslee, W. R. (2009). The prevention of depression in children and adolescents: A review. *La Revue Canadienne de Psychiatrie*, 54, 212–221.

Guzmán, M. P., Jellinek, M., George, M., *et al.* (2011). Mental health matters in elementary school: First-grade screening predicts fourth grade achievement test scores. *European Child and Adolescent Psychiatry*. DOI 10.1007/s00787-011-0191-3.

Instituto Nacional de Estadística Geográfica e Informática (INEGI) (2006). Regiones socioeconómicas de México. Viewed May 19, 2006, www.inegi.gob.mx/est/contenidos/espanol/sistemas/regsoc/default.asp?c=5688

Instituto Nacional de Estadística Geografía e Informática (INEGI) (2012). Encuesta Nacional de Victimización y Percepción sobre Seguridad Pública. Viewed September 8, 2013, www.inegi.org.mx/est/contenidos/proyectos/encuestas/hogares/regulares/envi pe/default.aspx

JUNAEB (Ministry of Education in Chile) (2014). Habilidades para la vida. Viewed October 23, 2014, www.junaeb.cl/habilidades-para-la-vida

Microdata Center of the University of Chile. (2012). Centro Microdatos. Viewed September 24, 2013, www.microdatos.cl

Microdata Center of the University of Chile. (2013). Encuesta Longitudinal Primera Infancia 2012. Viewed September 24, 2013, www.elpi.cl

MINEDUC (2003). Constitutional amendment establishing the obligation and fee for secondary education. Law 19.876. Viewed September 24, 2013, www.mineduc.cl.

Ministry of the Interior and Public Security, Secretariat for Crime Prevention, Prevention Area (2010). Programa PreVe. Viewed May 21, 2014. www.programapreve.gob.cl

Ministry of Health (1999). *National Mental Health Plan and Psychiatry*. Santiago de Chile.

Ministry of Health (2011). National Mental Health Strategy: a leap forward. Proposal for collective construction. Working Paper.

Ministry of Social Development. (2011). CASEN survey: Education module. Viewed May 19, 2014 www.ministeriodesarrollosocial.gob.cl

National Registry of Evidence-Based Programs and Practices (NREPP) (2014). Viewed March 9, 2014, www.nrepp.samhsa.gov/ViewIntervention.aspx?id=334

Neil, A. J. & Christensen, H. (2009). Efficacy and effectiveness of school-based prevention and early intervention programs for anxiety. *Clinical Psychology Review*, 29, 208–215.

Organización para la Cooperación y el Desarrollo Económico (OCDE) (2013). *Panorama de la Educación, México.* Viewed September 8, 2013, www.oecd.org/edu/Mexico_EAG2013%20Country%20note%20%28ESP%29.pdf

Patel, V. & Sumathipala, A. (2001). International representation in psychiatric journals: a survey of 6 leading journals. *British Journal of Psychiatry*, 168, 406–409.

Ruvalcaba, N., Salazar, J., & Gallegos, J. (2012). Competencias socioemocionales y variables sociodemográficas asociadas a conductas disociales en adolescentes mexicanos. *Revista CES Psicología*, 5, 1–10.

Secretaría de Educación Pública (SEP) (2008). 1era Encuesta Nacional de Exclusión, Intolerancia y Violencia en Escuelas públicas de Educación Media Superior. Viewed August 10 2013, www.sems.gob.mx/es_mx/sems/encuestas_de_exclusion_intolerancia_y_violencia

Secretaría de Seguridad Pública (SEP) (2010). Pandillas: Análisis de su presencia en Territorio Nacional. Viewed August 10, 2013, www.ssp.gob.mx/portalWebApp/ShowBinary?nodeId=/BEA%20Repository/1214175//archivo

Secretaria General de Gobierno. (2014). Consejo Nacional de la Infancia. Viewed October 17, 2014, www.consejoinfancia.gob.cl

Sectoral System of Social Protection. (2009). Chile Crece Contigo. Viewed September 24, 2013, www.crececontigo.gob.cl

SENAME and INE. (2005). Childhood and adolescence in Chile: census 1992/2002. SENAME and INE.

SENDA (2011). Chile prevents. Viewed September 24, 2013, www.senda.gob.cl

Stallard, P., Simpson, N., Anderson, S., Carter, T., Osborn, C., & Bush, S. (2005). An evaluation of the FRIENDS programme: A cognitive behaviour therapy intervention to promote emotional resilience. *Archives of Disease in Childhood*, 90, 1016–1019.

UNICEF, México (2011). La Adolescencia. Viewed August 18, 2013, www.unicef.org/mexico/spanish/ninos_6879.htm

University of Chile (2014). Faculty of Medicine, Graduate School, Specialist Training Program in Child and Adolescent Psychiatry 2014. Viewed October 17, 2014, www.postgradomedicina.uchile.cl.

Vicente, B., Saldivia, S. de la Barra, F., et al. (2012). Prevalence of child and adolescent mental disorders in Chile: A community epidemiological study. *Journal of Child Psychology and Psychiatry*, 53, 1026–1035.

World Health Organization (2004). *Prevention of mental disorders: Effective interventions and policy options.* Geneva: World Health Organization.

World Health Organization and Chilean Ministry of Health (2006). *Report of the evaluation of the mental health system in Chile using World Health Organization assessment instrument for mental health systems (WHO-AIMS).* Santiago, Chile: World Health Organization and Chilean Ministry of Health.

Zertuche, C. (2012). Efectividad del Programa AMISTAD y Diversión en el desarrollo de la resiliencia en niños de edad preescolar. Master thesis in Education. Universidad de Monterrey.

Chapter 16

Flourishing Schools in Aotearoa, New Zealand
The Wellbeing in Schools Model

Pauline Dickinson and Rebecca Peterson

Overview

Schools are both learning environments and social places. Quality relationships with peers, teachers, families, and the wider school community help provide a sense of safety, security, and connection – factors that contribute to positive mental health. The development of social and emotional learning skills in children and young people has resulted in enhanced positive attitudes toward self and others, strengthened connections to school and improved educational outcomes, as well as reductions in aggression, conflict, low mood, and anxiety (Catalano, Berglund, Ryan, Lonczak, & Hawkins, 2002; Zins, Weissberg, Wang, & Walberg, 2004). School-based initiatives focusing on promoting mental health and emotional competence have been shown to have a direct effect on educational achievement, as well as factors such as strengthened connections to school, a more positive school ethos, enhanced positive attitudes toward self and others, reductions in aggression, conflict, low mood, and anxiety, and the development of listening and communication skills among children and young people (Webster-Stratton & Reid, 2004).

Poor mental health is commonly associated with low academic achievement and higher rates of school suspension and expulsion (Zubrick, Silburn, Burton, & Blair, 2000). Schools have become concerned about increases in behavior problems, including aggression and bullying, which impacts on the wellbeing of children, peers, parents and family/whānau (which is a Māori-language word for extended family), the climate of schools, and academic achievement. Current approaches to addressing these behaviors in schools focus on promoting competence and developing social skills rather than using punitive and exclusionary disciplinary strategies (Weare & Markham, 2005). Better educational outcomes for children and young people have been associated with protective factors such as individual resilience, coping, connectedness to school, caring adults and peer group, and social support (McNeely, Nonnemaker, & Blum, 2002).

Schools with a focus on promoting mental, emotional, and social wellbeing will reap the following benefits: positive atmosphere; warm and settled tone; safe emotional environment; nurturing and caring attitudes; warm relationships between staff and students; respectful communication; meaningful participation by students; acknowledgement of positive effort and achievement; a sense of self-worth of all members of the school community; enhanced student learning and achievement; social cohesion and social connection; well-supported students and staff; and mental health needs will be addressed (Department of Education and Skills, Health Service Executive, & Department of Health, 2013).

School Mental Health: Global Challenges and Opportunities, ed. Stan Kutcher, Yifeng Wei and Marc D. Weist. Published by Cambridge University Press. © Cambridge University Press 2015.

Flourishing Schools provides a framework for schools to implement strategies to promote and support children and young people's wellbeing. The theoretical approaches that underpin the model are: mental health promotion; the Five Winning Ways to Wellbeing (Connect, Be Active, Take Notice, Learn, and Give); a socioecological perspective; community action; and community development. The model provides an evidence-informed framework consisting of core elements, a whole-school approach, and best practice principles for promoting mental, emotional, and social wellbeing. The implementation of the model involves four steps: preparation and planning; discovery; initiatives planning and initiative rollout. To assist schools there are practical ideas, activities, programs, and resources provided on how to build a flourishing school community. The model allows flexibility for schools to develop their own wellbeing initiatives according to their unique character and needs. There is also provision for staff professional development and time for planning and preparation that fits within the school calendar year, charter, and annual planning cycles.

The initiative was piloted and evaluated in two primary schools in Hawke's Bay, where children have been identified as a priority population for the promotion of mental, emotional, and social wellbeing. In 2008 children aged 0–14 years comprised 22.4% of the Hawke's Bay population (projected) compared with 20.8% nationally (Dickinson & Peterson, 2010). Rates of anxiety, stress, conduct, and attention disorders among children are higher in Hawke's Bay than nationally.

The model consists of

- a theoretical framework comprising
  - core elements
  - a whole-school approach
  - best-practice principles;
- a four-step process comprising
  - preparation and planning
  - discovery
  - initiatives planning and evaluation
  - initiative rollout;
- practical ideas, activities, programs, and resources on how to
  - build a flourishing school community
  - promote personal and social skills
  - target support for children with mental health concerns;
- professional development opportunities;
- evaluation support to assess quality and success.

Theoretical framework

This framework (Figure 16.1) consists of core elements, a whole-school approach, and best-practice principles for promoting mental, emotional, and social wellbeing. The core elements include a focus on the whole school community, the promotion of personal and social skills, and the provision of targeted support for children with mental health concerns. The whole-school approach shows the target population and the key policies and strategies that promote and support mental, emotional, and social wellbeing. The framework is underpinned by seven best-practice principles: whole-school approach, social competence approach, the implementation of initiatives that are grounded in theories of child

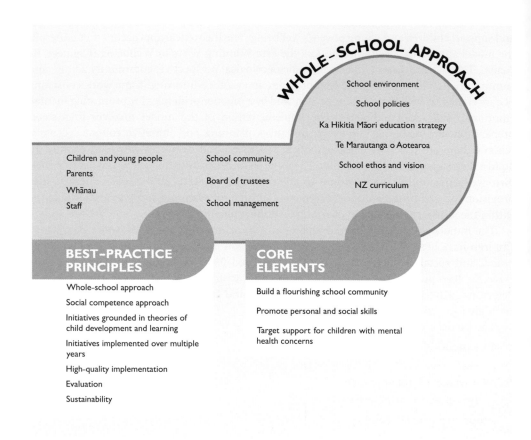

Figure 16.1 Whole-school approach.

development and learning, initiatives implemented over a number of years, high-quality implementation, evaluation, and sustainability (Barry & Jenkins, 2007).

The model provides a broadly focused framework to: strengthen individuals (e.g., life skills, coping, self-esteem to increase emotional resilience); strengthen schools and their communities (e.g., increasing social connections, inclusion, participation, and improving environments); reduce structural barriers to mental health in schools and communities (e.g., reducing discrimination and inequalities; provide schools with a multilayered, flexible, and diverse range of initiatives and opportunities rather than a one-size-fits-all approach); and consider all aspects of school life and the impact of these on mental health (e.g., school climate, policies, practices, events, teaching and learning; Adi, Killoran, Janmohamed, & Stewart-Brown, 2007; Catalano *et al.*, 2002; Lister-Sharp, Chapman, Stewart-Brown, & Sowden, 2000). Thus the model is not limited to one part of the school, but is integrated across the school and the curriculum (Weare, 2011).

Theoretical underpinnings

The Wellbeing in Schools Model is underpinned by: mental health promotion; Five Winning Ways to Wellbeing; a socioecological perspective; community action; and community development.

Mental health promotion focuses on the notion of positive mental, emotional, and social wellbeing. Mental health promotion involves building individual resilience in the context of supportive environments (Joubert & Raeburn, 1998). In school settings, mental health promotion includes initiatives that build social skills, promote self-esteem, teach problem solving and conflict resolution skills, increase social connections and foster inclusion and participation. It involves implementing multiple strategies and multiple levels in a wide range of settings (e.g., school, home, and community) to address mental, emotional, and social wellbeing needs.

Five Winning Ways to Wellbeing was developed in the UK as a result of the government's Foresight program and the 2008 Mental Capital and Wellbeing project. Subsequently, the New Economics Foundation was commissioned to develop a set of five evidence-based actions to improve wellbeing – connect, be active, take notice, learn, and give, which are described below (New Economics Foundation, 2011).

Connect

> Connect with people around you. With family, friends, colleagues and neighbours. At home, work, school or in your local community. Think of these as the cornerstones of your life and invest time in developing them. Building these connections will support and enrich you everyday

Feeling close to, and valued by, other people is a fundamental human need and one that contributes to functioning well in the world. School connectedness is positively associated with academic achievement and students' sense of belonging and self-esteem (Jané-L lopis 2005). Community connections enable children and young people to identify with positive role models and engage in community activities where they feel safe, valued, and have opportunities to become meaningfully involved, which contributes to positive mental, emotional, and social wellbeing (Health Canada, 2008).

Be active

> Go for a walk or run. Step outside. Cycle. Play a game. Garden. Dance. Exercising makes you feel good. Most importantly, discover a physical activity you enjoy, one that suits your level of mobility and fitness.

The overall consensus is that physical activity is essential for wellbeing. In the case of children, it has been argued that "action is central to cognition" (Goswami, 2008, p. 19). It is recommended that children and young people participate in moderate exercise for a minimum of one hour, five or more times per week. Slower-paced physical activity such as walking has social benefits at the same time.

Take notice

> Be curious. Catch sight of the beautiful. Remark on the unusual. Notice the changing seasons. Savour the moment, whether you are on a train, eating lunch or talking with friends. Be aware of the world around you and what you are feeling. Reflecting on your experiences will help you appreciate what matters to you.

Taking notice, or mindfulness, means attending to and being aware of what is happening in the present moment with curiosity and kindness. Recent research shows that students who develop mindfulness are: able to think flexibly, retain knowledge, and be more creative; able to draw on previous knowledge to approach new learning in innovative ways; more engaged in learning; calm; able to manage stress effectively; and to relate well to others. Developing the skills to take notice will enhance children's self-awareness and understanding about what is happening here and now, thus linking their thoughts, emotions, and behaviors. This can help them respond more positively to situations by thinking before they act (Davis & Hayes, 2011; Rempel, 2012).

Learn

Try something new. Rediscover an old interest. Sign up for that course. Take on a different responsibility at work. Fix a bike. Learn to play an instrument or how to cook your favourite food. Set a challenge you will enjoy achieving. Learning new things will make you more confident as well as being fun to do.

For children, learning contributes to their social and cognitive development (Goswami, 2008). When they are engaged in learning, they attend better, increase their efforts, and enjoy challenges and mastering them. These skills can contribute to a love of life-long learning. Adults are positive role models for children when they extend themselves by developing new skills and interests.

Give

Do something nice for a friend, or a stranger. Thank someone. Smile. Volunteer your time. Join a community group. Look out, as well as in. Seeing yourself, and your happiness linked to the wider community can be incredibly rewarding and will create connections with the people around you.

Giving is a strategy that contributes to flourishing. Fostering a generous attitude is important for strengthening social bonds and this can enhance connectedness in a school environment. Working in teams, helping others, sharing and giving have been associated with a positive sense of self-worth. These kinds of behaviors help with children's social cognitive development and wellbeing. Promoting connection between children's wellbeing and wellbeing of the wider community can lay the foundation for future meaningful community connections (Health Canada, 2008).

In addition to mental health promotion and the five winning ways to wellbeing, a socioecological approach and community action and community development frameworks underpin the Flourishing Schools Model.

A socioecological approach positions individuals within the context of their social and physical environment and recognizes cultural influences, family influences, and society and peer influences on behavior. Children and young people in schools are constantly deriving meaning and understanding from these different influences as they navigate through school (Jané-Llopis, Barry, Hosman, and Vikram Patel, 2005).

Community action uses both research evidence and local expertise to focus on the environmental factors that influence mental health (that is, school and community systems rather than individuals). In schools the focus is on changing practices and developing effective policies (Brown, 1991).

Community development is used to describe approaches that focus on community empowerment through building capacity of community members. Within schools the aim is to enable school staff and students to define local issues and develop local solutions (Kretzmann, Mcknight, Dobrowolski, & Puntenney, 2005).

The core elements

Three core elements underpin the model (Figure 16.2). Each core element has a list of different initiatives that schools can implement. For example, the element "Build a flourishing school community" includes initiatives designed to increase social connections and a sense of belonging and increase social inclusion and participation.

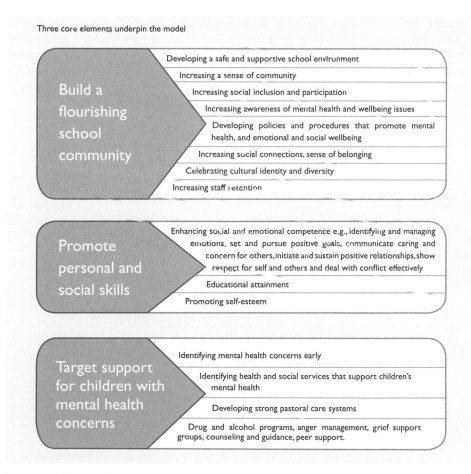

Three core elements underpin the model

Build a flourishing school community
- Developing a safe and supportive school environment
- Increasing a sense of community
- Increasing social inclusion and participation
- Increasing awareness of mental health and wellbeing issues
- Developing policies and procedures that promote mental health, and emotional and social wellbeing
- Increasing social connections, sense of belonging
- Celebrating cultural identity and diversity
- Increasing staff retention

Promote personal and social skills
- Enhancing social and emotional competence e.g., identifying and managing emotions, set and pursue positive goals, communicate caring and concern for others, initiate and sustain positive relationships, show respect for self and others and deal with conflict effectively
- Educational attainment
- Promoting self-esteem

Target support for children with mental health concerns
- Identifying mental health concerns early
- Identifying health and social services that support children's mental health
- Developing strong pastoral care systems
- Drug and alcohol programs, anger management, grief support groups, counseling and guidance, peer support.

Figure 16.2 The core elements.

Whole-school approach

The most effective approach to promoting mental, emotional, and social wellbeing is to take a school-wide approach which focuses on all members of the school community, as well as providing additional support for children who may be at risk of developing mental health difficulties (Patton, Glover, Bond, Butler, & Godfrey, 2000). Figure 16.3 shows a model for school mental health promotion adapted from the World Health Organization's School Change Model (Wynn, Cahill, Rowling, Holdsworth, & Carson, 2000). The model highlights the multiple layers necessary to support children and young people's wellbeing. Building a flourishing school community is represented in the widest part of the triangle, and this involves a whole-school approach, with the emphasis being on creating an environment that is conducive to learning. The second layer of the triangle signals the need to educate for and about mental health for everyone. In this way, children, young people, and adults can gain understanding, knowledge, and skills to support their own mental health and the mental health of others. The third level of the triangle signals the need for some targeted initiatives to support those children and young people with high mental health needs. These initiatives may be in the form of peer support groups, peer mediation programs, counseling and guidance, drug and alcohol programs, grief support groups, and anger management programs. The tip of the triangle signals the need for some professional support, which may involve individual, school-based counseling or referral when necessary to community agencies, and child and adolescent mental health services.

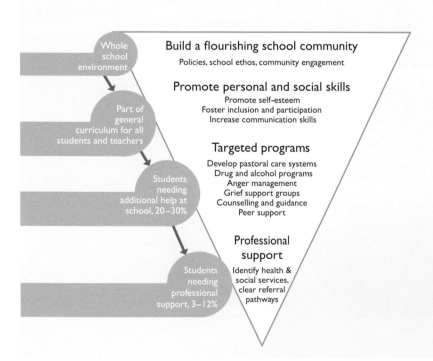

Figure 16.3 School mental health promotion model

Working within a geographic area

In keeping with the whole-school approach there are opportunities for schools to maximize wellbeing outcomes for children and young people by networking with other schools in a geographic area. The known benefits of working in this way include: more effective allocation and use of available resources such as finances, personnel time, space, and equipment; wellbeing initiatives being implemented at multiple levels; working with school systems rather than being individually focused, wider support for children and young people as they navigate through transitions and shared professional development opportunities (Adelman & Taylor, 2004).

Implementing the four-step process

The Wellbeing in Schools Model is designed to ensure schools have the best chance of achieving successful outcomes.

Step one: preparation and planning: the wellbeing team

The wellbeing team is led by a staff or board member and is made up of people with expertise and an interest in mental, emotional, and social wellbeing. This may be an existing committee or group who is willing to undertake this task, or a new group can be established. The wellbeing team is responsible for leading the school through implementation of the model and communication with the wider school community.

Step two: discovery

To assist schools to assess their mental, emotional, and social wellbeing needs and to help determine what initiatives to implement, the following tools are used: the Flourishing Environment Analysis Tool (FEAT), Photovoice, and a School Community Survey.

Flourishing Environment Analysis Tool

FEAT is a tool designed to help schools analyze policies, practices, and environments that influence flourishing and wellbeing. FEAT consists of four sections:

- *Discover* is the section for entering exactly what is happening in the school environment in relation to each FEAT question.
- *Analyze* helps question how useful or successful current practices are.
- *Aspire* requires consideration of what more can be done and is the section for creative visioning.
- *Action* provides the opportunity to choose one or two activities to implement.

FEAT questions

The following questions guide the discovery phase of FEAT. Questions can be asked in any order and answered over time. Actions can be implemented for one question while raising other questions at the same time. This allows for continuous reflection and refinement of wellbeing initiatives.

- How do school policies contribute to a sense of belonging and inclusion among staff and students and whānau/families?

Table 16.1 FEAT example

How do school policies contribute to a sense of belonging and inclusion among staff and students, and their whānau/families?			
Discover What is happening now?	**Analyze** How well is it happening?	**Aspire** What more could be done?	**Action (SMART)**
Example only: Whānau Ora policy has been written to ensure that the wellbeing needs of children are always considered along with those of their whānau.	It is too early to tell as the policy is very new.	The policy could be reviewed by a third party kaupapa Māori agency to ensure its cultural integrity and relevance.	**Action 1: third-party review of Whānau Ora Policy** • Identify appropriate agency to review the policy. • Agency reviews the policy and makes recommendations (if required). • Recommendations implemented and policy adopted prior to commencement of 2012 school year.

- How are relationships between all members of the school community fostered so that a warm and caring learning environment is created?
- What programs/activities exist that foster generosity, kindness, and gratitude among students and staff and their whānau/families?
- Are staff and students encouraged to be attentive to their immediate experience and surroundings? How does the school support this practice?
- Are staff and students encouraged to reflect on their own thoughts and feelings and how these impact on their day-to-day functioning?
- How are students supported to express and pursue their own interests?
- What processes are in place to identify the unique strengths and talents of students, staff, and whānau/families?
- How is choice and creativity being promoted for students in their learning?
- How are staff supported to pursue their own interests?
- How is being active for wellbeing promoted beyond health and physical education?
- Are the mental wellbeing and social benefits of being active well understood and promoted by the whole school community?
- How is physical activity used to promote teamwork and kindness?
- What are some of the emerging issues in your school community that may currently be impacting on the emotional and mental wellbeing of students, staff, and the wider school community?
- What is your school's vision statement and values? Do they promote flourishing/ wellbeing?

• Considering all of the above questions, which areas do you think could be developed further to help create a flourishing school environment?

Photovoice

Photovoice is an effective way of engaging children and young people to share concerns, ideas, and issues about school that are important to them. It also provides an opportunity to bring students and teachers together to share viewpoints and find out more about each other (Wang & Burris, 1997).

The benefits of Photovoice include: the ability to provide instant results from digital cameras; the development of creative skills; providing an opportunity for reflection and review of a familiar environment; anyone can take a photograph and tell a story; "a picture can show a thousand words"; photographs can provide more information than words alone; a method to convey messages to people in power such as school managers, policy makers, local councils, and community members (Wang & Burris, 1997).

Questions are developed to focus the Photovoice research. Students discuss the questions to ensure they understand them. Photovoice is best implemented over approximately eight to ten weeks using a team of 20–25 students with a range of abilities, cultures, and ages. The team attend training to explore the meaning of wellbeing at school, learn how to use a camera and the ethics of taking photographs. Below are some general and more specific questions that could be used.

General questions

• What is good about our school?
• What is not so good about our school?
• What would you like to keep about school?
• What would you like to change about school?
• What makes your school safe and supportive?
• What does your school do to promote a sense of community?

More specific wellbeing questions

• What does wellbeing mean to you?
• What helps you/students feel good at school?
• What makes you/students not feel good at school?
• What could be changed to make you/students feel good at school?
• What things at school make you feel worried or anxious?
• What things at school make you feel you belong?
• How do people care for each other at school?

School community survey

Schools interested in promoting student wellbeing understand the importance of building relationships with parents, carers, and families. The school community survey is a mixture of statements with rating scales and open-ended questions, such as how the school supports family wellbeing; local issues that may be affecting children and family wellbeing; whether the school is welcoming and inclusive; whether the school promotes home and school links;

how wellbeing could be promoted at school; whether the school fosters a sense of belonging; and the value placed on cultural difference.

Initiatives planning and evaluation

Once the discovery phase is completed, schools receive a report which identifies key areas of focus on which to base wellbeing initiatives. For example, one of the pilot schools identified the need to build student social and emotional competence and the initiative selected was the FRIENDS program (Barrett, Farrell, Ollendick, & Dadds, 2006).

An overarching logic model was developed to show the expected outcomes from school-based initiatives. The model (Figure 16.4) is read from bottom to top and shows the short-, medium-, and longer-term outcomes. Schools then developed their own logic models to reflect their areas of focus and outcomes. The logic model was used to develop a framework for the evaluation.

Exemplar schools

This section describes the two exemplar schools, Porritt Primary School and Tamatea Primary School, the initiatives implemented, and a brief summary of the evaluation findings. The two schools conducted needs assessments using the FEAT tool, a parent survey, and a Photovoice project with children to identify the focus of their initiatives, which aimed to promote mental, emotional, and social wellbeing.

Porritt Primary School

Porritt is a Decile 4 primary school located in Napier. The school roll is approximately 320. The gender composition is female, 43%; male, 57%. The ethnic composition is New Zealand European/Pakeha 58%; Māori 41%; and Pacific 1%.

The wellbeing initiatives

The initiatives were a values-based program focusing on the school motto "Porritt PRIDE" and the implementation of a police education program "Doing the Right Thing" (New Zealand Police, 2005). This is a school-wide program that consists of classroom teaching about values and school-wide practice of these values. The program has regular sessions that have been adapted to meet the needs of different age groups. The focus for the first part of the program was on the value of respect and the second part focused on "right and wrong."

A *culturally responsive curriculum* responding to the needs of Māori children (Māori are the indigenous people of Aotearoa, New Zealand) was implemented through a whānau group held weekly. Children's learning occurred through storytelling and practicing traditional skills. The whānau group addressed key aspects of the Māori Education Strategy – Ka Hikitia (Ministry of Education, 2013) through emphasizing the importance of ako – effective and reciprocal teaching and learning – for and with Māori learners and the conditions that support it.

Evaluation findings

The values-based program evaluation findings

The values program enabled teachers to incorporate their own ideas as well as those from a prescribed values education program based around the teaching of core values. Teachers

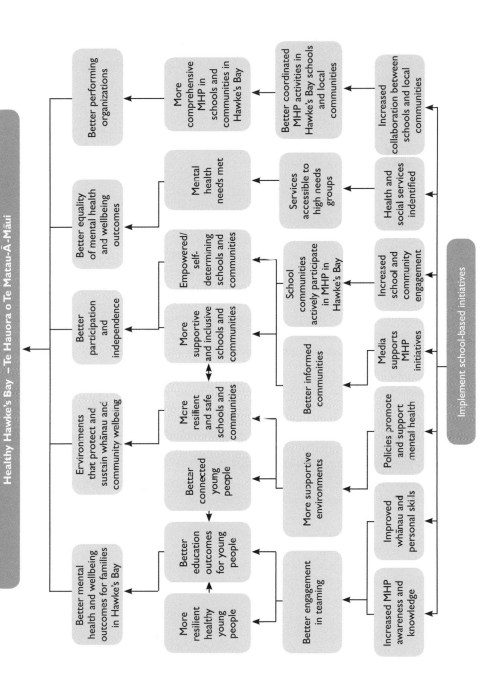

Figure 16.4 Overarching logic model.

were confident to deliver the program which was in keeping with the requirements of the New Zealand curriculum. There is clear evidence that the strong focus on respect and right and wrong across the whole school impacted positively on children's understanding and behavior in relation to these values, both in the classroom and in the wider school environment. The school experienced an improved tone and culture, fewer behavioral problems, decreased need for anger management support, and children were more settled, tolerant, accepting, and supportive of each other.

> I quite openly say to anybody who says "How is the school going at the moment?" Well, in the nine years I have been there this is the best our school has been running and one of our teachers who has been there for I imagine close to 25 years now said "This is my best year teaching ever." So those sort of comments coming spontaneously from people does say that we are making a difference at the moment. *(Principal)*

The culturally responsive curriculum findings

The whānau group program involved 45 Māori children with a mixture of girls and boys. The group met weekly for 45 minutes. The group ethos is about affirming a sense of belonging and connections through whakapapa[1] and whanaungatanga.[2] The group engaged in activities that promoted the five winning ways to wellbeing – being active, connecting, taking notice, learning, and giving. These evidence-based activities promote positive mental health.

Children learned through practical application of skills (such as making waka[3] from harakeke[4]), storytelling, and dialogue between the leader and the students. The leader commented that students were developing pride from being involved in practical activities.

> I actually made it a really hands-on activity. We took the stalks out of flax bushes and we've cut them and shaped them and we've made waka. You know, model wakas and we've talked about the things associated with that and the tribal groups and so on but being hands-on the kids have all liked it, they've really enjoyed it and they've actually ended up with a product at the end of it that they're proud of . . . there's a certain pride in what they've done.

Children expressed their enthusiasm for what they were learning in the whānau group.

> I learnt karakia.[5] I made a model waka. I learnt to cut carefully. I used flax stalks for the first time. I learnt about the wakas and where they came from.

Tamatea Primary School

Tamatea is a Decile 3[6] primary school located in Napier, providing education for students in Years 1–6. The school roll is approximately 184 and the gender composition is female 46%

---

[1] Whakapapa refers to geneology.
[2] Whanaungatanga refers to attaining and maintaining relationships and connections.
[3] Waka is a Māori canoe. [4] Harakeke is a New Zealand flax. [5] Karakia refers to prayer.
[6] A school's decile rating indicates the extent to which it draws its students from low socioeconomic communities. Decile 1 schools are the 10% of schools with the highest proportion of students from low socioeconomic communities, whereas decile 10 schools are the 10% of schools with the lowest proportion of these students.

and male 54%. The ethnic composition is Māori 62%, New Zealand European Pākehā 26%, other ethnic groups 10% and Pacific 2%.

The wellbeing initiatives

FRIENDS for Life is an evidence-based early intervention and prevention program that focuses on preventing anxiety and developing social and emotional skills in children. Teachers participate in a one-day professional development session prior to implementing the program. It is classroom-based and delivered as part of the curriculum throughout the whole school. FRIENDS is designed to encourage peer and experiential learning in a safe and supportive environment.

Promote a safe and caring environment: Tamatea Primary School teachers identified the promotion of a safe and supportive environment as a priority area. The school behavior policy is the guiding document that contributes to this. Six core values being taught were: cooperation, responsibility, perseverance, tolerance, honesty, and kindness. Recognition and reward schemes which acknowledged children practicing these values at school were displayed in classrooms and around the school. The school prides itself on having an open-door policy and provides weekly breakfasts where families are welcomed to regularly meet and build relationships and a sense of belonging with teachers and the wider school community.

Evaluation findings

Positive results from the implementation of the FRIENDS program were that children experienced enhanced personal and social skills which included: more positive self-esteem; more positive interactions with teachers and peers; improved ability to understand emotions and how to respond; and being able to think about challenging situations in more positive and powerful ways; they also showed a clear understanding of the value of respect.

Conclusion

The Flourishing Schools initiative is based on sound mental health promotion principles, is evidence-informed, and has a logical sequence of expected outcomes from the interventions implemented. To date, the initiative has been piloted in two schools in Hawke's Bay and the evaluation findings are promising and contribute to the evidence base for what works to promote mental, emotional, and social wellbeing in school settings.

The two schools have implemented different initiatives to promote and support the mental, emotional, and social wellbeing of children using the Flourishing Schools Model. Both initiatives are showing some promising early outcomes. Both schools have adopted a school-wide approach which has focused on creating change at the individual, classroom, and school levels. The initiatives implemented are based on a social competence approach which focuses on the promotion of resourcefulness and generic coping and competence skills rather than focusing on specific problems. The initiatives have used interactive and participatory approaches and have provided children with the opportunity to apply the skills they have learned in the classroom to wider social contexts. The two interventions are grounded in theories of child development and learning (Barry & Jenkins, 2007).

The two schools recognize the need for the interventions to be ongoing in order to produce lasting effects for children. The implementation of the initiatives has had a high level of support from school management and children are engaged and are enjoying their learning. Teachers have been trained and are confident in their ability to deliver the initiatives. They have access to quality resources which they have adapted to better meet the learning needs and styles of the children.

The next step for flourishing schools is to roll-out the initiative to more schools in the Hawke's Bay region and to continue to evaluate the quality and success of the initiative. The authors have also developed a Flourishing Schools resource to assist schools with implementation of the initiative.

References

Adelman, H., & Taylor, L. (2004). *Mental health in schools: Reflections on the past, present and future – from the perspective of the Center for Mental Health in Schools at UCLA.* Los Angeles, CA: Department of Psychology, UCLA.

Adi, Y., Killoran, A., Janmohamed, K., & Stewart-Brown, S. (2007). *Systematic review of the effectiveness of interventions to promote mental wellbeing in primary schools: Universal approaches which do not focus on violence or bullying.* London: National Institute for Clinical Excellence.

Barrett, P. M., Farrell, L. J., Ollendick, T. H., & Dadds, M. (2006). Long-term outcomes of an Australian universal prevention trial of anxiety and depression symptoms in children and youth: An evaluation of the FRIENDS Program. *Journal of Clinical Child and Adolescent Psychology*, 35, 403–411.

Barry, M., & Jenkins, R. (2007). *Implementing mental health promotion.* Philadelphia, PA: Churchill Livingstone Elsevier.

Brown, E. R. (1991). Community action for health promotion: A strategy to empower individuals and communities. *International Journal of Health Services*, 21(3), 441–456.

Catalano, R. F., Berglund, L., Ryan, A. M., Lonczak, H. S., & Hawkins, J. (2002). Positive youth development in the United States: Research findings on evaluations of positive youth development programmes. *Prevention and Treatment*, 5(1), n.p.

Davis, D. M., & Hayes, J. A. (2011). What are the benefits of mindfulness? A practice review of psychotherapy-related research. *Practice Review*, 48(2), 198–208.

Department of Education and Skills, Health Service Executive, & Department of Health. (2013). *Wellbeing in post-primary schools: Guidelines for mental health promotion and suicide prevention.* Ireland Department of Education and Skills, Health Service Executive, and Department of Health.

Dickinson, P. & Peterson, R. (2010). Mental health promotion plan, Hawke's Bay District Health Board.

Goswami, U. (2008). *Learning difficulties: Future challenges.* London: The Government Office for Science.

Health Canada. (2008). *Outreach, early intervention and community linkages for youth with problem substance use.* Ottawa: Government of Canada.

Jané-Llopis, E. (2005). From evidence to practice: Mental health promotion effectiveness. *Promotion & Education*, 1 (suppl), 21–27.

Jané-Llopis, E., Barry, M., Hosman, C., & Vikram Patel, V. (2005). *Mental health promotion works: A review. Promotion & Education*, 12(9), 9–25.

Joubert, N., & Raeburn, J. (1998). Mental health promotion: People, power and passion. *International Journal of Mental Health Promotion*, 1, 15–22.

Kretzmann, J. P., Mcknight, J. L., Dobrowolski, S., & Puntenney, D. (2005). *Discovering community power: A guide to mobilizing local assets and your organisation's capacity.* Evanston, IL: Asset-Based Community Development Institute.

Lister-Sharp, D., Chapman, S., Stewart-Brown, S. L., & Sowden, A. (2000). Health promoting schools and health promotion in schools: Two systematic reviews. *Health Technology Assessment*, 3(22), whole issue.

McNeely, C. A., Nonnemaker, J. M., & Blum, R. W. (2002). Promoting school connectedness: Evidence from the national longitudinal study of adolescent health. *Journal of School Health*, 72(4), 138–146.

Ministry of Education (2013). *Ka Hikitia Accelerating Success 2013–17*, Wellington: Ministry of Education.

New Economics Foundation. (2011). Winning ways to wellbeing: new applications, new ways of thinking. Available from www.neweconomics. org/publications/entry/five-ways-to-wellbeing (accessed November 3, 2013).

New Zealand Police (2005). *Doing the Right Thing, Fostering Positive Values, Lessons for Primary School Classes.* Auckland: New Zealand Police.

Patton, G. C., Glover, S., Bond, L., Butler, H., & Godfrey, C. (2000). The Gatehouse project: A systematic approach to mental health promotion in secondary schools. *Australian and New Zealand Journal of Psychiatry*, 34, 586–593.

Rempel, K. (2012). Mindfulness for children and youth: A review of the literature with an argument for school-based implementation. *Canadian Journal of Counselling and Psychotherapy*, 46 (3), 201–220.

Wang, C., & Burris, M. A. (1997). Photovoice: Concept, methodology, and use for participatory needs assessment. *Health Education Behavior*, 24 (3), 369–387.

Weare, K. (2011). Mental health and social and emotional learning: Evidence, principles, tensions, balances. *Advances in School Mental Health Promotion* 3(1), 5–17.

Weare, K., & Markham, W. (2005). What do we know about promoting mental health through schools? *Promotion & Education*, X11 (3–4), 118–122.

Webster-Stratton, C., & Reid, J. (2004). Strengthening social and emotional competence in young children: The foundation for early school readiness and success – Incredible Years classroom social skills and problem-solving curriculum. *Infants and Young Children*, 17 (2), 96–113.

Wynn, J., Cahill, H., Rowling, L., Holdsworth, R., & Carson, S. (2000). Mind Matters, a whole-school approach to promoting mental health and well-being. *Australian and New Zealand Journal of Psychiatry*, 34 (4), 594–601.

Zins, J. E., Weissberg, R. P., Wang, M. C., & Walberg, H. (2004). *Building academic success on social and emotional learning.* New York: Teachers College Press.

Zubrick, S. R., Silburn, S. R., Burton, P., & Blair, E. (2000). Mental disorders in children and young people: Scope, cause and prevention. *Australian and New Zealand Journal of Psychiatry*, 34, 570–578.

Universal schooling and mental health

Toward school mental health in northern Ghana

Amanda Lee, Marissa Smith-Millman, Heather McDaniel,
Paul Flaspohler, Peter Yaro, and Mark D. Weist

School mental health (SMH) in Ghana is virtually non-existent; this is especially so in the northern regions of the country. Universal schooling in Ghana is similarly under-prioritized, though to a lesser extent. That is, many children in northern Ghana have either never been to school or have not completed basic education. This chapter aims to address the lack of SMH in northern Ghana within the greater context of the country's struggles with universal schooling and the provision of mental health services to children and youth. Further, the chapter aims to function as a "call to arms" for implementation of SMH services in northern Ghana. Throughout the chapter, the authors will interweave vignettes and quotes from informal interviews conducted with teachers and principals from Yumba Special School, one of northern Ghana's two schools for children with special needs, and members from a non-profit organization involved with Yumba Special School, BasicNeeds. Finally, we will provide suggestions about how to begin implementing quality SMH services and move forward. The chapter represents a "far left" example in the left to right continuum of very limited to advanced SMH development, with lessons relevant to other developing nations with significantly underdeveloped education and mental health systems, and essentially non-existent SMH systems.

The chapter consists of five sections. The first section provides a brief history of universal schooling in Ghana. It explains the current state of universal schooling throughout the country, with an emphasis on northern Ghana, and discusses what Ghanaian schools are doing to address mental health in schools. The second section broadens the discussion to include what is known about child and adolescent mental health and treatment in Ghana. The third section describes existing barriers to the further development of the education and mental health system in northern Ghana. This is followed by a section highlighting innovative strategies aimed at addressing the gap between child and youth mental health problems and available mental health services. Finally, the chapter ends with suggestions about how to promote key stakeholder collaboration as a guide for beginning to implement SMH services in northern Ghana.

School Mental Health: Global Challenges and Opportunities, ed. Stan Kutcher, Yifeng Wei and Marc D. Weist. Published by Cambridge University Press. © Cambridge University Press 2015.

Universal schooling in northern Ghana

A brief history of universal schooling

Ghana has been striving to achieve universal basic education for over half a century (Agbemabiese, 2010; Akyeampong, 2006; 2009; 2010). After declaring independence from Britain in 1957, the new Ghanaian government pushed for universal education in hopes of accomplishing three goals: having a scientifically literate population, overcoming the environmental causes of low productivity, and creating the knowledge needed to bolster Ghana's economy (Akyeampong, 2010). In 1961 Ghana's first president, Dr. Kwame Nkrumah, signed a new Education Act that made primary and middle education both free and compulsory (Akyeampong, 2006; 2009; 2010). This mandate included six years of primary school beginning at age six, and four years of middle school to follow. Although tuition fees were waived, students were still responsible for paying for transportation, uniforms, and school supplies. This reform had a major impact on school enrollment, with rates doubling between 1961 and 1966 (Akyeampong, 2006). However, this expansion came at a cost. Ghana lacked the necessary number of trained teachers to cope with the increasing numbers of students, and quality of education suffered accordingly (Akyeampong, 2006). Further, the education expansion was greater in the southern region of Ghana than in the north. This created a gap in access to education between the south and north that still persists (Akyeampong, 2009).

The country experienced educational and economic decline in the 1970s and 1980s (Akyeampong, 2006; 2009; 2010). In response to this decline, the government passed another set of education reforms in 1987. These reforms restructured primary and secondary education by shortening it from 17 years to 12 years. In addition, the Ghanaian government also passed the Free, Compulsory and Universal Basic Education amendment, a constitutional amendment that deemed education a basic right and abolished all educational fees in hopes of increasing rates of enrollment and abolishing the education gap between the north and south (Akyeampong, 2009; Nudzor, 2012). However, by abolishing additional school fees, this amendment caused schools countrywide to lose revenue. As a result, schools enforced a variety of indirect fees, and students who failed to pay were sent home. This furthered the education gap because schools in wealthy areas were able to sustain themselves, whereas schools in poor areas were not (Akyeampong, 2009).

Current state of universal schooling

In 2011, 77% of primary school aged children in Ghana were enrolled in schools (The United Nations Educational, Scientific and Cultural Organization [UNESCO], 2011). Though this rate may seem high, rates of enrollment from 2011 show that pre- and post-primary school enrollment rates were very low, with only 18% of children enrolled in pre-primary education, 41% in secondary education, and a mere 8% in tertiary education (UNESCO, 2011). Further, when viewed by region, the massive education gap between the north and south of the country becomes apparent. That is, the three northern regions of Ghana, the Upper East, Upper West, and Northern Regions, have a much higher proportion of people who have never been to school, ranging from 44.5% to 54.9%, than regions in the south, ranging from 10.1% to 26.4% (Ghana Statistical Service [GSS], 2010).

Special and inclusive education

Special education and inclusive education are other important facets of universal education with which Ghana struggles (Adera & Asimeng-Boahene, 2011; Agbenyega, 2007; Kuyini & Mangope, 2011). That is, Ghana struggles to provide education to students with disabilities because most basic schools are ill equipped to provide such a service and there are very limited numbers of special schools. The Ghanaian government has created various policies throughout the years to address these issues. In 1951, Dr. Kwame Nkrumah introduced the concept of inclusive education into Parliament through the Education Reform under the Accelerated Development Plan. This reform cancelled school fees and introduced compulsory basic education for all children. With the subsequent formation of the National Education Act in 1961, these policies were enacted and the Ghana government assumed responsibility for the education of children with disabilities (Anthony & Kwadade, 2006). This act encouraged parents of children with intellectual disabilities to form the "Society of Friends of the Mentally Retarded "association in 1964. Following their strong advocacy campaigns, Ghana's first "home for the mentally handicapped" was established in 1966 (GES Special Education Division, 2005). The development of this home initiated a rapid growth in the number of segregated special schools for the visually impaired, the hearing impaired, and the mentally disabled through the 1980s. In 1985 the increasing national and international recognition of the need for special education services led the Ghana Education Service to form the Special Education Division (GES Special Education Division, 2005).

Ghana adopted several policies to further address inclusive education in subsequent years. In the 1998 constitution, the Children's Act imparted responsibility onto the government to promote the physical, mental, and social wellbeing of every child. Later, in 2006, the Persons with Disability Act was adopted; this act provided for the establishment of special education schools for children with severe special needs. Parents and guardians/caregivers assumed responsibility to enroll their children in schools that accommodated their level of disability. In the Education Act of 2007, all district-level government agencies were explicitly instructed to provide inclusive education; this policy is now under the new Mental Health Law Act.

Over the past decade there has been a significant increase in the number and types of special education institutions, from 22 to 200 special education schools, including inclusive education schools, special schools, schools for the deaf, schools for the blind, and schools for the developmentally disabled (Ministry of Education, 2008). Among these schools are 13 special schools for the mentally handicapped and 24 integrated schools for persons with intellectual disabilities (Casely-Hayford et al., 2011). However, the rapid growth of these special schools has largely been limited to the southern sectors of Ghana. Indeed, only a handful of the special education schools in the country are located in the northern regions. Of the 24 integrated schools in the country, only four are located in the northern sectors.

Providing inclusive education and/or education at special schools is how schools in northern Ghana have come to address mental health concerns in schools. To date, there exists no body of literature regarding school mental health in northern Ghana. In the subsequent sections of this chapter, we will discuss the similarly scarce information about child and adolescent mental health in northern Ghana, the barriers that impede the improvement of universal schooling and mental health services, as well as the few initiatives in place to address the mental health gap and future directions in SMH services.

Child and youth mental health in Ghana

Prevalence of child and youth mental health problems

It is estimated that one in five people suffer from a diagnosable mental illness in their lifetime (Patel *et al.*, 2007; WHO, 2001; 2003; 2005a). Among adults with a diagnosable mental disorder, approximately 75% developed the disorder in their youth, between the ages of 12 and 24 (Patel *et al.*, 2007). Despite the apparent burden of child and adolescent mental illness, there has been very little research conducted on the prevalence rates of child and adolescent psychopathology in low- and middle-income countries, and no prevalence rate studies have been conducted in Ghana (Cortina *et al.*, 2012). However, in a meta-analysis of community-based prevalence rate studies conducted in sub-Saharan Africa, Cortina and colleagues (2012) found that 14.3% of children have some form of emotional/behavioral disorder and 9.5% have a specific psychiatric disorder. These rates may be under-reported due to cross-cultural differences; for example, in traditional African cultures there is a tendency to express mental illness through somatic symptoms or to diagnose mental illness as "social problems" (Patel, 1995; Rahman *et al.*, 2000). Taking the WHO (2001; 2003; 2005a) estimates that approximately 20% of children worldwide suffer from mental disorders. Given this estimate, and that 29.5% of Ghana's population of 24 658 823 is under the age of 15 years (GSS, 2010; WHO, 2007), it is estimated that approximately 1 454 870 children and youth are suffering from mental health problems in Ghana, underscoring an urgent and largely unaddressed mental health need.

Risk factors for child and youth mental health problems

Given the pressing mental health needs of children and youth in Ghana, it will be critical to understand factors that contribute to and perpetuate these issues. Poverty and stigma are major risk factors for mental health problems in low- and middle-income countries. These factors may put children in Ghana at higher risk for developing mental illness than other populations (Earls & Carlson, 2001; Patel & Kleinman, 2003; Patel *et al.*, 2007; WHO, 2005a).

Poverty

Studies have shown that those living in lower socioeconomic areas are at greater risk of developing mental health problems as a result of the stress accompanying deprived living conditions, risk for trauma, or other negative life events, social exclusion, and food insecurity (Chatterjee *et al.*, 2009; Lund *et al.*, 2011; Raja *et al.*, 2008). Additionally, those suffering from mental health problems are at greater risks of financial struggle, as mental health problems are often associated with unemployment, increased health expenditure, and reduced productivity (Social Enterprise Coalition, 2011). This "vicious cycle" – where poor mental health leads to a greater risk of poor socioeconomic performance, while poor socioeconomic conditions leads to a greater risk of poor mental health – is a major barrier to treatment, and is likely especially so in the developing world.

Several poverty-related risk factors that increase morbidity and mortality of children in Ghana must also be considered. The first is malnutrition; children who are malnourished are more likely to suffer from poor mental development and poor school performance (Granthan-McGregor & Fernald, 1997; Pelletier *et al.*, 1993; 1995; Schroeder & Brown, 1994). In Ghana, 28% of children under the age of five have stunted growth, indicating chronic malnutrition. Moreover, the stunting rate among children in the poorest 60% of the country was found to be more than twice the rate of children in the richest 20% (GSS, 2008). With the poorer regions in the north, it is not surprising that higher levels of malnutrition have been observed for over a decade (Alderman & Mundial, 1990). Further, child labor is another poverty-related risk factor for child mental illness (Edmonds & Pavcnik, 2005; WHO, 1987). In sub-Saharan Africa one in three children between the ages of five and fourteen are economically active (Bass, 2004); this is recognized as the world's highest concentration of child labor. Within Ghana, 2.47 million children were identified as economically active through a survey conducted by GSS in 2003.

Despite the relationship between poverty-related risk factors and mental health among the younger population (Costello *et al.*, 2003), children and adolescents with disabilities are not currently integrated into the government's poverty-alleviation strategies. In a situational analysis of four African countries, researchers found that apart from the disability grants offered in South Africa, children and adolescents with mental health problems are not considered eligible beneficiaries of grants or paid support services. Further, current poverty-reduction strategies in developing countries have been generally targeted toward those with physical disabilities and not mental disabilities (Kleintjes *et al.*, 2010). Thus, despite the role poverty and its related risk factors play in the perpetuation of mental health problems in youth, these risk factors are not addressed in current policies.

Stigma and cultural perspectives on mental health problems

The burden of mental illness is further compounded by discrimination, often as a result of spiritual beliefs prominent throughout Ghana. Studies show that in Ghana, as in other African countries such as Uganda, Zambia, and South Africa, disabilities are often conceptualized through religious and spiritual beliefs (Kleintjes *et al.*, 2010; Mawutor & Hayford, 2000; Nukunya, 2003; Salm & Falola, 2002). People are more likely to give spiritual explanations for mental illness than scientific ones, particularly in the northern regions (Quinn, 2007). Discussions with teachers at Yumba Special School in the Northern Region reaffirm the results of these studies; "people do not believe it is a mental disability or mental retordation . . . they attribute it to something else."

Kleintjes and colleagues (2010) indicated that discrimination and violation of the rights of individuals with mental health problems extends to the familial level. Mental health workers in Ghana report that family members have been known to mistreat, alienate, or disown their relatives with mental health problems. For example, parents may attribute spiritual factors to child and adolescent mental illnesses and thus are often blamed or blame themselves for their child's struggles. This can result in denial of the child's right to education; teachers report that they "are not admitted into [main stream] schools. At times parents may also neglect the child, "They don't want to say 'This is my child'," and they may "allow them to go out roaming and begging" in the streets. In some extreme cases, parents may lock up their children. A teacher at Yumba special school describes one such case:

> I'm very close to Jonas. For a very long time, I've known him. I came here in 2007. At that time, he could not stand on his own feet. His parents had kept him locked up for a very long time. And because he consumed a lot of carbohydrates, he put on a lot of weight. So when he came, we gave him a stick to use, and we taught him first to take a step, and now he can move.

Many in the community "feel that [mental illness] is contagious," and they may refuse to touch children and adolescents with mental disabilities; at times, others "may even hit them." Teachers also report that some students are verbally or even sexually abused on the streets:

> There's this one girl I've heard about. Because this woman had this child, her husband divorced her. Now, she can't take care of her child alone. So the girl roams around. People abuse her sexually. People throw stones and call her by names.

Given these experiences, it is extremely probable that stigma and discrimination maintain and worsen mental health problems for children and youth in Ghana. However, here and throughout this chapter is the caveat that conclusions to be drawn on the status of affairs related to children and youth are based on very limited quantitative and qualitative data, and the experiences of the authors, three of whom have done significant work in the nation (AL, PY, PF).

Programs for child and youth mental health

Despite the vast need for mental health services, child and adolescent mental health programs are still scarce in most developing countries (WHO, 2005a). Many governments have under-prioritized the development of child mental health programs and have therefore not created policies to address these issues (WHO, 2001). In a study conducted by the WHO (2005b), only one-third of the 15 respondents, out of a total of 46 African WHO member states that were contacted, endorsed having any policies about child and adolescent mental health in their country. Notably, even within the five countries that responded favorably to having a child and adolescent mental health policy, there is a lack of human and material resources. This lack of resources often leads to the coexistence of many child and adolescent mental health programs within adult facilities, thus decreasing the focus on youth (Patel *et al.*, 2007).

Ghana is one such country without a national child and adolescent mental health policy. It has an overwhelming under-representation of child and youth mental healthcare throughout the country (Kleintjes *et al.*, 2010). Out of 70 outpatient facilities across the country, none exclusively address child and adolescent mental healthcare (Kleintjes *et al.*, 2010). Further, of the three total inpatient facilities in Ghana, the Accra Psychiatric Hospital, the premiere mental health facility in Ghana, is the only hospital with a unit specifically for children. This unit contains approximately 20 beds for children with a wide variety of conditions, ranging from developmental disorders to attention deficit hyperactivity disorder (Yaro, witness account). Moreover, there are no child and adolescent day treatment facilities in the country (Kleintjies *et al.*, 2010). Even within the mixed child and adult facilities, limited support is provided to children and adolescents. For example, only 4% of psychiatric beds throughout Ghana are allocated for children and adolescents (Kleintjies *et al.*, 2010). This begins to cast light on the dearth of services available for children and adolescents throughout Ghana, and given the immense demand for mental health services, it highlights the need to implement additional mental health services.

Barriers to improving universal schooling and mental health services

There are myriad reasons for the education and mental health services gaps in northern Ghana, including poverty and a dearth of economic resources, rurality, and a lack of trained personnel. Universal education and child and adolescent mental healthcare face similar challenges to effective practices. In the following section we outline how these factors serve as barriers to the improvement of the education and mental health systems in northern Ghana.

Poverty and a dearth of economic resources

Poverty is a major barrier to both universal education and child and adolescent mental healthcare. In terms of universal education, poverty has a major effect because it may necessitate the use of child labor. Many families in northern Ghana rely on agriculture and farming to make a living, and often their children start working on the farm around age eight (Akyeampong, 2009). Further, the GSS Ghana Child Labour Survey (2003) found that parents perceived their children's financial contributions to the household to be significant, indicating that the monetary incentive of keeping children out of school to work is high in this part of the country. Child labor also contributes to dropout and non-completion rates in the north because parents sometimes send their children to school during a lean season (a season of little or no harvest), but then withdraw them so that they can help during the harvest (Akyeampong, 2009).

On the other hand, special schools, like the Yumba Special School, struggle to retain students due to the lack of government and/or private funding. On a related note, mental health in Ghana, like many other developing countries, is severely underfunded by both the government (Saxena et al., 2007) and private donors such as pharmaceutical companies, charity trusts, and foundations (Raja et al., 2012). This, in turn, leads to a lack of service provision to children with special needs. Without external funding, these schools do not have a long-term financial solution to maintain their institution. A conversation with the headmistress of Yumba Special School illustrates the challenge of underfunding by the government and therefore overreliance on outside donors and NGOs:

> We have worked with so many groups, but they didn't come out so well to support us. But with a few NGOs, like RAINS, the support we had from them was great (like building a washroom and giving us a bus). And CAMFED, they have given us so far gas burners for the home economics department, cutlery and saucepans. . . . They have a fund called the Safety Net Fund, and with that fund we look out for needy children – those who do not have sandals and schoolbags . . . We need funding in order for as to use it for some things that the school really needs improving upon – things like infrastructure. The children still need classrooms. Also boarding structures . . . because we have most of the children staying in other districts. Apart from the health of the children, we also look for their welfare, looking at their feeding and what the child is wearing. . . . We are still praying and waiting we get support from the government, the NGO or any other place. Parents support a little, and government too, but it is still not enough. We need more to support the work of this school.

It is due to financial stressors that of the 110 students enrolled at Yumba Special School, only around 80 students report to class each day. While the Ghana Ministry of Education covers school fees and one of two school buses, caregivers are responsible for transportation costs (e.g. fuel for the school bus) to and from school. Additional costs associated with bus maintenance and repairs are deducted from teachers' salaries. At Yumba Special School, the annual fee for fuel is approximately GHS₵180 (US$75) per student. With an average annual income per household of GHS₵1,452 (US$702) in the Northern Region, GHS₵616 (US₵298) in the Upper East Region, and GHS₵606 (US$293) in the Upper West Region (GSS, 2008), many families cannot afford this "small fuel donation." Six children from the Sagnarigo District in the Northern Region alone were reported to have permanently withdrawn from Yumba Special School as they were unable to afford the annual fee for fuel. Although attempts were made to contact their parents, Yumba Special School teachers have been unable to follow-up on the schooling status of these children. As for students who live farther than 30 minutes from the school, they must be rejected due to transportation costs and also because the school does not have enough funds for a boarding facility.

To address some of these issues, mental health workers and special education teachers have petitioned for an increased budget in mental health, an increased number of mental health professionals in the northern regions, and a budget to cover student transportation. Discussions with teachers indicate that the Ministry of Health has not yet taken any concrete, practical steps to address the situation; this further highlights how critical economic resources are to the development of school mental health services in northern Ghana.

Given the poverty and lack of governmental support, it is clearly challenging to implement quality education and mental health services for children and youth with mental health problems in northern Ghana. And, as mentioned above, poverty and poverty-related risk factors perpetuate these issues. Thus, it will be critical to move forward to try to integrate funding streams from the government as well as outside donors and NGOs, when possible, to create more comprehensive services for children and youth.

Lack of trained personnel

Another barrier to the provision of universal schooling and mental health services in northern Ghana is the shortage of trained education and mental health professionals. The lack of trained teachers and lack of resources have a major impact on enrollment rates in schools in northern Ghana. Many teachers in Ghana refuse to accept positions in the northern regions due to the lack of opportunities, which leads to a major shortage of trained teachers in northern Ghana (Akyeampong, 2009). Because of this shortage, schools have had to rely on untrained or undertrained teachers. This degrades the quality of education provided to northern Ghanaian students and acts as another disincentive to sending children to schools (Akyeampong, 2009).

Ghana has also struggled with providing inclusive education for students with special needs due to the lack of educational resources. In a study of student teachers' perceptions of inclusive education in Botswana and Ghana, Kuyini and Mangope (2011) found that while Ghanaian student teachers held more positive attitudes toward inclusive education than their counterparts from Botswana, they also had more concerns about inclusive education than student teachers from Botswana. Ghanaian student teachers' concerns were mainly based around lack of resources like adequate time to attend to students with special needs, lack of training in how to teach and manage children with special needs, and access to para-professionals.

The barrier of lack of teachers trained in special education is particularly apparent in northern Ghana. The headmistress at Yumba Special School notes that, despite "children with intellectual disabilities in all the northern regions, schools cannot be open." This results in crowded and loud classrooms where special education is offered. Such an environment inhibits educational progress and may endanger students. For instance, at Yumba Special School, in a crowded classroom, students would exit the classroom many times throughout the day without the teachers' knowledge, and would sometimes wander into the nearby fields where poisonous snakes breed. Teachers were also observed to be absent from the classroom for up to two hours at a time, often to attend to individual children who had wandered away. Teachers at Yumba Special School noted that due to the shortage of teachers, many students are unable to receive the necessary amount of attention to improve academically and behaviorally. Discussions with these teachers also reveal that they "did not receive practical training" during their tertiary studies.

There also have been very few Ghanaian teachers who specialize in special education. This is because there is very little incentive for teachers to pursue a career in that field. Special education teachers from Yumba Special School note that the pay is poor relative to other teaching jobs and that levels of stigma are high. One teacher said "They don't pay much attention to special educators in Ghana here. The way they treat special educators in Ghana is discouraging. I would not like to continue because [even] if you want to advance, you can't." Another teacher says: "In the community where we work, the community does not see the need. They feel like they are wasting their time. So there is a stigma attached to it. They call us teachers taking care of mad people."

Similarly, in regards to mental health, there is a lack of trained mental health professionals, with only 0.05 psychiatrists per 100 000 people in the country (Kleintjes *et al.*, 2010). In addition, throughout the country there are only 12 practicing psychiatrists, two clinical psychologists, and 12 700 psychiatric nurses (Amoakwa-Fordjour, 2013). Of these mental health professionals, none currently specialize in child psychiatry (GSS, 2010), and none work in school settings (Kleintjes *et al.*, 2010). Therefore, the lack of trained mental health professionals and teachers severely limits both the quantity and quality of schooling and mental health services for students with mental health problems in Ghana.

Inequities related to rurality

Northern Ghana comprises approximately 40% of Ghana's land area, but is home to only 10% of Ghana's population (Akyeampong, 2006). This rural landscape and low population density leads to difficulties in building centrally located schools (Akyeampong, 2006; Fentiman *et al.*, 1999). Since settlements are often small and far away from one another, it is difficult for the government to decide where to build schools. Further, the cost of transportation to a school far away from the home is another disincentive for parents to send their children to school (Akyeampong, 2006; 2009; Fentiman *et al.*, 1999; Senadza, 2012).

Similarly, northern Ghana is at a disadvantage due to the centralization of institutions providing mental health care. Mental health resources are concentrated in the more affluent, urban areas of Ghana. All psychiatric hospitals, all 12 psychiatrists and the only three clinical psychologists in the country are located in the more densely populated sectors of the southern regions of Ghana, leaving northern Ghana without access to higher-level mental health care (GNA, 2013).

Religious and cultural beliefs

Religious practices in Ghana and the imbalanced distribution of human resources (WHO, 2007) also exacerbate the problem of stigma and access to mental health services, as community members often approach religious counselors before turning to the less accessible formal mental healthcare system (Appiah-Poku *et al.*, 2004). The widespread appeal for traditional healers to treat mental illness in Ghana is reflected in the distribution of workers within the mental health sector; while there are only 12 psychiatrists working in Ghana, there are around 45 000 traditional healers in the country (Roberts, 2001).

While they are more accessible, traditional healers may at times violate human rights and patient safety by implementing controversial treatment methods. Some practices involve chaining or beating mental illness out of patients (Read *et al.*, 2009). In an interview with the headmistress of Yumba Special School, an example of the questionable methods employed by spiritual healers to treat mental illness is mentioned:

> There are people who believe magic men can change the child into animals and release them into the bush. So when you ask the parents where their child is, they say they gave the child to a magic man and that their child is now in the bush.

These discussions indicate that traditional practices are still deeply rooted within historically and culturally accepted responses and are not immediately seen as a human rights issue (Read *et al.*, 2009). Thus, the community's trust in its spiritual leaders cannot be ignored when considering an alternative, innovative response to treating mental illness in northern Ghana.

Innovative strategies

Ghana and the mhGAP

To address the under-prioritization of mental healthcare in developing countries, the WHO (2008) created a Mental Health Gap Action Programme (mhGAP), which makes child mental healthcare a priority condition and provides recommendations for community-based child mental healthcare in low- and middle-income countries. The mhGAP suggests that one way to address the current child mental health gap in Ghana is to introduce affordable community-based treatment programs and integrate mental and primary healthcare at the community level. This proposed model targets both reduction of stigma, by educating the general community about mental illness, and treatment of mental illnesses, by training select community members to become mental health workers. While the mhGAP has not yet been adapted to address child mental health in Ghana, progress has been made to address epilepsy, a neuro-psychiatric disorder, in Ghanaian children. Ghana was one of the countries selected by the WHO to pilot a four-year project entitled Fight Against Epilepsy, which aims to work with communities across Ghana to decrease stigma surrounding epilepsy, increase awareness about the disorder, and educate and train healthcare providers about treatment (WHO, 2012). Since the project was recently launched in 2012, there are no data on the program's efficacy yet.

BasicNeeds: a holistic approach to a community-based mental health model

Another innovative strategy aimed to reduce the gap between mental health needs and available services is BasicNeeds. Founded in 1999 and based in Ghana, BasicNeeds developed an innovative community-based approach to mental health in developing areas using their Mental Health and Development Model (BasicNeeds, 2008). The purpose of developing this model was to introduce affordable community mental healthcare into low- and middle-income countries, and to enable people with mental illness or epilepsy to live and work successfully in their own communities (BasicNeeds-Ghana, 2011). The link between mental health and the community is highlighted in this model. Underhill emphasizes that "the community [is] the essential crucible for a model" (BasicNeeds, 2008). The model addresses the interaction between mental health and poverty by acknowledging the importance of social development and economic stability, as well as of the pharmacological needs of individuals with mental health problems or epilepsy. The model simultaneously addresses the needs of the individual, the family, and the larger community. Concurrently addressing related health, social, and economic concerns, BasicNeeds has created a holistic way to bring about sustainable positive change for individuals with mental health problems living in poverty (BasicNeeds-Ghana, 2010; 2011; 2012). Their model comprises five modules (BasicNeeds-Ghana, 2010):

1. Capacity building: building the capacity of partners, including self-help groups, NGOs, government health workers, and community-based workers.
2. Community mental health: mobilizing psychiatric clinicians from the public sector and health workers from the community to coordinate mental health clinics in community centers.
3. Sustainable livelihoods: supporting individuals with mental illness or epilepsy, their families, and self-help groups in engaging in productive activities, by linking them to employers and/or through micro financing.
4. Research: bridging the gap between policy and practice by conducting research on program outcomes and promoting mental health policy reforms.
5. Management and administration: managing partnerships, human resources, accounts, and information systems to inform program evaluation and planning.

As of June 2012, BasicNeeds has supported more than 104 234 people affected by mental illness and epilepsy. Their innovative model continues to receive funding from trusts, foundations, corporations, and individual donors, allowing them to fund vital parts of free care in India, Sri Lanka, Lao PDR, Uganda, Kenya, Tanzania, Pakistan, China, Vietnam, South Sudan, Nepal, and Ghana.

BasicNeeds began operations in Ghana in 2002, following a feasibility study conducted to understand the mental health situation in the country. Afterwards, a three-year pilot project, known as *New Initiatives in Mental Health and Development*, commenced to implement the model. BasicNeeds-Ghana has operated in some of the most deprived locations of Ghana, particularly in the northern parts of Ghana, which includes the Northern Region. Over the decade that BasicNeeds-Ghana has been active, a total of 23 870 (8986 men, 10 631 women, 2381 boys, and 1872 girls) mentally ill persons have participated in the program (BasicNeeds-Ghana, 2013). Thus, BasicNeeds is a promising model for implementing mental health services in under-resourced areas.

Toward school mental health for youth and families in northern Ghana

While Ghana still struggles to implement universal schooling, much improvement has been made over the past 50 years. More concerning, however, is the lack of mental health services for children, youth, and families, despite pressing mental health needs. While neither BasicNeeds nor mhGAP have appropriated their models to address child and adolescent mental health, these innovative models serve as important references for the development of child mental health services, including SMH programs, in northern Ghana. Within this context, SMH services are a future direction for connecting resources currently available through the education and mental health systems, as well as BasicNeeds and mhGAP, and overcoming the numerous barriers to system development.

Promoting SMH stakeholder collaboration

In northern Ghana, both school and mental health systems are currently under-resourced and burdened with great need for services. In addition, these systems appear to be operating in isolation. However, given the intense social, emotional, and behavioral needs of children and youth in northern Ghana, it seems unreasonable that any one system, agency, or organization would be able to meet this demand. In the United States there is growing understanding that collaboration among key systems, including education, mental health, primary care, and others, is critical to the provision of services to youth with social, emotional, and behavioral needs (Dryfoos, 1994; Flaherty et al., 1998). However, collaboration can occur at multiple levels, either at the systems level or at the organizational or individual stakeholder level, or a combination of various levels. Key disciplines to involve as SMH stakeholders include, but are not limited to, nursing, psychology, psychiatry, school counseling, social work, and education (Flaherty & Osher, 2003). While it is understood that there are barriers to collaboration, such as inadequate funding and resources, disciplinary "turfism," and bureaucratic practices, pursing a joint agenda, promoting Ghanaian children and youth's mental wellbeing, may incrementally advance SMH services in northern Ghana.

In fact, the BasicNeeds model promotes the mobilization of psychiatric clinicians from the public sector and health workers from the community to coordinate mental health clinics in community centers (BasicNeeds-Ghana, 2010). In the case of implementing SMH, schools can be conceptualized as the "community center." Thus, given the successes of the BasicNeeds model in Ghana, it can serve as an important model for creating collaborations aimed at implementing SMH services.

University–community partnerships are a particular type of collaboration that has emerged as the key in implementing mental health services in school settings (Owens et al., 2011; Ringeisen et al., 2003). These partnerships may be able to help leverage university resources for use in the community. For example, similar to northern Ghana, there are little to no SMH services in India, in large part due to a lack of trained personnel (Kumar et al., 2009). To bridge the gap, a university in India organized an interdisciplinary training workshop for teachers, hosted by psychologists, psychiatrists, and psychiatric social workers; this workshop provided teachers with a framework for identifying emotional or behavioral problems, implementing appropriate interventions, and understanding the role of mental health in students' lives (Kumar et al., 2009). After the workshop, teachers had more knowledge about psychiatric problems, were more accepting of children with mental health problems in the classroom, and felt more confident in identifying children with mental health problems as well as assisting students with mental health problems (Kumar et al., 2009). Further, teachers who attended the workshop reported that they attempted to disseminate information learned at the workshop to other teachers and to families (Kumar et al., 2009). This seems a feasible and promising first step to follow for the collaboration in northern Ghana. Such a workshop for teachers in northern Ghana led by mental health professionals would begin to fulfill teachers' needs for additional training in mental health and would also allow for widespread dissemination of knowledge without excessive burden on the limited number of mental health professionals.

Another strategy that may be particularly helpful in the initial implementation of SMH services in northern Ghana is the active involvement of important religious and cultural leaders in the community. Quality indicators for SMH suggest that "students, families, teachers and other important groups are actively involved in the program's development, oversight, evaluation, and continuous improvement" (Weist *et al.*, 2005). Mobilizing an advisory board composed of youth, families, administrators, educators, school health staff, community leaders, and others may assist with the cultivation of school and community buy-in. Since traditional cultural and religious practices are still deeply rooted in northern Ghana, involving spiritual leaders and traditional healers on an advisory board may be critical to success. This may promote a program that is more culturally appropriate and well received by the community.

Overall, strategic collaborations seem key to the implementation of SMH services in northern Ghana. University–community partnerships and engaging spiritual and community leaders may address some of the barriers discussed earlier in this chapter. In addition, the provision of mental health services in schools allows for greater accessibility to services in comparison to the existing mental health services located in more southern, urban regions. Furthermore, SMH services also allow for the provision of mental health services in a more natural setting, promoting ecological validity, and may help to overcome the stigma associated with seeking mental health services. This has been shown to work in rural areas of the United States (for example, Owens, Watabe, & Michael, 2013). Therefore, promoting collaborations to move toward the provision of SMH seems a critical next step in improving services for children and youth with social, emotional, and behavioral problems in northern Ghana.

References

Adera, B. A., & Asimeng-Boahene, L. (2011). The perils and promises of inclusive education in Ghana. *Journal of the International Association of Special Education,* 12(1), 28–32.

Agbemabiese, P. E. (2010). Are the Schools We HAVE the Schools We NEED in Ghana? A Contribution to the Ongoing Debate on Ghana's Education Reform. *The Ghanaian Times,* January 4.

Agbenyega, J. (2007). Examining teachers' concerns and attitudes to inclusive education in Ghana. *International Journal of Whole Schooling,* 3(1), 41–56.

Akyeampong, A. K. (2006). Extending basic education to out-of-school children in Northern Ghana: What can multigrade schooling teach us? In Little, A.W. (ed.) *Education for All and Multigrade Teaching: Challenges and Opportunities.* Amsterdam: Springer, 215–238.

Akyeampong, K. (2009). Revisiting free compulsory universal basic education (FCUBE) in Ghana. *Comparative Education,* 45(2), 175–195.

Akyeampong, K. (2010). 50 years of educational progress and challenge in Ghana, CREATE, University of Sussex.

Alderman, H., & Mundial, B. (1990). *Nutritional status in Ghana and its determinants.* Washington, DC: World Bank.

Amoakwa-Fordjour, G. (2013) The breakdown of Ghana's mental healthcare Retrieved, August 12, 2013, from: www.ghanaweb.com/GhanaHomePage/features/artikel.php?ID=289180

Anthony, J. H., & Kwadade, D. D. (2006), *Inclusive education: Master teacher trainer manual.* Accra, Ghana: Education Quality for All (EQUALL) Special Education Needs (SEN) Component, United States Agency for International Development.

Appiah-Poku, J., Laugharne, R., Mensah, E., Osei, Y., & Burns, T. (2004). Previous help sought by patients presenting to mental health services in Kumasi, Ghana. *Social Psychiatry and Psychiatric Epidemiology*, 39(3), 208–211.

BasicNeeds (2008). *Mental health and development: A model in practice*. Leamington Spa: BasicNeeds.

BasicNeeds-Ghana (2010). 2010 annual impact report. Retrieved August 12, 2013, from: www.basicneedsus.org/blog/wp-content/uploads/2010/01/2010-Annual-Impact-Report_Screen-version.pdf

BasicNeeds-Ghana. (2011). Consolidating gains made in mental health and development in Ghana: Annual evidence-based report. Retrieved August 12, 2013, from: www.basicneedsghana.org/images/PDF/Report%202011-revised.pdf

BasicNeeds-Ghana (2012). Annual impact report 2012. Retrieved February 25, 2013, from: www.basicneedsghana.org/index.php/publication/downloads

BasicNeeds-Ghana (2013). Statistical tracking sheet.

Bass, L. E. (2004). *Child labor in sub-Saharan Africa*. Boulder, CO: Lynne Rienner Publishers.

Casely-Hayford, L., Quansah, T., Tetteh, P., Adams, R., & Adams, I. (2011). *Inclusive education in Ghana. A look at policy, and practice in Northern Ghana*. Ghana: Voluntary Service Organisation.

Chatterjee, S., Pillai, A., Jain, S., Cohen, A., & Patel, V. (2009). Outcomes of people with psychotic disorders in a community-based rehabilitation programme in rural India. *British Journal of Psychiatry*, 195: 433–439.

Cortina, M. A., Sodha, A., Fazel, M., & Ramchandani, P. G. (2012). Prevalence of child mental health problems in sub-Saharan Africa: A systematic review. *Archive of Pediatric and Adolescent Medicine*, 166(3), 276–281.

Costello, E. J., Compton, S. N., Keeler, G., & Angold, A. (2003). Relationships between poverty and psychopathology. *JAMA*, 290(15), 2023–2029.

Dryfoos, J. G. (1994). *Full-service schools: A revolution in health and social services for children, youth, and families*. San Francisco, CA: Jossey-Bass.

Earls, F., & Carlson, M. (2001). The social ecology of child health and well-being. *Annual Review of Public Health*, 22(1), 143–166.

Edmonds, E. V., & Pavcnik, N. (2005). Child labor in the global economy. *The Journal of Economic Perspectives*, 19(1), 199–220.

Fentiman, A., Hall, A., & Bundy, D. (1999). School enrolment patterns in rural Ghana: A comparative study of the impact of location, gender, age and health on children's access to basic schooling. *Comparative Education*, 35(3), 331–349.

Flaherty, L. T., Garrison, E. G., Waxman, R., Uris, P. F., Keys, S. G., Siegel, M. G., & Weist, M. D. (1998), Optimizing the roles of school mental health professionals. *Journal of School Health*, 68, 420–424.

Flaherty, L. T., & Osher, D. (2003). History of school-based mental health services in the United States. In M. D. Weist, S. W. Evans, N. A. Lever (Eds.), *Handbook of school mental health: Advancing practice and research* (pp. 11–22). New York: Kluwer Academic/Plenum Publishers.

Ghana Education Service Special Education Division. (2005). Special educational needs policy framework. Ghana Education Service Special Education Division

Ghana Statistical Service (GSS) (2003). Ghana child labour survey. Accra, Ghana: Ghana Statistical Service, Ghana Health Service, and ICF Macro.

Ghana Statistical Service (GSS). (2008). Ghana Living Standards Survey, report of the fifth round (GLSS 5). Accra: Ghana Statistical Service.

Ghana Statistical Service (GSS). (2010). *Population and housing census; Summary report of final results*. Ghana Statistical Service.

GNA. (2013). The breakdown of Ghana's mental healthcare. Retrieved August 12, 2013, from: www.ghanaweb.com/GhanaHomePage/NewsArchive/artikel.php?ID=289180

Grantham-McGregor, S. M., & Fernald, L. C. (1997). Nutritional deficiencies and subsequent effects on mental and behavioural development in children. *Southeast Asian Journal of Tropical Medicine and Public Health*, 28, 50–68.

Kleintjes, S., Lund, C., Flisher, A. J., & MHAPP Research Programme Consortium. (2010). A situational analysis of child and adolescent mental health services in Ghana, Uganda, South Africa and Zambia. *African Journal of Psychiatry*, 13(2), 132–139.

Kumar, D., Dubey, I., Bhattacharjee, D., Singh, N., Dotiwala, K. N., Siddiqui, S., & Goyal, N. (2009). Beginning steps in school mental health in India: A teacher workshop. *Advances in School Mental Health Promotion*, 2(4), 28–33.

Kuyini, A. B., & Mangope, B. (2011). Student teachers' attitudes and concerns about inclusive education in Ghana and Botswana. *International Journal of whole schooling*, 7(1), 20–37.

Lund, C., De Silva, M., Plagerson, S., Cooper, S., Chisholm, D., Das, J., & Patel, V. (2011). Poverty and mental disorders: Breaking the cycle in low-income and middle-income countries. *The Lancet*, 378(9801), 1502–1514.

Mawutor, A., & Hayford, S. (2000). Promoting inclusive education in basic schools in Winneba Circuit: The role of school attachment programme. A paper presented at International Special Education Congress: Including the Excluded, University of Manchester, EENET, July 24–28.

Ministry of Education (2008). *Complementary education policy (draft)*. Accra, Ghana: Ministry of Education Accra:

Nudzor, H. P. (2012). Unmasking complexities involved in operationalising UPE policy initiatives: Using the "fCUBE" policy implementation in Ghana as an exemplar. *Journal of Educational Change*, 13(3), 347–371.

Nukunya, G. K., (2003), *Tradition and change in Ghana: An introduction to sociology* (2nd edn). Accra, Ghana: Ghana Universities Press.

Owens, J. S., Andrews, N., Collins, J., Griffeth, J. C., & Mahoney, M. (2011). Finding common ground: University research guided by community needs for elementary school-aged youth. In L. Harter, J. Hamel-Lambert, & J. Millesen (Eds.), *Participatory Partnerships for Social Action and Research* (pp. 49–71). Dubuque, IA: Kendell Hunt Publishers.

Owens, J., Watabe, Y., & Michael, K. D. (2013). Culturally responsive school mental health in rural communities. In C. S. Clauss-Ehlers, Z. N. Serpell, & M. D. Weist (Eds.), *Handbook of culturally responsive school mental health: Advancing research, training, practice, and policy* (pp. 31–42). New York: Springer Science + Business Media.

Patel, V. (1995). Explanatory models of mental illness in sub-Saharan Africa. *Social Science & Medicine*, 40(9), 1291–1298.

Patel, V., Flisher, A. J., Hetrick, S., & McGorry, P. (2007). Mental health of young people: A global public-health challenge. *The Lancet*, 369(9569), 1302–1313.

Patel, V., & Kleinman, A. (2003) Poverty and common mental disorders in developing countries. *Bulletin of the World Health Organization*, 81: 609–615.

Pelletier, D. L., Frongillo Jr, E. A., & Habicht, J. P. (1993). Epidemiologic evidence for a potentiating effect of malnutrition on child mortality. *American Journal of Public Health*, 83(8), 1130–1133.

Pelletier, D. L., Frongillo Jr, E. A., Schroeder, D. G., & Habicht, J. P. (1995). The effects of malnutrition on child mortality in developing countries. *Bulletin of the World Health Organization*, 73(4), 443.

Quinn, N. (2007). Beliefs and community responses to mental illness in Ghana: The experiences of family carers. *International Journal of Social Psychiatry*, 53(2), 175–188.

Rahman, A., Mubbashar, M., Harrington, R., & Gater, R. (2000). Annotation: Developing child mental health services in developing countries. *Journal of Child Psychology and Psychiatry*, 41(5), 539–546.

Raja, S., Boyce, W. F., Ramani, S., & Underhill, C. (2008). Success indicators for integrating mental health interventions with community-based rehabilitation projects. *International Journal of Rehabilitation Research*, 31(4), 284–292.

Raja, S., Underhill, C., Shrestha, P., Sunder, U., Mannarath, S., Wood, S., & Patel, V. (2012) Integrating mental health and development: A case study of the BasicNeeds model in Nepal. *PLoS Medicine*, 9(7): e1001261.

Read, U. M., Adiibokah, E., & Nyame, S. (2009). Local suffering and the global discourse of mental health and human rights: An ethnographic study of responses to mental illness in rural Ghana. *Globalization and Health*, 5(1), 13.

Ringeisen, H., Henderson, K., & Hoagwood, K. (2003). Context matters: Schools and the "research to practice gap" in children's mental health. *School Psychology Review*, 32(2), 153–168.

Roberts, H. (2001). Accra: A way forward for mental health care in Ghana? *The Lancet*, 357(9271), 1859.

Salm, S. J., & Falola, T. (2002). *Culture and customs of Ghana*. Westport, CT: Greenwood Publishing Group.

Saxena, S., Thornicroft, G., Knapp, M., & Whiteford, H. (2007). Resources for mental health: Scarcity, inequity, and inefficiency. *The Lancet*, 370(9590), 878–889.

Schroeder, D. G., & Brown, K. H. (1994). Nutritional status as a predictor of child survival: Summarizing the association and quantifying its global impact. *Bulletin of the World Health Organization*, 72(4), 569.

Senadza, B. (2012). Education inequality in Ghana: Gender and spatial dimensions. *Journal of Economic Studies*, 39(6), 724–739.

Social Enterprise Coalition (2011). *The social franchising manual*. London: Social Enterprise Coalition. Retrieved November 10, 2013, from: www.socialenterprise.org.uk/uploads/files/2011/11/social_franchising_manual.pdf

UNESCO. (2011). UIS statistics in brief. Retrieved November 8, 2013, from: http://stats.uis.unesco.org/unesco/TableViewer/document.aspx?ReportId=121&IT_Language=en&BR_Country=2880

Weist, M. D., Sander, M. A., Walrath, C., Link, B., Nabors, L., Adelsheim, S., & Carrillo, K. (2005). Developing principles for best practice in expanded school mental health. *Journal of Youth and Adolescence*, 34(1), 7–13.

World Health Organization. (1987). Children at work: special health risks, report of a WHO study group [meeting held in Geneva, December 10–16, 1985].

World Health Organization. (2001). *World health report 2001: mental health – new understanding, new hope*. Geneva: World Health Organization.

World Health Organization. (2003) *Caring for children and adolescents with mental disorders: Setting WHO directions*. Geneva: World Health Organization.

World Health Organization (2005a). *Child and adolescent mental health policies and plans: Mental health policy and service guidance package*. Geneva: World Health Organization.

World Health Organization (2005b). Atlas: Child and adolescent mental health resources. Global concerns, implications for the future. Retrieved August 12, 2013, from: www.who.int/mental_health/resources/child_ado_atlas.pdf

World Health Organization. (2007). *Ghana a very progressive mental health law*. Geneva: World Health Organization.

World Health Organization. (2008). *mhGAP: Mental Health Gap Action Programme – scaling up care for mental, neurological and substance use disorders*. Geneva: World Health Organization.

World Health Organization. (2012). mhGAP Newsletter: Mental health gap action programme. Retrieved November 10, 2013, from: www.who.int/mental_health/mhGAP_nl_December_2012.pdf

A Singapore model – REACH

Yuhuan Xie, Jillian Boon, Wan Hua Sim, and Daniel Fung

Singapore is a small island with a land area of slightly over 700 square kilometers, at the tip of the Malaysian Peninsula. It is one of the wealthiest countries, ranked 35th in the world by gross domestic product (GDP) (World Bank, 2012). The state of physical health in Singapore is good by international standards, ranked sixth in the world by the World Health Organization in 2000. Singapore has one of the lowest rates of infant mortality (2.1 per 100 000 live births) and highest life expectancy (81.6 years) in the world (World Economic Forum, 2012–2013). The leading causes of morbidity and mortality are the major non-communicable diseases such as cancer and coronary heart disease (Ministry of Health, 2013a). While Singapore's health and primary education systems are ranked among the best in terms of the ability to meet the needs of a competitive economy, the country contends with significant population and health challenges. This includes having one of the lowest fertility rates in the world (1.15 per female), growing divorce rates, and a rapidly aging population. Healthcare expenditure as a percentage of total government spending has risen from 6.7% in 2006 to 9.4% in 2012 (Ministry of Health, 2013b). Mental health expenditure constitutes less than 10% of healthcare expenditure and the burden of disease for mental health disorders is unlikely to change in the next decade. In a 2004 study (Phua *et al.*, 2009) mental health disorders contributed to 11.8% of the overall burden of disease.

In response to the increasing healthcare needs and challenges, mental health services in Singapore have evolved to shift the delivery of care from specialist hospital care and institutions to the community. To support the mental healthcare needs of children and adolescents, a community-based mental health service was inaugurated in 2007 to work closely with schools, physicians, and community agencies to help students below 19 years old with mental health problems. The community mental health team is known as *R*esponse, *E*arly Intervention and *A*ssessment in *C*ommunity Mental *H*ealth, or by its acronym, REACH. This chapter presents a description of the major changes in the mental health service delivery model for children and adolescents in Singapore, and it highlights the principles that guided the system and program development of REACH. The chapter also outlines the nature of the services resulting from the model and concludes with a discussion of lessons learned from the program and a peek into the possible future.

Developing community models of care

Despite advances in technological innovation and cutting-edge thinking, Singapore contends with significant mental healthcare challenges and disparities across its diverse

School Mental Health: Global Challenges and Opportunities, ed. Stan Kutcher, Yifeng Wei and Marc D. Weist. Published by Cambridge University Press. © Cambridge University Press 2015.

population. Representative surveys of mental health in Singapore have been conducted regularly for service development and disease surveillance since 1978. All are merely cross-sectional snapshots with only one (Woo *et al.*, 2007), focused on children, reporting an overall prevalence of mental health disorders to be 12.5%. In a recent survey of adults aged 18–65, large treatment gaps for mental health disorders were noted (Chong *et al.*, 2012a). In addition, many conditions, such as anxiety disorders, depression, and alcohol dependence, had early childhood and adolescent onset (Chong *et al.*, 2012a; 2012b).

Until recently, mental healthcare for psychiatric illnesses had been predominantly provided by specialized services in both public and private sectors. The Institute of Mental Health (IMH) is the nation's tertiary specialty center for psychiatric care and it is the largest provider of in-patient care and specialist out-patient and community services. It has just under 2000 beds, of which 20 are for individuals under 19 years of age. In the traditional model of care, psychiatrists are the key health providers involved in diagnosing and treating the mentally ill. Students with emotional and behavioral problems commonly present themselves for treatment in community hospitals by direct referrals from schools, family physicians, and community agencies on a first-come-first-served basis. Accordingly, this model of service delivery resulted in long wait times or no care at all for certain individuals. The fragmentation and duplication of services across public health and social services providers often make it difficult for young people and their families to access mental healthcare.

Besides structural barriers to accessibility of services, stigma discourages early help-seeking behaviors. Having a child with a mental disorder is considered shameful in many families. For some, cultural and religious beliefs play a role in shaping their attribution of the causes of psychiatric disorders and might influence them to turn to practitioners of traditional medicine or indigenous spiritual healers for treatment (Ow, 1998). Consequently, only about 25% will seek help from primary care physicians, psychiatrists, or psychologists when dealing with a mental disorder (Chong *et al.*, 2012c). There is a need for innovative approaches for delivering timely mental healthcare for those who need it.

Recognizing the importance of a population-based approach to healthcare, a committee comprising representatives from public health, mental health, education, and the social services sectors was convened in 2005 to develop a national program that supports the mental healthcare needs of different groups in Singapore. These collaborative efforts led to the formulation of the National Mental Health Blueprint in 2007 (Ministry of Health, 2010). The Blueprint aims to promote primary prevention, improve access to mental health services, and enhance the quality and monitoring of mental health services. It is envisioned that a population-based model that emphasizes the dispensing of care at appropriate sites and a continuum of care will optimize preventive care and early intervention for the individual. In 2007 the REACH program was established as one of the pillars of the Blueprint to support the mental healthcare needs of children and adolescents under 19 years of age. The REACH program is organized according to three main objectives that are the underpinnings on which advances to child and adolescent mental health services are to be made (Fung *et al.*, 2013). The objectives are to:

1. improve mental health of children and adolescents through early assessment and intervention;
2. enhance the capacity of schools and community partners to detect and manage mental health problems through support and training; and

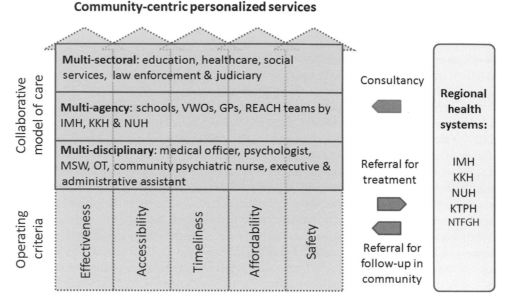

Figure 18.1 The REACH model.

3. develop a mental health support network for children and adolescents in the community involving schools, general practitioners, and voluntary welfare organizations (or nongovernmental organizations).

The REACH model is intended to provide responsive services based on five operating criteria of quality care and a support mechanism involving regional health systems (see Figure 18.1). In the REACH model, regional hospital systems (IMH,[1] KKH,[2] NUHS,[3] KTPH[4], and NTFGH[5]) are placed at the center of an effort to create regional networks of mental healthcare and social services for a seamless continuum of care for children, adolescents, and their families. Together, the hospitals host four REACH mobile teams that comprise medical doctors, psychologists, medical social workers (MSWs), occupational therapists (OTs), and community psychiatric nurses.

The initial focus of the Blueprint for children and adolescents was the school. Most children in Singapore attend six years of compulsory mainstream primary school education, except for children with special needs who are supported by a customized educational program in special education schools. By building on the legacy of schools in providing pastoral care (Ministry of Education, 2013a) or allied health services for students (Ministry of Education, 2013b), the delivery of mental health services in schools was considered to

---

[1] IMH: Institute of Mental Health – located in the northeast of Singapore.
[2] KKH: KK Women's and Children's Hospital – located in the east of Singapore.
[3] NUHS: National University Hospital System – located in the west of Singapore.
[4] KTPH: Khoo Teck Puat Hospital – a regional general hospital in the north of Singapore with psychiatrists interested in caring for youths.
[5] NTFGH: Ng Teng Fong General Hospital – a regional general hospital opening in 2015 in the west of Singapore.

potentially demonstrate a positive impact on child and adolescent health and academic achievement, while simultaneously increasing visibility and viability of mental wellness in schools. Beginning with a prototype program in 12 schools in the north of Singapore, by 2012 REACH services had been extended to more than 350 schools, 7 voluntary welfare organizations, and 29 general practitioners (GPs). The phased approach to implementation allowed opportunities for program refinement as the REACH program expanded.

Response to intervention and continuum of care

Schools in Singapore have a long history of collaboration with GPs and specialists in the management of health and wellbeing of students. School support services for students with social, emotional, or behavioral problems are organized in a tiered system, beginning with first-level intervention by teachers who have undergone training in basic counseling and behavioral management skills. If the intervention is unsuccessful or if the student requires more specialized attention, a referral is made to the appropriate school-based allied educators (in mainstream schools) or allied health professionals (in special education schools). In the case where the student needs more intensive specialized intervention, the student may be referred to specialists of the Ministry of Education, or to external agencies such as hospital-based clinics and family service centers. The REACH program is intended to build on schools' existing support structures to provide a more accessible and responsive service for students with mental health problems before a referral to a tertiary healthcare system is warranted.

The REACH component that supports the implementation of its clinical services is the dedicated telephone consultation service or helpline that can be accessed by its school and community partners to seek advice in the management and referral of students with mental health problems. During the telephone consultations, referred students are evaluated by the REACH team through a triage system, which helps to ascertain mental health concerns and the level of urgency for assessment and intervention. All referrals are then tabled for team discussion and the outcomes of the referral will be communicated to the referring school. When a referral is accepted, mental health assessment for the student is conducted by REACH member(s) at the school or home, together with the family and school liaison. Assessments conducted at school or home have several benefits, such as reducing the chance of no-show for appointments, attaining better quality of interaction at the setting natural to the student and caregivers, and increasing the likelihood that a comprehensive understanding of the student's problems is achieved. When a referral is not accepted for intake (e.g., deemed to have no mental disorder or substantial mental health problem after team discussion), the team will provide recommendations that are more appropriate for the student's challenges.

Following the initial REACH assessment, treatment plans are reviewed and endorsed by the REACH team's consultant psychiatrist so as to ensure a high standard of case formulation and care for the students assessed by the team. Various treatment options may be recommended based on the nature and level of care needed. The options could include further individual or group intervention services by the REACH team and/or a transfer of care to GPs, family service centers, or psychiatric clinics. For students who are referred for specialist care in the clinics, the team helps to ease the transition for the students and their caregivers by helping them to understand the clinic processes and accompanying them for the first visit. This process reflects the principle of appropriate care and the commitment to provide quality care.

To ensure that an effective partnership with schools can be formed, the REACH teams also embarked on providing training and resources to support schools in identification and management of mental health problems. In the REACH model for schools, the school counselor plays a central role in working with the students and their families in collaboration with REACH, providing information to the school staff, and communicating effectively with various community mental health and social service providers. Based on the "train the trainer" model, REACH team members conduct regular workshops that cover topics ranging from clinical interviewing to knowledge of specific child and adolescent mental health disorders to school counselors. School counselors and other community partners are also invited to training conducted by overseas experts and monthly inter-agency case conferences organized by the Child Guidance Clinic of the IMH to encourage participation in multi-agency exchanges on case formulation and treatment issues. Such training strategies strengthen the capacity and confidence of traditionally non-mental health professionals in detecting and managing affected children and adolescents.

With enhanced accessibility to mental health services and support offered by REACH, schools are empowered to support students with a variety of mental health problems and mental disorders, as specialized help is now more readily available than through traditional hospital-based services. Providing on-site help in problem solving about emotional and behavioral issues and offering training reflects another strategy for establishing a mental health perspective in schools. The REACH program augments the work of school-based non-mental health professionals, and emphasizes an effort by schools to fill gaps and improve support services in a collaborative, interdisciplinary, and inter-agency team effort for the holistic wellbeing of students. These service developments, along with the establishment of REACH, further provide an opportunity for hospitals to work with schools in their regions to provide timely interventions for children, their parents, and teachers. Through REACH, an integration of the response-to-intervention model used by educators and the principle of continuum of care advocated by health systems becomes possible.

Building bridges for better access

Implementing and sustaining initiatives that build community networks and promote community capacity building may have far-reaching impact beyond what the clinical component of the REACH program can offer. Apart from schools, the REACH program recognizes the important linkages to other community providers of health and social services, while taking into account regional variations as well as demographic realities. To achieve its objectives of developing a mental health support network for children and adolescents, REACH started identifying and training voluntary welfare organizations (VWOs) and GPs who demonstrate interest and capability to take on the additional role of providing mental health services to their clients. In Singapore, VWOs have had a long-standing influence in their communities through their provision of social services such as counseling, befriending, parenting, and financial assistance for children, youth, and their families. Being the primary healthcare providers in the neighborhoods close to homes, GPs are often the first point of contact for young people and their caregivers. Thus a more formalized collaboration with VWOs and GPs can offer not only improved access to treatment for children and adolescents, but also avenues for prevention through early identification of mental health problems.

Similar to the partnership with schools, VWOs and GPs are able to access the REACH helpline to consult the team for advice on the referral and management of their clients with mental health problems. The training programs are customized to suit the unique needs of the community partners and may include group seminars, clinical attachments, and live supervision at the psychiatric clinics in the hospitals. There are also ongoing efforts to attract new community partners on board the REACH program and to maximize their engagement with the project. The partnership with general practitioners and VWOs has opened doors for two-way referrals and consultations, improving accessibility and continuity of care for children and adolescents. Through REACH, schools have also developed liaisons with their regional VWOs and GPs to co-manage the diverse needs of children and their families. By offering a range of mental health and social services in the least restrictive environment as close to their communities as possible, significant impacts can be made in many areas of a child's and his or her family's life.

With no end in sight to the dearth of child and adolescent psychiatrists and practitioners in related disciplines, it is acknowledged that broader systemic approaches in building mental healthcare competencies in service providers to meet the mental healthcare needs of the nation are required. One such effort was taken when the Ministry of Health collaborated with the Accreditation Council for Graduate Medical Education in the United States to improve the local postgraduate training system to educate larger numbers of specialists and family physicians in Singapore. In 2010, the country achieved a milestone in its psychiatric training with the launch of the Graduate Diploma in Mental Health, where family physicians enrolled in the course have to undertake six modules dedicated to child and adolescent mental health. Other efforts to prepare doctors in community mental healthcare consist of including a core posting in psychiatry during their training programs. For example, medical officers posted to IMH are expected to serve a posting in the REACH team so as to equip them with knowledge and skills in working with children and adolescents in the community. Together, these strategies support the objectives of the National Mental Health Blueprint to strengthen mental health human resources and service provisions to meet the mental healthcare needs of the nation.

Understanding outcomes, challenges and learning points of the REACH program

Various sources of data were captured to track the effectiveness of the REACH program since its inception in 2007. Data collected indicated that the REACH program had been successful in achieving its overarching goal of improving the emotional and social wellbeing of children and adolescents in Singapore. This was done through providing prompt delivery of services using a community-based approach.

Ensuring that the REACH program is effective in meeting its objectives is an ongoing process. Key performance indicators (KPIs), measuring both process and outcomes, were decided upon for each objective. These KPIs act as markers to monitor whether goals were attained for each objective. The KPIs chosen were simple to monitor and reflected the intent of measurement. As REACH is a funded program under the National Mental Health Blueprint, these KPIs are submitted to the Ministry of Health on a bi-annual basis to ensure accountability. Small-scale research studies have been carried out over the years looking at various outcome indicators of the REACH program (e.g., Koh et al., 2011; Soo et al., 2011; Sulaiman, Ong, & Fung, 2009). The outcome and effectiveness of the REACH program will be best evaluated through looking at each objective

Objective 1: improve mental health of children and adolescents through early assessment and intervention

Clinical outcomes were deemed the most important measurement marker for this objective. The clinical effectiveness of the REACH program is demonstrated if students referred through

Table 18.1 Brief summary of instruments administered

Instrument	Domains measured	Population administered
Strengths and Difficulties Questionnaire (SDQ)	A 25-item brief questionnaire measuring behavioral and emotional problems of children and youths (Goodman, 1997) in five domains: emotional symptoms, conduct problems, hyperactivity, peer relationship problems, and pro-social behaviors.	• Teacher • Voluntary Welfare Organization (VWO) case worker
Clinical Global Impression (CGI)	Consists of two items – the Severity of Illness item (CGI-Severity) and the Global Improvement item (CGI-Improvement). The severity of illness was rated on a seven-point scale.	• School counselors • VWO case workers • GP partners
European Quality of Life: 5 Dimensions (EQ-5D)	Five domains of health outcomes and general health state: mobility, self-care, usual activities, pain/discomfort, and anxiety/depression	• Students, 11 years old and above
Children's Global Assessment Scale (CGAS)	General functioning of children (Schaffer et al., 1983)	• GP partners

the REACH program eventually improved in clinical markers of mental health. Hence, all students who passed through the REACH program were assessed on a number of clinical scales prior to a REACH assessment, and again six months after the assessment. These clinical scales used to assess and evaluate clinical effectiveness included the Strengths and Difficulties Questionnaire, Clinical Global Impression scale, the European Quality of Life: 5 Dimensions questionnaire and the Children's Global Assessment Scale. A summary of the instruments, the domains they measured and the population administered to are reflected in Table 18.1.

Figures 18.2, 18.3, and 18.4 reflect the KPIs attained for the first objective. The clinical indicators for students' mental health as rated by school counselors demonstrated that more than half of referred youths from schools who went through the REACH program showed improvement in their emotional and behavioral symptoms (as rated on the SDQ in Figure 18.2). Similar overall improvements in mental health (as rated on the CGI) were noted six months after the first assessment by the REACH team (see Figure 18.2).

All cases referred by VWO partners showed improvement on these same clinical indicators since the REACH VWO partnership started in FY 2010 (data not included in

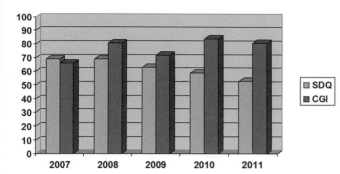

Figure 18.2 Percentage of students referred by school with improvement in SDQ (teacher's rating) and CGI (school counselor's rating).

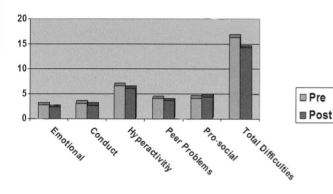

Figure 18.3 Pre- and post-SDQ ratings on five domains of Problem and Total Difficulties by teachers.

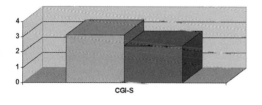

Figure 18.4 Pre- and post-REACH intervention CGI ratings by school counselors

this chapter). Youths referred by REACH to be managed by REACH GP partners showed that over two-thirds of these students improved in their overall mental health (as rated on the CGI by the GP partners). A majority of children and youths referred to GP partners every year were rated as having improved in their general functioning (as rated on the CGAS), with the exception of FY 2010, where only 25% showed improvement. Further investigation of the data in FY 2010 revealed that many of the ratings on the CGAS indicated that referred cases in FY 2010 might only have mild impairment in a single area before intake, therefore the further improvement was not significant.

Clinical improvements have been examined by looking at the pre- and post-six-month SDQ (teacher-rated) and CGI (school counselor-rated) scores of students referred from schools. Previously, small-scale research on clinical outcomes of youths referred through schools and managed by REACH had demonstrated the clinical effectiveness of the program. Sulaiman *et al.* (2009) found that six months after referral to REACH, there was a statistically significant reduction in the Total Difficulties, Emotional, and Hyperactivity subscales scores for students on the SDQ ($N = 26$). In addition, the ratings of the severity of problems on the CGI ($N = 36$) were significantly lower when a comparison was conducted between CGI-Severity (CGI-S) at the first assessment and six months following. Similarly, Koh et al. (2011) found that at six months post-assessment of students referred to REACH ($n = 276$) there were statistically significant improvements on the CGI-S scores, and also statistically significant improvements on all subscales of the SDQ.

A statistical analysis using pair-wise t-tests analyses on the pre-assessment and post-six-months data collected from July 2007 to December 2011 for all referred cases consistently indicated positive improvements of the students referred to REACH on the clinical indicators of mental health. Figures 18.2 and 18.3 reflect the outcomes for the SDQ and CGI data, respectively.

SDQ ratings ($n = 690$) reflected statistically significant improvements after six months on the mean of Total Difficulties score, $p < 0.00$. Statistically significant improvements were also found on the means of raw score of the five subscales of Emotional Symptoms, $p < 0.00$, Conduct Problems, $p < 0.00$, Hyperactivity, $p < 0.00$, Peer Problems, $p < 0.00$ and Pro-social, $p < 0.00$ (see Figure 18.3). However, effect sizes were found to be small for the change in scores on the subscales (Cohen's d ranging from 0.16 to 0.23), while the effect size for the change in scores on the Total Difficulties score was slightly larger ($d = 0.32$). Thus, it can be said that emotional and behavioral improvements in referred students were noticeable but not dramatic.

Looking at the school counselors-rated CGI-S item ($n = 718$) in Figure 18.4, improvement in ratings six months after the first assessment were found to be statistically significant among the students who were referred to REACH, $t (717) = 13.51$, $p < 0.00$. In this analysis, the effect size ($d = 0.50$) was medium. Hence, school counselors did observe reasonable improvements in the severity of problems among referred students.

Limitations of the evaluation

An estimate of 1500 students was referred to REACH since its establishment. However, only a percentage of these students' clinical indicators could be assessed with the presence of the post-KPIs completed. Therefore, the data may not fully reflect the intervention outcomes achieved by the REACH program. The difficulty of attaining post-KPI evaluation measures from respective stakeholders (teachers, REACH partners) could be due to several factors such as change of teachers or students leaving the school, among others.

A limitation of the self-report surveys also allowed for the possibility of response bias. The response bias of each rater (teachers and REACH partners) could affect the validity and generalization of the study findings. As such, the data should be interpreted with some caution.

It was also found by Koh et al. (2011) when comparing clinical outcomes of students referred to REACH with patients managed after admission to a child and adolescent psychiatric in-patient unit, that the improvements on the CGI-Improvement item were significantly higher in the in-patient group than the REACH group. The authors acknowledged that management plans in such community-based programs may not be as efficacious in a short time frame compared with that of an in-patient setting. Of course, the different baseline levels in two populations also have significant contribution to how fast and how much improvement can be gained by a short treatment intervention. Therefore, one suggestion for future analysis on the effectiveness of REACH might be to look at cost-effectiveness to clarify the efficacy and efficiency of the REACH model of care.

The current data provide a good general overview of the improvements made by the students referred to REACH from various levels (primary, secondary, and junior college). Noticeable improvements also signify a good indication of attaining REACH's objectives. However, it did not allow us to know the relationship of outcomes and the specific diagnosis. It would be helpful to know which specific disorders might benefit the most from REACH services. As such, future considerations can look at the associations of various disorders with the outcomes of REACH interventions.

In general, the ratings completed by teachers and school counselors have demonstrated that REACH has been effective in improving the mental health of many children and adolescents under its care. This is evidenced by the improvements on indicators of severity of problem, and behavioral and emotional symptoms as rated on the CGI and SDQ, respectively. Ongoing data monitoring and research will allow further examination of the clinical effectiveness of the REACH program.

Objective 2: enhance the capacity of schools and community partners to detect and manage mental health problems through support and training

Capacity building of resources in the community was a clearly targeted objective from the conceptualization of the REACH program. This was achieved through supporting and training school personnel and staff of social service agencies. Table 18.2 shows the KPIs for the second objective. These statistics were collated through sources such as: (1) attendance records during training; (2) scheduling of training; (3) feedback provided after training; (4) record of helpline referrals and calls; and (5) feedback provided after assessments, case consultations, and interventions.

In the first five years of its roll-out, various training was offered at no cost to REACH partners (i.e., schools, VWOs, and GPs partners). Furthermore, to ensure a holistic approach to empowering partners in the community, support and trainings did not merely encompass didactic-style lectures, but also included practice of skills learned and case consultations. Exclusive trainings conducted by overseas guests and typically reserved for clinical staff of hospitals were often extended to REACH partners (schools, VWOs, and GP partners).

To ensure that REACH training was relevant to the work done by community partners, school counselors and VWO partners were asked after every training session they attended if they had found the training to be satisfactory and effective. The figures in Table 18.2 indicate that over the period from 2007 to 2011, over 90% of school counselors and VWO staff felt the training had been effective in providing them necessary skills and were satisfied with the training provided.

It was important to evaluate the effectiveness of the training provided and whether it benefited the counselors in the community. Soo and her colleagues (2011) conducted a study on the mental health literacy (i.e., knowledge on identifying and managing mental health conditions) of school counselors who have been partners with the REACH program for a year. Results indicated that school counselors showed significant improvement in general mental health literacy, specifically in identifying mental health conditions, and knowledge of mental health conditions. Despite the suggested improvements in mental health literacy, there was no improvement in their confidence in managing mental health conditions. The authors postulated that self-report modesty may partly explain the lack of significant improvement in school counselors' confidence in managing mental health conditions. Results of the study also showed that, unexpectedly, the number of training sessions did not predict improvement in identification and knowledge of mental health conditions, suggesting that the improvements may have been due to factors not considered in the study, e.g., experience and knowledge gained through use of REACH and its helpline, self-study, and peer discussions. Soo *et al.* (2011) concluded that the study highlighted that although school counselors' knowledge and ability to identify mental health conditions in students increased over time, more had to be done to empower school counselors in managing students with mental health problems/disorders.

As part of the holistic approach to providing mental health support to the community, the REACH helpline was established for the purposes of supporting our school counselors and VWO partners. As shown in Table 18.2, the number of calls on the helpline has increased over the years with the establishment of REACH teams in the various zones.

Table 18.2 KPIs for Objective 2: "Enhance the capacity of schools and community partners to detect and manage mental health problems through support and training"

Key performance indicators	FY 2007	FY 2008	FY 2009	FY 2010	FY 2011
School counselors					
No. of school counselors trained	13	176	197	198	413
No. of trainings conducted for school counselors	6	4	17	26	116
Effectiveness of training (% of school counselors who agreed that the training has equipped them with the necessary skills to manage students)	–*	100	99	98	92
Satisfaction with training (% of school counselors who are satisfied with the training)	–	91	99	100	98
No. of calls/workload received by helpline from school counselors	306	1418	3444	4620	8371
No. of case conferences with school counselors	29	35	134	513	726
School counselor satisfaction with support from REACH	–	92	100	97	99
No. of cases referred from school	14	111	241	376	734
% of urgent cases from school seen within one week of referral	–	100	98	87	100
% of non-urgent cases from school seen within four weeks of referral	–	98	100	99	100

Table 18.2 (cont.)

Key performance indicators	FY 2007	FY 2008	FY 2009	FY 2010	FY 2011
VWOs					
No. of VWO staff trained	NA**	NA	27	2	53
No. of training session conducted for VWOs	NA	NA	10	45	23
Effectiveness of training (% of VWO staff who agreed that the training has equipped them with the necessary skills to manage the students)	NA	NA	95	100	100
Satisfaction with training (% VWO staff who are satisfied with the training)	NA	NA	97	100	100
No. of calls/workload received by helpline from VWO partners	NA	NA	3	62	102
No. of case conferences with VWO partners	NA	NA	NA	6	20
VWO partners' satisfaction with support from REACH (%)	NA	NA	NA	100	100
No. of cases referred from VWO partners	NA	NA	NA	5	6
% of urgent cases from VWO partners seen within one week of referral	NA	NA	NA	NA	100
% of non-urgent cases from VWO partners seen within four weeks of referral	NA	NA	NA	67	100

* –: Data not requested at that point in time
** NA: Data not collected at that point in time as process not started

Furthermore, case conferences are now the routine practice after the assessment of each child, to ensure that the school counselors or VWO partner is involved and supported in the future management of the child. As demonstrated in Table 18.2, over 90% of school counselors and VWO partners were consistently satisfied with this form of support.

Process indicators such as the number of referrals and number of calls received by the REACH helpline (refer to Table 18.2) from schools and VWO partners were captured as well. These figures were consistently monitored by the respective REACH teams to ensure that youths with mental health problems were being detected and referred. Furthermore, the responsiveness of REACH in meeting timelines for cases which were classified as "urgent" and "non-urgent" was also monitored. With such a monitoring system, obstacles to early responsiveness (i.e., when KPIs are not met) were addressed and rectified regularly by the individual REACH teams.

Thus, it can be seen that much has been done for REACH to achieve its second objective. REACH partners have generally been satisfied with the support and training that REACH provides. However, it is noted that empowering community partners in managing youths with mental disorders remains a challenge for future program improvement for REACH.

Objective 3: develop a mental health support network for children and adolescents in the community involving schools, GPs, and VWOs (or NGOs)

A mental health network in the community would benefit Singaporean children and adolescents who may be at risk of developing mental health disorders, or who require less intensive treatment. Such a community network would also reduce the stigma of seeking help for mental health-related problems. With that in mind, KPIs for this objective looked at the recruitment of REACH partners and appropriate care and management for children and adolescents with less severe mental health problems. Table 18.3 shows the KPIs for the third

Table 18.3 KPIs for Objective 3: "Develop a mental health support network for children and adolescents in the community involvings schools, general practitioners and voluntary welfare organizations (or NGOs)

Key performance indicators	FY 2007	FY 2008	FY 2009	FY 2010	FY 2011
VWOs					
No. of referrals to a social service agency	NA**	NA	NA	6	36
GPs					
No. of GPs/pediatricians recruited as partners	9	13	7	3	8
No. of GPs/pediatricians trained	62	40	67	83	25
Effectiveness of training (% of GPs who agreed that the training has equipped them with the necessary skills to manage the patients)	–*	100	100	92	95
% of GP-managed patients who returned to specialist's care (not due to worsening condition)	17	13	0	2	3
No. of cases discharged to GPs	6	8	9	26	37
% of patients who rejected the referral to GP's care	33	60	72	14	35
% of patients discharged without E-room visits	100	100	100	100	100
% of patients discharged without hospitalization	100	100	100	100	100
% of caregivers satisfied with GP services after six months	–	100	100	93	88

* –: Data not requested at that point in time
** NA: Data not collected at that point in time as process not started

objective. These KPI statistics were collated through sources such as: (1) records of GPs recruited over the years; (2) scheduling of training for GPs; (3) feedback provided after training; (4) record of referrals that are appropriately sited to GPs.

The relationship of REACH and social service agencies is a bidirectional one. As seen in Table 18.3, REACH VWO partners consult with REACH and refer cases of suspected mental health issues. Similarly, REACH refers to VWO partners and other social service agencies if the cases seen by REACH require support from social service agencies. This way, a step-down approach to care is implemented. Similarly, students with no mental disorders but who are grappling with social problems, can be referred to appropriate agencies.

As indicated in Table 18.3, the majority of GPs who attended training organized by REACH agreed that the training has equipped them with the necessary skills to manage patients. In addition, parents of referred students were increasingly more open to the idea that a GP could manage their child's mental health condition. REACH started the initial referrals to GP partners with much caution in FY 2007 as it was a new partnership. Only students who presented with mild mental health problems were referred to the GP partners. Hence, very few parents rejected the idea of a referral to a REACH GP partner. With increasing confidence in the GP partnership, REACH referred more students to GP partners in FY 2008 and FY 2009. However, as seen in Table 18.3 many parents in FY 2008 and FY 2009 turned this option down, possibly because seeing GPs in the community for a mental disorder was still uncommon.

Over time, schools with students who were referred to and managed by REACH GP partners were able to give testimony to their confidence with the GP partners. Hence, the percentage of patients who rejected a referral to a GP decreased drastically after FY 2009. The success of this partnership was especially illustrated in the data, which illustrated that over the years, patients who were referred to REACH GP partners were managed well by the GPs, and were eventually discharged without any visits to the hospital. A large proportion of caregivers rated their experience with our REACH GP partners to be satisfactory (Table 18.3).

One of the limitations of the collected data on the satisfaction of REACH training was that the background profiles of the REACH partners were not specified. The feedback forms given to the REACH partners after trainings and workshops did not reflect their educational qualifications or work experience. As such, this limited our ability to understand the profile of the individuals who had benefited or not benefited from the REACH trainings. Therefore, future data collection should include more information about the profile of our REACH partners to allow us better understanding of the needs of different partners, improve the satisfaction rating, and provide skill training to fulfill our partners' needs.

On the whole, maintaining a network of community resources to support at-risk children and adolescents requires continuous effort that ties in with needing to train our partners in the community to detect and manage childhood mental health issues. Community partners need to be well-trained and know that they always have the support to manage such issues before they can feel confident to take on this task.

Conclusion

Overall, the effectiveness of REACH has been demonstrated, and the program objectives were generally met. More than half of the students referred to REACH improved on clinical indicators of emotional, behavioral, and mental wellbeing. Training and support in the area of mental health were continuously provided for community partners to ensure they were able to better detect and provide holistic management for children and adolescents with mental health issues. This training has proven to provide better mental health literacy in REACH partners, thereby increasing the rate of screening for mental illnesses in children and adolescents in Singapore. Finally, REACH continues its effort to improve the community mental health network through appropriate triaging and ensuring youths at risk receive appropriate support in the community.

Future directions

Despite the positive outcomes of the REACH program, there remain challenges in maintaining smooth operation of the program, securing funding for program development, and ensuring its primary objectives are met.

Future plans to address the above challenges are considered by the REACH teams and IMH leadership. The REACH teams have weekly meetings to discuss and resolve ongoing operating issues. However, schools and community partners are not regularly involved in those meetings, and scheduling regular meetings with those partners will help the teams to identify the needs of the community partners and service gaps or overlaps among different sections. There are also plans to expand the collaboration with special education schools so to enhance the capacity of those schools to meet the mental healthcare needs of children with special needs. Ultimately, the goal is to improve the effectiveness of the program. Further data collection and exploration will allow us to have a better understanding of the reasons or barriers for students' lack of improvement despite REACH's comprehensive assessment and involvement.

References

Chong, S. A., Abdin, E., Sherbourne, C., et al. (2012a). Treatment gap in common mental disorders: The Singapore perspective. *Epidemiology and Psychiatric Sciences*, 21, 195–202.

Chong, S. A., Abdin, E, Vaingankar, J. A., et al. (2012b). A population-based survey of mental disorders in Singapore. *Annals of the Academy of Medicine Singapore*, 41, 49–66.

Chong, S. A., Vaingankar, J. A., Abdin, E., Kwok, K. W., & Subramaniam, M. (2012c). Where do people with mental disorders in Singapore go to for help? *Annals of the Academy of Medicine Singapore*, 41, 154–160.

Fung, D., Ong, L. P., Tay, S. L. & Sim, W. H. (eds.). (2013). *REACH chronicles: A community mental health model for children and adolescents in Singapore*. Singapore: World Scientific.

Goodman, R. (1997). The strengths and difficulties questionnaire: A research note *Journal of Child Psychology and Psychiatry*, 38, 581–586.

Koh, D., Sulaiman, R., Ooi, Y. P., and Fung, D. (2011). Clinical outcomes of a community mental health programme for youths in Singapore. *Annals of the Academy of Medicine Singapore*, 40, S43.

Ministry of Education. (2013a). Pastoral care. (Online) Available at www.moe.gov.sg/education/programmes/social-emotional-learning/pastoral-care (accessed August 24, 2013).

Ministry of Education. (2013b). Special education schools. (Online) Available at www.moe.gov.sg/education/special-education/ (accessed August 24, 2013).

Ministry of Health. (2010). Health minds, healthy communities: National mental health blueprint 2007–2012. Available at www.imh.com.sg/uploadedFiles/Publications/IMH%20National%20Mental%20Health%20Blueprint.pdf (accessed October 19, 2014).

Ministry of Health. (2013a). Principal causes of death. Available at www.moh.gov.sg/content/moh_web/home/statistics/Health_Facts_Singa

pore/Principal_Causes_of_Death.html (accessed August 24, 2013).

Ministry of Health. (2013b). Healthcare financing: Government health expenditure. (Online) Available at www.moh.gov.sg/content/moh_web/home/statistics/Health_Facts_Singapore/Healthcare_Financing.html (accessed September 29, 2013).

Ow, R. (1998). Mental health care: The Singapore context. *Asia Pacific Journal of Social Work and Development*, 8, 120–130.

Phua, H. P., Chua, A. V. L., Ma, S., Heng, D., & Chew, S. K. (2009). Singapore's burden of disease and injury 2004. *Singapore Medical Journal*, 50, 468–478.

Schaffer, D., Gould, M. S., Brasic, J., *et al.* (1983) A children's global assessment scale (CGAS). *Archives of General Psychiatry*, 40, 1228–1231.

Soo, G., Ong, J. G. X., Chen, A., and Ong, L. P. (2011). Mental health literacy of Singapore school counselors: A preliminary study.

Annals of the Academy of Medicine Singapore, 40, 214.

Sulaiman, S. R., Ong, L. P., & Fung, D. (2009). Preliminary Evidence for the Effectiveness of the REACH Community Mental Health Programme. Poster presented during the National Healthcare Group Annual Scientific Congress, October 16–17, 2009.

Woo, B. S. C, Ng, T. P., Fung, D. S. S, *et al.* (2007). Emotional and behavioural problems in Singaporean children based on parent, teacher and child reports. *Singapore Medical Journal*, 48, 1100–1106.

World Bank. (2012). Gross domestic product 2010. (Online) Available at http://databank.worldbank.org/data/download/GDP.pdf (accessed October 19, 2014).

World Economic Forum (2012–2013). *The global competitiveness report 2012–2013*. Geneva: World Economic Forum. (Online) Available at www3.weforum.org/docs/WEF_GlobalCompetitiveness Report_2012–13.pdf (accessed August 24, 2013).

Chapter 19

Improving mental health via schools

A perspective from Istanbul, Turkey

Yanki Yazgan and Selin Karacam

Turkey and its K-12 educational system

In the 2012–2013 academic year, Turkey had 16 156 519 students (5 593 910 in primary, 5 566 986 in junior high, and 4 995 623 in secondary education) enrolled in its 12-year compulsory educational system, a high proportion (96.97%) of whom attended public schools (Ministry of National Education Turkish Statistical Institute, 2013). The private school system admitted 488 340 students and it complies with the same regulations as the public school system. Of all the students in the compulsory education system, only 252 052 (less than 2%) were classified as students with special needs, either with physical, academic/intellectual, or emotional disabilities.

The Ministry of Education is the primary governing source for all public and private schools in Turkey, with the exception of a few internationally governed schools. Consequently, school mental health services across the country are closely tied to the centralized policies of the Ministry of Education in the capital.

School mental health services in Turkey, both in the public and private schools, are at best limited to the services of the Psychological Counseling and Guidance Units (Units) within the schools. Whereas not every public school has an on-site counselor, a rotating guidance counselor serves a large number of students and teachers, and district-based "Guidance Research Centers" serve as outside support agencies, which are overloaded by documentation needs of children who present with a wide range of disabilities (*The Official Gazette*, 2001). Despite the efforts of the professionals in these units, the resources for the school and educational psychologists and teachers such as training programs, child psychiatry supervision and support, and research opportunities remain limited for meeting the needs of both students and educators.

The Units in schools address student mental health through a number of responsibilities and activities. This includes: implementing the guidance curriculum and modifying it to the needs of the individual school; organizing educational and career development seminars; providing individual guidance; engaging in psychological counseling; generating a report for graduating students in cooperation with their teachers, families, administrators, and themselves for the purposes of documenting the student's educational history and providing relevant guidance; providing necessary guidance to students and families who need special education or inclusion services; and cooperating with the homeroom teacher in guiding the student for appropriate extracurricular activities.

Counselors at the Guidance Research Centers address mental health needs of the students through a number of roles and responsibilities. This includes engaging in activities

School Mental Health: Global Challenges and Opportunities, ed. Stan Kutcher, Yifeng Wei and Marc D. Weist. Published by Cambridge University Press. © Cambridge University Press 2015.

to raise self-awareness in students or individuals; conducting assessments for students if necessary; partaking in the referral process; partaking in report generation and consolidation; engaging in research and development of services; supervising counselors in schools; organizing meetings, panels, and conferences to explain the needs of students to teachers, administrators, and families, especially in those schools with no guidance counselor (*The Official Gazette*, 2009). The role of the psychologist at Guidance Research Centers includes evaluating and diagnosing children with atypical characteristics, adaptation difficulties, and disabilities; providing psychological support and therapy; and conducting appropriate outside referrals (*The Official Gazette*, 2012). The role of the social worker at the Guidance Research Centers includes gathering family information and finding appropriate referral resources for families based on their socioeconomic background.

In addition to the above-mentioned school professionals, there are special education teachers, homeroom teachers, and administrators who are indirectly involved in sustaining school mental health initiatives, especially in monitoring the overall health of students, developing and implementing supportive social-emotional programs, and documentation.

In this chapter we focus on the services provided to support the Units in schools by the Guzel Gunler Private Clinic, which is a privately funded, independent clinic in Istanbul, serving children, adolescents, and young adults on a fee-for-service basis on a sliding scale. This chapter is not intended to provide comprehensive information about the school mental health services in Turkey, but rather to share what we propose as a working model of school and clinic collaboration, to guide and empower the "manpower" in schools while providing support to foster the development of children with a range of specific social, emotional, and behavioral needs. This approach arose from the unmet needs of the Units at schools. In order to foster the empowerment of the school-based manpower whose priority is to support the mental health needs of the students, we set the goal as to collaborate with the families and all the related school professionals in order to facilitate better communication between parties and provide research-based alternatives or enhancements to the already implemented strategies. Our mission in writing this chapter is to share our vision, knowledge, experiences, and framework to help serve as one of the consultation and collaboration models in the field.

School-related services at the clinic

The Guzel Gunler Private Polyclinic is a privately funded, independent clinic which serves families of children from birth until their late twenties. The clinic hosts a resident child and adolescent psychiatrist (CAP), an adolescent and adult psychiatrist, a pediatrician, a school psychologist (SP), a clinical child psychologist (CCP), and a learning specialist (LS). The most common reasons for referral to the psychiatric department in our clinic is attention issues, developmental abnormalities, learning difficulties, behavioral disorders, social communication difficulties, and autism. As a part of our work with the families to ameliorate the overall functioning of their children, in addition to providing direct medical, counseling, and academic remediation services, we cooperate with schools and the families in order to provide the best care and support for children and adolescents in the school setting, as a third-party provider. We are funded by the families and occasionally take on corporately funded projects or public grants to do community service. Our clinic also archives the data we obtain from our patients, such as behavioral checklists, observational information, treatment information, demographic information, and diagnostic information. We use this data to guide the professionals in our clinic to enhance their efficiency in treatment.

Our clinic engages in school mental health services in two main forms. The first is through teacher and parent training and seminars. The second is through direct observation of the student and subsequent consultation with the faculty and staff.

Our clinic's system of working with children is significantly different compared to other similar mainstream privately funded mental health clinics in Istanbul. Initially, it is important to highlight that the consultation we provide aims to stay as objective as possible: we hold a "360-degree multi-perspective by collecting observational, anecdotal, and written record data about behavioral problems, social and emotional functioning, and scholastic functioning of the child, as well as the measures and accommodations at school by the teaching and counseling staff. In addition, and more importantly, our work is free of conflicts of interest in terms of the direct clinical or psychoeducational services provided to students in the schools by the school system. This is because the clinicians involved in the information gathering and observation, as well as consultation with the school, are not otherwise involved with the family, nor are working directly with the students who are the subject of the consultation. The therapeutic and educational needs continue to be addressed by other professionals. This gives us the opportunity to objectively observe the environment in which concerns are formed, as well as all parties contributing to the concerns. Through our objectivity and intended neutrality, our goal is to support the student by supporting all parties involved. These are some key differentiating characteristics between the services provided by our clinic and some other more mainstream private clinic practices. This difference in approach to school mental health increases our efficiency in providing the support needed by the children.

The second important characteristic to highlight is that, contrary to common practice, our intervention recommendations are tailor-made and are context-specific – that is, specific to the student, the family, the school, the content, and the social dynamic. Although we base our recommendations on examples of best practice both in Turkey and in international grounds, we look for individualization and practical applicability of each strategy we generate.

The third and most critical characteristic to highlight is our role. Families or schools typically choose to consult with us as the ultimate and last resource. This is at least partly due to our longstanding position as a tertiary-care and academically oriented clinic, while it is also a freestanding, private one. Therefore, many strategies have been tested and implemented, techniques have been tried, and contracts have been typically made prior to our involvement in the system. More often than not, this history brings along pre-formed dynamics and experiences within the system. We pay extra attention to these sensitive dynamics. Our approach is to analyze the efficiency of previously used techniques and pinpoint how they failed, and to use this information as a precaution in implementing other techniques. Our goal is to be creative in finding novel strategies and also implement research-based interventions.

Finally, we recognize that we cannot succeed in ameliorating all aspects of a situation at once. We try to prioritize the areas of functioning that need improvement by their urgency in terms of the level of harm to the child we work with, and harm to his or her age peers. In some cases, the needs of the child, the family, and the school may not overlap. Such a case may be seen where a child is hitting other children, suffering from anxiety, and failing academically, all at the same time. In such a case, while the teacher's main concern may be that the child is hitting other children, his parents' main concern may be academic achievement. Usually, the child's main concern is the level of anxiety he experiences on a daily basis. We try to prioritize where we will start based on the immediacy of the harm a situation is causing this child. Then we gradually try to support all parties involved.

Box 19.1 Key elements of our service

- Specifically trained professionals in the area.
- Two types of consultation models: indirect and direct.
- Multi-dimensional, multi-perspective data gathering.
- Tailor-made, context-specific, research-based and novel intervention strategies.
- Response to pre-existing dynamics between school, family, and other support professionals.
- Development and modification of strategies through progress monitoring.

Indirect school mental health services

Here, we elaborate on the developmental history of the therapeutic school consultation in our experience in order to understand how we formulated our approach to school mental health and developed the therapeutic school consultation in response to the needs we identified.

Thinking of schools as a mental health base addressing critical incidents

Our clinic has developed programs to help educators appropriately respond to critical and traumatic incidents and alleviate their impacts on students. For example, in August of 1999, Turkey was hit by one of the strongest earthquakes of its recent history, resulting in the loss of lives of thousands of people, and homes of hundreds of thousands. Dr. Yazgan and his colleagues implemented a preventative teacher-mediated intervention program to help support children of 320 families living in a village outside of Adapazari, a middle-sized city outside of Istanbul, in one of the areas largely affected by the earthquake (Wolmer et al., 2003). The goal was to help minimize the number of post-traumatic stress cases, and provide emotional support to these children and their families during those difficult times. Meanwhile, we measured the effectiveness of the interventions and the required teacher training. The methods included a three-stage process approach. During the first stage, teachers (who were exposed to the disaster) were involved in a group session to help them process and restructure their own experiences and responses, as well as their roles as educators, after the earthquake. In the second stage, teachers were educated about children's responses to trauma, and trained in what the researchers called the "Disaster Related School Reactivation Program." In the third stage, teacher-mediated group sessions were held with the children (during regular school hours), involving their parents in separate sessions, where during eight two-hour sessions over a span of four weeks, the groups focused on recovery from trauma. Those children who were involved in the intervention study had not received any organized mental health support prior to the study. Six weeks after the completion of the interventional group sessions, the students showed a significant decline in post-traumatic and dissociative symptoms, whereas there was a significant increase in grief symptoms. While 30% of these children warranted a diagnosis of post-traumatic stress disorder at the beginning of the intervention, only 18% still met the criteria for the diagnosis at the six-week follow-up, a percentage similar to that of the control group at the city of Izmir, which was not physically affected by the earthquake. In total, 39% of the children showed less severe symptoms, whereas 27.5% of the children showed more severe symptoms; 33.5% of the children remained unchanged (Wolmer *et al.*, 2003). Teacher and student feedback suggested that the intervention eased the grief process, as it also helped the students to better concentrate in class, improved the classroom climate, and increased motivation both in students and in teachers.

Three and a half years after the earthquake, a follow-up study was conducted by Wolmer *et al.* (2005) on the recovery rates of PTSD symptoms and children's adaptive functioning as measured on academic, social, and behavioral subdomains. The study found that when compared to a control group with similar demographics, risk, and exposure factors, the intervention group had similar rates of improvement for post-traumatic, grief, dissociative symptomatology in the period. However, the intervention group scored significantly higher in adaptive functioning than the control group. These results obtained in a most extraordinary and tragic context inspired Dr. Yazgan to focus on finding ways to increase the power of school-based mental health services in "regular" contexts.

General psychoeducation about mental disorders

Initially, the psychoeducation efforts were toward raising awareness among school counselors and faculty focusing on parent and classroom management of behavior and conduct problems, and a few diagnostic categories such as anxiety disorders, attention deficit hyperactivity disorder (ADHD), and autism spectrum disorders (ASD). Lectures were delivered to small groups of mental health professionals, or larger groups of school staff in collaboration with the educational districts or with the private school group. Lectures covered one or more of these topics and addressed questions from the audience. Parents and faculty both attended some sessions, and these were reported as the most productive based on the feedback from the participants.

Short-term intensive psychoeducation for parents, teachers, and school counseling staff was also offered at the clinic on the topic of ADHD, focusing on the diagnostic symptoms, associated conditions, treatment options, and implications for schools.

ASD, comorbid to ADHD in most cases, also constitutes a major part of the school-based consultation cases and attracts more attention from the public education system. However, this area is heavily commercialized by individuals and professionals who aggressively market their skills and unproven treatments and techniques, leading to a direct conflict of interest and exploitation of children awaiting effective treatments of autism. In order to counter this potential complication in our efforts to disseminate the best evidence-based scientific knowledge, we took advantage of our connections with scientists and renowned experts who visited Istanbul and invited them as speakers in our public education meetings. Parallel to that we were able to bring together a group of parents who organized monthly open meetings about the genetics, symptoms, educational intervention opportunities, other intervention options, and research updates in autism. Participants, who averaged to approximately 200 for each meeting, were mainly parents, teachers, therapists, and administrators. This little group of parents further established an active website (www.otizmakademisi.org) to share video recordings of the lectures with Turkish subtitles.

Public psychoeducation for increasing awareness about social and emotional development of children and adolescents

Social media has provided significantly more coverage of children's mental health within the past decade in Turkey. Although no study was found to provide exact numbers, considerably more people, especially in the urban areas, are interested in their child's mental health, in addition to their physical health and academic success. More families consult with professionals in their upbringing practices, and more articles are published on how to best support your child both in schools and the community. More coverage has been allocated both in written press as well as news broadcasts to the healthy mental development of children.

School-based research on case identification

Our accumulated experience with public pscyhoeducation and other educational derivatives enabled us to build long-term close relationships with the schools (teachers, parents, students, and administrators) and the educational system, leading us to develop a consultation algorithm that would enhance the clinical understanding and treatment of the child within the system where problems arise.

However, in order to promote support and treatment for a child with a mental health difficulty, the adults in his surroundings must understand and recognize the problem. Our school-based research suggested that the discrepancy between the reports of different stakeholders can be first observed even at the point of diagnosis. De Los Reyes and Kazdin (2004, 2005) identified how informant discrepancies between children, parents, and teachers influence the assessment, classification, and treatment of childhood psychopathology. Rettew *et al.* (2011) also found within a sample of 1730 Dutch children that home-specific problems were quite common, which were reported by parents but not by teachers. Indeed, Wolraich *et al.* (2004) noted that low agreement between parent and teachers "may be the rule rather than the exception." In our research, too, about case identification and informant discrepancy in ADHD, we reached the conclusion that parents and teachers significantly disagree about what qualifies as a case, even though they each were able to identify cases correctly. Thus, we suggested a parent- *or* teacher-based case identification algorithm, which should be the basis for better explaining to the parents and teachers about the inevitability of their disagreement and the necessity of managing this conflict during the treatment process (Güler *et al.*, 2011). The research we have conducted in the schools helped us understand the process from multiple perspectives. We could also establish a trusting relationship that would serve as a basis for our proposed model of therapeutic school consultation.

Direct school mental health services: therapeutic school consultation

The more commonly implemented type of services that our clinic engages in are direct services to the children, their families, and their educators on an individual case basis. These children's families initially apply to our clinic either independently as a result of their own needs, or when they are referred to a mental health professional by their school. Although in our indirect services we provide insight and support to schools when working with children, we never service a child directly upon a school referral. In our direct services, the child's family is always our patient and the child is always who we serve.

In supporting the child referred by his parents, we first obtain consent from the parents to work with the school. Next, we obtain agreement from the school for a collaboration focusing on one individual child. Our goal is to help support the child by supporting the teachers. Consultants at our clinic review all types of information that is obtainable about the child through the school system and the parents, namely anecdotal information from the teachers, staff, and administrators, behavioral checklists filled out by teachers, counselors, parents, and the child himself or herself when age-appropriate, in-vivo classroom observations of the child, and record review focusing on attendance, academic, and disciplinary aspects. Occasionally, we enrich the data collected from the child by conducting psycho-educational testing privately in our clinic. When developing an intervention plan, our main focus is on enhancing the teacher's toolbox in supporting the individual child, as well as strengthening the system so the teacher can get the support he or she needs from the administrators and staff. This empowers the teachers to try alternate, unorthodox techniques to accommodate the child and facilitate his or her learning and adaptation to the classroom.

Therapeutic school consultation: the nine-step process

Step one: referral

Once a family applies to our clinic and is approved for evaluation, the attending CAP conducts the initial psychiatric evaluation, during which the patient's need for a school intervention is determined. The CAP then refers the family to the Therapeutic School Consultation Team for further evaluation of the presenting issue, as well as to determine whether the student and the family would be a good candidate to benefit from the services we offer in our clinic.

Following this step, the team members, typically either one or two of an SP, a CCP, and an LS, contact the family to schedule an intake session, briefing the referral made. The team also sends the family a document detailing the therapeutic school consultation process for them to review and familiarize themselves with the information prior to the meeting.

Step two: family intake

During the intake session, the consultants listen to the family's concerns and obtain detailed information such as anecdotal information, school report cards, weekly behavior charts, emails, etc. Once the problem area is identified in detail, the family's needs are evaluated. This step is especially important in determining what type of intervention is needed, and whether it is appropriate for the intervention to be school-based or not.

Step three: a bimodal approach

In step three, the selected consultants engage in contact with the school and commence the process. Due to differing needs of students, two types of consultation are available, which we call *modes*. These two modes were determined according to the extent and depth of data gathered regarding the referred child, as well as the degree and extent of the collaboration and consultation with the school. Geographic factors (in Istanbul vs. in other parts of Turkey vs. outside Turkey), type of school (public vs. private), the mental health and special

Table 19.1 Informative pamphlet for families on therapeutic school consultation steps 1 and 2, referral and family intake

THERAPEUTIC SCHOOL CONSULTATION (TSC) PROCESS

1. **REFERRAL: Need is determined by the CAP. The patient coordinator assigns the appointment.**
2. **FAMILY INTAKE:** 1 SESSION

   - Determines the need and suitability for the TSC process.
   - TSC is described in detail.
   - One of the two options for step three is determined with the family based on the identified needs.

     a) Distant consultation in TSC.
     b) School visit in TSC.

THERAPEUTIC SCHOOL CONSULTATION (TSC) PROCESS

3. **REFERRAL: Need is determined by the CAP. The patient coordinator assigns the appointment.**
4. **FAMILY INTAKE:** 1 SESSION

   - Determines the need and suitability for the TSC process.
   - TSC is described in detail.
   - One of the two options for step three is determined with the family based on the identified needs.

     a) Distant consultation in TSC.
     b) School visit in TSC.

educational resources available at the school, openness of the school for collaboration, the family's reservations, fiscal concerns, and the gravity of the presenting issue are key factors considered in determining which type of consultation will best fit the student's and the family's needs.

In Mode A, consultation is provided from a distance, using telecommunication technology (e-mail, telephone, Skype, YouTube video clips, to name a few). In Mode B, information is gathered on-site, in schools, and occasionally at home, by direct observation and anecdotal reports from teacher and administrator interviews. In both modes, we collect information by asking the teachers and parents to complete checklists, as well as do a record review on the referred student. Whether to proceed in Mode A or Mode B is decided upon in step three. During steps four through eight, the depth and extent of the information obtained from school, as well as the intervention designed for the child, vary according to the mode. Regardless of complexity, both modes are aimed to be concluded in eight steps. Upon the conclusion of these eight steps, both modes are preceded by a follow-up process, resulting in conclusion of a total of nine steps, regardless of which mode you pursue.

Steps four, five, six, seven, and eight – Mode A: distant individualized consultation

Mode A features consultation from a distance, without an actual site visit and on-site observation of the child. Once the family intake session is completed and the route that shall be taken is determined, the consultants contact the school, which constitutes step three. Upon first contact, the consultants obtain information regarding the student's school performance. The point of contact is either the homeroom teacher or the guidance counselor. Besides obtaining information from the guidance counselor, we value perspectives of the homeroom teacher since they typically are the ones with the most significant amount of information regarding the student's overall functioning, especially when the student is in earlier grades. Both the guidance counselor and the homeroom teacher determine together whether other key educational professionals need to be involved. When available, the guidance counselor arranges for the consultants to have conversations with other teachers. The roles of the homeroom teacher and the guidance counselor are especially critical in determining how welcoming the school is of third-party providers and how involved the consultants are expected to be. Following this, other identified teachers, administrators, and teachers' aides are contacted to get a full picture of the student's functioning.

In addition to anecdotal information, any or preferably all teachers of the core courses (reading, writing, math, science, and social studies) are asked to complete standardized checklists regarding the student. If the problem area involves any elective courses, obtaining anecdotal and structured information from the teacher of that subject (e.g. foreign languages, physical education) is of significant value as well.

In step four, further information from parties outside of the school, such as tutors, coaches, home-based teachers, occupational therapists, speech and language pathologists, or other support professionals, are gathered.

In step five, information collected from all parties involved is processed, and the student's case is conceptualized. Areas of strength and weakness, both within the student and within the system, are identified. Hypotheses regarding these issues are formed; strategies to intervene with the current situation are generated. The case is then presented at the weekly team meeting, discussing the observations, hypotheses, and potential intervention strategies. The case is open for suggestions from a psychiatrist, clinical psychologists, and a pediatrician on the team. Upon completion of the team meeting, a report is generated, documenting the information obtained, the results of standardized measures such as checklists, identifying the common problem areas, and describing detailed intervention techniques and strategies. Each suggested intervention is presented to address a particular area of difficulty, and at least one alternative technique is provided to address the same issue. Interventions are designed considering the daily workload and dynamics of the school system where the intervention will occur.

In step six, the report is initially shared with the family, and later discussed to help answer questions or address any issues or areas of concern. The necessary modifications to the report are made following the consultation with the family. Once the report is finalized and approved for sharing by the family, it is sent to the school via e-mail in step seven.

Finally, in step eight direct contact is made with either the guidance counselor or the homeroom teacher at the school, addressing any issues or questions they may have about the report. After reviewing the report together with the contact person, a mutually agreed implementation plan is generated. In addition, a follow-up plan is discussed and the schedule of future contacts is determined. Usually, a follow-up phone call is recommended two weeks and four weeks following this conversation, and it is communicated to the school that they may contact the consultants at any point regarding any concerns that may arise. In step nine the follow-up phases are developed upon conclusion of step eight, which will be discussed in further detail later in this chapter.

Table 19.2 Informative pamphlet for families on therapeutic school consultation (TSC) step 3A: distant consultation

3.A. Distant consultation process in TSC	DURATION
3.A.1. **Collecting information from the school** • E-mail exchanges and phone conversations with all teachers involved with the student in order to obtain information regarding the child's overall functionality in the school * This step may be repeated as needed throughout the process, and the information obtained will be reprocessed as updated	2 sessions
3.A.2. **Putting together information** *When applicable*, obtaining information from other professionals the student works with outside of school	1 session
3.A.3. **Evaluation, generating an intervention plan and report** • Processing and organizing the obtained information • Sharing the information with the CAP at the team meeting for supervision • Documenting the areas and behaviors of concern • Generating an intervention plan to address the areas and behaviors of concern • This step will be completed within the first ten days of the initial contact made to gather information	3 sessions
3.A.4. **First family feedback session** • Sharing the report with the family via e-mail • Answering related questions and making necessary revisions upon family feedback • Family feedback session in the clinic upon request	1 session
3.A.5. **Sharing the report with the school** With the family's permission, sharing the revised report with the school via e-mail	(1 session, not subject to billing)
3.A.6. **Contact with the school** • Follow-up contact is made with the school one week following the e-mail sharing the report • Feedback is obtained regarding the implementation of the interventions • A common action plan is generated	(1–2 sessions, not subject to billing)

Steps four, five, six, seven, and eight – Mode B: school visit and direct observation

Prior to step three, Mode B can be applied either after steps in Mode A are exhausted, or according to the shared decision of the clinicians and the family to take a more intensive intervention route early in the process. Different than Mode A, in step three the consultants contact the school, either the homeroom teacher or preferably the guidance counselor, to arrange for a school visit date. They also obtain brief information about the student's general presenting problems, and formulate a plan for the visit. The plan includes the key classes to be visited, and direct interviews with the relevant parties in the school (teachers, administrators, counselors, etc.) The visit date is scheduled for when the student has core classes. Initial observations are intended to be on a regular school day. If the particular problem area exists outside of a school day, such as on field trips or during show rehearsals or sports practices, we find it best to observe both occasions on separate days.

The visit starts with the school day and covers at least a half-day, including one long recess and lunch periods. Observations are conducted during core and elective classes, recess, free time (if applicable), and lunch time. Interviews with the homeroom teacher, relevant elective subject teachers, guidance counselor, and administrators, when necessary, also occur during this time. Observers follow the school schedule and regulations rather than imposing a fixed agenda onto the school. However, ensuring that all necessary information is collected is a crucial part of the school visit.

The process we follow in steps four, five, and six of Mode B are similar to those of Mode A.

In step seven, phone contact with the school is made, informing them that the report will be shared via e-mail. During this conversation, a date is determined for a school–family–clinic meeting to serve as a feedback session, which is intended to be held in school grounds. The report is then shared with the guidance counselor, and also the homeroom teacher, so that they have a chance to review the report prior to the meeting. The school visit, as well as the report, are then discussed at the school–family–clinic meeting, which constitutes step eight.

In step eight of Mode B, the report is discussed by all parties involved. Any updates regarding the student's performance are shared with the group and relevant modifications to the report are noted. Once all questions regarding the observations and recommendations are answered, an action plan is generated and agreed to by all parties, namely, the school, the family, and the consultants. At the end of the meeting, mutual understanding of the duties of each individual is intended to be established. The follow-up plan is generated by scheduling upcoming phone conversations and e-mail reports. Typically, the consultant's role is to highlight the three most significant intervention strategies, generate implementation plans, identify areas where the school personnel will need further support and resources, and provide them. It is also for the consultants to implement the follow-up plan, which we summarize in the next section.

Step nine: follow-up in three phases

Once the report is shared, our clinic assumes responsibility of the case for three months following the feedback session or date on which the report is shared. During these three months, we follow up on the case to make sure the intervention is implemented by the teachers and administrators as planned and agreed upon during the school–family–clinic feedback session; we monitor the change in the frequency of unwanted behavior; we monitor the academic progress the child makes; and we monitor the child in other

Table 19.3 Informative pamphlet for families on therapeutic school consultation (TSC) step 3B: school visit

3.B. School visit process in TSC	DURATION
Scheduling a visit date with the school via telephone	
3.B.1. **School visit** • Direct observation during main subjects, elective subjects, recess, and lunch • Meetings with the homeroom teacher, counselor, elective teachers, and all other relevant school personnel regarding the student's functioning • *If necessary*, meeting with administrators	5 sessions
3.B.2. **Putting together information** *When applicable*, obtaining information from other professionals the student works with outside of school	1 session
3.B.3. **Evaluation, generating an intervention plan and report** • Processing and organizing the obtained information • Sharing the information with the CAP at the team meeting for supervision • Documenting direct observation data and the areas and behaviors of concern • Determining the problem areas and behaviors • Generating an intervention plan that can be implemented in a school setting to address the areas and behaviors of concern • This step will be completed within the first ten days of the initial contact made to gather information	5 sessions
3.B.4. **First family feedback session** • Sharing the report with the family via e-mail • Family feedback session at the clinic within one week after the report has been shared with the family, where the report and intervention plan will be reviewed in detail • Responding to the family's questions and making possible revisions	1 session
3.B.5. **Sharing the report with the school** With the family's permission, sharing the revised report with the school via e-mail	(1 session, not subject to extra billing)

Table 19.3 (cont.)

3.B. School visit process in TSC	DURATION
3.B.6 **School–family–clinic feedback session** • Sharing the report with the school in the presence of the family • Determining the plausible and inapplicable intervention strategies for the school • Determining role assignments for the implementation of the plan • Determining the follow-up plan	2 sessions

Table 19.4 Follow-up to Mode A of the therapeutic school consultation

4.A. **Follow-up process** Duration of three months following the date of report shared with school	
4.A.1 **Active follow-up** • Covers duration of one month following the date of report shared with school • Contact is made with the school on a predetermined schedule to obtain feedback on the implementation of intervention strategies	(2–4 sessions not subject to extra billing)

4.A.2
Second family feedback session
• One month after the school–family–clinic feedback session, a family meeting is held at the clinic to discuss the effectiveness of the interventions
• As a result of the needs-assessment conducted in this meeting:
  a) option 3.B school visit can commence
  b) individual sessions can be held on a "per-need" basis
  c) Process can evolve into case coordination
  d) A different plan formed in collaboration with the family can be implemented
  e) Passive follow-up phase can begin
	1 session

Table 19.4 (cont.)

4.A.3
Passive follow-up
• The second and third months proceeding the first month of active follow-up
• During passive follow up, information exchange and consultation continues (if needed) via e-mail and telephone
• Should there be a need for active intervention during the passive follow-up stage:
  a) option 3.B school visit can commence
  b) individual sessions can be held on a "per-need" basis
  c) process can evolve into case coordination
  d) a different plan formed in collaboration with the family can be implemented
	(1–3 sessions not subject to extra billing)

Table 19.5 Follow-up to Mode B of the therapeutic school consultation

4.B. **Follow-up process** Duration of three months following the date of report shared with school	
4.B.1 **Active follow-up** • Covers one month following the date of report shared with the school • Implemented per follow-up plan determined at the school–family–clinic feedback session • Contact is made with the school on a predetermined schedule to obtain feedback on the implementation of intervention strategies • Regular contact with the family is sustained	(2–4 sessions not subject to extra billing)

4.B.2
Second family feedback session
• One month after the school–family–clinic feedback session, a family meeting is held at the clinic to discuss the effectiveness of the interventions
• As a result of the needs-assessment conducted in this meeting:
  (a) individual sessions can be held on a "per-need" basis
  (b) process can evolve into case coordination
  (c) a different plan formed in collaboration with the family can be implemented
  (d) passive follow-up phase can begin
	1 session

Table 19.5 (cont.)

4.B.3
Passive follow-up
• The second and third months proceeding the first month of active follow-up
• During passive follow-up, information exchange and consultation continues (if needed) via e-mail and telephone
• Should there be a need for active intervention during the passive follow-up stage:
  (a) individual sessions can be held on a "per-need" basis
  (b) process can evolve into case coordination
  (c) A different plan formed in collaboration with the family can be implemented
	(1–3 sessions not subject to extra billing)

designated areas we set as goals for the child to obtain. The first month is called the "Active Follow-Up" period, which is phase one of follow-up. During this time, the consultants contact the school on a regular basis. In addition to these regular contacts, any phone call requests, e-mails, additional documents, or information are welcomed and added to the evaluation. Feedback is given both to the school and to the family on a regular basis.

Upon the conclusion of the Active Follow-Up period, a second feedback session is held with the family as step two of follow-up. During this session, consultants share with the family their impression on the efficacy of implementation of the plan and the student's progress. Also during this session, the family and the consultants determine the nature of their relationship for the next two months, which constitutes step three, Passive Follow Up. During these two months, contact with the school and the family is on an irregular, as-needed basis. Sessions, phone conversations, and e-mail exchanges requiring further consultation result in additional sessions. If a passive follow-up is apparently not suitable to fulfill the needs of the student (i.e., if too many additional sessions are required), either Mode B is implemented if it has not already been implemented (i.e., only Mode A has been exhausted), or a case management approach is taken. As an alternative, a different arrangement suggested by the family can also be implemented if the efficacy of the program is not compromised.

Case study: Derrick S.

In this section we present one of the first cases from our pilot year. The first case played a crucial role in determining the protocol, and still provides valuable information for future directions, which will be discussed in the next section. Identifying information of the patient has been modified.

Toward the end of the fall term, Derrick's parents visited the CAP's office for a psychiatric consultation regarding Derrick's behaviors both in school and at home.

Derrick was described as a smart but difficult child who is insistent on routines, does not like interruptions, has a preference of the use of some words over others, and has issues with "getting stuck" on some issues and not being able to let go. Derrick was also reported to have some issues adapting to the school, non-compliance with classroom instructions, hitting other children, and not being able to perform his curriculum tasks.

The CAP evaluated Derrick and described him as an overly sensitive child with high anxiety, and having significant difficulties in the domains of sensory processing, social communication, cognitive flexibility, and self-regulation. He referred Derrick to the Therapeutic School Consultation Team (TSCT) for an evaluation and consultation for the most efficient ways to include him in the classroom, socially and academically.

The TSCT also reconnected parents with the school to clear their miscommunications. The school had no intention of making the necessary adjustments for Derrick according to the parents' report. The school principal, reportedly, used Derrick's repetitive behavior as the pretext for excluding him from different activities, and she implicitly remarked about the "negative" diagnostic implications of his social communication difficulties. The parents felt intimidated by the school administration; on the other hand, the teacher's reports complained about the parents' denial of the problems and not adhering to the school's recommendations and requests.

The TSCT initially contacted the parents and asked for permission to reach out to the school. Once contact was made with the school, preliminary information was obtained via telephone and e-mail, and a date for a school visit was scheduled. Two professionals (a school psychologist and a general psychologist) made the visit, beginning with an interview with Derrick's counselor, followed by a meeting with his classroom teacher, multiple classroom and playground observations, and interviews with the school's administrators. During all the interviews, we obtained information regarding Derrick's academic, social, behavioral, and emotional functioning in school, during class, in the playground, in transitional activities, and during mealtimes.

We used an overt observation technique for the school visit, identifying to the school personnel who we were, but a covert observation technique with the student, only being introduced as visitors to the classroom. We used both running records of our direct observations of our subject, as well as anecdotal records we obtained from different school personnel. Although we observed the classroom as a whole, our focus was primarily on Derrick, and secondarily on the teachers.

Once the school visit was completed, the consultants analyzed the observational data. Problem areas were identified based on teacher reports as well as observational data. Collectively, teachers reported problems in a total of 12 areas. These areas involved hitting other children, not following instructions, resistance to change and transition activities, repetitive and self-harming behaviors such as hitting his head, impaired social relationships, resistance during literacy activities, and overall lack of readiness for elementary school. Box 19.2 shows the problem areas in detail.

Box 19.2 Reorganization of problem areas in school, reported by school personnel

Description of the problem in the school setting

Based on the information obtained through interviews and observations, we can describe the behaviors of primary concern that impede Derrick's academic, behavioral, and social-emotional functioning in school. These descriptions can serve as a guideline to identify the target behaviors to be modified with interventions.

1. Inappropriate interactions with Sam in the classroom.
2. Hitting other children on the playground.
3. Difficulty with following instructions during literacy class.
4. Intolerance of spontaneous changes in daily routines.
5. Difficulty adapting to transition activities.
6. Difficulty following instructions in the classroom that include remaining seated, or working on a challenging activity for a prolonged period of time.
7. Repetitive and self-harming behaviors.
8. Social stigmatization within the classroom by Derrick's peers when they witness an uncommon behavior of Derrick's.
9. Intolerance of irregular rules of the English language, and not wanting to spell his full name.
10. Elementary school readiness level.
11. Difficulty with writing activities.
12. Only speaking in English with everyone in the school.

Due to the difficulty of addressing so many issues all at once, we prioritized the target behaviors based on urgency within a school setting. We divided these 11 areas into two, labeling them the "primary focus group" and the "secondary focus group." The report and recommendations were generated addressing each problem area, in both the primary and the secondary focus groups. It is important to note that although these behaviors may be related to different psychopathological conditions, the grouping in this section aims to differentiate the behavior based on the impact it has on daily functioning and within the contextual priorities (such as behaviors that affect the safety of the child himself or another child). A psychopathological diagnosis is pertinent for understanding the mechanism.

Box 19.3 Description of target areas for intervention

In order to increase the efficiency of interventions, we suggest that the school address the more imminent behaviors first, and address the less imminent behaviors secondarily. For the purposes of this report, we will call this group of more imminent behaviors "primary focus group" and the less pressing behaviors with a lower degree of priority, "secondary focus group."

In our opinion, "Inappropriate interactions with Sam in the classroom," "Hitting other children on the playground," "Difficulty with following instructions during literacy class," "Intolerance of spontaneous changes in daily routines," "Difficulty adapting to transition activities," "Difficulty following instructions and sustaining attention on activities that include remaining seated, or working on a challenging activity for a prolonged period of time," and "Repetitive and self-harming behaviors" (items 1–7) are considered in the "primary focus group"; the remaining behaviors (items 8–12) are best left to be addressed subsequently, in the "secondary focus group."

The report was then shared with the family during a feedback session. This was one of the first TSC cases we took on, and therefore the model was still a work in progress. The family feedback session consisted of listening to the family's perspective on what was going on in school, as well as sharing our ideas of what could be done to best support Derrick in the school. The family was then asked to review the report at home and suggest any changes they found appropriate. Once the family approved the report, we shared it with the school and scheduled a school–family–clinic feedback session. During this session we went over the reported risk behaviors, the target behaviors we found appropriate to address, and we discussed which strategies were plausible for implementation in the school. We made a plan to implement a weekly report card system for which we would score Derrick's behavior in five target areas, on a Likert scale of 1–5. For the report card, we chose five of the seven behaviors we classified to be within the "primary focus group." This report card would not be used as a behavior reinforcement system, but rather as a way for the teachers, family, and clinic to track the progress of Derrick's behavior. In addition, the school firmly requested that Derrick be accompanied by a "shadow teacher," a one-on-one aide, in literacy classes, and the family requested that the school find one for him.

Box 19.4 Sample of recommendations in therapeutic school consultation report

For the playground

Primary focus group

1. Derrick's play area in the playground should be more clearly defined and designated.
2. In order to better monitor his behavior, he would benefit from having to choose between two activity options, and having a more restricted area in which he could play. For example, for the first playground break of the day, Derrick can be offered to choose either "riding a scooter" or "jumping on the trampoline."
3. Instead of monitoring Derrick one-on-one, the designated area where Derrick will remain for the duration of the break (i.e., where he will exercise the chosen activity) can be monitored by one teacher.
4. Derrick's developed math skills, and his natural tendency to engage in repetitive behavior, can be exploited in order to facilitate him remaining on one activity throughout the break. Derrick can be told that his task during the break is to perform a certain behavior, a certain number of times. For example, if he chooses to ride the scooter during playground time, then his task can be "riding the scooter under the bridge 25 times." This way, Derrick will stay on task.
5. Derrick can be informed that upon completion of a certain task, he will be rewarded. It is important to choose the rewards based on what Derrick will perceive as a reward. The rewards need not have monetary value, they only need to be of perceived value for Derrick.
6. In order to prevent Derrick from hurting himself by engaging in repetitive behaviors, instructing him to engage in an alternative behavior will help him to discontinue the destructive repetitive behavior and commence a constructive, alternative behavior.

Secondary focus group

1. In order to address the issue of Derrick and Sam playing together, Derrick can once again be given a choice about whom he will play with. The choices are best to be limited to two or three options, and not include Sam.
2. Using Derrick's natural tendency to engage in repetitive behavior, assigning tasks for Derrick to complete, such picking up toys, picking up fallen leaves, putting toys back in their designated places, etc., can be used as an activity to keep Derrick engaged in a productive activity.
3. At times when Derrick is visibly tense, or significantly non-compliant, making physical contact (such as a hug, a caress, a pat on his shoulder, or simply physical proximity) may help him calm down.

During the follow-up period, weekly report cards of daily behavior ratings were reviewed, and the process of selecting a shadow teacher was closely monitored. We generated a progress-monitoring chart on which we recorded the results from each week's report card on a graph. We shared this graph with the school upon the completion of the first eight weeks. There was no evident progress within this time. Therefore, we adapted the rating scale and lowered the thresholds for obtaining a high score for the target behavior. Although this chart was never shared with Derrick himself, and therefore used as a reinforcer, it was indeed shared with his parents simply to monitor his progress. During this time, the school did not further consult with the clinic about problems that remained; however, the family continued to seek out the support of the consultants in dealing with the issues that arose from Derrick's presence in the school and later transitioning into primary school. The school maintained a positive attitude for collaboration.

This case was one of our pilot cases where we hoped to perfect the model. In fact, we learned plenty from the positive and the negative outcomes of this case, and changed our model accordingly. Due to the continued requirement of our support for Derrick's functioning in school throughout the year, and later when transitioning into the primary school, this is a case we took on for continued case coordination.

Our role in Derrick's case involved direct observation of the child in the school environment, cooperation with the teachers to generate better solutions to help him by empowering them with new tools and strategies, supporting the family in working with the school, and supporting the school in working with the family. Our function was to provide mental health services and support as an outside professional collaborator. We played the school social worker's role by helping the family in navigating the school's system and helping the child transition into the primary school. We also had to play the school psychologist's role by conducting direct behavioral observations, generating interventions and monitoring the implementation and progress.

One of the most important lessons we derived from this experience was to conduct an intake session specifically for the therapeutic school consultation. Typically, families visiting our clinic treat our service as well-linked with other services. Therefore, as a part of the diagnostic procedure with the CAP, they go through a very detailed intake process. The families may find providing further information as repetitive, and therefore feel hesitant to provide the background information at a different point in the process. However, due to the difference in the nature of the work we do when working with schools than when providing medical/psychiatric care, it is of crucial importance to have a family intake session prior to visiting the school to better understand the dynamics between the family and the school, the demands and expectations of the family, and the starting point. Getting families and schools to commit to the implementation and follow through our system is a process involving sensitive boundaries and fine lines, which are best assessed prior to contacting the school.

During this process, we always described to both the family and the school the differences between a medical consultation with the aim of making a diagnosis and a treatment plan, and a therapeutic school consultation with the aim of not only improving the identified difficulties or impaired behaviors but enhancing communication and cooperation between all parties involved in the child's life.

Conclusions and future directions

Since our therapeutic school consultation model is still fairly new, our primary goal is to solidify the definition of our roles and our functions when working with schools.

Second, we hope to be able to empower families to reserve their rights to demand the highest quality of services for their children.

Next, we hope to empower schools with better tools, strategies, techniques, and resources to better support their students. Teachers play a crucial and pivotal role in students' functional adaptation and learning in the schools. When teachers feel overwhelmed, which is a common occurrence in both public and private schools in Turkey, it is harder for them to find the enthusiasm and courage to come up with innovative ideas, implement novel strategies and take alternative approaches. We hope to be able to provide the support to the teachers so they feel more empowered to go the extra mile in helping those children in need.

Although we have conducted most of the therapeutic school consultations in Istanbul, the largest city of Turkey and also the city in which our clinic resides, our goal is to extend those services to other smaller cities with even more limited mental health service providers at schools and no tradition of having psychiatrists or psychologists work in collaboration with the schools.

Our main goal is to help implement our model within schools, so that schools have trained personnel to conduct unbiased observations, generate alternate solutions to problems arising in the classroom, and closely and empirically monitor students' progress rather than rely on qualitative information obtained from teachers, mostly based on their overall "feeling" about the student's functioning. This will enable the outside clinicians to provide better diagnostic and therapeutic services, based on the enhanced quality of the school-based information.

The "outside" clinicians, on the other hand, should improve their skills in working with the schools for more effective treatments and better understanding of the condition. One of our colleagues has conducted a "travelling" workshop at different departments of child and adolescent psychiatry across the country, focusing on how to work with schools and parents for the child's best interest. Although we do not yet know about the impact of this educational effort, we designed a similar workshop with a similar aim, but this time to provide school personnel with the necessary skills in collaborating with "outside" clinicians.

Lastly, our experience working with schools is that clinical recommendations and interventions cannot find their way into practice (i.e., school life, classrooms) unless there is an established working relationship between the clinical team, parents, and the school. Our goal in formulating therapeutic school consultation as a "method" is to emphasize the necessity of developing ways to make the clinical recommendations, formulations, and therapies work and make an impact on the child's life by improving the social, academic, and behavioral functioning. This is a barely achievable goal if we restrict ourselves to decreasing symptoms or developing skills in our "outside" clinical work.

We encourage our readers from different parts of the world to actively contribute to this chapter by sharing their own methods of therapeutic school consultation to bringing together the parties in a working relationship for the interest of the child.

References

De Los Reyes, A., & Kazdin, A. E. (2004). Measuring informant discrepancies in clinical child research. *Psychological assessment*, 16(3), 330.

De Los Reyes, A., & Kazdin, A. E. (2005). Informant discrepancies in the assessment of childhood psychopathology: A critical review, theoretical framework, and recommendations for further study. *Psychological Bulletin*, 131(4), 483.

Güler, A., Scahill, L., Jeong, S., Taskin, B., Dedeoglu, C., & Yazgan, Y. (2011). Use of multiple informants to identify children at high risk for Attention Deficit Hyperactivity Disorder in a school sample in Turkey. Poster presentation at the Annual Meeting of AACAP.

Ministry of National Education Turkish Statistical Institute. (2013) *National education statistics: formal education 2012–2013*. Republic of Turkey Ministry of National Education.

The Official Gazette, Ministry of National Education guidance and psychological counseling services regulation. Number: 24376. April 17, 2001. Prime Ministry Printing House.

The Official Gazette, Ministry of National Education guidance and psychological counseling services regulation: amendments. Number: 27169. March 14, 2009. Prime Ministry Printing House.

The Official Gazette, Changes in the special education services regulation. Number: 28360. July 21, 2012. Prime Ministry Printing House.

Rettew, D. C., Oort, F. V., Verhulst, F. C., *et al.* (2011) When parent and teacher ratings don't agree: The Tracking Adolescents' Individual Lives Survey (TRIALS). *Journal of Child and Adolescent Psychopharmacology*, 21(5): 389–397.

Wolmer, L., Laor, N., Dedeoglu, C., Siev, J., & Yazgan, Y. (2005). Teacher-mediated intervention after disaster: A controlled three-year follow-up of children's functioning. *Journal of Child Psychology and Psychiatry*, 46(11), 1161–1168.

Wolmer, L., Laor, N., & Yazgan, Y. (2003). School reactivation programs after disaster: Could teachers serve as clinical mediators?. *Child and Adolescent Psychiatric Clinics of North America*, 12(2), 363–381.

Wolraich, M. L., Lambert, E. W., Bickman, L., Simmons, T., Doffing, M. A., & Worley, K. A. (2004). Assessing the impact of parent and teacher agreement on diagnosing attention-deficit hyperactivity disorder. *Journal of Developmental & Behavioral Pediatrics*, 25(1), 41–47.

Chapter 20

School and community mental health promotion strategies for youth in Ukraine

Nataliya Zhabenko and Olena Zhabenko

Introduction

Ukraine is the second largest country on the European continent, and as of August 2012 is home to 46 million people. Ukraine is still recovering from the collapse of the Soviet Union in 1991, which was plagued by a number of difficult stages of development, including the Soviet stagnation era since the mid 1960s and Perestroika since 1986, as well as the Russian financial crisis in 1998 and Ukraine's Orange Revolution in 2004 (Samokhvalov *et al.*, 2009). Ukraine is classified by the World Bank as a lower middle income country, and nearly one-third of the population currently lives in absolute poverty – that is, on less than US$2.15 per person per day (World Health Organization, 2005). Table 20.1 provides an overview of the country statistics (World Health Organization, 2012). These political and economic crises in Ukraine and the Soviet Union have resulted in substantial negative impacts to the health, including mental health, system in Ukraine. Substantial efforts to address these are now beginning. These include the development and application of school-based mental health promotion. This chapter describes current Ukraine mental health promotion strategies for youth in schools and communities.

Table 20.1 Description of Ukraine

Total population	45 530 000
Gross national income per capita (purchasing power parity international $)	7040
Life expectancy at birth male/female (years)	65/76
Probability of dying under five (per 1000 live births)	11
Probability of dying between 15 and 60 years male/female (per 1000 population)	310/120
Total expenditure on health per capita (International $, 2011)	528
Total expenditure on health as % of GDP (2011)	7.2

School Mental Health: Global Challenges and Opportunities, ed. Stan Kutcher, Yifeng Wei and Marc D. Weist. Published by Cambridge University Press. © Cambridge University Press 2015.

Psychiatric epidemiology in Ukraine

Prevalence of psychiatric disorders among children and adolescents worldwide is striking, with approximately 20% of youth (aged 12–25) suffering from mental illness over their life span (World Health Organization, 2001). While Ukraine statistics are consistent with world data, rates of mental disorders have been increasing over the past few decades. Prevalence of any mental disorder in Ukraine is 20.5% (95% CI = 17.7–23.2), among the highest in Europe: Spain (9.2%; 7.8–9.6); Germany (9.1%; 7.3–10.8); Italy (8.2%; 6.7–9.7); Belgium (12.0%; 9.6–14.3). According to the Ukrainian Ministry of Health, one in 4–5 children suffer from at least one mental disorder, every fifth child has either behavioral, cognitive, or emotional disturbances, and every eighth child is diagnosed with a chronic mental illness (UA Reporter, 2008). Ukrainian researchers conclude that the most prevalent mental health problems in childhood and among adolescents are emotional disturbances, deviant forms of behavior, and social maladaptation (Gura, 2008). However, one of the most serious problems of youth is increasing drug addiction. The most commonly consumed illicit drugs are marijuana and ecstasy. Of a random sample of 1800 people aged 15–34 from different regions of Ukraine, 32% used illicit drugs for the first time between the ages of 12 and 16 (European Monitoring Centre for Drugs and Drug Addiction, 2010). A recent epidemiological study in Dnepropetrovsk (one of the Ukrainian regions) has shown that psychiatric disorders have the third highest cause of disease burden (Vashchenko *et al.*, 2012).

Morbidity of mental disorders among children and adolescents in different regions of Ukraine during 2012 in absolute numbers is presented in Table 20.2. The morbidity of mental illness ranges from 419 in Chernovetska region (Chernivtsi) to 2595 in Lvivska region (Lviv) (Ukrainian Ministry of Health, 2013).

Table 20.2 Morbidity of mental disorders (F00–F09, F20–F99) among children and adolescents (0–17 years) in different regions of Ukraine during 2012 (absolute numbers)

Cherkasy	875
Chernihiv	1325
Chernivtsi	419
Crimean Peninsula	1525
Dnepropetrovsk	1716
Donetsk	2594
Ivano-Frankivs'k	991
Kharkiv	1857
Kherson	1510
Khmel'nyts'kyy	787
Kirovohrad	723
Kyiv	1039

Table 20.2 (cont.)

Luhansk	1624
Luts'k	468
Lviv	2595
Mykolayiv	661
Odesa	1760
Poltava	983
Rivne	691
Sumy	748
Ternopol	869
Uzhhorod	838
Vinnytsya	1038
Zaporizhzhya	1011
Zhytomyr	1895

The mental health care system in Ukraine

Prior to Ukrainian independence, the psychiatric services system was inherited from the Union of Soviet Socialist Republics (USSR). It was not effective in addressing child and youth mental healthcare needs and was chronically under-funded (Martsenkovsky, 2011). The Ukrainian healthcare system currently is based mostly on specialized secondary and tertiary care, and does not focus on primary care or prevention. Compared to current Western European and North American standards, much existing child and adolescent psychiatric care is archaic, based on outdated clinical psychiatric practice and still follows the direction of the old Soviet authoritarian traditions (Martsenkovsky, 2011). As of 2009, there were approximately 5000 psychiatrists and addiction psychiatrists (who receive separate training in Ukraine) and over 500 child psychiatrists (Martsenkovsky and Ougrin, 2009). The number of child and adolescent psychiatrists is decreasing every year; from 521 in 2010, to 512 in 2011, and 498 in 2012. Moreover, there are no child psychiatry departments at medical universities in Ukraine, and there are no residency programs in child psychiatry in Ukraine. A license in child psychiatry, however, can be obtained after six months of training following a general psychiatric internship. Pediatricians often identify children with and at risk for behavioral health problems who may not receive evidence-based interventions through either the mental health or educational systems (Kazak, 2010). There are social services run by the government for children, youth, and families, and they are responsible for promoting healthy life skills. Social services exist in at least two forms: social service centers and social work mobile advisory points. Services include individual and group counseling, lectures, talks, workshops, videos, outdoor games, and other non-evidence supported preventive measures in summer camps, as well as distribution of promotional and informational materials. The dominant topic for prevention focuses on the prevention of drug/alcohol problems. In 2010, 13 685 children and young people accessed services from the 468 social work mobile advisory points (European Monitoring Centre for Drugs and Drug Addiction, 2010). However, it also should be noted that public awareness about the types of social services available and the opportunities to obtain them is low within Ukraine (European Monitoring Centre for Drugs and Drug Addiction, 2010).

Ukraine has been accepted into the International Association for Child and Adolescent Psychiatry and Allied Professions as a full member, and this is a hopeful step in the direction of increasing and improving the role of child psychiatry in the country to address child and youth mental health needs. The section of Child Psychiatry of the Scientific Society of Neurologists, Psychiatrists, and Addiction Psychiatrists of Ukraine plans to reform the children's mental health system in Ukraine, together with colleagues from the United Kingdom, Poland, and the United States (Martsenkovsky, 2011).

School and community mental health infrastructure in Ukraine

The Ukrainian Ministry of Health reports that the health system is not ideal and should be reorganized, and that mental disorders in children and adolescent are a heavy economic burden for society (Design Concept for improving mental health care for children in Ukraine, 2012). As a result, a number of national and international policies have been endorsed by the government to support mental health initiatives in Ukraine, including:

- the United Nations (UN) Convention on the Rights of the Child (UN Convention on the Rights of the Child, 1989);
- Ukrainian Law "Protection of Childhood" (Supreme Council of Ukraine, 2001). It is a strategic national priority legislation, enacted for the purpose of ensuring the implementation of children's rights to life, health, education, social protection, and development overall.

In 2011 the President of Ukraine made a political decision to reform the psychiatric healthcare system, and in December 2011 Presidential decree No. 1163/2011 emphasized the importance of promotion of mental health and prevention, with the first paragraph of the decree calling for the "development and implementation of specific prevention programs for schools that will promote the mental health for students, prevent antisocial behavior, abuse, and ensure the formation of students' social and adaptive behaviors" (Design Concept for improving mental health care for children in Ukraine, 2012).

Meanwhile, Ukrainian researchers, medical practitioners (both psychiatrists and psychologists), social workers, as well as educators have invested significantly in the promotion of mental health and prevention of psychiatric illness due to the high prevalence of mental disorders, indicating that approximately 50% of all mental disorders in adults have an onset before the age of 14 years (Atlas: Child and Adolescent Mental Health Resources, 2005). In a recent survey of teachers, researchers found that 28% of teachers believed that students' knowledge about the risks and harms of drug use was not sufficient (European Monitoring Centre for Drugs and Drug Addiction, 2010). These results underscore the importance of improving programs for promotion of mental health.

Although youth mental health need has been identified and policies have been created to support addressing this need, there are no specific governmental organizations that are involved in mental health promotion and prevention of mental disorders in Ukraine, although some private and public agencies have started some work in this field. For example, psychologists in secondary schools are trained to diagnose the psychological status of youth, to document what they find, and refer students at risk of mental health problems/ disorders to psychiatrists when warranted. This is usually conducted through group testing on psychological functioning in the classroom, rarely as an individual examination, and if it is done, it is made by psychologists in collaboration with teachers. Psychologists also directly intervene and rehabilitate in cases where this level of care is available and effective. Promotion of mental health in schools includes traditional lectures to the students and discussions about substance abuse and consequences of risk-taking behavior. However, these kinds of programs are voluntary for students to take. The Ministry of Education of Ukraine has recommended implementing a monthly psychological hour into the school schedule to provide psychological support for children and to deliver psychoeducation information to all students to prevent behavioral and emotional disorders. The main directions of psychological services in schools include the following:

- Diagnostic and psychological examination of children and adolescents. Assessment of learning and development abilities.
- Behavior correction. The implementation of psychoeducation with the goal of modification of different pathological behaviors and predisposition to crime.
- Rehabilitation. Provision of psychological and educational assistance to children and adolescents who suffer from emotional and social distress, including crises such as natural disasters, etc.
- Prevention. Assessment of early-warning deviations in personality development, interpersonal relationships, interpersonal conflict, and other kinds of psychosocial distress.
- Psychological expertise. Evaluation of new training and educational technologies and innovations for their appropriate use in the school (Regulations on the psychological service in the educational system of Ukraine, 1993).

At the primary and secondary school level, teachers, school nurses, speech specialists, and psychologists work together to support mental health promotion and prevention strategies for youth in Ukraine. Teachers usually explain classroom rules in detail, encourage respectful behaviors toward other students in class, and reward students in order to consolidate pro-social skills. Students who do not respond well to ordinary classroom discipline are sent to the nurse and/or psychologist for further evaluation and recommendations. Schools for children and young adults with special needs (e.g., blindness, deafness, some mental health concerns, mostly mental retardation and speech problems) are available in Ukraine, predominantly (more than two-thirds of them) for children with mental retardation. Special needs students have choices to go to regular schools, but in many cases concerns about academic difficulties and social avoidance will bring them to these subsidiary schools. These special schools offer an excellent opportunity to provide services to this population; however, in some ways the separation of these children from healthy children creates avoidance of the problem and stigmatization of children with psychiatric and other neurological disabilities (Martsenkovsky, 2011).

At the post-secondary school level, information about mental health is included in elective courses on topics related to healthy lifestyles, and less than 25% of students voluntarily take part in such classes, as reported by a study conducted on the prevalence of preventive programs (European Monitoring Centre for Drugs and Drug Addiction, 2010). The goal of mental health promotion in college and university students is to help students transition and adjust to a new level of education (to increase protective factors, and to decrease risk factors). A good example is that in January 2002, Governmental University in Sumy created a psychological service in response to the needs of students and teachers to assist all those attending the university. This service provides help at the psychological office (staffed by psychologists and other mental health providers) and hopes to improve the social and psychological climate of the university. Psychological support of students is an important focus of practical psychology, mainly addressing the following areas: psychoeducation, preventive work, diagnostic work (individual and group), counseling (individual and group), and psychotherapy (group and individual). Psychoeducational interventions are usually delivered via lectures, newsletters, and posters, such as "Psychological Service – how it works," "Leadership school," and "School of supervisors." The main topics of prevention works are: "Suicide – the problem of modern life," "Stress and coping strategies," "How to be prepared for the exam," "How to plan your day," "How to deal with fatigue," etc.

School and community mental health initiatives in Ukraine

Recently, there have been a number of major mental health initiatives designed to promote mental health in Ukrainian schools and the community. For example, the research project "Psychological, educational, medical and social rehabilitation of children with deviant and delinquent behavior" was introduced at the Centre of Psycho-Pedagogical Correction in the Fontanskaya rehabilitation school in Odesa region. It was later extended to social rehabilitation secondary schools in some other regions of Ukraine (Lviv, Donets'k, Mykolayiv, Luhansk, Kharkiv). A pilot project has been done with the following objectives: development of behavioral plan for each individual in specific social conditions; social adjustment of children; reducing social deprivation; development of methods of psychological and pedagogical studies; development of methods to diminish illiteracy and school maladaptation; improvement of creative abilities and talents of each child according to its natural inclinations; development of labor education of children on the basis of the professional orientation of each individual. To address these challenges in the process, the following directions were pursued: (1) implementation of technology called Case Study (investigates a contemporary phenomenon within its real-life context, capturing information on "how," "what," and "why" questions); (2) overcoming students' illiteracy and building motivations to learn; (3) labor education, supporting creative work of students; (4) treatment at school; (5) social support students and graduates of the institution. Experimental results showed that these institutions were able to provide educational, medical, psychological, and social assistance to children who could not adapt to normal schools (European Monitoring Centre for Drugs and Drug Addiction, 2010).

In 2010 a series of developmental-educational programs for young students in governmental general education schools were voluntarily created and implemented by social educators and practical psychologists. Some examples include: "Preventing aggressive behaviors and formation of legal culture"; "Programme of correction of anxiety level in teenagers"; "Saving mental health and prevention of emotional disorders"; "Dealing with anxiety in teenagers"; "Anxiety reduction and prevention of affective manifestations of behaviors of elementary school students"; "Psychological correction of teenagers with psychopathic and accentuation of character"; and "Correction of children deviant behavior." However, such programs have been operated independently, are not evidence-based, and their impacts have not been analyzed. Their primary purpose has been to deliver information and educate students about mental health (European Monitoring Centre for Drugs and Drug Addiction, 2010).

In addition, a psychoactive substance-use prevention project named "Peer-to-peer education" was conducted in 2009–2010 in five regions (Vinnytsya, Ternopol, Khmel'nyts'kyy, Chernivtsi, and Kyiv) of Ukraine. Almost 7000 schools (100 000 students) took part in the following related sub programs: "Peer-to-peer education"; "Safe behaviors"; "Attention! Drugs"; "School against AIDS"; "Youth and the law"; "The influence of smoking, alcohol, drugs on the human body"; and others. More than 5000 peer trainers and over 20 000 teachers were trained to deliver the program. From all participants of the survey, only one-quarter took part in the prevention project. There was not a great interest in participating (programs are not held for the general public on a regular basis); only 1% of participants watched the movie that showed the alcohol- and drug-related problems; and the exhibition about healthy lifestyle was visited by 1% of students (European Monitoring Centre for Drugs and Drug Addiction, 2010).

Positive results were shown after implementing the selective preventive program for the children whose parents work abroad, for the parents and tutors of these children, and teachers. The project "Child protection service," however, was conducted only in the Kirovohrad region and the experience was not spread throughout Ukraine. The purpose of the project was to test positive behavior strategies among social orphans (in Ukraine, this expression indicates that a child has no adults looking after him/her, but one or both parents are still alive), raise children's awareness and responsibility, substitute aggressive behaviors with the ability to conduct a constructive dialogue, and to create a new model of social assistance (European Monitoring Centre for Drugs and Drug Addiction, 2010).

In 1998 the Youth for Health Ukraine–Canada project was launched, funded by the Canadian International Development Agency and managed by the Canadian Society for International Health. This initiative aimed to address the large and increasing percentage of youth in Ukraine who are demonstrating at-risk drug-taking behaviors by empowering youth, promoting healthier living and behaviors, and emphasizing gender equity and youth involvement. The initiative was conducted by a consortium of agencies and systems and lasted till 2008. The Ukrainian Institute for Social Research was the lead organization and built partnerships with Ministries of Health, Education and Family and Youth, another research institute, the Kyiv City Government, and a youth non-governmental organization (NGO) which collaboratively ran the initiative. When they adopted their project model in the regions, the institute worked mainly with different levels of government and youth NGOs. The mutual collaboration of all partners has been key to the success of the project model. The project's activities have included partnership building; the development and implementation of an integrated health education curriculum in schools; the development of a training program for service providers to promote youth health; the engagement of youth and practitioners in designing educational materials, resources, and programs to promote healthy youth behaviors; and evaluation of the strategies and research on youth behaviors, existing law and policy on youth health, and the influence of the media on youth. This project has gained strong public and political support at the national level to create a national health-promotion policy and it led to improvements in the quantity and quality of youth health promotion policies and programs at national, regional, and local levels (World Health Organization, 2008). The project ran in two regions, two cities, and two villages in

Kviv, Cherkassy region, and Rivne region, and focused on HIV/AIDS prevention, drug and alcohol harm reduction, smoking cessation, physical activity, healthy nutrition, gender equality, mental health, and youth health promotion policy proposals. Thirty Regional Resource Centers were established in the pilot districts, benefiting more than 3000 youth (Canadian Society for International Health, 2014).

In 1993, in Lviv, an educational-rehabilitation center entitled "Source" was created (Source, 2014). Since 1993 almost 2500 children and youth from birth to age 35 received help. Meanwhile, "Source" provides social services to the medical, psychological, educational, physical, social, and vocational rehabilitation for disabled children and persons with disabilities through mental retardation, mental illness, and violation of physical development. Daily, children with cerebral palsy, autism, Down syndrome, attention deficit hyperactivity disorder (ADHD), and other physical and mental illnesses get help. There are four branches in the center: (1) social, psychological and educational rehabilitation (ages 3–18 years); (2) Department of Labor Rehabilitation of Disabled Persons (persons aged 18–35 years); (3) Department of Child Development (ages birth to seven years); and (4) Office of Medical Support. In 2006 a new project for children with ADHD was created. The aim of the project was to generate a program of early intervention for children with ADHD. This was a multidisciplinary program with family-centered (providing services to children and families) help for children with ADHD, in which family relationships were emphasized as an important factor in psychological health. Among others goals, one is making education work with parents, professionals, and the general population to better understand the needs of child support and to strengthen the family, reducing social stigma and isolation.

Furthermore, a number of initiatives addressing ADHD have been created. For example, a psychoeducation program on child ADHD was delivered in Ukraine via the Internet in 2009 (Ukrainian National Resource Center, 2009). This online psychoeducational project delivers information about ADHD, and the website consists of the home page which welcomes everyone and gives an overview of ADHD, public announcements, information sources, gallery, archive of stories of individuals with ADHD, a forum, and contact information. The "public announcements" section contains key information related to ADHD in a chronological order. The website provides the most up-to-date information and activities related to ADHD. The "information sources" section of the child ADHD website contains an e-library, references, and websites related to ADHD in Russian and English languages. The "gallery" section includes real-life stories of children with ADHD, as well as pictures drawn by patients. The site also has a forum where parents, children, or specialists can easily interact with others. The website's information is also divided for different target groups: for children, for their parents, and for professionals. Each section contains information, useful videos, bulletins, pictures, information of upcoming seminars, etc. This website was created for psychoeducational and not for research purposes.

According to the website, the first publications on ADHD in Ukraine appeared in 2006, by Martsenkovsky and Tkachova. In 2008 the first book about ADHD in Ukrainian was published by Romanchuk, and in 2010 it was translated and published in Russian (Romanchuk, 2010).

As a result of the success of these programs, there were several steps forward made in 2008. First, the Ministry of Health in Ukraine conducted a focus group with those who worked on local guidelines for children with ADHD, the goal of which was to describe professionals' experiences and points of view of challenging public health issues such as diagnosis and treatment of children with ADHD. The professional educational training project for child psychiatrists was delivered together by the Section of Child Psychiatry in the Ukrainian Psychiatric Association, the P. L. Shupyk National Medical Academy of Postgraduate Education (Department of Child, Social, and Forensic Psychiatry), Ukrainian Research Institute of Social and Forensic Psychiatry and Drug Abuse, and with colleagues from the United Kingdom. Press conferences by the Ukrainian Independent Information Agency discussing ADHD in children and youth were held. Also, mass media started describing ADHD. In 2009, guidelines on "Health care of children with ADHD" were approved by the Ministry of Health and a great number of related activities have taken place. For example, the first ADHD conference for parents and children was held in February 2009. The "Our range plus" association for parents whose children suffer from ADHD was established. The summer school "Health care of children with ADHD and autism" was convened. ADHD medicine such as Concerta and Strattera became available in Ukraine. The DVD "Parent's school" by Romanchuk was created, and the workshop "Diagnosis of ADHD" taught by colleagues from the Netherlands and United Kingdom was held. Other psychological and mental health services based on national and regional programs are described in the Table 20.3.

Discussions and conclusions

Although some mental health infrastructures for children and youth have been established in Ukraine, such as mental health promotional activities in schools and mental health interventions at work, there has been a lack of mental health promotion services in Ukraine, and the mental health infrastructure in this country should be improved in specific ways, as recommended by the World Health Organization (WHO). This should start with the early childhood interventions in support of child and youth development. It should empower women socially and economically and provide social support for elderly populations. And it should further its efforts to develop community-based programs with a focus on schools, engaging collaborations from different sectors.

Some Ukraine institutions have initiated groundbreaking work to bring the community together to address child and youth mental health needs in the country. For example, the Institute of Mental Health at Ukrainian Catholic University (Lviv), with the support of the Swiss Cooperation Office in Ukraine, has implemented the project "Creating a model to improve the availability, efficiency and quality of mental health service for children and adolescents in Ukraine at the example of Lviv." This project tries to achieve a number of main goals. First, it aims to increase awareness of the community and parents about mental health problems to enhance early identification and provide early treatment opportunities. Second, it will modify and improve basic and continuing education of child psychiatrists at the Department of Psychiatry and Psychotherapy in order to ensure early detection and timely referral of children and youth to appropriate programs by specialists and primary care providers. Finally, it will develop a two-year training program in cognitive-behavioral therapy (CBT) for psychologists who wish to acquire a specialization in CBT focusing on mental health of children and adolescents.

In addition, there are several initiatives that could be considered for implementation in Ukraine. First, it is necessary to establish child and adolescent psychiatry residency programs. Currently licensure can be obtained after six months of training following general psychiatric residency, which is apparently not sufficient to appropriately deal with mental health problems/disorders among children and youth. Second, the work to reduce stigma

Table 20.3 Psychological services of mental health in Ukraine

Program name	Program content	Target group	Report
Multidiscipline program "Healthy nation," 2002–2011 (Decree on approval of interbranch complex program "Health of the Nation" for 2002–2011)	Stress management: how to reduce, prevent, and cope with acute and chronic stress. Creating healthy life-styles in the school community	Pupils	Training of practical psychologists and social workers of the program included interviews, lectures, training sessions, role-plays, and discussions. Several training seminars were organized and conducted on preventive education: "Useful Habits" and "Interesting hobbies." The program "Culture of life" was implemented in schools.
Complex program "Prevention of Crime 2006–2011," by the General Prosecutor of Ukraine	Early identification of dysfunctional families	Pupils and parents	Social workers arrange additional tutoring for children; attract this category of children to participate in work groups and sections in free time. School psychologists carry out child support through individual consultation with correction and development of personal and cognitive functioning. Psychologists develop and implement programs of social and psychological support for children with deviant and delinquent behavior.

European Network of Health Promoting Schools	Prevention of smoking, alcohol, and drug use among adolescents	Adolescence	The programs have been implemented in high school "Holosiyivsky" № 241, School number 59, Secondary School № 286 since 2004. The program is implemented via workshops in schools, prevention activities, prevention of smoking, alcohol, and drug use. Positive experiences are provided through seminars for psychologists and social workers, e.g., "The factors that lead to the first use of drugs among children"
The program "Culture of self-determination in life." Ministry of Education and Science of Ukraine. The Institute of Education of Pedagogical Sciences of Ukraine. UNICEF in Ukraine (The Law of Ukraine on Protection of Childhood)	The program teaches how to react in different situations (involving moral, social, communicative, aesthetic, and professional values)	Pupils	The integrated course for students of secondary schools (1 to 11 classes) has been successfully implemented in the gymnasium № 48 Shevchenko district (Kyev), and had positive results. Expertise is distributed among employees of psychological services through seminars and grand rounds.
The "Dialogue" Project	Promoting healthy lifestyles in children and adolescents	Children and adolescents	It is performed in 34 schools of different Ukrainian cities. Focused on psychoeducation about drug addiction.

and discrimination against children, adolescents, and youth who suffer from mental disorders could be very important for adaptation. Stigma toward mental disorders has been considered a significant barrier to help-seeking and access to care, and therefore, it should be prioritized as the foundational component in mental health promotion, prevention, and intervention. Schools could be an ideal setting for such interventions. Third, it is imperative to improve accessibility of psychoeducational programs not only in settings such as clinics and schools, but also for more general populations; mental health promotion should occur in "everyday" contexts, with actions such as conducting evidence-based research, monitoring, and evaluating current programs and interventions, and promoting mental health literacy. Fourth, it is essential to develop a cadre of researchers who can develop best evidence-based interventions and evaluate their outcomes, in school settings and in the community.

The importance of mental health promotion strategies for Ukrainian youth could not be overestimated since mental health is an essential component of social functioning and productivity. Mental health promotion improves the quality of life at the individual level as well as for the whole population. Ukraine has started working toward improving the mental health of its children and youth through a variety of innovations. The challenges for the next years include continuing development, analyzing the effectiveness of current programs, and working on improving promotion strategies among youth in Ukraine.

Declaration of interest

The authors report no conflicts of interest. The authors alone are responsible for the content and writing of this chapter.

Acknowledgements

We would like to thank Amy R. Krentzman for English copy-editing the manuscript.

References

Atlas: Child and Adolescent Mental Health Resources. (2005). *Global concerns: implications for the future*. Available at: www.who.int/mental_health/resources/Child_ado_atlas.pdf (accessed September 29, 2013).

Decree on Approval of interbranch complex program "Health of the Nation" for 2002–2011. Available at: http://zakon4.rada.gov.ua/laws/show/14-2002-п (accessed September 29, 2013).

Design concept for improving mental health care for children in Ukraine. (2012) Available at: http://moz.gov.ua/ua/portal/Pro_20120405_3.html (accessed September 29, 2013).

European Monitoring Centre for Drugs and Drug Addiction (2010). Country overview: Ukraine. Available at: www.emcdda.europa.eu/publications/country-overviews/ua (accessed September 29, 2013).

Gura, E. I. (2008). *Mental and behavioral disorders in adolescent, deprived of parental care. Abstract of dissertation*. Kharkiv.

Kazak, A. E., Hoagwood, K., Weisz, J. R., *et al.* (2010). A meta-systems approach to evidence-based practice for children and adolescents. *American Psychologist*. 65 (2). 85–97.

Martsenkovsky, I. (2011). The Section of child Psychiatry of the Scientific Society of Neurologists, Psychiatrists and Narcologists of Ukraine. *International Association for Child and Adolescent Psychiatry and Allied Professions*. 28. 5–8.

Martsenkovsky, I. and Ougrin, D. (2009). Delivering psychiatric services in primary care: Is this the right way to go for Ukraine? *International Psychiatry*. 5 (1). 2–5.

Martenkovsky, I. A. and Tkachova, O. V. (2006). Hyperactivity disorder in children: principles of diagnosis and therapy. *Therapy: Ukrainian Medical News*. 3 33–38.

Regulations on the psychological service in the educational system of Ukraine (1993). Available at: http://zakon1.rada.gov.ua/laws/show/z0101-93 (accessed September 29, 2013).

Romanchuk O. I. (2008). ADHD among children: practical guide. Lviv, Greo.

Romanchuk O. I. (2010). *ADHD among children* (translation from Ukrainion). Moscow, Genesis.

Samokhvalov, A. V., Linskiy, I. V., Minko, O. I., *et al.* (2009). Alcohol use and addiction services in Ukraine. *International Psychiatry*. 6 (1). 5–7.

Source (2014). Available at: www.dzherelocentre.org.ua/uk/ (accessed May 17, 2014).

Supreme Council of Ukraine (2001). The law of Ukraine on protection of childhood. №30, article 142. Available at: http://zakon2.rada.gov.ua/laws/show/2402-14 (accessed September 29, 2013).

UA Reporter (2008). In Ukraine each fourth baby suffers from mentally disorders. Available at: http://ua-reporter.com/novosti/43704 (accessed October 1, 2013).

Ukrainian Ministry of Health (2013). *Mental health and psychictric care in Ukraine (review 2008–2012)*. Kyiv.

Ukrainian National Resource Center, The problem of attention deficit hyperactivity disorder. Available at: www.adhd.org.ua/ditjam.html (accessed September 29, 2013).

UN Convention on the Rights of the Child (1989). Available at: www.unicef.org.uk/UNICEFs-Work/Our-mission/UN-Convention/ (accessed September 29, 2013).

Vashchenko, L. V., Rubaschnaya, O. F., Vakulenko, L. I., *et al.* (2012). Status of the problem of child disability (analysis 1997–2011). *Health of the Child*. 6 (41). 20–23.

World Health Organization (2001). *The world health report 2001: Mental health – new understanding, new hope*. Available at: www.who.int/whr/2001/en/ (accessed September 29, 2013).

World Health Organization (2005). Highlights on health in Ukraine. Available at: www.euro.who.int/__data/assets/pdf_file/0016/103615/E88285.pdf (accessed September 29, 2013).

World Health Organization (2008). *Integrating mental health into primary health care, a global perspective*. Available at: www.who.int/mental_health/policy/Integratingmhintoprimarycare2008_lastversion.pdf (accessed September 29, 2013).

World Health Organization (2012). Ukraine: Country statistics. Available at: www.who.int/countries/ukr/en/ (accessed September 29, 2013).

Innovative contemplative/ mindfulness-based approaches to mental health in schools

Katherine Weare

Aims of this chapter

The term mindfulness refers to the ability to direct the attention to experience as it unfolds, moment by moment, with open-minded curiosity and acceptance (Kabat-Zinn, 1996). It is learned through practices which might be termed meditations or exercises which train concentration of the attention. It enables those who practice it to be more able to be with and accept their present experience, and respond more skillfully to whatever is actually happening. The teaching of mindfulness is increasing rapidly across the world in a wide range of contexts, including most recently for young people and in schools, and the evidence base for its usefulness is growing. This chapter will explore the state of mindfulness in schools, the evidence of its various types of impact, and what this suggests about where mindfulness may best fit into mainstream schools.

   The chapter will give an overview of the state of the evidence but will then be illustrative rather than exhaustive, as the number of empirical studies is now large and the chapter will not cite every reference, although it will indicate the number of studies that have shown the impact of mindfulness on particular examples. It will highlight particularly the .b Mindfulness in Schools Programme from the UK to provide a thumbnail of how mindfulness programs work in practice and the evaluated impacts they can achieve (.b is pronounced dot-be, which stands for "Stop, Breathe and Be" – the core practice). Shorter illustrations from a range of other programs and research interventions will also be included.

Mental health and young people

As we shall see, mindfulness is starting to be helpful in preventing and relieving the mental health difficulties of children and young people. This is a welcome contribution as the level of mental health problems is indeed alarming, increasing, and mars young peoples' lives in many interconnected ways, including negatively influencing school performance by disrupting thinking and hindering learning (Barnes *et al.*, 2003). One typical estimate for the UK (Mental Health Foundation, 2014) placed the number of children and young people with an identifiable mental health problem, such as depression or anxiety, at 25%, 10% of whom fulfill criteria for a mental health disorder which justifies specialist assessment and treatment. This number of young people with a diagnosed problem is likely to be the tip of the iceberg, as most young people with mental health problems never have a diagnosis

School Mental Health: Global Challenges and Opportunities, ed. Stan Kutcher, Yifeng Wei and Marc D. Weist. Published by Cambridge University Press. © Cambridge University Press 2015.

(Farrell & Barrett, 2007). A great many more young people who would not meet the diagnostic criteria have their ability to function, including in school, but their enjoyment of life has been undermined by low level but persistent mental health difficulties and stress, a state which has been called "languishing" (Keyes, 2002).

Furthermore it is increasingly recognized that it may be helpful to focus on positive strengths and capacities and the ability to be resilient when faced with difficulties, rather than solely on people's weaknesses and problems. There is much to build on: Graham (2004) concluded that, contrary to the stereotype, most young people enjoy reasonable levels of positive mental health, and work hard at school, get along with their parents, and do not engage in high levels of risky behavior, while many young people move along a continuum or spectrum of mental health throughout their young lives, some of them toward a state of optimum mental health which has been termed "flourishing" (Keyes, 2002). Mindfulness has a key role to play in this move to the positive.

The growth of interest in mindfulness

Mindfulness can be said to have originated in Buddhist philosophy and meditation practice over 2500 years ago, the mission of which was to address and relieve the suffering caused by the dysfunctional ways people habitually respond to their experience. The secularization and popularization of mindfulness was initiated in the 1970s by Jon Kabat-Zinn, an experienced meditator in the Buddhist tradition, working at the Medical Center at the University of Massachusetts, who introduced an eight-week structured mindfulness skills training program based on his own knowledge of meditation techniques, greatly simplified, and manualized (Kabat-Zinn, 1996). The short course he devised gave demonstrable and relatively rapid psychological, and often physical, relief to a range of adults experiencing intractable severe pain and distress from a wide range of chronic physical and mental health conditions, and is the foundation for much of what followed.

Since then, mindfulness interventions and research have proliferated across the world, and the emerging evidence base suggests that mindfulness has a wide range of potential applications (Kabat-Zinn, 1996; Baer, 2006). The most common form of mindfulness intervention for adults is still a version of the classic Kabat-Zinn course, usually experienced as a weekly 2–3 hour session over eight weeks, which aims to reduce stress (mindfulness-based stress reduction, or MBSR) (Kabat-Zinn, 1996) or to prevent depressive relapse (mindfulness-based cognitive therapy, or MBCT) (Ma & Teasdale, 2004). MBCT is now a therapy officially recommended for publicly funded treatment for recurrent depression by the UK National Institute for Clinical Excellence, having proved to be three times more effective than treatment as usual (NICE, 2009).

How is mindfulness learned?

There are a growing number of types of mindfulness interventions, including, and increasingly, ones for children and young people. They include long and short taught courses, one-to-one or group therapy, tailor-made interventions for specific groups, self-help manuals and CDs, and online versions. Contexts include clinical settings, the workplace, schools, universities, and the community. Although details and exemplifications vary in different contexts, the core activities, rationale, and mechanisms for how mindfulness appears to work are essentially the same.

In line with the original MBSR course devised by Kabat-Zinn (1996), participants are led in simple meditation/concentration exercises which enable them to become more able to be "with" their present experience. Through giving close attention to feelings and sensations, such as the breath, sound, contact, and the fluctuating sensations that arise in different parts of the body, participants gradually acquire the ability to be aware of the passing and changing nature of all experience – thoughts, emotions, and physical sensations.

How does mindfulness work?

Over time participants, young and old, who practice regularly report that they gradually learn to sustain and focus their attention and accept experiences of all kinds in a more curious, interested and open minded rather than a judgmental way; they also discover how to use felt physical sensations of the breath and the body as "anchors" to return to when their minds wander and negative, ruminative, and repetitive thoughts take over (Kabat-Zinn, 1996). They come to see that thoughts are mental events rather than facts and can be allowed to let come and go: this realization helps loosen the grip of habitual, mindless activity, including negative ruminations and worries, and produces less reactivity and impulsiveness, and a greater ability to examine thoughts more rationally (Ma & Teasdale, 2004). This gradually modifies habitual mental and behavioral patterns which otherwise create and maintain negative mental states, such as stress, anxiety, and depression, and makes for greater mental stability, calm, acceptance, appreciation, and higher levels of happiness and wellbeing (Hölzel *et al.*, 2011b).

Mindfulness for young people and in schools

Mindfulness in education is not completely new: There have been calls for an increase in mindfulness in schools by academic educators such as Langer (1993) since the early 1990s, and the alternative educational approach of Montessori schools has long incorporated practices to help students develop concentrated attention to sensory experience (Lillard, 2011). However, over the last ten years mindfulness for children and young people in mainstream settings has developed apace, initially in therapeutic contexts, most recently in schools.

The country with the greatest number of programs is the United States, where the Garrison Institute (2014a), who are helping lead the field, lists 45 "contemplative education programs," all of which nominate "mindfulness" as their core philosophy; and the list is steadily growing. As a perusal of the database shows, mindfulness programs represent a wide scope. They range from short practices designed to be taught by any teacher to provide mindful pauses throughout the school day (e.g., Inner Explorer, 2014), to lesson-based curriculum interventions (e.g., Learning to Breathe, 2014; Broderick & Metz, 2009), to outreach programs which work with adults such as school staff, parents, and the community (e.g., Mindful Schools, 2014), and to programs that aim to be socially and personally transformative through the development of ethically based values, empathy, compassion, a sense of interconnectedness, and social and ecological engagement (e.g., Wake up schools, 2014).

Teaching mindfulness to young people in schools

The basic intentions of mindfulness approaches for the young are the same as for adult mindfulness, and some programs for adolescents, such as the Stressed Teens program (Biegal, 2009) stick to age-adapted versions of adult mindfulness practices outlined in the original Kabat-Zinn eight-week MBSR course, and with demonstrated success (Biegal *et al.*, 2009). However, there is a rich diversity, innovation, and experimentation, accompanied by considerable discussion and exchange of ideas around the appropriate formats, teaching methods, resources, and practices in the attempt to engage the hearts and minds of modern youth (Meiklejohn *et al.*, 2012). Some interventions include contemplative approaches such as yoga, tai chi, and relaxation, which may be more likely to appeal to energetic youth than sitting meditation alone. Some, such as the Mindup program (Hawn Foundation, 2014), use larger frameworks, such as social and emotional learning, which can help young people and school staff integrate mindfulness more easily into existing learning.

The .b Mindfulness in Schools Project (MiSP, 2014) has put considerable energy into creating lively child- and teen-friendly materials and methods, while attempting to retain the integrity of the basic practices of the eight-week course at the core, possibly because it was created by practicing classroom teachers who are also long-term mindfulness meditators. It is a positively evaluated mindfulness in schools program (Huppert & Johnson, 2010; Kuyken *et al.*, 2013) based in the UK, and advised by staff from three universities, with a rapidly growing presence across the world, translated into ten languages, and with several developing interconnected strands of work. The stated aim of the non-profit which runs it is to encourage, support, and research the teaching of secular mindfulness in schools.

The flagship course, ".b," is aimed at adolescents. It was first taught in a four-lesson version, evaluated by Huppert and Johnson (2010), and the most recent nine-lesson version was recently evaluated by Kuyken *et al.* (2013): findings were positive, as will be discussed later. The course aims to help students experience greater wellbeing, fulfill their potential, and pursue their own goals, improve their concentration and focus, work with difficult mental states, and cope with the everyday stresses and strains of adolescent life. The lessons typically include a brief presentation by the teacher with the help of engaging and punchy visual, film, and sound images, and practical and fun exercises and demonstrations which attempt to make mindfulness vivid and relevant to students' lives. Practices are relatively brief, lessons are closely structured, with repetition, home practice is regular but optional, and there are clear explanations about the purpose of the activity, as sometimes initially cynical students usually have no choice about attending. The course is supported by a student handbook, and teachers are given detailed scripted lesson plans with accompanying PowerPoints, film and sound files, an overall guidance book on how to teach mindfulness in the classroom, and access to an online community of fellow students and .b developers with whom to consult and share. In order to be eligible to attend the four-day training to teach .b, teachers need to have attended at least an eight-week basic course and have a regular mindfulness practice.

MiSP now also offers a version of the .b course for adults (which also provides an alternative eligibility route for teachers who wish to train to teach .b in schools), a version for primary schools in development ("Paws b"), and taster sessions.

The evidence base for mindfulness in schools

There is a sound evidence base, based on well-conducted randomized control trials (RCTs), for the impacts of mindfulness for adults on most aspects of wellbeing: on physical health problems – such as pain, blood pressure, and the immune function; on mental health – such as depression, anxiety, and stress; and on cognitive development – such as executive function, attention, and metacognition (Baer, 2006). Amalgamating the results of the studies by meta-analysis (Zoogman *et al.*, 2014) results in a medium effect size overall (Cohen's d = 0.30–0.60), which is usually taken to be convincing as an indicator of serious impact (Lipsey & Wilson, 2001). Work with adults shows that mindfulness training is cost-effective, with long-term effects often apparent after three years, and relatively short inputs producing discernable results: Four days of mindfulness training was sufficient to improve mindfulness, visual-spatial memory, working memory, and sustained attention (Hölzel *et al.*, 2011a). Even short periods of mindfulness practice have been shown to reshape the neural pathways in the brain in ways which increase the areas associated with kindness, compassion, and rationality, and decrease those involved in anxiety, worry, and impulsiveness (Davidson and Lutz, 2008).

Work on mindfulness and children is more recent, still relatively thin, and thus less definitive, but results so far are generally positive and promising. At the time of writing there are around 35 studies of mindfulness interventions which can be said to form its evidence base. (This refers to interventions which include some form of practice that might be termed meditation, aimed at children and young people in school contexts, published in peer-reviewed journals, and which include some quantitative assessment of impact.) There is also an expanding literature on mindfulness for school staff, on related areas of yoga and tai chi, on mindfulness in clinical and community contexts, on qualitative research, and on the theoretical base. A fairly comprehensive, and rapidly growing, set of articles of "contemplative approaches in education" can be found on the website of the Garrison Institute database of programs (2014b).

The literature on mindfulness for the young includes, to date, seven reviews of the published quantitative studies (e.g., Rempel, 2012). The most recent of these is a meta-analysis by Zoogman *et al.* (2014) which concluded from the 20 studies that met their inclusion criteria that mindfulness was helpful and did no harm, and had an overall effect size in the small to moderate range (0.23, $p < 0.0001$), a respectable result in research terms (Lipsey & Wilson, 2001).

Evaluated interventions are usually short, 6–8 sessions being common, but often originate in programs with broader intentions and aspirations. They are a mixed bag, and currently represent between them nearly twice as many targeted (22) as universal (13) programs. In terms of setting, the majority (21) took place in schools (mostly for age 11-plus), with the rest in clinical settings (11) and the remaining three in the community.

As may be anticipated in a new field, there are as yet weaknesses in this empirical evidence base on which all the reviews comment (e.g., Greenberg & Harris, 2012). Many studies are underpowered small pilots; there are only nine RCTS of varied quality, nine further studies with an element of control (mostly wait list), and 15 before and after. Descriptions of the methodology and the details of the intervention are often thin, and few studies have adequate follow-up. Studies cover a very wide range of conditions, problems, age groups, and contexts: there is therefore very little replication. There are as yet few measures designed for young people specifically, with no standardization or much overlap in the use of measures, and a good deal of emphasis on self report. Bias is a problem, with the frequent use of the same teams to design, deliver, and evaluate programs.

However, there is much to conclude already from this evidence base that is positive. Interventions tend to be highly "acceptable," i.e., well received, and there have been no reports of any adverse effects. Outcomes are in line with the convincing evidence base for adults, giving rise to the belief that the same processes and mechanisms are at work. Calls for better-quality research are widespread and many programs are now putting serious efforts into robust evaluation.

Targeted mindfulness

Groups of children and young people so far targeted by mindfulness interventions represent a wide range of problematic conditions. Informed by the impacts shown by the evidence base for adults, targeted interventions have focused particularly on mental health problems, both in clinical and school contexts, particularly depression, anxiety, and behavior problems (such as ADHD, behavior-control problems, and substance abuse). There are a few studies aimed at young people with sleep problems, learning difficulties/low academic performance, and economic disadvantage.

For example, one of the most methodologically sound studies in the field was of a targeted intervention, using an RCT and a large sample. Biegel *et al.* (2009) studied the effects of a modified eight-week MBSR course for 102 4–18 year olds with a wide range of mental health diagnoses. When compared with a control group, the young people who received MBSR self-reported significantly reduced symptoms of anxiety, depression, and distress, and increased self-esteem and sleep quality. At three-month follow-up, those who practiced more showed improved clinician's ratings of anxiety and depression compared with those who did not.

Targeted mindfulness interventions for children and young people have been shown to be significantly helpful, in line with the common finding that mental health interventions tend to have the largest impact on those with most need (Weare & Nind, 2011). The recent meta-analysis (Zoogman *et al.*, 2014) found a moderate effect size for studies drawn from clinical samples (i.e., with a defined problem) compared to non-clinical samples of 0.50 vs. 0.20, $p = 0.024$, commenting that this effect was nearly three times the magnitude. It would therefore appear to be worthwhile for schools to consider adding mindfulness to any targeted efforts they may be making to help children and young people with mental health difficulties, and to support any mindfulness therapy offered to their students by the specialist services.

Towards wellbeing: the universal targeted balance

As well as targeted approaches, the case is clear that we also need universal approaches that push the whole population toward a "flourishing" state of optimal functioning (Keyes, 2002), not only for the good of the majority but also to have the greatest impact on those at the sharp end of difficulty (Huppert, 2014). Many children and their carers never seek clinical interventions for emotional disorders (Farrell & Barrett, 2007) and so providing universal prevention programs in schools is an attractive and cost-effective way to reach this needy population. Providing a basic program with entitlement for all helps avoid the persistent problem of stigma that makes those in need of special help reluctant to attend or cooperate. It also engenders a humane and respectful culture across the school, and helps provide a broad base of helpful skills and attitudes by the whole community to support young people with problems. Ultimately, the evidence suggests that we need a balance between targeted and universal approaches, and that they need to be well coordinated with one another (Adi *et al.*, 2007; Weare & Nind, 2011).

Mindfulness and wellbeing

Mindfulness as a trait is generally associated with better health and wellbeing in adults and young people. Children and teens who are more mindful generally experience more positive emotion, better relationships, greater wellbeing, and less negative emotion and anxiety (Ciarrochi et al., 2010). It is not surprising, then, that five mindfulness interventions, representing a range of approaches, have been shown to have a measurable impact on young people's levels of happiness, calmness, relaxation, and overall wellbeing (e.g., Huppert & Johnson, 2010; Van de Weijer-Bergsma et al., 2012); Wisner et al., 2010).

An example of a well-established program which had a wide range of impacts on mental health and wellbeing is the universal "Learning to Breathe" curriculum, an MBSR-derived manualized mindfulness program which was evaluated by Broderick and Metz (2009). Their study, a non-randomized quasi-experimental pilot trial of a year group of 137 17–19-year-old female students in a US independent girls' school showed decreases in negative affect, tiredness, and aches and pains, and increases in calm, relaxation, self-acceptance, emotional regulation, awareness, and clarity.

Mindfulness and mental health problems

Both targeted and universal interventions have shown to have a significant impact on mental health problems in the young: indeed, it is in the addressing of problems that mindfulness interventions appear so far to have had the most impact. In the recent meta-analysis (Zoogman et al., 2014), in which 16 of the 20 studies were universal interventions, a significantly larger overall effect size was found on psychological symptoms compared to other outcomes measured by studies of mindfulness interventions for youth (0.37 vs. 0.21, $p = 0.028$), i.e., nearly twice the effect.

The evidence base for the impact on mindfulness in adults on depression is particularly strong (Ma & Teasdale, 2004). This impact is generally thought to be connected to the reduction of worry and negative rumination by allowing people to unhook from their recurrent depressive thoughts (Ma & Teasdale, 2004), a process which has been observed in young people (Ciesla et al., 2012). In line with this evidence, a relatively impressive and growing number of studies, seven to date, in both school and clinical contexts, are noting a fairly reliable impact from a range of different mindfulness interventions on child and adolescent depression (e.g., Biegal et al., 2009; Mendelson et al., 2010; Raes et al., 2013).

For example, the MiSP .b program has had clear impact on mental health problems in young people. An early four-week version was evaluated in a control trial of 173 teenage boys by Huppert and Johnson (2010) and produced significant effects on wellbeing among students who regularly did ten minutes of home practice each day. A later nine-lesson version had more substantial impact. It was evaluated in a non-randomized controlled study of 522 young people aged 12–16 in 12 secondary schools (Kuyken et al., 2013). The young people who participated in the program reported fewer depressive symptoms post-treatment ($p = 0.004$) and at follow-up ($p = 0.005$), along with lower stress ($p = 0.05$) and greater wellbeing ($p = 0.05$) at follow-up. Again, the amount of home practice mattered: The degree to which students in the intervention arm practiced the mindfulness skills was associated with better wellbeing ($p < 0.001$) and less stress ($p = 0.03$) at three-month follow-up.

Anxiety is the most reported psychopathology in childhood, often coexisting with depression, often persists into adulthood, and causes considerable impairment in many areas of life, including the ability to focus on school work and make friends (Rempel, 2012). The increasingly pressurized and fast-changing nature of modern life, and the increasing demands being placed on young people by schools, are risking the whole generation, including the very able, chronically anxious. Nine mindfulness interventions have shown an impact on anxiety in the young in both clinical and school contexts (e.g., Beauchemin *et al.*, 2008; Semple *et al.*, 2005). For example Napoli *et al.* (2005) reported on a project which integrated mindfulness and relaxation work with children aged 5–8 with high anxiety in a school context. The research was good quality and used an RCT design with 228 participants who were participating in the Attention Academy Program (AAP) intervention, which was 12 45-minute sessions of mindfulness and relaxation over 24 weeks. Post-treatment measures showed significant improvement in self-rated test anxiety, teacher-rated attention, social skills, and selective (visual) attention. Reported effect sizes ranged from small to medium. The study is unusually strong methodologically compared with most in the field, with its RCT design, reasonable sample size, and use of objective measures of attention.

It would appear that the impact of mindfulness on anxiety may work through its ability to improve students' attentional focus (Semple *et al.*, 2005), anxiety being often associated with attention problems. Other mechanisms at work may be the improvement in the ability to relax (Singh *et al.*, 2003), as well as the already noted ability to "catch" negative ruminative thought processes. This may all help explain the fairly regular impact shown by mindfulness on sleep problems in both adults and the young (e.g., Biegal *et al.*, 2009), which is most welcome as many young people are chronically tired, making concentrating in school and behaving well difficult.

Mindfulness and behavior

Schools may or may not be interested in mental health for its own sake, but all of them are necessarily involved in encouraging good behavior. It will interest them that mindfulness is having an impact in reducing the so-called "externalizing" disorders connected with difficult behaviors in adolescents, with four studies to date showing impact on ADHD, impulsiveness, aggression, and oppositional behavior (e.g., Bogels *et al.*, 2008; Zylowska *et al.*, 2007). The underlying reason why mindfulness improves behavior may lie in its ability to develop the vital skill of "emotional regulation." Mindfulness has been shown to help control impulses, delay gratification, and monitor attention (Hölzel *et al.*, 2011b), and a significant number (12) of mindfulness interventions for the young are showing an impact on improving emotional regulation. The training of the ability to be "with" experience rather than react appears to be able to increase the crucial time lapse in the brain pathways between the stimulus or impulse to act and the response in action (Goleman, 2006), allowing time for better choices to be made.

Mindfulness and learning

It is important to remember that the key business of schools is learning, not wellbeing, and that the case has to be made for why efforts put into wellbeing, or social and emotional learning (SEL), support learning. Making this case is increasingly easy to do, as the hard data on links between SEL and school achievement accumulates (Durlak *et al.*, 2011; Zins *et al.*,

2004), while neuroscience has long been clear about the fundamental link between the emotional and cognitive functions in the brain (Ledoux, 1998).

However, for those in education who have not caught up, or remain unconvinced, the growing evidence that mindfulness can impact directly on cognitive processes is potentially helpful in encouraging all in education to take mindfulness seriously. Mindfulness interventions have been shown to have the ability to enhance "executive function" in both adults and young people – executive functioning referring to cognitive processes such as working memory, problem solving, attention, planning, and self-management (Elliott, 2003).

Six studies from varied contexts demonstrated impact on executive function in the young. For example, Flook *et al.* (2010) conducted an RCT of 64 children aged 7–9 years to evaluate school-based program of mindful awareness practices, delivered for 30 minutes twice a week for eight weeks. The program was based on the well-respected "Mindful child" curriculum approach of Kaiser-Greenland (2009). It included exercises and games to promote: awareness of self through sensory awareness, attentional regulation, and awareness of thoughts and feelings, awareness of others, and awareness of the interconnectedness of the environment. The course showed significant impact on executive function, particularly, and predictably as we are seeing, in the children who had the lowest levels to begin with.

Schools are likely to be particularly drawn to the emphasis within mindfulness on the training of attention. The ability to "pay attention" is fundamental for learning and, often, from the teacher's point of view, frustratingly lacking in today's distracted adolescents. Indeed, Goleman (2013) recently claimed that the ability to "focus" is for all of us the critical skill underlying emotional intelligence and personal success. There is growing empirical evidence, from eight wide-ranging studies to date, of the impact of mindfulness with children and young people on improving awareness and clarity (e.g. Napoli *et al.*, 2005; Schonert-Reichl & Lawlor, 2010; Zylowska *et al.*, 2007).

Mindfulness has shown to increase metacognition (the ability to stand back from the thought stream and to appraise thoughts in a reflective manner) (e.g., Napoli *et al.*, 2005; Flook *et al.*, 2010). This is useful for any school working on the process of learning as well as the content; for example, for those engaged with teaching the "thinking skills" that underlie cognition, honing their students' capacity to form concepts, plan, reason, imagine, solve problems, and make decisions and judgments (Butterworth & Thwaites, 2013).

The most attractive evidence of all from the school's point of view comes from three evaluations which show that programs have been associated directly with improvements in academic learning, academic performance, and school achievement. For example, an evaluation by Beauchemin *et al.* (2008) conducted a pre/post no-control design intervention of a five-week mindfulness meditation with 34 volunteer students with learning difficulties, aged 13–18 years, in classrooms in a special school. The authors hypothesized that mindfulness meditation decreases anxiety and negative self-belief, which in turn promotes social skills and academic outcomes. All outcome measures showed significant improvement, with participants who completed the program demonstrating decreased state and trait anxiety, enhanced social skills, and improved academic performance. This demonstrated link with academic learning may encourage teachers to integrate mindfulness into their everyday practice and the mainstream curriculum, which is the point social and emotional learning starts to really make a strong difference in terms of demonstrable impact on learners (Weare & Nind, 2011).

Mindfulness and social and emotional learning

Many schools have already "got" the link between wellbeing and academic learning, and the last few decades have seen a major shift in the widening role of the school, with a cluster of interventions under a plethora of names including "social and emotional learning," "emotional intelligence/literacy," "resilience," "lifeskills," "character education," and more recently, "flourishing." The evidence base suggests that the best of the interventions, when well implemented, are effective in promoting positive wellbeing, helping those with problems, and improving behavior and learning (Adi *et al.*, 2007; Shucksmith *et al.*, 2007; Weare & Nind, 2011).

Mindfulness for adults has been shown to impact on the ability to feel calm and in control of the emotions, to make meaningful relationships, and to experience compassion, empathy, and attunement, to accept experience, to manage difficult feelings, and to be resilient, motivated, persistent, and optimistic (e.g., Mendelson *et al.*, 2010). Seven varied mindfulness interventions have detected direct impacts on self-awareness, self-esteem, and self-acceptance in the young (e.g., Biegal *et al.*, 2009). Mindfulness-based interventions are showing similar promise in helping children develop sociability and relationships (two studies, e.g., Kerrigan *et al.*, 2010); the resilience to manage stress (five studies, e.g., Kuyken *et al.*, 2013); optimism (Schonert-Reichl & Lawlor, 2010); and set goals more effectively (Bogels *et al.*, 2008).

Mindfulness appears, then, to have something valuable to add to existing inputs on the promotion of mental health and on SEL. As Shucksmith *et al.* (2007) concluded, if we look beneath the branding, effective mental health/SEL interventions offer a very similar mix of CBT and social skills training for children in self-regulation, and for parents and teachers in appropriate reinforcement and better methods of discipline: the formula is generally the same whatever the problem or diagnosis. Mindfulness has been termed the "missing piece" that has the potential to work alongside these rather cognitive, wordy, and teacher-driven approaches and make them more effective with a relatively small additional input (Lantieri & Nambiar, 2012). It can help rather cerebral practices, and take on the new depth that comes from the work of quiet exploration of mind and body, the objectivity that comes with relaxed and acceptant awareness of passing thoughts, feelings, and sensations, and the empowerment that comes from developing the inner self-management techniques to take charge of one's own growth and development.

Mindfulness and school staff

So far, this chapter has looked at interventions for school students, but there is a strong argument for starting further back, with school staff. There is a consensus among those responsible for training mindfulness teachers that those who would teach mindfulness need to learn and practice it first if they are to understand its somewhat paradoxical processes from within and embody its (educationally non-traditional) attitudes of open-minded non-judgmentalism, in an authentic and convincing way (Albrecht *et al.*, 2012; Crane, 2010).

The .b project has adopted a useful phraseology to distinguish three levels at which mindfulness may impact on school staff (MiSP, 2014). The first is that they "be mindful" themselves, i.e., learn and practice mindfulness for their own benefit and wellbeing. The second is that they "teach mindfully," i.e., allow mindfulness to impact on the way they teach in their normal line of duty. The third is "teach mindfulness," i.e., to impart mindfulness through directly teaching it to their students.

Teaching is a tough job, mental health problems are endemic, and the human and financial costs in terms of staff stress, absenteeism, and attrition are high for both teachers and students (Brouwers & Tomic, 2000). So the requirement that teachers are first able to "be mindful" is a benign one as mindfulness has been shown to support teachers with their own health and wellbeing. As we have seen, there is sound evidence that mindfulness can produce improvements in physical and mental health of adults in general, and more recently five studies with teachers specifically have indicated improvements particularly relevant to the teaching profession such as reducing burnout and stress (e.g., Albrecht *et al.*, 2012).

The benefits of teachers then being able to go on to "teach mindfully" are also showing up in terms of their improved classroom performance. Mindfulness can enable teachers to be more effective in most aspects of their everyday work in classrooms, for example by improving their ability to relate supportively to their students, managing their own emotions, and staying calm and in control, attuning more empathically with greater "presence" and reciprocity, managing student behavior more effectively, being more flexible and responsive in their responses, and staying on track with their intentions through the course of a lesson (Albrecht *et al.*, 2012; Meiklejohn *et al.*, 2012; Napoli *et al.*, 2005).

Thus, it is unsurprising then that most effective mindfulness-in-schools courses incorporate a strong element of teacher education, and indeed some programs concentrate solely on this – for example, the Cultivating Awareness and Resilience in Education (CARE) program of the Garrison Institute in the United States. This program (Garrison Institute, 2014c) has been developed by a team of researchers, educators, and psychologists over the last six years. Its intentions are to help teachers reduce stress through greater calm, and bring greater awareness into the classroom to enhance their relationships with their students, their classroom management, and their curricular implementation. It aims to do this through promoting awareness, presence, compassion, reflection, and inspiration, seen as the inner resources teachers need to help students flourish socially, emotionally, and academically. The program introduces basic mindful awareness activities, such as periods of silent reflection, caring practice, and mindful listening activities to promote empathy, and progresses to activities that demonstrate how to bring mindfulness to challenging situations teachers often encounter.

The program has been subject to several evaluations. Two pilot studies (Jennings *et al.*, 2011) examined program feasibility, attractiveness, and efficacy. They found that while teachers in the high-stress, high-risk urban settings showed significant pre/post improvements in mindfulness and a reduction in a sense of burnout/time-related stress, those teaching in less challenging school environments did not, suggesting that this program, and possibly mindfulness more generally, may be more efficacious in supporting teachers working in high-risk settings, another example of the tendency for mental health interventions to be of most help to those with most need.

A more rigorous RCT (Jennings *et al.*, 2011) examined a sample of 50 teachers randomly assigned to CARE or wait-list control condition and showed more general usefulness for a wider range of teachers. Participation in the CARE program resulted in significant improvements in teacher wellbeing, efficacy, burnout/time-related stress, and mindfulness compared with controls. Qualitative data showed that teachers viewed CARE as a feasible, acceptable, and effective method for reducing stress and improving their own performance, and reported that, as a result of applying the skills and knowledge they learned from the CARE program, their students spent more time on task and showed improvements in academic performance. It would appear, then, that mindfulness for school staff shows a good deal of promise for hard-pressed schools.

Conclusions

Innovative and exciting mindfulness-in-school programs for students and their teachers are being developed, and outcomes from the evaluations of various interventions, both targeted and universal, look promising, although there is an urgent need for more robust studies to support the exponential growth in practice. Well-conducted mindfulness interventions have been shown to be popular with students and staff, capable of addressing the many and varied problems of young people and their teachers, and helping them positively flourish. There are several possible promising locations for mindfulness within mainstream education, for example within SEL/mental health, behavior improvement, the process of learning, and staff development. Mindfulness deserves serious attention by all who would seek to help our young people grow into well-balanced, successful, and caring adults.

References

Adi, Y., Killoran, A., Janmohamed, K., & Stewart-Brown, S. (2007). *Systematic review of the effectiveness of interventions to promote mental wellbeing in primary schools: Universal approaches which do not focus on violence or bullying.* London: National Institute for Clinical Excellence.

Albrecht, N. J., Albrecht, P. M., & Cohen, M. (2012). Mindfully teaching in the classroom: A literature review. *Australian Journal of Teacher Education*, 37(12), Article 1.

Baer, R. A. (ed.) (2006). *Mindfulness-based treatment approaches: Clinical guide to evidence base and applications.* London: Elsevier Academic Press.

Barnes, V., Bauza, L., & Treiber, F. (2003). Impact of stress reduction on negative school behaviour in adolescents. *Health and Quality of Life Outcomes*, 1(7). doi:10.1186/1477-7525-1-10.

Beauchemin, J. Hutchins, T. L., & Patterson, F. (2008) Mindfulness meditation may lessen anxiety, promote social skills and improve academic performance amongst adolescents with learning difficulties. *Complementary Health Practice Review*, 13, 34–45.

Biegal, G. (2009) *Stress reduction workbook for teens.* Oakland, CA: Instant Help/Harbinger.

Biegel, G. M., Brown, K. W., Shapiro, S. L., & Schubert, C. M. (2009) Mindfulness-based stress reduction for the treatment of adolescent psychiatric outpatients: a randomized clinical trial. *Journal of Consulting and Clinical Psychology*, 77(5), 855–866.

Bogels, S., Hoogstaf, B., Van Dun, L., De Schutter, S., & Restifo, K. (2008) Mindfulness training for adolescents with externalizing disorders and their parents. *Behavioural and Cognitive Psychotherapy* 36(2), 193–209.

Broderick, P. C. & Metz, S. (2009) Learning to BREATHE: A pilot trial of a mindfulness curriculum for adolescents. *Advances in School Mental Health Promotion*, 2(1), 35–45.

Brouwers, A. & Tomic, W. (2000) A longitudinal study of teacher burnout and perceived self-efficacy in classroom management. *Teaching and Teacher Education*, 16(2), 239–253

Butterworth, J. & Thwaites, G. (2013) *Thinking skills: Critical thinking and problem solving.* Cambridge: Cambridge University Press.

Ciarrochi, J., Kashdan, T. B., Leeson, P., Heaven, P., & Jordan, C. (2010). On being aware and accepting: A one year longitudinal study into adolescent well-being. *Journal of Adolescence*, 34(4), 695–703.

Ciesla, J. A., Reilly, L. C., Dickson K. S., Emanuel, A. S., & Updegraff, J. A. (2012). Dispositional mindfulness moderates the effects of stress among adolescents: Rumination as a mediator. *Journal of Clinical Child & Adolescent Psychology*, 41(6), 760–770.

Crane, R. S., Kuyken, W., Hastings, R. P., Rothwell, N., & Williams, J. M. G. (2010). Training teachers to deliver mindfulness-based interventions: Learning from the UK experience. *Mindfulness*, 1(2), 74–86.

Davidson, R. & Lutz, A. (2008) Buddha's brain: Neuroplasticity and meditation. *IEEE Signal Process Mag.* 25(1), 176–174. www.ncbi.nlm.nih.gov/pmc/articles/PMC2944261 (accessed January 30, 2012).

Durlak, J. A., Weissberg, R. P., Dymnicki, A. B., Taylor, R. D., & Schellinger, K. (2011). The impact of enhancing students' social and emotional learning: A meta-analysis of school-based universal interventions. *Child Development*, 82, 474–501.

Elliott, R. (2003). Executive functions and their disorders. *British Medical Bulletin*, 65, 49–59.

Farrell, L. & Barrett, P. (2007). Prevention of childhood emotional disorders: Reducing the burden of suffering associated with anxiety and depression. *Child and Adolescent Mental Health*, 12(2), 58–65. doi:10.1111/j.1475–3588.2006.00430.x

Flook, L., Smalley, S. L., Kitil, M. J., *et al.* (2010). Effects of mindful awareness practices on executive functions in elementary school children. *Journal of Applied School Psychology*, 26(1), 70–95.

Garrison Institute (2014a). *Contemplative education programme database.* www.garrisoninstitute.org/contemplation-and-education/contemplative-education-program-database (accessed February 10, 2014).

Garrison Institute (2014b). *Database of programmes.* www.garrisoninstitute.org/contemplation-and-education/article-database (accessed February 10, 2014).

Garrison Institute (2014c). *The CARE programme.* www.garrisoninstitute.org/contemplation-and-education/care-for-teachers (accessed February 15, 2014).

Goleman, D. (2006). *Social intelligence: The new science of human relationships.* London: Random House.

Goleman, D. (2013). *Focus, the hidden driver of excellence.* New York: Harper Collins.

Graham, P. (2004). *The end of adolescence.* Oxford: Oxford University Press.

Greenberg, M. T. & Harris, A. R. (2012). Nurturing mindfulness in children and youth: Current state of research. *Child Development Perspectives*, 6: 161–166.

Hawn Foundation (2014). *MindUp Programme.* http://thehawnfoundation.org/mindup (accessed February 10, 2014).

Hölzel, B. K., Carmody, J., Vangel, M., *et al.* (2011a). Mindfulness practice leads to increases in regional brain gray matter density. *Psychiatry Research Neuoroimaging* 191(1), 36.

Hölzel, B., Lazar, S., Gard, T., Schuman-Olivier, Z., Vago, D., & Ott, U. (2011b). How does mindfulness meditation work? Proposing mechanisms of action from a conceptual and neural perspective. *Perspectives on Psychological Science*, 6, 537.

Huppert, F. A. (2014). The state of well-being science: Concepts, measures, interventions and policies. In: F A. Huppert & C. L. Cooper (eds.), *Interventions and policies to enhance well-being.* Oxford: Wiley-Blackwell.

Huppert, F. A. & Johnson, D. M. (2010). A controlled trial of mindfulness training in schools: The importance of practice for an impact on well-being. *The Journal of Positive Psychology*, 5(4), 264–274.

Inner Explorer (2014). Mindfulness in schools, learning from the inside out. http://innerexplorer.org/mindfulness-in-education-programs (accessed February 15, 2014).

Jennings, P., Snowberg, K., Coccia, M., & Greenberg, M. (2011). Improving classroom learning environments by cultivating awareness and resilience in education (CARE): Results of two pilot studies. *Journal of Classroom Interaction*, 46(1), 37–48.

Kabat-Zinn, J. (1996) *Full catastrophe living.* London: Piakus Books.

Kaiser-Greenland, S. (2009). *The mindful child.* London: Simon and Schuster.

Kerrigan, D., Johnson, K., Stewart, M., *et al.* (2010). Perceptions, experiences, and shifts in perspective occurring among urban youth participating in a mindfulness-based stress reduction program. *Complementary Therapies in Clinical Practice*, 17(2), 96–101.

Keyes, C. L. M. (2002). The mental health continuum: From languishing to flourishing in life. *Journal of Health and Social Behavior*, 43, 207–222.

Kuyken, W., Weare, K, Ukoumunne, O., *et al.* (2013). Effectiveness of the .b mindfulness in schools program: A non-randomized controlled feasibility study. *British Journal of Psychiatry.* http://bjp.rcpsych.org/content/203/2/126.full. pdf±html (accessed October 22, 2014).

Langer, E. (1993). A mindful education. *Educational Psychologist*, 28(1), 43–50.

Lantieri, L. & Nambiar, M. (2012). Social emotional learning and mindfulness-based contemplative practices in education. http://wh atmeditationreallyis.com/index.php/home-blo g/item/380 (accessed February 10, 2014).

Learning to Breathe (2014). A mindfulness curriculum for adolescents http://learning2 breathe.org (accessed February 15, 2014).

LeDoux, J. (1998). *The emotional brain*. New York: Simon and Schuster.

Lillard, A. S. (2011). Mindfulness practices in education: Montessori's approach. *Mindfulness* 2, 78–85.

Lipsey, M. W. & Wilson, D. B. (2001). *Practical meta-analysis*. Thousand Oaks, CA: Sage.

Ma, S. & Teasdale, J. (2004). Mindfulness-based cognitive therapy for depression: Replication and exploration of differential relapse preven- tion effects. *Journal of Consulting and Clinical Psychology*, 72(1), 31–40.

Meiklejohn, J., Phillips, C., & Freedman, M. L. (2012). Integrating mindfulness training into K-12 education: Fostering the resilience of teachers and students. *Mindfulness*, 3(4), 291–307.

Mendelson, T., Greenberg, M. T., Dariotis, J. K., Gould, L. F., Rhoades, B. L., & Leaf, P. J. (2010). Feasibility and preliminary outcomes of a school-based mindfulness intervention for urban youth. *Journal of Abnormal Child Psychology*, 38(7), 985–994.

Mental Health Foundation (2014). Mental health statistics and children. www.google.co. uk/search?q=mental+health+statisics+children %26sourceid=ie7%26rls=com.microsoft:en-G B:IE-Address%26ie=%26oe= (accessed February 10, 2014).

Mindful Schools (2014). Integrating mindfulness into education. www.mindfulschools.org (accessed October 22, 2014).

MiSP (2014). The mindfulness in schools project. http://mindfulnessinschools.org (accessed February 10, 2014).

Napoli, M., Krech, P. R., and Holley, L. C. (2005) Mindfulness training for elementary school students: The attention academy. *Journal of Applied School Psychology*, 21(1), 99–125.

NICE (National Institute for Health and Clinical Excellence) (2009) *Depression: The treatment and management of depression in adults.* London: NICE.

Raes, F., Griffith, J. W., Van der Gucht, K. J., & Williams, G. (2013). School-based prevention and reduction of depression in adolescents: A cluster-randomized controlled trial of a mindfulness group program. *Mindfulness*. doi: 10.1007/s12671-013-0202-1.

Rempel, K. D. (2012). Mindfulness for children and youth: a review of the literature with an argument for school-based implementation. *Canadian Journal of Counselling and Psychotherapy*, 46(3), 201–220.

Schonert-Reichl, K. A. and Lawlor, M. S. (2010). The effects of a mindfulness-based education program on pre- and early adolescents'well-being and social and emotional competence. *Mindfulness*, 1(3), 137–151.

Semple, R. J., Reid, E. F., & Miller, L. (2005). Treating anxiety with mindfulness: An open trial of mindfulness training for anxious children. *Journal of Cognitive Psychotherapy*, 19(4), 379–392.

Shucksmith, J., Summerbell, C., Jones, S., & Whittaker, V. (2007). *Mental wellbeing of children in primary education (targeted/indicated activities).* London: National Institute of Clinical Excellence.

Singh, N., Wahler, R., Adkins, A., & Myers, R. (2003). Soles of the feet: A mindfulness-based self-control intervention for aggression by an individual with mild mental retardation and mental illness. *Research in Developmental Disabilities*, 24(3), 158–169.

Van de Weijer-Bergsma, E., Langenberg, G., Brandsma, R., Oort, F. J., & Bögels, S. M. (2012). The effectiveness of a school-based mindfulness training as a program to prevent stress in elementary school children. *Mindfulness*. doi: 10.1007/s12671-012-0171-9.

Wake up schools (2014). Cultivating mindfulness in education. http://wakeupschools.org (accessed February 15, 2014).

Weare, K. & Nind, M. (2011) Mental health promotion and problem prevention in schools:

What does the evidence say?. *Health Promotion International*, 26(S1), 29–69.

Wisner, B. L., Jones, B., & Gwin, D. (2010). School-based meditation practices for adolescents: A resource for strengthening self-regulation, emotional coping, and self esteem. *Children and Schools*, 32(3), 150–159.

Zins, J. E., Weissberg, R. P., Wang, M. C., & Walberg, H. (2004). *Building academic success on social and emotional learning*. New York: Columbia Teachers College.

Zoogman, S., Simon, B., Goldberg, S., Hoyt, W. and Miller, L. (2014). Mindfulness interventions with youth: A meta-analysis. *Mindfulness*. doi: 10.1007/s12671-013-0260-4.

Zylowska, L., Ackerman, D. L., Yang, M. H., *et al.* (2007). Mindfulness meditation training in adults and adolescents with ADHD: A feasibility study. *Journal of Attention Disorders*, 11(6), 737–746.

The Life Course Model for providing empirically supported school-based services for adolescents

A. Raisa Petca, Allison K. Zoromski, Steven W. Evans, and Yuko Watabe

In the United States (see Figure 22.1 for education structure in the United States), 22% of 13- to 18-year-olds experience a mental health disorder and associated impairment within a lifetime, with anxiety, behavior, mood, and substance use disorders being most prevalent (Merikangas *et al.*, 2010). Yet only 20% of youth needing mental health services receive any (Kataoka, Zhang, & Wells, 2002). Entry into mental health services in the United States often begins in school settings (Farmer *et al.*, 2003), with 90% of schools providing assessment and referrals for mental health services and 75% of them providing direct services via psychologists, social workers, or nurses (Foster *et al.*, 2005). Federal regulations (e.g., special education) indicate that educators should meet the academic and vocational needs of students with emotional and behavioral problems. Therefore, the impetus is on school professionals to implement mental health services that can (1) identify adolescents with emotional and behavioral problems; and (2) address these problems with the goal of

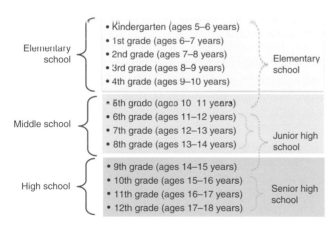

Figure 22.1 Structure of education provision in the United States. As indicated in the figure, the actual grades included in each level of school vary across districts partly as a function of size of buildings and staffing. Schooling is mandatory for all children in the United States, but the age range for which school attendance is required varies from state to state. Some states allow students to drop out with parental permission before finishing high school, between the ages of 14 and 17, but other states require students to stay in school until age 18. Students can attend public or private schools or be home-schooled by their parents or via online schooling programs.

School Mental Health: Global Challenges and Opportunities, ed. Stan Kutcher, Yifeng Wei and Marc D. Weist. Published by Cambridge University Press. © Cambridge University Press 2015.

effectively educating students. School districts have employed school mental health professionals (SMHPs; e.g., counselors, school psychologists) and resources have been developed to help SMHPs learn evidence-based practices to achieve these goals. For example, two large web-based systems have been developed, including one operated by the Substance Abuse and Mental Health Services Administration (SAMHSA; www.nrepp.samhsa.gov) and another by the Institute of Education Science (IES; http://ies.ed.gov/ncee/wwc), as well as some published evidence-based treatment guidelines (e.g., Evans, Owens, & Bunford, 2014) to highlight evidence-based treatments for use in schools.

Some education and mental health models of care in the United States have borrowed their structure from the Institute of Medicine model of prevention and service provision across three tiers: (1) universal, (2) indicated, and (3) targeted prevention/intervention (Springer & Phillips, 2006). Two similar tiered service delivery models have emerged to help educators organize academic and mental health services: School-Wide Positive Behavior Support (SWPBS; Simonsen, Sugai & Fairbanks, 2007) and Response to Intervention (RTI; National Center on Response to Intervention, 2010). Tier 1 strategies include universal/primary prevention services aimed at teaching and reinforcing the expected behavior in schools (Caldarella *et al.*, 2011) and may entail system-wide evaluations such as screening of all students or a needs analysis of the school system. Tier 2 tactics emphasize improving functioning and include selective interventions for at-risk students who are inadequately responsive to Tier 1 strategies. For the students who are unresponsive to Tier 1 and 2 strategies, individualized interventions at Tier 3 are provided. These interventions are intensive, function-based strategies employed by specialized staff (Crone, Horner & Hawken, 2004).

Overall, the tiered models have important strengths, including that they are flexible, may contain a wide variety of evidence-based interventions, and emphasize prevention, including school-wide assessments and observations to identify when, where, and why students may fail (e.g., Scott *et al.*, 2010). Their emphasis on prevention may lead to reductions in unnecessary labeling, special education placement, or pharmacotherapy for youth with behavioral and emotional problems (Froiland, 2011) by attempting to address issues before they become impairing. Additionally, these models are conceptualized as problem-solving models at the level of each tier (Burns, Deno & Jimerson, 2007) so they allow for adapting interventions to the needs of the student, based on outcomes. The tiered models also have several limitations. First, the tiered model is not prescriptive, in that it does not provide guidance about the interventions that should be used for particular problems. Instead, tiers differ based on the intensity of the intervention as guided by the allocation of time and resources per student served. Second, we believe that the tiered model lacks adequate emphasis on the long-term benefits of services (Forrest & Riley, 2004). Possibly as a result of this lack of emphasis, many services often provided in the tiered model emphasize short-term accommodations that are unlikely to improve the competencies of the students (Harrison *et al.*, 2013). Third, professionals implementing services within the tiered model typically only incorporate interventions that can be provided in schools and do not include implications for community-based services. As a result, the tiered model does not adequately provide guidance to parents or educators about the breadth of services available.

Recently, a Life Course Model (LCM) has been proposed as an alternative or augmentation to the tiered model that focuses on long-term outcomes and emphasizes the provision of care following a referral (Evans *et al.*, 2014a). The LCM is structured in four layers that inform the sequencing and selection of evidence-based services for youth with emotional and behavioral problems. Services provided in each layer can vary in intensity, in accordance with the individualized needs of each child, as long as they are consistent with the seven principles of the model (see Figure 22.2). Although, typically, the provision of services begins at Layer 1 and continues to higher layers if the lower layer does not trigger an adequate treatment response, the provision of services at different layers may also occur concurrently, to accommodate individual needs. Importantly, within the LCM, the progression through the layers leads to a coordinated set of school and community services, as the provision of interventions from lower layers does not need to end when services are initiated at higher layers.

In this chapter, we discuss school-based mental health services for adolescents, as promoted and studied in the United States. We provide an in-depth account of the LCM and the services that can be offered within each layer. Lastly, we illustrate the application of the LCM via a case example of an adolescent with disruptive behavioral problems.

The Life Course Model

The Life Course and tiered models of care are complementary and each presents unique strengths (see Evans *et al.*, 2014b for a comparison of the two models). Figure 22.2 provides a graphic overview of the LCM. As indicated in the figure, there are seven principles that are prioritized throughout the four layers of service delivery that guide the provision of specific services within each layer. The LCM principles entail: (1) implementing interventions with an understanding of contextual and cultural factors; (2) promoting engagement of parents and youth; (3) tailoring interventions to the youth's developmental level; (4) addressing individual youth and family needs; (5) including progress monitoring tools to evaluate treatment response; (6) facilitating alliances within and between systems of care; and (7) including ongoing practice supports for those implementing interventions (for a comprehensive description, see Evans *et al.*, 2014a).

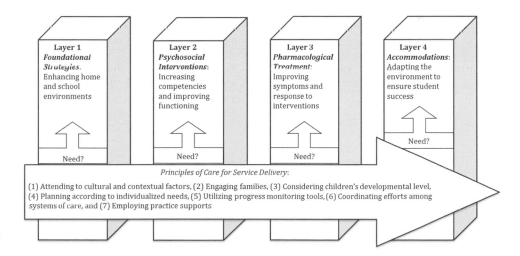

Figure 22.2 Illustrative depiction of the Life Course Model. From Evans *et al.* (2014b). Copyright 2014 by Guilford Press. Reprinted with permission.

Layer 1 involves services that address problems in the student's environment that may be causing or exacerbating the problems leading to a referral. These services address serious contextual problems at home, in the community, or in the classroom, such as chaotic settings, repeated exposure to trauma, or significant neglect. Addressing these problems first can enhance the benefits of all services that may follow. The rationale for the sequence of the remaining three layers is based on prioritizing services that are most likely to enhance competencies that enable the student to independently meet age-appropriate expectations related to academic and social functioning. Psychosocial services (e.g., organization interventions, cognitive behavioral therapy) are recommended as a starting point, as many of them are intended to increase students' abilities to independently complete assignments, relate effectively to others, and follow rules. The LCM lists medication next because, for some youth, it can directly improve functioning and it may enhance the benefits of psychosocial services; however, the benefits tend to be limited to when the adolescents are taking the medication. Finally, accommodations are listed as a last resort. They do not typically enhance competencies and often involve reducing expectations such that low levels of functioning are acceptable (e.g., extended time to complete tasks, giving students copies of class notes). Thus, a reliance on accommodations alone should be avoided when possible, but the *temporary* use of accommodations while providing services at Layers 1 and 2 may be a valuable approach for some students. Descriptions of the services at each layer and a case example are below.

Layer 1: foundational strategies

Layer 1 includes foundational strategies that are aimed at ensuring that the environments at home and school are not contributing to the presenting problems. Services from Layer 1 are not intended to address the specific needs of an adolescent, but rather to diminish the contextual influences to the youth's problems by establishing environments that are supportive, nurturing, and safe (Evans *et al.*, 2014a). Some referred adolescents may not need Layer 1 services if these settings are well-managed and supportive. For others, addressing the context can improve functioning and establish a foundation that increases the likelihood that services in the other layers will be effective.

In classroom settings, the environment can be enhanced by increasing student engagement in educational activities, making setting changes, and improving classroom behavior management. Activities such as peer tutoring and cooperative learning can improve student engagement and subsequently reduce disruptive behavior (Little & Akin-Little, 2009). Setting changes such as allowing only relevant materials on students' desks or using assigned seating can facilitate a task-oriented environment. Increased teacher movement through the classroom can enhance behavior management because the teacher can quickly detect and address problems (Shores, Gunter, & Jack, 1993). Models of teacher consultation have been developed and can be used to help teachers provide a safe and supportive environment for all students (Pas, Bradshaw, & Cash, 2014).

In home settings, helping parents understand the importance of monitoring their adolescent's activities and locations is a Layer 1 service that is associated with a reduction in delinquent behavior (Walther *et al.*, 2012). Conversely, parent behaviors that reinforce the adolescent's maladaptive behaviors (e.g., encouraging compulsive rituals in adolescents with obsessive compulsive disorder) can exacerbate problems (e.g., Storch *et al.*, 2010). Parents can be educated about helpful strategies to modify these parenting behaviors in parent training programs offered either in schools or community settings.

Layer 2: strategies to increase competencies and address functional impairments

Layer 2 is the first point where individualized psychosocial interventions are selected and implemented to address the specific needs of an adolescent (e.g., improving academic performance; reducing anxiety levels). Services from Layer 2 include strategies that can increase competencies (e.g., taking effective class notes) and address functional impairments (e.g., improving interaction with peers). Contrary to the exclusive use of school-based interventions in tiered models, services within the LCM may be provided at school (e.g., academic interventions, cognitive behavior therapy), in community agencies (e.g., individualized parent training), or in ways that involve professionals from both school and community. Layer 2 allows for the concurrent implementation of multiple interventions with varying degrees of intensity that may be adjusted based on assessment and response to interventions.

Layer 2 services for adolescents with externalizing disorders

Services addressing impairment related to externalizing disorders include behavioral modifications, parent training (often with the adolescent present), organizational and note-taking skills training, and self-management. Some examples of psychosocial intervention programs that have been designed for adolescents with externalizing problems are the Challenging Horizons Program (CHP; Evans et al., 2011); the Adolescent Transitions Program (ATP; Dishion & Kavanagh, 2003); Check and Connect (C&C; Christenson et al., 2008); and the adolescent version of the Summer Treatment Program (STP-A; Sibley et al., 2011). The comprehensive approach of these programs incorporates a mixture of specific interventions that are unlikely to be adequately effective on their own (e.g., family therapy; Barkley et al., 2001). The first three (CHP, ATP, and C&C) are school-based programs and the first two (CHP and ATP) include a significant family component, as does the STP-A. Organization interventions that involve helping adolescents with attention deficit hyperactivity disorder (ADHD) organize their time and materials were developed in the CHP (Storer, Evans, & Langberg, 2014) and these interventions have continued to be developed and refined in other school-based programs for adolescents, such as the Homework, Organization, and Planning Skills (HOPS) intervention (Langberg et al., 2012). Other interventions targeting specific impairment associated with ADHD were developed in the CHP and have been evaluated individually, such as note-taking instruction (Evans, Pelham & Grudberg, 1994), training in interpersonal skills (Sadler et al., 2011), and a homework management plan (Raggi et al., 2009). Other techniques such as self-management training (Gureasko-Moore, DuPaul, & White, 2007), an adaptation of the Daily Report Card for adolescents (DRC; Evans & Youngstrom, 2006), the Family Check-up (part of ATP; Dishion & Kavanagh, 2003), mentoring (part of C&C; Christenson, 2001), and parent–adolescent therapy (Robin & Foster, 1989) are incorporated into some of these comprehensive treatment programs.

Some adolescents with externalizing problems exhibit problems with delinquency and substance use. Two types of interventions targeting adolescents with these maladaptive and disruptive behaviors are Functional Family Therapy (FFT; Alexander et al., 2013) and Multisystemic Therapy (MST; Henggeler & Lee, 2003). FFT is a three-phase intervention delivered in 3–30 home- or clinic-based sessions over a three-month period, to 11- to 18-year-old adolescents and their families. The focus of FFT is on enhancing protective factors for and reducing risk of negative parent–child interactions and adolescents' behavior problems. MST is a three- to five-month family- and community-based intervention for 10- to 17-year-old adolescents with serious conduct problems and includes cognitive behavioral approaches, behavior therapies, parent training, pragmatic family therapies, and pharmacological services. MST was found to be superior to community services in addressing problems of youth with criminal offences and is a recommended intervention of evidence-based guidelines (Eyberg, Nelson, & Boggs, 2008). These two interventions differ from the ones listed above in their focus on delinquent behavior and substance use, but they also address many of the problems in the previous paragraph.

Layer 2 services for adolescents with internalizing disorders

Adolescents with internalizing disorders experience sad, irritable, or fearful states, generally accompanied by somatic and cognitive changes that result in functional impairment and maladaptive behavior. One of the most recognized evidence-based interventions for internalizing disorders is cognitive behavioral therapy (CBT; David-Ferdon & Kaslow, 2008). CBT includes the use of various techniques to target (1) distressing physical symptoms such as excessive fatigue or hyperventilation (e.g., sleep hygiene; breathing retraining); (2) maladaptive behavioral patterns such as systematic withdrawal from activities or avoidance (e.g., behavioral activation, graded exposure); and (3) irrational negative thoughts (e.g., cognitive restructuring).

There are several school-based programs that have yielded good results with adolescents. Examples of programs targeting anxiety disorders are the CAT Project (adaptation of Coping Cat for adolescents; Kendall et al., 2002), Cool Kids (Mifsud & Rapee, 2005), the Baltimore Child Anxiety Treatment Study in the Schools (BCATSS; Ginsburg et al., 2008), and the Skills for Academic and Social Success (SASS; Masia et al., 1999). The CAT Project is delivered in 16 individual sessions of CBT that consist of both learning ways of coping with anxiety and practicing skills in imaginary and real-life situations. The other programs entail 8–12 group sessions of CBT, which are supplemented by other components (Cool Kids and SASS) such as individual sessions or meetings with parents or teachers. Unique to BCATSS is the adaptation of CBT to include culturally relevant examples and interactive techniques targeted at adolescent populations (ages 14–17) with typically unmet mental health service needs (i.e., inner-city, low-income, ethnic minorities). One CBT school-based program, Cognitive-Behavioral Intervention for Trauma in Schools (CBITS; Jaycox, 2003) targets both anxiety (i.e., post-traumatic stress disorder) and depression symptoms common when youth experience trauma. CBITS has been found effective with students in Grades 4–8 who were exposed to hurricane trauma (Stein et al., 2003), and consists of ten one-hour group sessions, 1–3 individual sessions, two optional parent education meetings, and one teacher education meeting. Examples of CBT school-based programs targeting depression are Adolescents Coping with Emotions (ACE; Wignall et al., 1998) and Adolescent Coping with Depression (CWD-A; e.g., Lewinsohn et al., 1990). Both ACE and CWD-A consist of eight weeks of CBT group sessions. One school-based program targeting depression utilizes Interpersonal Psychotherapy (IPT), the other evidence-based treatment for depression (David-Ferdon & Kaslow, 2008). IPT-Adolescents (IPT-A) is an individually delivered 12-session program focused on relating depression symptoms to one or more of four problem areas (grief, role disputes, role transitions, and interpersonal deficits) and on developing strategies for dealing with these problems (Mufson et al., 1999). IPT-A led to faster and significantly better outcomes than treatment as usual in 12- to 18-year-olds treated in school-based health clinics for depression (Mufson *et al.*, 2004).

Due to the myriad specific problems and impairments that adolescents experience, a multitude of Layer 2 school-based programs have been evaluated. Although these interventions have been empirically studied, their application within the framework of the LCM has not yet been investigated. Research is needed to test decision-making models that can help guide the sequencing and selection of programs within Layer 2 that can address the individual needs of adolescents with emotional and behavioral problems and the efficacy of combining several multi-component treatments. Because many services involve the participation of parents, teachers, and SMHPs, researchers should also investigate ways in which alliances can be enhanced. Despite the comprehensive approach to treatment inherent in Layer 2 services, some adolescents may need additional support, which can be provided via services in subsequent layers.

Layer 3: medication

The third layer consists of pharmacological treatment provided by physicians in the community. Generally, within the LCM, medication is not viewed as a standalone treatment, although there may be instances in which medication is the primary treatment. In many situations, medication can be used as a supplement to the psychosocial interventions, when response to treatment is insufficient. However, in some cases treatment plans may take a combined approach from the outset (i.e., services from Layers 1, 2, and 3). Reasons for combining medication and psychosocial treatment may include (1) a need for acute symptom reduction, (2) a comorbid disorder that requires concurrent treatment, and (3) a limited response to psychosocial treatment and potential for better outcomes with combined treatment (March, 2002). Multimodal approaches including psychosocial treatments alongside medication are supported by some studies. For example, the combination of CBT and medication was found more effective than CBT and placebo in adolescents with anxiety-based school refusal and comorbid depression (Bernstein *et al.*, 2001). Similarly, for some children with ADHD, maximum treatment benefits were obtained when psychosocial and pharmacological services were provided concurrently (e.g., MTA Cooperative Group, 1999).

Educators and SMHPs do not prescribe medication and many are discouraged from recommending them. Nevertheless, SMHPs can play an important role in educating parents about available interventions for adolescents, and medications should be considered when discussing the LCM with parents. In fact, avoiding discussions of medication with parents may be detrimental and limit the parents' ability to effectively meet the needs of their child. SMHPs may explain the benefits and disadvantages of pursuing pharmacological treatment within the context of the LCM and help parents make informed decisions about care for their child.

Layer 4: accommodations

Within the LCM, services in Layer 4 are considered a last-resort attempt to address an adolescent's problems, as these services are inconsistent with the goals of the LCM. Services from Layer 4, typically referred to as accommodations, often involve the modification of the expectations of adults for a youth to perform at the level similar to same-aged peers. Students may be provided classroom accommodations such as preferential seating (e.g., near the door to allow leaving class for breaks or shelter from distractions) or testing accommodations such as extended time on tests or having the test questions read aloud. Students may also be given assignment/homework accommodations such as having to turn in portions of an assignment consecutively rather than concurrently or receiving full credit for late assignments or partially completed assignments. However, providing these services is an indication that attempts to improve the adolescent's competencies have not been successful and that the adolescent can only function adequately in an environment in which expectations for behavior or achievement have been significantly reduced compared to those of same-aged peers. In fact, research indicates that accommodations do little to improve the competencies of students with emotional and behavioral problems and do not provide the "differential boost" or "leveling of the playing field" that they were initially intended to achieve (Harrison *et al.*, 2013). Therefore, Layer 4 is only recommended for adolescents who have been inadequately responsive to a combination of services from Layers 1, 2, and 3. Additionally, they may be useful on a temporary basis for students who are learning new skills. For example, it may be reasonable to give a student a copy of a classmate's notes while he is learning to take notes independently. Complete reliance on accommodations suggests that parents, educators, and SMHPs believe the adolescent cannot be helped to function independently at an age-appropriate level. Therefore, accommodations are the last approach in the LCM.

Case example

Paul Hammond (alias) is a 14-year old boy in Grade 8, who was referred for an assessment for school-based services. During the first semester of Grade 8 he earned Fs in Algebra and Earth Science, a C in English and a D in Government. Paul talked to his peers during class and teachers saw him drawing in the margins of his notebook instead of taking notes. During seatwork, Paul was off-task. These problems were most apparent during Algebra and Earth Science, but his Government teacher also mentioned that Paul had not been taking notes. Mrs. Stone, his Algebra teacher, felt that he did not care about academics. At parent–teacher conferences, she learned that Paul was diagnosed with ADHD-Combined Type in Grade 2. Paul's father, Mr. Hammond, reported that Paul typically earned Cs or better in prior years. In elementary school, Paul's teachers sent home a list of homework assignments at the beginning of each week and Mr. Hammond would help Paul complete them. When Paul entered middle school, this kind of support was not provided. Mr. Hammond asks Paul about his homework, but he always says that he finished his homework in study hall. Mr. Hammond has no way of verifying it. When Paul was diagnosed with ADHD, his pediatrician offered stimulant medication. However, Mr. Hammond was hesitant to have Paul take medication due to stories he heard from coworkers and a history of maternal substance use. Mr. Hammond felt Paul's strength was his outgoing and comedic nature, and feared that medication would impact his personality. Historically, Paul did not have significant social problems; however, in the past month, he was in trouble three times for fighting on the bus. In one instance, he reportedly gave a student a black eye.

Layer 1

The SMHP, Miss Clark (school counselor), first assessed Paul's school and home context. During meetings with Paul's teachers, Miss Clark learned that the teachers received little training in classroom behavior management and Paul's classes were large (over 30 students). Particularly, she noted that Mrs. Stone (Algebra teacher) was struggling with classroom management. Miss Clark scheduled an observation during Paul's Algebra class. She tracked Mrs. Stone's use of labeled praise, effective and ineffective commands, consequences, and references to classroom rules, as well as Paul's disruptions and off-task behavior. Mrs. Stone and Miss Clark met to discuss strategies to enhance classroom rules and routines. Mrs. Stone had not posted classroom rules because she thought that a brief explanation of rules at the beginning of the school year would be sufficient for Grade 8 students. Miss Clark reviewed Mrs. Stone's rules and helped her modify them to capture the key problem behaviors she was noticing (e.g., "Don't fight, yell, swear, or disrespect the teacher!" was changed to "Be Respectful!"). The SMHP also helped Mrs. Stone think of consequences for rule violations (e.g., first violation results in a warning, subsequent violations result in being held back from the passing period between classes for one minute) (Teach for America, 2011). Miss Clark talked with Mrs. Stone about using specific labeled praise for desirable behaviors and ignoring mildly annoying behaviors that did not violate classroom rules. They collaboratively developed a classroom routine to increase structure: review rules, review homework, teach the lesson of the day, and complete a practical application of the lesson. Mrs. Stone expressed concerns about implementing these changes in the middle of the year, but agreed to try them. Miss Clark scheduled follow-up observations, during which she continued to track the frequencies of teacher and student behaviors and used these data as part of her consultation and performance feedback.

Miss Clark also contacted Mr. Hammond. She learned that, after Paul was first diagnosed with ADHD, Mr. Hammond participated in a parent training group. Mr. Hammond had learned to use praise for expected behaviors and time-out for non-compliance. Mr. Hammond still tried to use these strategies, but felt he could no longer make Paul stay in time-out. Mr. Hammond had some remaining concerns about Paul's non-compliance. Mr. Hammond also shared that his wife was recently sentenced to six months in prison due to repeated driving under the influence offences. Mrs. Hammond has struggled for years with addiction to alcohol and Oxycodone. Mr. Hammond felt that Paul had become more irritable, and seemed less interested in seeing friends since his mother was arrested last month. Overall, Mr. Hammond reported that he was somewhat satisfied with the level of parent–teacher communication, but he was interested in more information about teachers' expectations of Paul (e.g., homework assignments, test dates). Thus, it appeared that Mr. Hammond provided a supportive home environment and Layer 1 services were not necessary. Miss Clark had worked with Mrs. Stone to improve order in her classroom, and observations in other classrooms indicated adequate levels of behavior management and quality instruction. Although additional services appeared to be needed to help Paul succeed, there was nothing else that was needed in Layer 1.

Layer 2

Miss Clark continued to observe and assess Paul's progress. She noted that Paul's locker contained a scattered mixture of clothing, papers, notebooks, and folders, and he did not appear to have any system for organizing materials. The SMHP also learned that Paul was assigned daily Algebra seatwork, but rarely completed it. Paul did poorly on tests in multiple subjects and he was observed doodling during lessons and interrupting frequently. Overall, Miss Clark concluded that Paul was experiencing problems with organization, task completion, and attending to lessons, as well as problems with compliance to his father's requests at home.

Paul's organization difficulties, coupled with evidence suggesting that disorganization plays a central role in ADHD (Langberg *et al.*, 2011), contributed to the decision to implement an organization intervention for Paul. Mr. Pratt, Paul's English teacher, agreed to implement the organization intervention (Evans *et al.*, 2009). Paul was given a binder, and criteria for organizing his materials. At least weekly, Mr. Pratt completed a nine-item organization checklist (e.g., Are all worksheets [non-homework papers/notes] in the correct subject folders?). When Paul failed a criterion on the checklist, he was required to correct the error (e.g., place loose papers in proper folders) and the item was marked as failed on his tracking sheet. His locker was checked and corrected using similar criteria and procedures. Paul's scores on the checklists were recorded as a percentage of criteria met out of total criteria. Additionally, an electronic assignment notebook was established for Paul using his smartphone. After Paul inputted his assignments for his four core classes, his teachers electronically signed off on them. His father had access to this system and could review Paul's assignments on his computer (alternatively, paper assignment notebooks and teacher hand signatures can also be used). The number of assignments entered completely and accurately out of his four core classes was recorded electronically each day. Paul's percentages on both the organization and assignment notebook interventions were graphed, so that his progress could be monitored and additional rewards or negative consequences could be added, if needed. Miss Clark met with Mr. Pratt biweekly to discuss progress and check whether modifications needed to be made.

Because Paul's difficulty with completing Algebra seatwork negatively impacted his grade, Mrs. Stone, his Algebra teacher, implemented a DRC intervention. Mrs. Stone used data from her grade book over the prior week as a baseline to set his initial DRC goal. Given his average of 50% completion during the baseline week, an initial DRC target of 65% completion was established for Paul. Typically, teachers remind students of their DRC goals at the beginning of each class. Because there was concern that publicly reminding Paul of his DRC goals might embarrass him, Mrs. Stone wrote a reminder note on his seatwork worksheet. After class, Mrs. Stone sent Mr. Hammond an e-mail telling him the percentage of seatwork completed that day. Mr. Hammond limited video-game time at home each evening based on the daily report from Mrs. Stone (e.g., Evans & Youngstrom, 2006).

Due to Paul's poor grades, a study hall class period was added to his schedule, during which he participated in a group note-taking intervention to improve attention to instruction and reduce off-task behavior. The instructor taught a basic outline format for taking notes from class lessons and books. In subsequent classes, the teacher presented a lecture on relevant class material, using think-aloud techniques to guide students in creating an outline (for procedures, see Evans, Pelham & Grudberg, 1994). Note-taking scores (number of main ideas and supporting details written correctly/total number of main ideas and supporting details) were recorded daily. As Paul progressed, prompting was tapered and student-generated notes were emphasized. Occasionally, teachers were asked to give Paul a score on his in-class notes and give him feedback on the quality of his notes to facilitate generalization.

Finally, given Paul's compliance issues at home, it was determined that his father may benefit from parent training sessions. Because this was not a service available at the school, Miss Clark referred Mr. Hammond to a community clinic that provided parent training. Miss Clark released relevant assessment information to the community clinic after receiving Mr. Hammond's consent. Paul's father is currently the sole caregiver in the home. He works until 5 p.m., and does not have evening childcare for his six-year-old daughter. To accommodate this problem, the community provider suggested that Paul stay home with his sister while his father attended evening parenting sessions. The provider suggested that Mr. Hammond could interrupt their meetings to call home to check on his children as needed. Mr. Hammond learned about other consequences he could use for problematic behaviors including removal of privileges (e.g., TV time) and the enhancement of desirable privileges (e.g., extended curfew). The community provider gave Mr. Hammond a tracking sheet to document non-compliance frequency during a baseline week and to monitor Paul's progress after new home consequences were implemented. Having Mr. Hammond's approval for release of information, the community provider shared updates regarding progress with Miss Clark.

Layer 3

After implementing the classroom behavior management in Paul's Algebra class (Layer 1), organization intervention, assignment notebook intervention, note-taking intervention, and parent training sessions (Layer 2) for two months, Paul improved his work completion in Algebra, took some notes in class, turned in more of his homework than he had in the past, and used a binder and kept it organized. However, Paul's grades were still a concern; he made careless mistakes on tests and quizzes and continued to interrupt frequently in class. Mr. Hammond asked Miss Clark about medication for Paul. Although school district policy did not allow Miss Clark to recommend medication for a student, she was able to discuss the layers in the LCM and the rationale for that sequence of interventions. This included providing basic information about medication treatment for ADHD and a recommendation to consult Paul's physician for additional information. Thus, Miss Clark did not recommend medication, but helped Mr. Hammond understand and make informed choices about his pursuit of services across the four layers of the LCM.

Layer 4

Although Paul's note-taking improved, he had not demonstrated the ability to independently take notes in class at the expected level after two months of intervention. Thus, an accommodation was considered. A graduated approach was taken such that, initially, while Paul learned how to take notes, he was provided with a model set of notes from his teachers. Initially, he was given a set of notes with spaces left blank, in which he was to insert the appropriate phrase as he read or listened during class (cloze procedure). After class, he would compare his document to the model set to determine whether he entered the correct phrases. Gradually, Paul began taking notes independently, and continued to compare his notes to the model until a month later, when he no longer needed the notes provided.

Throughout the academic year described in this example, the SMHP had the opportunity to consider all four layers of the LCM. Moreover, her work was consistent with the overarching principles of the model. First, Miss Clark modified the procedure for providing a daily reminder of DRC goals, to ensure that it was age-appropriate (Principle 3) and did not result in unwanted attention and embarrassment to Paul. The SMHP reached out to Paul's father multiple times, to gather information about his concerns and his perception of Paul's problems (Principle 2). Mr. Hammond's attendance with the community provider was problematic due to his work schedule and childcare responsibilities. In order to accommodate his needs, the community provider proposed the solution that Paul stay home with his younger sister, while his father attended evening parent training sessions (Principle 4).

Within Paul's family there was an important contextual factor to consider regarding the use of medication. Mr. Hammond had reservations about stimulant medication that emerged from communication with his coworkers and Paul's mother's history of substance abuse. Thus, the SMHP explained to Mr. Hammond that alternative medications to stimulants were available, but recommended that he contact the family physician for further information (Principle 1). Finally, data were collected for each of the interventions implemented (e.g., scores on organization checklist, frequency of non-compliance at home; Principle 5). These data, along with data collected during Miss Clark's observations, were used to inform decisions about changes to services (i.e., progress monitoring) and to provide performance feedback to staff members implementing interventions (Principles 6 and 7).

Conclusion

Although the case example of Paul may differ from how services are provided at many schools in the United States, it represents an important and achievable ideal for SMHPs who adopt an LCM approach. School mental health in the United States has experienced remarkable development in recent years, as government directives have made the use of evidence-based interventions a high priority. Despite the recent proliferation and availability of evidence-based school mental health services, usage of these practices in schools is not always optimal. In fact, Ennett and colleagues (2003) found that nearly 40% of schools are providing services that have not been demonstrated to work, even when an available effective alternative exists. Thus, more work is needed to decrease the research–practice gap. The LCM has the potential to contribute to closing that gap, but there are many changes needed to training programs, quality assurance systems, and accountability before the gap can close completely. We are cautiously optimistic about the wide-reaching utility of this model, as it is derived from empirical literature, but research is needed to validate it. We hope that this depiction of coordinated community and school-based care will fuel the discussion of optimizing services for adolescents and families.

References

Alexander, J. F., Waldron, H. B., Robbins, M. S., et al. (2013). *Functional family therapy for adolescent behavior problems*. Washington, DC: American Psychological Association.

Barkley, R. A., Edwards, G., Laneri, M., et al. (2001). The efficacy of problem-solving communication training alone, behavior management training alone, and their combination for parent–adolescent conflict in teenagers with ADHD and ODD. *Journal of Consulting and Clinical Psychology*, 69, 926–941.

Bernstein, G. A., Hektner, J. M., Borchardt, C. M., et al. (2001). Treatment of school refusal: One-year follow-up. *Journal of the American Academy of Child and Adolescent Psychiatry*, 40, 206–213.

Burns, M.K, Deno, S., & Jimerson, S. R. (2007). Toward a unified model of response to intervention. In S. R. Jimerson, M. K. Burns, & A. M. VanDerHeyden (Eds.), *The handbook of response to intervention: The science and practice of assessment and intervention* (pp. 428–440). New York: Springer.

Caldarella, P., Shatzer, R. H., Gray, K. M., et al. (2011). The effects of school-wide positive behavior support on middle school climate and student outcomes. *Research in Middle Level Education Online*, 35, 1–14.

Christenson, S. L. (2001). *Promoting engagement with school and learning: A resource for Check & Connect mentors to enhance student success*. Early Risers "Skills for Success" Project, University of Minnesota.

Christenson, S. L., Thurlow, M. L., Sinclair, M. F., et al. (2008). *Check and Connect: A comprehensive student engagement intervention manual*. Minneapolis, MN: University of Minnesota, Institute on Community Integration.

Crone, D. A., Horner, R. H., & Hawken, L. S. (2004). *Responding to problem behavior in schools: The behavior education program*. New York: Guilford Press.

David-Ferdon, C. and Kaslow, N. (2008). Evidence-based psychosocial treatments for child and adolescent depression. *Journal of Clinical Child and Adolescent Psychology*, 37, 62–104.

Dishion, T. J. & Kavanagh, K. (2003). *Intervening in adolescent problem behavior: A family-centered approach*. New York: The Guilford Press.

Ennett, S. T., Ringwalt, C. L., Thorne, J., *et al.* (2003). A comparison of current practice in school-based substance use prevention programs with meta-analysis findings. *Prevention Science*, 4, 1–14.

Evans, S. W., Owens, J. S., and Bunford, N. (2014). Evidence-based psychosocial treatments for children and adolescents with attention-deficit/ hyperactivity disorder. *Journal of Clinical Child and Adolescent Psychology*, 43 (4), 527–551.

Evans, S. W., Owens, J. S., Mautone, J. A., *et al.* (2014a). Toward a comprehensive Life Course Model of care for youth with Attention Deficit Hyperactivity Disorder. In M. D. Weist, N. A. Lever, C. P. Bradshaw, & J. S. Owens (Eds.), *Handbook of school mental health* (2nd ed.; pp. 413–426). New York: Springer.

Evans, S. W., Pelham, W. E., and Grudberg, M. V. (1994). The efficacy of notetaking to improve behavior and comprehension of adolescents with Attention Deficit Hyperactivity Disorder. *Exceptionality*, 5, 1–17.

Evans, S. W., Ryback, T., Strickland, H., *et al.* (2014b). The role of school mental health models in preventing and addressing children's emotional and behavioral problems. In H. Walker & F. Gresham (Eds.), *Handbook of evidence-based practices for school-related behavior* (pp. 394–409). New York: The Guilford Press.

Evans, S. W., Shultz, B. K., DeMars, C. E., *et al.* (2011). Effectiveness of the Challenging Horizons after-school program for young adolescents with ADHD. *Behavior Therapy*, 42, 462–474.

Evans, S. W., Schultz, B. K., White, L. C., *et al.* (2009). A school-based organization intervention for young adolescents with ADHD. *School Mental Health*, 1, 78–88.

Evans, S. W. & Youngstrom, E. (2006). Evidence-based assessment of attention-deficit/ hyperactivity disorder: Measuring outcomes. *Journal of the American Academy of Child and Adolescent Psychiatry*, 45, 1132–1137.

Eyberg, S. M., Nelson, M., and Boggs, S. R. (2008). Evidence-based psychosocial treatments for children and adolescents with disruptive behavior. *Journal of Clinical and Adolescent Psychology*, 37, 215–237.

Farmer, E., Burns, B. J., Phillips, S. D., *et al.* (2003). Pathways into and through mental health services for children and adolescents. *Psychiatric Services*, 54, 60–66.

Forrest, C. B. & Riley, A. W. (2004). Childhood origins of adult health: A basis for life-course health policy. *Health Affairs*, 23, 155–163.

Foster, S., Rollefson, M., Doksum, T., *et al.* (2005). *School mental health services in the United States: 2002–2003*. Rockville, MD: Center for Mental Health Services, Substance Abuse and Mental Health Services Administration.

Froiland, J. M. (2011). Response to intervention as a vehicle for powerful mental health interventions in the schools. *Contemporary School Psychology*, 15, 35–42.

Ginsburg, G., Becker, K., Kingery, J., *et al.* (2008). Transporting CBT for childhood and anxiety disorders into inner city school based mental health clinics. *Cognitive and Behavioral Practice*, 15, 148–158.

Gureasko-Moore, S., DuPaul, G. J., & White, G. P. (2007). Self-management of classroom preparedness and homework: Effects on school functioning of adolescents with attention deficit hyperactivity disorder. *School Psychology Review*, 36, 674–664.

Harrison, J., Bunford, N., Evans, S. W., *et al.* (2013). Educational accommodations for students with behavioral challenges: A systematic review of the literature. *Review of Educational Research*, 83, 551–597.

Henggeler, S. W. & Lee, T. (2003). Multisystemic treatment of serious clinical problems. In A. E. Kazdin & J. R. Weisz (Eds.), *Evidence-based psychotherapies for children and adolescents* (pp. 301–322). New York: The Guilford Press.

Jaycox, L. H. (2003). *Cognitive behavioral intervention for trauma in schools.* Longmont, CO: Sopris West Educational Services.

Kataoka, S., Zhang, L., & Wells, K. B. (2002). Unmet need for mental health care among U.S. children: Variation by ethnicity and insurance status. *American Journal of Psychiatry*, 159, 1548–1555.

Kendall, P. C., Choudhury, M., Hudson, J., *et al.* (2002). *"The C.A.T. Project" manual for the cognitive behavioral treatment of anxious adolescents.* Ardmore, PA: Workbook Publishing.

Langberg, J. M., Epstein, J. N., Becker, S. P., *et al.* (2012). Evaluation of the Homework, Organization, and Planning Skills (HOPS) intervention for middle school students with Attention Deficit Hyperactivity Disorder as implemented by school mental health providers. *School Psychology Review*, 41, 342–364.

Langberg, J. M., Epstein, J. N., Girio-Herrera, E., *et al.* (2011). Materials organization, planning, and homework completion in young adolescents with ADHD: Impact on academic performance. *School Mental Health*, 3, 93–101.

Lewinsohn, P. M., Clarke, G. N., Hops, H., *et al.* (1990). Cognitive-behavioral group treatment of depression in adolescents. *Behavior Therapy*, 21, 385–401.

Little, S. G. & Akin-Little, A. (2009). Classroom management. In W. T. O'Donohue & J. E. Fisher (Eds.), *General principles and empirically supported techniques of cognitive behavior therapy* (pp. 173–180). Hoboken, NJ: John Wiley & Sons.

March, J. S. (2002). Combining medication and psychosocial treatments: An evidence-based medicine approach. *International Review of Psychiatry*, 14, 155–163.

Masia, C., Beidel, D. C., Albano, A. M., *et al.* (1999). Skills for academic and social success. Available from C. Masia Warner, New York University School of Medicine, Child Study Center.

Merikangas, K. R., He, J. P., Burstein, M., *et al.* (2010). Lifetime prevalence of mental disorders in US adolescents: Results from the National Comorbidity Study-Adolescent Supplement (NCS-A). *Journal of American Academy of Child and Adolescent Psychiatry*, 49, 980–989.

Mifsud, C. & Rapee, R. M. (2005). Early intervention for childhood anxiety in a school setting: Outcomes for an economically disadvantaged population. *Journal of the American Academy of Child and Adolescent Psychiatry*, 44, 996–1004.

MTA Cooperative Group. (1999). A 14-month randomized clinical trial of treatment strategies for attention-deficit/hyperactivity disorder. *Archives of General Psychiatry*, 56, 1073–1086.

Mufson, L., Dorta, K. P., Wickramaratne, P., *et al.* (2004). A randomized effectiveness trial of Interpersonal Psychotherapy for depressed adolescents. *Archives of General Psychiatry*, 61, 577–584.

Mufson, L., Weissman, M. M., Moreau, D., *et al.* (1999). Efficacy of Interpersonal Psychotherapy for depressed adolescents. *Archives of General Psychiatry*, 56, 573–579.

National Center on Response to Intervention. (2010). *Essential components of RTI: A closer look at response to intervention.* Washington, DC: US Department of Education, Office of Special Education Programs, National Center on Response to Intervention.

Pas, E. T., Bradshaw, C. P., and Cash, A. H. (2014). Coaching classroom-based preventive interventions. In M. D. Weist, N. A. Lever, C. P. Bradshaw, & J. S. Owens (Eds.), *Handbook of school mental health* (2nd ed.; pp. 255–267). New York: Springer.

Raggi, V., Chronis-Tuscano, A., Fishbein, H., *et al.* (2009). Development of a brief, behavioral homework intervention for middle school students with attention-deficit/hyperactivity disorder. *School Mental Health*, 1, 62–77.

Robin, A. & Foster, S. L. (1989). *Negotiating parent–adolescent conflict.* New York: The Guilford Press.

Sadler, J. M., Evans, S. W., Schultz, B. K., *et al.* (2011). Potential mechanisms of action in the treatment of social impairment and disorganization in adolescents with ADHD. *School Mental Health*, 3, 156–168.

Scott, T. M., Alter, P. J., Rosenberg, M., *et al.* (2010). Decision-making in secondary and tertiary interventions of school-wide systems of positive behavior support. *Education and Treatment of Children*, 33, 513–535.

Shores, R., Gunter, P., & Jack, S. (1993). Classroom management strategies: Are they setting events for coercion? *Behavioral Disorders*, 18, 92–102.

Sibley, M. H., Pelham, W. E., Evans, S. W., *et al.* (2011). Evaluation of a Summer Treatment Program for adolescents with ADHD. *Cognitive and Behavioral Practice*, 18, 530–544.

Simonsen, B., Sugai, G., & Fairbanks, S. (2007). School-wide positive behavior support: Preventing the development and occurrence of problem behavior. In S. W. Evans, M. D. Weist, & Z. N. Serpell (Eds.), *Advances in school-based mental health interventions: Best practices and program models* (pp. 8-1–8-17). New York: Civic Research Institute.

Springer, F. and Phillips, J. L. (2006). The IOM model: A tool for prevention planning and implementation. *Prevention Tactics*, 8, 1–8.

Stein, B. D., Jaycox, L. H., Kataoka, S. H., *et al.* (2003). A mental health intervention for schoolchildren exposed to violence: A randomized controlled trial. *Journal of the American Medical Association*, 290, 603–611.

Storch, E., Larson, M., Muroff, J., *et al.* (2010). Predictors of functional impairment in pediatric obsessive-compulsive disorder. *Journal of Anxiety Disorders*, 24, 275–283.

Storer, J. L., Evans, S. W., & Langberg, J. M. (2014). Organization intervention for children and adolescents with Attention-Deficit/Hyperactivity Disorder (ADHD). In M. D. Weist, N. A. Lever, C. P. Bradshaw, & J. S. Owens (Eds.), *Handbook of school mental health* (2nd ed.; pp. 385–398). New York: Springer.

Teach for America. (2011). Creating and implementing effective rules and consequences. In *Classroom Management & Culture* (pp. 15–26). New York: Teach for America.

Walther, C. P., Cheong, J., Molina, B. G., *et al.* (2012). Substance use and delinquency among adolescents with childhood ADHD: The protective role of parenting. *Psychology of Addictive Behaviors*, 26, 585–598.

Wignall, A., Gibson, J., Bateman, N., *et al.* (1998). ACE-Adolescents coping with emotions: Group leader manual and ACE student workbook. North Sydney: Northern Sydney Health.

Chapter 23

Interconnecting school mental health and school-wide positive behavior support

Jessica Swain-Bradway, Jill Johnson, Lucille Eber,
Susan Barrett, and Mark D. Weist

Introduction

One in five children in America have a significant mental health disorder (Merikangas *et al.*, 2010). These children and youth require multidimensional interventions but less than 20% of this group will receive any mental health services at all (Bazelon Center for Mental Health Law, n.d.; Katoka, Zhang, and Wells, 2002). For children and youth who do receive mental health services, schools typically serve as the primary setting for identification of mental health disorders, and delivering mental health services (Burns *et al.*, 1995). The public school as the primary setting for mental health service delivery is a logical fit – all children are required by law to attend school. However, despite the promise of the evidence-base for mental health promotion and intervention in schools (Kutash, Duchnowski, and Lynn, 2006), the traditional approach to mental health services in schools, which will be referred to as school mental health (SMH) for the duration of the chapter, is inadequate in the United States (Rowling and Weist, 2004; Weist, Evans, and Lever, 2003) along numerous dimensions.

The traditional approach to SMH often reflects a "standalone" arrangement, with SMH clinicians hired by districts, operating in an isolated manner, contradictory to the cohesive "system of care" model promoted by the US Substance Abuse and Mental Health Services Administration (SAMHSA; the federal agency most responsible for guiding and supporting mental health services) for nearly 30 years (Kutash *et al.*, 2006). Traditional SMH lacks consistent implementation of evidence-based practices (EBPs) as well as a lack of systematic evaluation of the impact of mental health services on students served or the school (Calhoun, Moras, Pilkonis, and Rehm, 1998; Evans and Weist, 2004; Graczyk, Domitrovich and Zins, 2003; Kratochwill, 2007; Kutash *et al.*, 2006; Weist, Lever, Bradshaw, and Owens, 2014). This approach is often associated with a "fee-for-service" model in which clinicians, hired by school districts, come into schools and work one-on-one with a few students who present more challenging problems. The mental health services students receive are dependent upon the training the clinician has received. The clinical services are provided in isolation from other facets of the students' school day, and life, often not in coordination with school-wide health/wellness promotion, prevention, or early identification/intervention (Weist, 2003).

This isolated approach is ineffective (Weist and Murray, 2007) due to: (1) low implementation fidelity of interventions, (2) lack of coordinated efforts by clinicians, teachers,

School Mental Health: Global Challenges and Opportunities, ed. Stan Kutcher, Yifeng Wei and Marc D. Weist. Published by Cambridge University Press. © Cambridge University Press 2015.

and other school personnel who interact with the students receiving mental health services, (3) lack of well-established selection criteria for identifying students who need mental health services, and (4) infrequent and inconsistent monitoring and adjustment of interventions. The traditional approach fails to provide any kind of preventative interventions to the broader student body and is marked by high levels of dissatisfaction with care by students, families, and school staff (Weist and Murray, 2007). In recent years, educational and clinical groups in the United States have given increased attention to the limitations of this standalone approach to SMH service provision and there has been a concerted, organized movement toward coordinated systems of mental healthcare. This chapter describes one approach to establishing a coordinated system of mental health service provision in schools, the Interconnected Systems Framework (ISF).

The ISF is an approach to coordinating efforts among educators, school administrators, and clinical mental health providers in order to embed SMH within the existing school and district systems to maximize resources, and create a foundation for efficient and effective delivery of SMH services. The ISF is marked by features that explicitly address the limitations to traditional SMH services: inclusion of a full continuum of EBPs for mental health promotion, prevention and intervention, data-based decision making for identification and monitoring outcomes, and collaboration among school, family, and community stakeholders. This chapter describes the ISF, its core components, and examples of those components working within various schools, districts, and states across the United States. These exemplars have prioritized the inclusion of SMH practices into the intervention systems they provide to students as a means to reduce and remove barriers to learning and school success.

The Interconnected Systems Framework: conceptual foundations

The ISF is a merger of EBPs in mental health service provision with positive behavioral interventions and supports (PBIS). PBIS is a decision-making framework that guides selection, integration, and implementation of the best evidence-based academic and behavioral practices for improving important academic and behavior outcomes for all students (Sugai et al., 2010). PBIS is not a prescriptive set of practices. Within the decision-making framework of the PBIS model, school personnel use data on student problem behaviors to select, match, and implement interventions that have evidence of reducing those problem behaviors. For example, students lacking social skills for peer interactions would receive instruction in an evidence-based curriculum for improving interpersonal skills.

The PBIS framework is a multi-tiered, layered approach and is organized to allow for intensifying interventions for students who require more intense, or more frequent behavioral interventions to be successful. Tier 1 interventions target the school population at large with a goal of establishing a core social behavior curriculum to prevent and reduce behaviors that would negatively impact academic achievement. Tier 2 is an additional layer of support for students requiring additional supports to be successful. It does not replace Tier 1 supports but supplements them by providing interventions at a high dosage to small groups of students with similar problem behaviors. The goal of Tier 2 interventions is to support students to attain a level of skill fluency that would make Tier 1 supports sufficient for student success. Tier 3 interventions are highly individualized and are designed to reduce the intensity and frequency of problems. Tier 3 includes function-based behavior plans and person-centered wraparound plans for students who require highly personalized support to be successful in the school setting. Students receiving Tier 3 supports would also receive interventions at Tiers 1 and

2 but would have additional interventions at the intensity necessary for reducing their problem behaviors. As an example, if a student requires social skills instruction they may participate in a small group (Tier 2) social skills class, but also have individual practice and/or intervention sessions with a clinical therapist as part of their individualized plan. As student needs intensify, the EBPs selected for implementation are more specific to the needs of a student and can include a range of academic, social emotional, psychiatric, and behavioral approaches. PBIS is grounded in implementation science (Fixsen *et al.*, 2005; Graczyk *et al.*, 2003), which provides guidance for organizing sustained, consistent implementation of practices.

PBIS foundations include data-based decision making by collaborative teams, tiered levels of support that enable increasingly intense intervention delivery, clearly defined outcomes, and monitoring of those outcomes. As typically implemented in schools, PBIS is a prevention-based system of behavioral interventions in which school systems are organized to support staff (policies, training, and resources), data and practices are aligned with the valued outcomes of the school community resulting in coordinated supports. However, despite the flexibility of the framework, implementing schools do not typically consider mental health services within the range of EBPs implemented to reduce problem behavior (Barrett, Eber, and Weist, 2013).

There are currently 20 000 schools in the United States implementing PBIS (www.PBIS. org) and a host of studies document evidence of impact on school-related student outcomes including: (1) improvements in academic instruction by teachers (Taylor-Greene *et al.*, 1997; McIntosh *et al.*, 2006a; 2006b); (2) increases in parent involvement (Ballard-Krishnan *et al.*, 2003); (3) decreases in student discipline referrals (Anderson and Kincaid, 2005); (4) decreases in suspension rates (Frey *et al.*, 2008); and (5) improvements in student academic performance (Kincaid *et al.*, 2002). In addition to student-related improvements, benefits to schools and staff – such as reduction in staff turnover, improved organizational efficiency, and increased perception of teacher efficacy and increasing quality of life for students (Kincaid *et al.*, 2002) – have also been documented.

Interconnected Systems Framework: core features

The ISF promotes a prevention-based continuum of mental health promotion and intervention by bringing school and community mental health providers into established PBIS systems. Building from the foundational framework of PBIS, core features of the ISF operationally align systems, data, and practices within the school to meet a common goal of mitigating the impact of mental health issues sufficient to support student academic and social achievement. The goal is to systematically build an expanded continuum of mental health supports integrated within an established three-tiered-system of academic and behavior supports. The expanded continuum of mental health supports is achieved by the overlap of the ISF core features: (1) *administrative leadership and priority* of team-guided decision making on the selection, implementation, and monitoring of evidence-based SMH practices; (2) *effective teams* that include community mental health providers and family members to help guide decision making; (3) *data-based decision making* to inform implementation activities; (4) formal processes for the selection and implementation of *EBPs*; (5) early access through use of *comprehensive screening for mental health disorders*; (6) rigorous *progress-monitoring* for both fidelity and impact; and (7) *ongoing coaching* of both systems and practices to ensure fidelity and impact. By building on the multi-tiered systems already in place within the PBIS framework and facilitating cross-disciplinary collaboration between educators and mental health professionals, the ISF is able to provide early identification and supports to students with mental health issues at multiple levels of intensity.

Tier 1 supports within the multiple tiers of ISF are universally available interventions, and primarily focused on preventative services. This includes mental health promotion and identification of students who have mental health disorders before those disorders impede learning. Tier 2 supports include interventions targeted to small groups of students with similar mental health disorders who are not responding to the preventative supports at Tier 1. The goals of Tier 2 include minimizing impact of current disorders through interventions delivered in small groups. Trauma-informed interventions, designed to miti- gate the impact of ongoing exposure to traumatic events (Jaycox, 2003), are one example of a Tier 2, group-delivered intervention. Tier 3 interventions are individually developed by a team of school, family, and the appropriate community mental health providers. They may include one-on-one service delivery, as well as family involvement, teacher-driven inter- ventions, and medical interventions. The goal is to decrease the intensity and duration of symptoms and to maximize day-to-day functioning across life domains, commensurate with typical peers to the greatest extent possible. The strategies included within the tiers of support demand that as mental health disorders intensify, school, community, and family members communicate and collaborate with increasing frequency. Communication and collaboration is facilitated by multidisciplinary teams who are responsible for monitoring services provided at Tiers 1, 2, and 3.

The multi-tiered teaming structure allows for schools to include more community mental health providers in decision making on the mental health services that will most appropriately address the students' mental health disorders. Schools implementing the ISF ideally have multiple community mental health services providers participating on the teams that monitor and modify SMH services at each tier. As an example, school teams may include clinicians with training in trauma-informed interventions, family therapy, and substance abuse treatment. At each level of intervention and support the community mental health providers, together with their school-based partners, can guide school policies, practices, and data to embed mental health services into the day-to-day operations of a school. A greater array of mental health supports for students and families can become available through school-based intervention systems involving collaboration between school and community mental health providers.

The ISF provides structures for more effective implementation of mental health promo- tion, early intervention, and treatment, with greater likelihood of impact for more students than separate or "co-located" mental health delivery systems can provide. The initial commitment to ISF in many of the early implementation sites generally included events such as a new funding source, new legislation or policy change. Other variables that influenced leaders to move toward an ISF approach included changing demographics, identified cost savings, or frustration with current outcomes; while the impetus for engaging in the ISF process varied, its core features are evident in each case example.

The following sections describe the core features of the ISF and provide case examples, generated from the ISF monograph (Barrett et al., 2013) and the ISF Work Group, a collaborative group of educators, researchers, program evaluators, administrators, and clinicians from various districts, states, and national groups. The examples generated by the monograph and the work group come from experiences at the state, district, and school level from various geographically diverse school sites in the United States. The depth and range of the examples show the synergistic potential of the ISF to increase the capacity of schools and districts to provide empirically supported SMH services.

While the case examples describe one component and one point in time, it is important to remember that the ISF implementation process is fluid and iterative. Districts and schools impacted by changes in funding, administration, and student and community population characteristics engaged in multiple implementation activities at one time, and not necessarily in a linear manner. The first core component of the ISF, administrative commitment and priority, is critical in consideration of the dynamic environment of school districts.

Administrative commitment and priority

Administrative commitment to the ISF process is the active and overt involvement and investment in multi-tiered prevention and intervention for improving student emotional/behavioral functioning. State, district, school, and community leaders are critical to each phase of implementation, from exploring the relevance of ISF in a district, to maintaining the implementation at full capacity. Note similarities here to points made by Rowling (2009) in discussing the global advancement of SMH and asserting the direct impact and relevance of school leadership in systems change contributing to school success and positive student outcomes. The examples included in this chapter demonstrate this leadership manifested through a variety of administrative activities that promote re-envisioning SMH services and promotion of a positive social climate around mental health disorders. In support of ISF implementation, leaders from early-implementing sites expressed support publicly, secured resources, allocated direct and in-kind funding, and participated in training and meetings at the state, district, and school levels. Administrative vision and commitment to ISF implementation allowed school district and community stakeholders to collaborate in the ISF process by dedicating time to examine current conditions, participating in resource audits and considering reallocation of resources. Additional examples of the ISF include supporting policy changes to facilitate integration of mental health practices in schools. The first example below, the National Community of Practice, documents the administrative commitment and priority to ISF at a national level.

Case example: national leadership

In 2004 a National Community of Practice (CoP) on Collaborative School Behavioral Health (IDEA Partnership, 2013) emerged out of collaboration between two federally funded groups, the Individuals with Disabilities Education Act (IDEA) Partnership and the Center for School Mental Health (CSMH). Communities of Practice are an approach to interdisciplinary collaboration, through which professionals from diverse disciplines, and representing diverse stakeholders, voluntarily work together to share ideas and strategies to promote a shared agenda (Wenger, McDermott and Snyder, 2002) and "can be viewed as a way to address complex social and population health problems by taking advantage of a broader set of resources and increased capacity" (p. 17, Pope, MacKean, Casebeer, Milward, and Lindstrom, 2013).

The CoP brought together 22 national organizations, nine technical assistance centers, policy and administrative leaders in 16 states, to facilitate a "shared agenda" across education, mental health, and families focused on specific issues or themes related to SMH, including, among other topics: (1) building a collaborative culture for student mental health; (2) connecting SMH and PBIS; (3) targeting education as an essential component of systems of care; (4) facilitating family leadership in SMH; (5) improving SMH for youth with disabilities; and (6) improving quality and EBP. The CoP facilitated conversations that resulted in the conceptual paper on the ISF (Barrett *et al.*, 2009), the ISF work group, including national, state, and school leaders that met regularly to discuss implementation activities, implications, and research agendas, and the comprehensive ISF monograph detailing the critical features and components of ISF systems, data, and practices (Eber, Barrett, and Weist, 2013). Without this leadership and involvement by administrators across political and educational environments, the collective knowledge and examples gained by the CoP members would not have been disseminated, leaving states and districts without guidance on the merger of the systematic framework of PBIS and evidenced-based SMH practices.

Case example: state leadership

In Montana in 2009, state and federal grant funds supported the formation of a statewide SMH CoP, and monthly meetings of licensed mental health centers providing comprehensive school and community treatment (CSCT). The intention of the colla-boration was to develop training in SMH and service delivery for community and school staff. In spring 2010 Montana's Department of Public Health and Human Services (DPHHS) and Montana's Office of Public Instruction (OPI) collaboratively agreed on the need to hire a researcher to develop and disseminate a White Paper on SMH best practices and EBPs to inform administrative rules for the state's prominent SMH initiative, CSCT, involving movement of the child and adolescent mental health services into schools (Butts, 2010).

At a statewide conference, the White Paper was presented as part of a general session as one strategy for helping participants learn from the research and prepare for new admin-istrative rules regarding SMH programs and CSCT. This was the first time state leaders invested in research to implement policy that would contribute to administrative rule changes in Montana. The administrative rule re-write process was facilitated by DPHHS and OPI administrators in a multidisciplinary work group. This process led to innovative rule changes and pooling of resources to increase mental health services accessibility in Montana's public schools. Importantly, a provision in new administrative rules as of August 2013 mandated that for community mental health service providers to access the CSCT funding they needed to work with schools already or beginning to implement the PBIS framework. This has ensured that mental health services are building from the platform of PBIS, as in the ISF, and is also directly leading to greater collaboration among community mental health providers and school staff in school-based planning teams (Butts, Casey, and Ewen, 2014). This collaboration is becoming particularly strong at Tier 3 (focusing on treatment services), but also beginning to be seen at Tier 2 (early identification and intervention) and Tier 1 (population-focused prevention).

Case example: district leadership

In the examples in Montana, state leadership impacted district and school activities. In some of the case examples, the impetus for ISF implementation originated within the district, such as in the Urbana School District, in Illinois. In 2009 district personnel in Urbana wrote a Safe Schools, Healthy Students grant, a federal grant focused on violence prevention, climate enhancement, and mental health promotion in schools. Although the district did not receive the grant, many of the district and community leaders, family members, and service providers felt that the work was important and decided, without additional funding, to implement the plan outlined in the grant. Community partners at the table were willing to work within existing funding structures to improve services according to the needs of students in the school setting. For example, community clinicians agreed to come to the school to implement a group intervention instead of requiring students to come to the community center, directly reflecting the access advantage of SMH (Weist, 1997). Also, community-based staff members were allowed to participate on school planning teams even though attending team meetings was not considered a billable service. This commitment by district and community leaders led to an expanded range of evidence-based SMH services available to students and increased access to services beyond what was previously available in either the school or community.

Effective teaming

Effective teams are inextricably linked to and guided by effective leadership. Within the ISF, state, district, and school teams are multidisciplinary, including personnel with background in education, mental health, policy, and community work, as well as family members from the school district. Teams share a local vision and carry out the daily tasks and activities necessary to implement and monitor ISF systems that support the SMH practices, including (1) student, school, and community needs assessment, (2) redirecting resources in response to needs assessments, (3) selecting and implementing EBPs that address school and community needs, (4) training and coaching of school and clinical staff who bear the responsibility of implementing the practices, and (5) reviewing data to monitor fidelity of implementation and impact on student outcomes (see Markle, Splett, Maras, and Weston, 2014).

For many of the early implementer examples in the ISF monograph (Eber *et al.*, 2013), an important first step in team creation and facilitating effective collaboration was to clarify and define the roles and responsibilities of the multidisciplinary partners working together on district/community leadership teams. Typical commitments from school systems included allocation of time from current staff, funding, administrative support, accountability, and assuring leadership by key staff. Commitments from community providers included allocating staff time to serve on teams, prioritizing school functionality in treatment planning, assisting in making connections to families, and using community data for determining priorities and monitoring progress toward valued outcomes. All activities were directly linked to specific and measurable outcomes for students.

Case example: effective teaming

In Champaign County, Illinois school community agreements (SCAs) between community and school providers illustrate the commitment process. School community agreements in Champaign County have included the following information to facilitate collaboration: (1) basic school and community agency contact information; (2) specifying individuals who serve as the primary contact for various services; (3) clarifying the process of releasing confidential of information; (4) defining what interventions may be delivered at different tiers of intervention (Tier 1, 2, or 3); (5) describing level of services at each tier; (6) expectations and strategies for communication between the school and community partner.

A significant part of the SCAs included agreements on funding sources to offset the cost of team activities and SMH service provision. Trauma-informed school-based groups had a history of funding by a SAMHSA System of Care Cooperative Agreement with groups jointly conducted by school and mental health clinicians. Over time, the SAMHSA funding diminished but the school and county leaders were committed to rethink funding to maintain the collaborative service delivery. The solution generated from a multidisciplinary team was to bill Medicaid (public health insurance) to cover the cost of the clinician and supplement with funding from community-based United Way (community foundation) dollars to allow access to the trauma-informed interventions by any student who needed the services. In addition, one local high-school that benefited from the district/community partnership contributed equitable funds for supplies, lunches for the group, and the in-kind benefits of office space and staff time allocation. The compiling of resources and information, and the ability to problem solve across disciplines, was facilitated by the school-based team, prioritized by committed administrative personnel.

Data-based decision making

Data-based decision making is a foundational component of the ISF and requires multiple systems and processes within the school and district to operate in alignment to guide team and administrator implementation activities. Multidisciplinary ISF teams utilize current, relevant data to improve accountability, increase effectiveness of practices, quicken the pace of identification, and progress monitor effectiveness and fidelity of practices and systems. Early implementing sites actively planned to develop or improve their systems for data-based decision making to include mental health issues, in addition to the typical academic and behavioral data typically maintained by schools (e.g., grades, attendance, office discipline referrals, graduation credits, etc.). As part of evaluation procedures, leaders and teams created action plans that prioritized a locally controlled data system with the capability to track, monitor, and generate reports on intervention fidelity and student response to interventions.

The long-term goal of a fully developed evaluation system is predicated on the need for early identification and access to appropriate SMH services as a means to prevent and reduce the impact of mental health disorders. Another core component of ISF, the goal of early access, is a direct response to the inability of SMH services to provide supports at the capacity necessary to support the over 80% of students with mental health issues who do not receive mental health services (Katoaka *et al.*, 2002). Early access is established and facilitated by a comprehensive data-based decision making system that includes the following critical features.

Universal screening

Universal screening is a component of PBIS, which some early ISF implementers have expanded to include screening for risk factors for mental disorder and mental health problems. Universal screening is a valid and reliable method for determining students with elevated levels of risk (Romer and McIntosh, 2005). It is a process in which the entire student population is screened via a validated measure. Some of the more commonly used measures include the BASC 2 Behavioral and Emotional Screening System (Kamphaus and Reynolds, 2007), the Student Risk Screening Scale (Drummond, 1994), and the Systematic Screening for Behavior Disorders (Walker and Severson, 1990). There is opposition to large-scale screening, including right to privacy laws, potential costs for screening, costs and resources necessary for providing more complete assessments, and intervention for students who are identified through the screener (Center for Mental Health in Schools at UCLA, 2005). Proponents of screening argue that early identification and access to interventions for students with mental health disorders decreases the likelihood that more intense problems may develop (Center for Mental Health in Schools at UCLA, 2005). Relying on crisis-level behaviors as a method of identification often results in intensive, costly services that are unlikely to achieve valued outcomes (Dowdy, Ritchey, and Kamphaus, 2010; Weist, Lever, Bradshaw, and Owens, 2014).

Monitoring progress and perception data

The ultimate goal of ISF is to positively impact student functioning within the school environment. To measure this impact, school teams must progress-monitor student outcomes across all facets of academic, behavioral, and mental health indicators. Monitoring progress of individual students allows for modification at the clinical level, while tracking group progress informs decision making at the systems level (e.g., resource allocation, potential training needs of clinicians and school staff, scheduling). In this progress-monitoring of student outcomes, the ISF provides protocols and policies that facilitate sharing relevant data with all stakeholders to encourage engagement and inclusion in the decision-making process. The process is fully informed when progress data are examined in conjunction with students', families', and teachers' regular assessment of their perceptions of areas of improvement, and non-improvement, or needs. Perception data are not only relevant to higher tiers of support and individualized therapeutic plans, but are necessary to ensure the contextual fit of interventions for students, families, teachers, and providers.

Supporting staff

Perception data are one way in which an ISF team can provide direct support to education and clinical staff. Supporting staff through established systems is critical to the ISF and sustained implementation of any practice (Fixsen *et al.*, 2005). Within the ISF, systems to support data-based decision making include ongoing assessment of current data sources to ensure multiple relevant sources of information are informing the ISF process. Accompanying the collection and organizing of those data, training of school and clinical staff is necessary on how to use the data for school-wide, small group, and individual student purposes. In the case examples from the ISF monograph (Eber *et al.*, 2013), school teams integrated academic behavioral and mental health data for a cohesive view of the "whole child," and conducted audits, or assessment of data types and sources that were easily available and/or missing from the decision-making process, including fidelity or treatment integrity data.

Measuring fidelity

Fidelity is a core component of ISF, intimately related to the data-for-decision-making process. Systematically measuring and addressing fidelity is robustly supported by research indicating that the magnitude of treatment effect is often associated with the level of implementation (Perepletchikova and Kazdin, 2005). Within the ISF, fidelity extends beyond integrity of the services delivered by clinicians and includes fidelity of the ISF systems that make delivery of those services feasible. In the ISF, clinicians would be responsible for utilizing fidelity measures that accompany evidence-based interventions, and sharing those data with the ISF team. The ISF team would use those data, in conjunction with student outcomes data to assess the overall implementation and impact of the ISF systems and practices. Examples of systems-directed questions that were developed collaboratively with the ISF work group include: Have teams defined roles and responsibilities? Is a universal screening process in place? Do teams regularly review and share school and community data with stakeholders? Do staff members have the required skills to implement the EBPs with fidelity? Are staff supported through a coaching model to ensure high-quality implementation? Reviewing critical systems features through fidelity checks allows the team to examine service delivery and student progress and thereby a team's ability to make meaningful decisions about implementation rather than assigning blame to students when interventions are unsuccessful.

Case example: data-based decision making, universal screening

A brief example of an informal school-developed nomination process to expand universal screening to include mental health concerns originates from Champaign County, Illinois. The school-based ISF team used a simple teacher nomination process to identify students in need of support who were not identified through typical universal screening systems (e.g., grades, attendance, and office referrals for problem behaviors). The teacher nomination was a list of students about whom teachers had concerns regarding internalizing behaviors (e.g., students experiencing depression, anxiety, and/or trauma). This provided information that was otherwise unavailable to the team and allowed the school to implement a school-based Tier 2 group intervention based on student needs.

Case example: data-based decision making, fidelity

Data collected for universal screening (as above) shape the resources allocated to SMH service delivery. For example, in Champaign County, Illinois, the school–community ISF team used fidelity data to support integrity of implementation of structured psychotherapy for adolescents responding to chronic stress (SPARCS: Derosa *et al.*, 2006). The team merged staff and student survey data with fidelity data to identify areas of strength and areas of weakness in implementation and were then able to target resources and training topics to address specific areas of need, including: (1) training teachers in the model to embed the SPARCS skills and language into the overall school culture as a preventative approach; (2) the training school social workers/counselors need to lead groups; and (3) training of mental health staff to participate meaningfully on school-based planning and problem-solving teams while expanding their role at the school.

Case example: data-based decision making, perception data

Another example of the data-based decision-making process and necessary systems comes from the ISF work group from a site in Scranton, Pennsylvania, a partnership between district personnel and a local behavioral health managed care organization, Community Care. In Scranton, mental health services were traditionally delivered in relative isolation from school settings and lacked cohesion and relevance for many students and families. Dissatisfied with this isolated approach, the school district and Community Care developed and installed an integrated school-based behavioral health and school-wide PBIS team. These partners convened leadership meetings with key stakeholders from the school, mental health, and community organizations. These school leadership teams began collecting data for the decision-making process by taking an inventory of local, available services and identifying potential data sources that would inform the team of student needs.

After careful consideration, the team identified several key measures and indicators in support of the goal of establishing the school as a clinical home for mental health interventions. The team used measures of student emotional/behavioral functioning (e.g., Youth Outcome Questionnaire; [Burlingame *et al.*, 1996]; Strengths and Difficulties Questionnaire [Goodman, 1997]), as well as informal measures, such as referrals to higher levels of mental healthcare, referrals to emergency evaluations, and measures to assess quality of interventions. This team also used formal PBIS data sources (e.g., the School Wide Information System, [May *et al.*, 2003]) and fidelity tools (e.g., the School-Wide Evaluation Tool [Sugai, Lewis-Palmer, Horner, and Todd, 2001]), as well as other school-level academic and behavioral indicators such as attendance, suspensions, and referrals to special education.

According to the partners, this was the first time that mental health and education professionals effectively shared data to inform intervention decisions and develop student-oriented action plans together to achieve valued outcomes. This collaborative approach overcame many of the limitations and barriers associated with a more isolated approach, and resulted in a more cohesive and effective system of care for students and families.

Selection and implementation of evidence-based practices

Selection and implementation of EBPs is a common barrier to SMH integration in the school setting (Evans and Weist, 2004; Weist *et al.*, 2009). There are a wide range of EBPs for school-aged youth. For example, SAMHSA maintains six online federal registries and 24 online resources for finding EBPs (www.samhsa.gov), including the Matrix of Children's Evidence-Based Interventions (Yannacci and Rivard, 2006) which lists over 90 evidence-based mental and behavioral health interventions for children and youth. However, due to the relatively isolated role of the SMH clinician in the school environment, these practices are often not known to the rest of the school personnel, including the administrator. Administrative commitment, expanded teams, and engaging in data-driven decision-making facilitates the selection and implementation of EBPs to best fit the needs of the student population.

In 2013 the OSEP National PBIS Technical Assistance Center initiated development of a "consumer guide" for selection of an EBP within the PBIS framework (Putnam *et al.*, 2012). As District Community teams were formed and resource-mapping activities allowed systems to list and examine current practices, it was clear that most systems did not have a formal process for selecting EBPs. Once the need was identified, the TA center partners developed a tool to examine the process by which needs are identified, practices were selected and implemented, and progress monitored.

Case example: selection of evidence-based practices

An example of the use of the *Consumer Guide for Selecting Evidence-based Practice Assessment* (Putnam *et al.*, 2012) was from the Champaign-Urbana community in Illinois. School social workers in the community used the *Consumer Guide* to (1) assess their process of selecting interventions based on student needs, and (2) assess the practice of progress monitoring interventions during and after treatment. Findings from the tool suggested that collaborative partnerships between school and community providers were lacking, implementation fidelity was not addressed, and progress monitoring of interventions was not a systematic process. Self-assessment of this kind allowed the social workers to be reflective on their practices, review the integrity of school systems, and provide concrete action steps to improve practices and systems. The information derived from completion of the *Consumer Guide* was organized and shared with the district leadership team, who then prioritized areas of need and training in the selection and monitoring of EBPs by the social workers.

Next, interventions, many of which focused on teaching students new skills, were selected after initial self-assessment of ISF systems and resource mapping, and an audit of the resources available within the community. This allowed schools to take inventory of current school practices, examine resource allocation, and assess impacts of current practices, including inefficiencies across both education and mental health systems. The school teams then identified possible overlap and determined current areas of need. Once a need was identified, a formal selection process ensured that there was a match for the presenting problem, but also a check to see if evidence-based strategies existed and were available and feasible to address the problem.

Ongoing coaching

Team-based selection and implementation of EBPs to meet emotional/behavioral needs of students can be a difficult and very different task than most school-based teams would engage in on a regular basis. Shifting to a comprehensive, ISF approach can require regular, systematic coaching and will be a shared responsibility across leadership and ISF teams. Two distinct types of coaching will be required for ISF to be effective.

Systems coaching requires a diverse set of skills to work with individuals and teams and usually requires skills that facilitate working across multiple levels of the system (Duda and Barrett, 2013). The specific skills needed are dependent on the level of work (e.g., individual, team, system) and the outcomes that the coach and his/her team are working toward. Systems coaches will focus on implementation structures such as professional development and training, as well data systems such as fidelity and performance feedback measures.

Coaching for practices occurs on-site and supports individuals and teams to develop fluency of newly acquired skills, and assist in adapting those skills to the unique challenges of the local context. Coaching is done by skilled members across the district/community who have the experience of implementing new skills/practices, and access to the supports needed to help others implement effectively. In schools, coaching is often done by school psychologists, social workers, counselors, special educators, or administrators. Within the ISF, coaching happens at both the systems and practices level to ensure fidelity of clinical services as well as the systems that support provisions of the services.

Effective use of ISF procedures is challenging. Not only must personnel be skilled in their focused professional area, but they need the skills to appreciate, integrate, and implement the talents of their cross-discipline partners. The lessons learned from the case examples are that effective implementation of ISF must include regular and systematic coaching for educational, behavioral, and mental health professionals to receive frequent, constructive feedback on how well they are applying core ISF features and practices.

Case example: ongoing coaching

Recent student populations in the Scranton School District have started including more children and families who are more likely to experience poverty, be a minority, and be at risk for needing additional interventions and supports. The previous system for delivering mental health services to children and families was restrictive, inefficient, and ineffective, and, as importantly as the additional mental health services, teachers and administrators needed professional development to better serve their students with mental health issues on a day-to-day basis. Community Care was committed to transforming this system and providing relevant training and coaching for school staff. Community Care personnel provided training, technical assistance, and coaching for merging SMH practices into the existing PBIS framework.

Ongoing dialogue with other community and school stakeholders guided embedding prevention, interventions, and supports at each tier. From the beginning, the staff members of the school–community team were integrated into the school building community. These team members were viewed as valued members of the educational team, providing clinical interventions including individual therapy, family therapy, and group therapy; case management; crisis intervention 24/7; and consultation to school staff on dealing with at-risk students. All staff at the building level received in-service training on the services offered to students during the school day, teachers' responsibilities in these services, and how these services could impact the youth and their families. Together, the coaches helped the teams install the service delivery process by establishing meeting norms, screening, and identification procedures, progress monitoring, and performance feedback measures to ensure fidelity.

Conclusion

In this chapter we have described the ISF, which has significant potential to improve SMH programs and services through embedding them within the platform of PBIS. Building SMH from the implementation structure of PBIS increases coherence of services and, in turn, SMH helps to improve the depth and quality of PBIS prevention/intervention. As our group and many others from around the nation have worked to develop and improve the ISF, many lessons are being learned at building, district, state, and national levels, and we have attempted to capture some of the more prominent lessons learned in this chapter. A major theme is that momentum is gained in improving and expanding SMH through connection to PBIS. As provided in examples in this chapter, schools and districts established which PBIS core components were fully implemented, which practices were in place to support the range of student needs and where gaps in services and practices existed. The process of effective collaboration between school and community partners helped to ameliorate these gaps. As a result of the established structures for training, coaching, and evaluation of PBIS, collaborative activities occurred rapidly. The case examples are brief illustrations of the ISF core components facilitated by the scalable platform of PBIS and illustrate a system of care that has the potential for broad-scale capacity building at state levels.

Stephan, Hurwitz, Paternite, and Weist (2010) report ten critical factors for capacity building. Many of the ten critical factors are illustrated in the examples of the ISF core components, while others, though explicit in the examples, can be facilitated by the inclusive teaming structures and expanded data sources included in the ISF process: (1) a unified, cohesive, and compelling vision and a shared agenda with stakeholders; (2) centralized organizational systems and accountability mechanisms to ensure implementation of the vision and action agenda; (3) feasible, sustainable funding models for comprehensive initiatives, including early intervention and prevention; (4) an understanding among state and local education leaders of the critical links between student academic success and mental health; (5) authentic engagement of diverse family members and youth in policy and program development; (6) recognition of the needs of culturally diverse populations and action planning that explicitly organizes policies, resources, and practices to reduce disparities to access to effective programs and services; (7) pre-professional and in-service training for educators and allied professionals related to youth development, youth mental health, and academic success, with emphasis on best practices; (8) support for practitioners in using evidence-based strategies; (9) equitable distribution of resources and services across schools related to ensuring student academic success, mental health, and wellbeing; and (10) focus on continuous quality improvement by collecting and using outcome data to inform decision making at the local school, school district, and state levels.

Building the ten critical factors for broad-scale capacity does not happen in a linear manner, as many of the ISF case examples in the monograph and ISF Work Group experienced; implementation is a process that occurs in stages (Fixsen *et al.*, 2005) from early exploration of the appropriateness and relevance of the ISF within a district to full implementation with the capacity to maintain and modify ISF core components to mitigate anticipated changes in the community, district, and school. The entire process is dependent upon administrative leadership and vision coupled with effective teams who are able to build and refine systems that support school and community staff in data-based decision making, spanning early identification and increased access, monitoring outcomes, aware-ness of stakeholder perceptions and scrutinizing fidelity of the empirically based practices in SMH that are necessary to support achievement and success of all students. The PBIS framework provides the implementation structures within the school to support this process on a broad scale, as evidenced by the over 20 000 schools that are in some stage of PBIS implementation (www.PBIS.org).

Promise of ISF

The early successes of the case examples are part of a growing base of promising documen-tation that a systematic application of SMH, through the PBIS framework, maximizes access, efficiency, and effectiveness of mental health interventions. We predict the synergis-tic benefits of merging PBIS and SMH through the ISF will potentiatate advantages of both systems, including: (1) improved access to care (Burns *et al.*, 1995; Catron, Harris, and Weiss, 1998; Rones and Hoagwood, 2000); (2) enhanced preventive services (Elias, Gager, and Leon, 1997); (3) increased early problem identification (Weist, Myers, Hastings, Ghuman, and Han, 1999): (4) less stigmatizing and more ecological programs (Atkins, Adil, Jackson, McKay, and Bell, 2001; Nabors and Reynolds, 2000); and (5) increased likelihood of generalization of intervention impacts across settings (Evans, Langberg, and Williams, 2003).

The need for comprehensive, systematic access to SMH services is relevant and pressing. A growing social climate in the United States is clamoring for schools to actively and effectively provide a full continuum of promotion/prevention, early intervention, and intervention to improve student health and wellness, reduce academic and non-academic barriers to learning, and improve school success. As attested to by the growing momentum, and hundreds of individuals involved in developing, expanding, testing, and refining the ISF, we believe this approach has the potential to dramatically enhance progress in school mental health, in the United States and beyond.

References

Anderson, C. and Kincaid, D. (2005). Applying behavior analysis to school violence and discipline problems: schoolwide positive behavior support. *The Behavior Analyst*, 28, 49–63.

Atkins, M. S., Adil, J. A., Jackson, M., McKay, M. M., and Bell, C. C. (2001). An ecological model for school-based mental health services. In C. Newman, C. Liberton, K. Kutash, and R. Friedman (eds.), *The 13th annual research conference proceedings, a system of care for children's mental health: Expanding the research base* (pp. 119–122). Tampa, FL: University of South Florida.

Ballard-Krishnan, S., McClure, L., Schmatz, B., Travnikar, B., Friedrich, G., and Nolan, M. (2003). The Michigan PBS Initiative: advancing the spirit of collaboration by including parents in the delivery of personnel development opportunities. *Journal of Positive Behavior Interventions*, 5, 122–126.

Barrett, S., Eber, L., and Weist, M. (2013). *Advancing educational effectiveness: Interconnecting school mental health and school wide positive behavior support*. OSEP Center on Positive Behavioral Interventions and Supports. Available at: www.pbis.org/common/pbisresources/publications/Final-Monograph.pdf (accessed March 22, 2014).

Barrett, S., Eber, L., and Weist, M. (2009). Development of interconnected systems framework for school mental health. Concept paper. Center for School Mental Health.

Bazelon Center for Mental Health Law. (n.d.). *Facts on children's mental health*. Washington, DC: Bazelon Center for Mental Health Law. Available at: www.bazelon.org/LinkClick.aspx?fileticket=Nc7DS9D8EQE%3dandtabid=378 (accessed June 14, 2013).

Burlingame, G. M., Wells, M. G., Hoag, M. J., et al. (1996). *Manual for the youth outcome questionnaire*. Stevenson, MD: American Professional Credentialing Service.

Burns, B. J., Costello, E. J., Angold, A., et al. (1995). Children's mental health service use across service sectors. *Health Affairs*, 14, 147–159.

Butts, E. (2010). *Advancing school mental health in Montana: A report on changes to administrative rules for comprehensive school and community treatment*. Helena: Montana Office of Public Instruction.

Butts, E., Casey, S., and Ewen, C. (2014). Advancing school mental health in Montana: Partnership, research, and policy. In M. Weist, N. Lever, C. Bradshaw, and J. Owens (eds.), *Handbook of school mental health: Research, training, practice, and policy*, (2nd edn.; pp. 75–86). New York: Springer.

Calhoun, K. S., Moras, K., Pilkonis, P. A., and Rehm, L. P. (1998). Empirically supported treatments: Implications for training. *Journal of Consulting and Clinical Psychology*, 66, 151–162.

Catron, T., Harris, V. S., and Weiss, B. (1998). Post treatment results after 2 years of services in the Vanderbilt School-Based Counseling project. In M. H. Epstein, K. Kutash, and A. Duchnowski (eds.), *Outcomes for children and youth with emotional and behavioral disorders and their families: Programs and evaluation best practices* (pp. 653–656). Austin, TX: PRO-ED, Inc.

Center for Mental Health in Schools at UCLA. (2005). *Screening mental health problems in schools*. Los Angeles, CA: UCLA Department of Psychology. Available at: http://smhp.psych.ucla.edu/pdfdocs/policyissues/mhscreeningissues.pdf (accessed March 25, 2014).

DeRosa, R., Habib, M., Pelcovitz, D., et al. (2006). Structured psychotherapy for adolescents responding to chronic stress. Unpublished manual.

Dowdy, E., Ritchey, K., and Kamphaus, R. W. (2010). School-based screening: A population-based approach to inform and monitor children's mental health needs. *School Mental Health*, 2, 166–176.

Drummond, T. (1994). *The student risk screening scale (SRSS)*. Grants Pass, OR: Josephine County Mental Health Program.

Duda, M. A. and Barrett, S. (2013). Systems coaching: Coaching for competence and impact. Brief #1. National Implementation research Network. Available at: nirn.fpg.unc.edu (accessed March 22, 2013).

Eber, L., Barrett, S., and Weist, M. D. (2013). *Advancing education effectiveness: An interconnected systems framework for Positive Behavioral Interventions and Supports (PBIS) and School Mental Health*. Eugene: University of Oregon Press.

Elias, M. J., Gager, P., and Leon, S. (1997). Spreading a warm blanket of prevention over all children: Guidelines for selecting substance abuse and related prevention curricula for use in the schools. *The Journal of Primary Prevention*, 18, 41–69.

Evans, S. W., Langberg, J. M., and Williams, J. (2003). Achieving generalization in school-based mental health. In M. Weist, S. Evans, and N. Lever (eds.), *Handbook of school mental health*. New York: Kluwer/Plenum.

Evans, S. W. and Weist, M. D. (2004). Implementing empirically supported treatments in the schools: What are we asking? *Clinical Child and Family Psychology Review*, 7, 263–267.

Fixsen, D. L., Naoom, S. F., Blase, K. A., Friedman, R. M., and Wallace, F. (2005). *Implementation research: A synthesis of the literature*. Tampa, FL: University of South Florida, National Implementation Research Network.

Frey, A., Lingo, A., and Nelson, C. (2008). Positive behavior support: a call for leadership. *Children & Schools*, 30, 5–14.

Goodman, R. (1997). The Strengths and Difficulties Questionnaire: A research note. *Journal of Child Psychology and Psychiatry*, 38, 581–586.

Graczyk, P. A., Domitrovich, C. E., and Zins, J. E. (2003). Facilitating the implementation of evidence-based prevention and mental health promotion efforts in schools. In M. D. Weist, S. W. Evans, and N. A. Lever (eds.), *Handbook of school mental health: Advancing practice and research* (pp. 301–318). New York: Springer.

IDEA Partnership. (2013). Communities of practice. Available at: www.ideapartnership.org (accessed May 20, 2013).

Jaycox, L. (2003). Cognitive behavioral intervention for trauma in schools. Longmont, CO: Sopris West Educational Services.

Kamphaus, R. W. and Reynolds, C. R. (2007). *Behavior assessment system for children – second edition (BASC-2); Behavioral and emotional screening system (BESS)*. Bloomington, IN: Pearson.

Katoaka, S. H., Zhang, L., and Wells, K. B. (2002). Unmet need for mental health care among U.S. children: Variation by ethnicity and insurance status. *American Journal of Psychiatry*, 159, 1548–1555.

Kincaid, D., Knoster, T., Harrower, J., Shannon, P., and Bustamante, S. (2002). Measuring the impact of positive behavior support. *Journal of Positive Behavior Interventions*, 4, 109–117.

Kratochwill, T. R. (2007). A report card on evidence-based practices in the schools: The good, the bad, the ugly. *Communique*, 36 (4).

Kutash, K., Duchnowski, A. J., and Lynn, N. (2006). *School-based mental health: An empirical guide for decision-makers*. Tampa, FL: University of South Florida, Louis de la Parte Florida Mental Health Institute, Department of Child and Family Studies.

Markle, R. S., Splett, J. W., Maras, M. A., and Weston, K. J. (2014). Effective school teams: Benefits, barriers, and best practices. In M. Weist, N. Lever, C. Bradshaw, and J. Owens (eds.), *Handbook of school mental health: Research, training, practice, and policy* (2nd edn.; pp. 59–74). New York: Springer.

May, S., Ard, W., Todd, A., *et al.* (2003). Schoolwide information system. Eugene, OR: University of Oregon, Educational and Community Supports.

McIntosh, K., Chard, D. J., Boland, J. B., and Horner, R. H. (2006a). Demonstration of combined efforts in school-wide academic and behavioral systems and incidence of reading and behavior challenges in early elementary grades. *Journal of Positive Behavior Interventions*, 8, 146–154.

McIntosh, K., Horner, R. H., Chard, D., Boland, J., and Good, R. (2006b). The use of reading and behavior screening measures to predict non-response to school-wide positive behavior support: a longitudinal analysis. *School Psychology Review*, 35, 275–291.

Merikangas, K. R., He, J., Burstein, M., *et al.* (2010). Lifetime prevalence of mental disorders in U.S. adolescents: Results from the National Comorbidity Study-Adolescent Supplement (NCS-A). *Journal of American Academy of Child and Adolescent Psychiatry*, 49, 980–989.

Nabors, L. A. and Reynolds, M. W. (2000). Program evaluation activities: Outcomes related to treatment for adolescents receiving school-based mental health services. *Children's Services: Social Policy, Research, and Practice*, 3, 175–189.

Perepletchikova, F. and Kazdin, A. E. (2005). Treatment integrity and therapeutic change:

Issues and research recommendations. *Clinical Psychology: Science and Practice*, 12, 365–383.

Pope, J. K., MacKean, G., Casebeer, A., Milward, H. B., and Lindstrom, R. (2013). *Inter-organizational networks: A critical review of the literature to inform practice*. Alberta: Alberta Centre for Child, Family and Community Outreach.

Putnam, R., Barrett, S., Eber, L., Lewis, T., and Sugai, G. (2012). Selecting mental health interventions within a PBIS Approach. In L. Eber, S. Barrett, and M. Weist (eds.), *Advancing education effectiveness: An interconnected systems framework for Positive Behavioral Interventions and Supports (PBIS) and School Mental Health*. Eugene, OR: University of Oregon Press.

Romer, D. and McIntosh, M. (2005). *The roles and perspectives of school mental health professionals in promoting adolescent mental health*. In D. Evans, E. Foa, R. Gur, H. Hendin, C. O'Brien, M. Seligman, and B. Walsh (eds.), *Treating and preventing adolescent mental health disorders: What we know and what we don't know* (pp. 598–615). New York: Oxford University Press.

Rones, M., and Hoagwood, K. (2000). School-based mental health services: A research review. *Clinical Child and Family Psychology Review*, 3, 223–240.

Rowling, L. (2009). Strengthening "school" in school mental health promotion. *Health Education*, 109, 357–368.

Rowling, L., and Weist, M. D. (2004). Promoting the growth, improvement and sustainability of school mental health programs worldwide. *International Journal of Mental Health Promotion*, 6, 3–11.

Stephan, S., Hurwitz, L., Paternite, C., and Weist, M. D. (2010). Critical factors and strategies for advancing statewide school mental health policy and practice. *Advances in School Mental Health Promotion*, 3, 48–58.

Sugai, G., Horner, R. H., Algozzine, R., et al. (2010). *School-wide positive behavior support: Implementers' blueprint and self-assessment*. Eugene, OR: University of Oregon. Available at www.pbis.org (accessed May 10, 2010).

Sugai, G., Lewis-Palmer, T. M., Horner, R. H., and Todd, A. W. (2001) *School-Wide Evaluation Tool version 2.1*. Eugene, OR: University of Oregon, Educational and Community Supports.

Taylor-Greene, S., Brown, D., Nelson, L., et al. (1997). School-wide behavioral support: starting the year off right. *Journal of Behavioral Education*, 7, 99–112.

Walker, H. M. and Severson, H. H. (1990). *Systematic screening for behavior disorders (SSBD): Users guide and technical manual*. Longmont: Sopris West.

Weist, M. D. (1997) Expanded school mental health services: A national movement in progress. *Advances in Clinical Child Psychology*, 19, 319–352.

Weist, M. D. (2003). Promoting paradigmatic change in child and adolescent mental health and schools. *School Psychology Review*, 32, 336–341.

Weist, M. D., Evans, S. W., and Lever, N. (2003). *Handbook of school mental health: Advancing practice and research*. New York: Kluwer Academic/Plenum Publishers.

Weist, M. D., Lever, N. A., Bradshaw, C. P., and Owens, J. S. (eds.) (2014). *Handbook of School Mental Health: Research, training, practice, and policy* (2nd edn.). New York: Springer.

Weist, M. D., Lever, N., Stephan, S., et al. (2009). Formative evaluation of a framework for high quality, evidence-based services in school mental health. *School Mental Health*, 1, 196–211.

Weist, M. D. and Murray, M. (2007). Advancing school mental health promotion globally. *Advances in School Mental Health Promotion*, 1, 2–12.

Weist, M. D., Myers, C. P., Hastings, E., Ghuman, H., and Han, Y. (1999). Psychosocial functioning of youth receiving mental health services in the schools vs. community mental health centers. *Community Mental Health Journal*, 35, 69–81.

Wenger, E., McDermott, R., and Snyder, W. M. (2002). *Cultivating communities of practice: A guide to managing knowledge*. Boston, MA: Harvard Business School Press.

Yannacci, J. and Rivard, J. C. (2006). *Matrix of children's evidence-based interventions*. Alexandria, VA: NASMHPD Research Institute, Inc.

Global school mental health
Considerations and future directions

Stan Kutcher, Yifeng Wei, and Mark D. Weist

Emerging themes

This rich and varied compilation of descriptions of school mental health (SMH) interventions in 18 different countries around the world raises numerous issues for our consideration, now and in the future. It is clear that SMH, which up until recently has been largely limited in its scope and development to North America, Europe, and Australia/New Zealand, is rapidly expanding and the complexities of SMH conceptualization and applications that globalization brings are considerable. It is one thing, for example, to apply theoretically sophisticated SMH approaches in settings of relative wealth and socio-political stability; it is quite another to do so in settings of severe or absolute poverty and civil unrest. It is one thing to apply SMH approaches in settings where basic literacy and numeracy are well established, and quite another to do so where these are not. It is one thing to apply SMH approaches in settings where basic health and human rights conditions are reasonable, and quite another to do so where these are not. We have much to learn from how SMH is applied in non-Western settings and those lessons should inform us everywhere (Wei and Kutcher, 2012).

This monograph has provided us with a glimpse of the depth and breadth of SMH initiatives globally. As such, it is, to our knowledge, the first such compilation. And, a number of themes have clearly emerged.

First, it is clear that in some jurisdictions, sophisticated frameworks have been developed to help guide the integration of schools with mental healthcare provision, as well as to address a variety of in-school mental health domains – such as mental health literacy and mental health promotion, prevention, and intervention. For example, in the United States (systems of care approach), Turkey (therapeutic school consultation), Canada (school-based integrated pathway to care approach), and Singapore (the REACH program approach), the roles of schools in enhancing access to mental healthcare delivery, integrated with existing health system structures and functions, demonstrates how SMH can be applied to this purpose. Such models may become useful templates, not in terms of the specific structures that they have identified, but in the conceptual approaches that they provide. As such, they may in whole or in part be able to be used to inform the development of comprehensive and sustainable but locally appropriate approaches in other settings worldwide.

Second, some of the chapters nicely summarize how thoughtful application of whole-school approaches can be established to advance a variety of SMH-based mental health promotion initiatives. For example, in Ireland the development and application of a national Social, Personal and Health Education Curriculum (Gabhainn, 2010) that is linked into the

School Mental Health: Global Challenges and Opportunities, ed. Stan Kutcher, Yifeng Wei and Marc D. Weist. Published by Cambridge University Press. © Cambridge University Press 2015.

Health Promoting Schools approach; in New Zealand Wellbeing at School (Adolescent Health Research Group, 2008; Darr *et al.*, 2014; Wellbeing at School, 2014); and in Australia MindMatters (Wyn *et al.*, 2000) and KidsMatter Early Childhood (KidsMatter, 2014). All of these impressive initiatives apply many of the components important for mental health promotion as identified by educators and mental health professionals (Joint Consortium for School Health, 2010; Weare and Nind, 2011; Wei and Kutcher, 2012). With these large-scale national initiatives the importance of evaluations and, whenever possible, application of RCT pilots to guide scale-up and scale-out activities is essential. Other settings can learn much from how these initiatives were developed, implemented, and evaluated.

Third, a number of chapters identify the many challenges and some possible solutions to building SMH initiatives in different countries (such as, for example: Ukraine, Iraq, Mexico, Chile, Ghana, China, India, and Israel) or within regions (such as, for example: British Columbia, Canada). A take-home lesson from these descriptions is the importance of adapting what is ideal to existing circumstances that can create the possible.

Finally, a number of chapters describe innovative interventions/models that are being applied in various jurisdictions (for example: Japan, Malawi, Brazil, the United States) or more generally (for example: the Mindfulness approach and teaching mental health literacy). These innovations have demonstrated their preliminary positive impact to support their application; it is essential that the highest standards of evidence be applied to research their impact so that policy makers and practitioners can be sure that they are implementing effective, safe, and cost-effective interventions. This is particularly important given that more methodologically rigorous investigations with negative results (for example in SMH prevention programs) are calling into question the impact of less rigorous research that has identified previously positive results (Araya *et al.*, 2013; Weare and Nind, 2011; Wei *et al.*, 2013).

This concluding chapter cannot be a complete summary or analysis of those that have gone before, but will try to bring some conceptual congruity and raise challenging issues for future consideration. There are many options to consider, directions to be followed, and choices about what to address in this concluding piece. We have chosen four issues to consider as SMH moves to the global stage: the challenges of language; an SMH framework based on a common language; the impact of site and purpose; and future globally applicable directions.

The challenges of language

As we have read in this monograph, there is tremendous variability in what is being implemented in SMH across the world. Many different components – including mental health promotion, attempts at prevention (of mental disorders and of psychosocial morbidity), interventions for treatment of mental illness, and interventions for enhancement of wellbeing in various iterations and combinations – seem to have sprung up all over. There seem to be literally hundreds if not thousands of things that are being done and even more ideas about things that can be done. There are favorite interventions, driven by solid research, and there are favorite interventions driven by novelty, personal preference, social ecology, ideology, and more. In many cases it is the presence of hard-working, dedicated, and committed individuals, with various backgrounds in mental health and education sectors, who by their vision and perseverance are able to overcome challenges and bring to the school stage one or more components of these mental health applications.

Given this plethora of approaches and buffet of offerings, it may be a good idea to provide a framework in which these may be considered and that educational and health systems can use to help inform what they will do and for which purpose. Ideally, this framework should allow for the fit of all useful and validated school-based mental health interventions and advance a conceptual model that can help decision makers, educators, health and mental healthcare providers and others, determine what needs to be done and decide on where specific types of interventions may best fit. It is within this need for a guiding framework that challenges of language – what do we mean by the words we use – need to be considered, clarified, and de-coded, so that that we can clearly communicate what we are doing with each other.

Commonly considered definitions about mental health, such as that of the World Health Organization (WHO) as a state of wellbeing (World Health Organization, 2014a) have been historically and politically useful in helping us consider the importance of mental health as well as mental disorders, and have drawn attention to the important social determinants of both health and disease. They are, however, complex, encompassing almost every aspect of social-cultural, civil, and economic life, and are often political in nature, giving responsible organizations (including governments and institutions) a vision for achievement rather than a plan. Such definitions can sometimes serve to obfuscate as well as to inform. If the definition of mental health covers every aspect of social, cultural, economic, and political life, what does it mean exactly? Indeed, this tension of understanding and the challenge of creating useful and valid operational definitions for the term have characterized our discussions since the early 1900s, when the term "mental hygiene" was coined and its congruence with "social hygiene" was noted (the Social Hygiene Movement, 1913; Cohen, 1983; Gale Group, 2008; Richardson, 1987; 1989). From the beginning of this convergence, the education system was intimately involved.

Other constructs, attempting to provide a blueprint for approaching mental health, have been recently applied. One such approach, the spectrum of mental health and mental disorders, suggests that an individual moves along a continuum that begins with mental health and that may end up with a mental disorder (e.g., Ontario Ministry of Education, 2013; Well-being Institute at the University of Cambridge, 2011; University of Michigan Health & Well Being Services, 2012). The predominant driver of movement on this spectrum is considered to be the presence of risk factors (primarily environmental) and protective factors (also primarily environmental) with the implicit message that decreasing risk and enhancing protective factors can position an individual on that spectrum and determine their progress across it. While this construct serves to highlight the importance of environmental factors across a host of outcomes, it does not explain why most individuals do not move from one part of the spectrum to another or why an individual can concurrently have a mental disorder and experience good mental health.

Furthermore, the spectrum construct has been applied to so many different components of the wider mental health field that it is often difficult to understand what particular spectrum is being referred to. For example, there are spectrums of services; there are policy and service delivery spectrums; there are spectrums which bridge prevention of mental disorders with care for mental disorders; there are spectrums of different mental disorders (such as autism spectrum disorder or obsessive compulsive spectrum); there are spectrums of "severity"; there are spectrums of symptoms that may or may not be congruent with current diagnostic categories; there is even a spectrum that combines two different spectrum – emotional wellbeing and severity of mental disorder. Indeed, there are so many different types and understandings of "spectrums" that they rival the different understandings of "mental health."

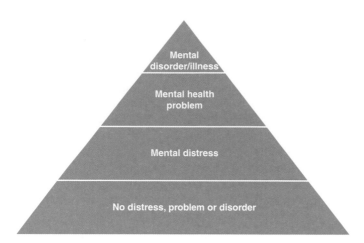

Figure 24.1 Mental health state.

Here, we propose an approach that considers the presence of mental disorders and also considers them as being able to exist concurrently with mental wellbeing as a potential helpful framework from which to be able to address the many nuances of SMH. In Figure 24.1, various components of the construct of "mental health" are identified and SMH interventions can be tailored to each of the domains described. None of the domains are exclusionary of any other domain, and at the level of the individual, a person can be in more than one domain at the same time. For example: a student can have a mental disorder (such as ADHD); be experiencing a mental health problem (such as a normal reaction to the death of a grandparent); be experiencing mental distress (such as an imminent examination); and be in a state of equilibrium (such as spending time playing a game with friends). And the impact of each of these domains may change over time (see Figure 24.1).

Mental disorder/mental Illness

For our purpose, we will define mental disorder/mental illness as synonymous and use globally accepted definitions as found in the two commonly applied medical diagnostic systems: the International Classification of Disease (World Health Organization, 2014b) and the Diagnostic and Statistical Manual (American Psychiatric Association, 2014). As those diagnostic systems change how mental disorders are defined globally, so our definitions of what constitutes mental disorders will also change.

Current understanding of mental disorders promotes a complex interrelationship between genetics and environmental factors that impact brain functioning, beginning from conception and continuing throughout the life span as our "best" perspective on what leads to mental disorders in any individual (Rutter *et al.*, 2008). Thus, a mental disorder is a perturbation in expected brain function that arises as a result of this complex interaction with, in some cases, genetic endowment that affects brain development bearing a greater weight of probable risk and in other cases environmental factors that affect brain development bearing a greater weight of probable risk. Even mental disorders that onset by definition due to environmental impacts (such as post-traumatic stress disorder) are strongly impacted by an individual's genes and other existing environmental factors (for example: social supports; access to healthcare; safety; etc.). Mental disorders signal that usual brain adaptive ability is substantially strained or failing and emotional, cognitive, behavioral, perceptual, and physical symptoms occur. These are of sufficient magnitude to cause noted functional impairment.

Individuals with mental disorders are usually provided assistance from medically related professionals (such as: physicians, nurses, psychologists, social workers, etc.) who have developed and apply specified competences that have stood the scrutiny of scientific research and are either regulated by governments or health institutions or endorsed by professional organizations. About 15% of young people (up to age 25 years) will meet criteria for a mental disorder during this part of the lifespan (Patel, 2007; Prince, 2007; World Health Organization, 2001).

Mental health problems

These are emotional, cognitive, and behavioral difficulties experienced by an individual arising from a substantive environmental stressor (such as loss of a loved one, loss of employment, migration, poverty, etc.). While there are substantial differences in how individuals experience and deal with such substantial stressors, all individuals will be impacted to some degree. Frequently, these stressors will result in significant emotional, cognitive, physical, perceptual, or behavioral symptoms, and even some short-term decrease in usual functioning, signifying difficulties in adaptation that are commonly addressed by community resources and community traditions (such as religious rituals regarding death, self-help organizations) or by socially sanctioned healers who may or may not be medical professionals (such as counselors, pastoral care workers, etc.).

Mental health problems are not mental disorders, and vice versa. Unfortunately, some jurisdictions confuse the two, and use data from mental disorders to define mental health problems. Such conceptual confusion can lead to medicalization of normal human experience (for example: treating with medications) or conversely, denial of needed treatment for a mental disorder by labeling the difficulties being experienced as a problem and thus not requiring mental health care. Depending on the social situation or geographic context, many individuals in a given population may experience a mental health problem during the school-aged years (up to age 25 years).

Mental distress

Mental distress is the common, ubiquitous, and normal experience of negative emotions, physical, cognitive, and behavioral symptoms that occur every day, arise from environmental challenges (for example: failing to make the chess club; preparing for an examination; experiencing romantic rejection; etc.) and are ameliorated with successful adaptation (leading to learning) and usual social, interpersonal, and family support. All students will experience some degree of distress in everyday life. Individuals experiencing mental distress do not require professional interventions and successful overcoming of distress is an essential component of developing resilience. Avoidance of usual distress can lead to incapacity to deal with "the slings and arrows of outrageous fortune . . . and by [so doing] end them" (Shakespeare et al., 2006).

Mental equilibrium: no distress, problem, or disorder

This is a point in time where the individual (even if they have been experiencing emotional, behavioral, perceptual, cognitive, or physical symptoms) are experiencing a positive sense of self, are adapting reasonably well to their environment, and are reasonably content with their state of being, however they define that state.

An SMH framework based on a common language

Clarification of meaning and establishing a common language can help set up a framework within which SMH can be developed and advanced globally. Under such a framework, interventions can be designed to meet the needs of a student in every domain, and these needs are not necessarily singular to one domain only. For example, the provision of "in-house" mental health assessment, treatment, and care through the vehicle of a school-based health center is an intervention designed to address mental disorders. The availability of school-based counseling services can help students who are experiencing mental health problems. Both of these types of interventions are targeted to young people who exhibit the characteristics that inform their need.

Interventions designed to help students develop competencies to better address usual distress can be either targeted or universal, but important considerations of need and cost must be addressed. For example, does a universal intervention designed to improve self-esteem of students actually result in other important outcomes rather than a change in self-esteem, and does the magnitude of those outcomes warrant the investment? Ideally, such determinations should be made prior to programs being implemented.

Furthermore, application of interventions designed to enhance outcomes for a specific domain may be inappropriate or unhelpful when applied to other domains. For example, an intervention designed to treat a mental disorder may not be appropriate for addressing mental distress: medications or evidence-based psychotherapies (such as cognitive behavioral therapy) are not used to "treat" normal negative emotions. And, important as support from a friend is, by itself it is not an effective treatment for a psychotic disorder. Failure to tailor application to need may result in over-intervention (at great cost and with wasted efficiency) or over-expectation (for example, improving the school environment may have no impact on the incidence of depression or obsessive compulsive disorder). This may result in applying interventions that are not needed or in not applying interventions that may be helpful for improving competencies to adapt to distress but not helpful for preventing a disorder (see Figure 24.2).

Here is where our language makes a significant difference. Every language provides a rich lexicon that describes important nuances in emotional, cognitive, perceptual, physical,

Enhancement of mental wellbeing ➡️ Health promotion

Addressing distress ➡️ Helping building resilience, Avoiding over-protection from stress

Addressing mental health problems ➡️ Enhancing supports, prevention

Addressing mental disorders ➡️ Prevention, best-in-class care

Figure 24.2 Relating intervention to mental health state.

Table 24.1 An example of language clarification

Distress	• Unhappy
	• Disappointed
	• Disgruntled
Problem	• Demoralized
	• Disengaged
	• Disenfranchised
Disorder/illness	• Depressed

and behavioral states. It is important to use language that best describes the domain to which it applies. For example, in the English language, the word "depression" is often applied to the domains of "distress," "problem," and "disorder" indiscriminately. Thus, when a young person answers affirmatively to a question such as: "Have you felt depressed this week?" they have no consideration as to what is being evaluated. And, an affirmative answer does not help distinguish which domain is being identified by the respondent. More careful attention to our language is needed. There is a huge difference between interventions that decrease the risk of symptoms of depression (such as feeling "depressed," "sad," "unhappy," etc.) and interventions that decrease the incidence of the mental disorder called depression. Unfortunately, this difference is often not explicitly stated, even in peer-reviewed research publications.

One issue that requires global attention as we move ahead to advance SMH is care given to the words we use and the meanings they have for us and the transparency and linking of good evidence-based interventions to the domains that they are most appropriate to address. Further, attention to this issue will also help guide policy makers and practitioners in focusing on those issues most important in their jurisdictions, helping SMH interventions develop based on local needs.

Impact of site and purpose

Globally, all schools have students, teachers, and a course of study (curriculum). Apart from those three commonalities, they can differ substantially from one another, depending on site and purpose. With the lead by the United Nations Educational, Scientific and Cultural Organization (UNESCO) in the global "Education for All" initiative (UNESCO, 2010; 2014), the importance of education as a foundation for achieving the United Nation's Millennium Development Goals (MDGs) has been acknowledged. The Dakar Framework for Action (World Education Forum, 2000) has thus become a milestone in global educational achievement. Important and essential as this has been for fundamental human rights such as gender equality, the application of what constitutes education and how education is delivered remains primarily locally defined. Thus, addressing mental health in the school setting is not universally acknowledged as either necessary or important. This issue can be considered to be partly addressed as a component of the health-promoting school initiative of the WHO (World Health Organization, 2014c) and can be embedded within the overall concept of whole-school approaches for health promotion. However, how this consideration plays out in different settings worldwide is not clear. Indeed, it was not until the mid 1990s that the WHO specifically noted the importance of linking mental health promotion to education (World Health Organization, 1996). The increasing importance of this direction, however, is now being recognized. For example, the WHO Regional Office for Europe report, *Mental health: facing the challenges, building solutions* has identified promotion of mental wellbeing in schools as one indicator for its "Reducing stigma ... mental health problems" indicator (World Health Organization, 2005). Such acknowledgements, however, are still narrowly conceived (for example, the 2005 WHO document does not consider schools as a potential site for mental healthcare) and to our knowledge are not widely promoted in other WHO regions.

Thus, in the global setting, the importance of schools as a place to address mental wellbeing and mental healthcare needs is a relatively recent consideration and one that does not necessarily fit easily into many existing sociocultural constructs about mental illness (World Health Organization, 2001). The ability to address mental healthcare needs of young people is also constrained by the unequal distribution of mental healthcare resources worldwide (World Health Organization, 2011; World Psychiatric Association, 2005). Thus, the ability, willingness, or capacity to effectively address one or more of the important components of SMH varies greatly from place to place.

One important corollary of this reality is that approaches that are being applied in Western or high-income (World Bank Group, 2014) countries may not be appropriate for transplantation into other countries, especially those where sociocultural, civil society, and economic factors are significantly different. For example, the chapter by Hamwaka addressing SMH in Malawi through training students in mental health literacy so that they can function in a peer health educator framework can be expected to impact not only students and teachers (who become trainers), but also the communities in which the students reside. This approach may have an impact on addressing stigma outside the school as well as inside the school – a challenge that is currently not well met with existing approaches. A similar approach is described by Lee *et al.*, where linking a long standing non-governmental organization involved in mental healthcare delivery and community-based stigma reduction (Basic Needs) to SMH initiatives offers an opportunity to change both within- and outside-school attitudes. The work of Estanislau in Brazil is another example of this approach, reaching from the school into the community to help drive change. Further research should inform us whether these types of innovative interventions work. Indeed, such innovations can also be transported into Western sites, where they may prove effective as well.

In situations where education is tightly controlled by the state, such as China, other factors may be at play. The chapters by Fang and Du demonstrate the complex interplay between state-driven expectations for specific learning outcomes and the realization that the education system may have more nuanced roles to play in promoting or addressing the mental and physical wellbeing of both students and teachers. In settings that are involved in or emerging from conflict, additional challenges including social and economic reconstruction, continued civil unrest, and basic considerations of safety and security have a tremendous impact on the ability of schools to address SMH. Parenthetically, perhaps, the greater the need the less capacity, as the chapter by Al Obaidi on SMH in Iraq demonstrates. In these settings, as in those that are significantly under-resourced and newly beginning to address mental health improvements in the health system, it is likely essential that SMH initiatives, such as Kumar *et al.* describe in

India and Gallegos-Guajardo *et al.* describe for Mexico and Chile, may need to be linked to reforms in mental healthcare. In this context, the model described by Xie *et al.* in Singapore may be instructive.

These illustrations (and many more in other chapters) stand in stark contrast to the well-developed integrated approaches presented by Rowling, Clarke, Wei, and Swain-Bradway from Australia, Ireland, Canada, and the United States, respectively. Further global developments in SMH will need to take into account these differences in site and process realities and it would be unrealistic to assume that what will be built in Africa, the Middle East, Latin or South America, or even Eastern Europe, will be a carbon copy of what exists currently in other locations. Hopefully, leaders in SMH in emerging regions and low-income situations will develop best-in-class indigenous models, perhaps borrowing what has shown promise elsewhere but interpreting, creating, developing, applying, and evaluating approaches that meet the exigencies of their realities and creating frameworks that can then inform further developments in more established, high-income settings.

Future globally applicable directions

Given that worldwide there are so many different types of schools, in so many different types of settings with so many different kinds of mandates, structures, and operational realities, clearly a one-size-fits-all approach to SMH globally is not appropriate (Wei and Kutcher, 2012). Instead, what will need to be developed are context-specific approaches that are based on and meet local needs and can be demonstrated to achieve specific goals and measurable outcomes. Within these, however, a number of key components, globally contextualized, could be considered and applied.

First, schools can be a place in which mental health is both promoted and mental healthcare can be delivered. It will be important as SMH is developed in different settings that attention is paid to both of these components and that resources be appropriate to meet these directions, and be prioritized and applied depending on local needs. This may be more easily initiated regarding mental healthcare, for although the structures through which mental healthcare can be delivered will vary from location to location, the care delivery competencies and the care interventions will be very similar and are universally applied (World Health Organization, 2014d).

This is a very important issue that has not achieved sufficient attention in high-income countries, but is recognized as an essential development for lower-income regions. It should be considered in wealthy countries as well as a possible model towards achieving health system reforms that more appropriately addresses mental health needs of populations. That is, the concept of health system strengthening. This does not mean the "health system" silo within human services organizations and activities as commonly considered in high-income countries, but a system of care that cuts across all human services organizations and activities (Global Fund, 2014; World Health Organization, 2007). Or, as more eloquently put by the Global Fund, "a health system consists of all organizations, people, and actions whose primary intent is to promote, restore or maintain health" (Global Fund, 2014). Thinking about SMH in this way can help all jurisdictions, worldwide, better understand the inexorable linkage between education and mental health, and may be a useful entry point for the initiation of SMH activities that can span the mental health needs of young people, from promotion to ongoing care.

Whole-school models, sophisticated and useful as they certainly are, tend to perpetuate silo structures that characterize "Western" human services systems, have been primarily developed from organizational and resource-supported constructs created in high-income nations, and it is not known how well these will translate into more resource-constrained and significantly different civic, political, cultural, and economic environments. Mental health promotion approaches have also been similarly determined. Further, they have often been applied without being subjected to prior controlled research, and thus, while usually evaluated after application, it is not possible to determine post-hoc their magnitude of impact or effectiveness from positive outcomes identified. Thus, attention should be paid, across all settings, to ensure that controlled research of high methodological rigor be conducted prior to interventions being rolled out or scaled up, to better determine the strengths and potential weaknesses of what is being implemented.

Another important global consideration is that of clarity in what schools are expected to do. In the high-income Western countries, the role and responsibilities of schools has changed substantially over time. For example, the focus on primarily preparing students with specific workplace-necessary skills has gradually been enhanced with inculcation of life-skills, social-emotional learning, and other competencies. Added to these relatively recent additions will be the impact of rapid social changes introduced by the electronic revolution just now beginning. These factors all create substantial demands on schools, educators, and others. However, basic structural components of how education is delivered (length of school day, holiday periods, classroom-based learning, etc.) has not similarly evolved. Thus, there will likely be a period of time when the social conversation will begin to focus on answering the question: "What exactly does our society want our schools to do, and how can they be best structured and resourced to do so?" Answers to this question may differ from place to place and how SMH will fit into what changes will be forthcoming based on how this conversation plays out cannot be predicted.

Finally, a common thread that should be applied globally is that of mental health literacy. Mental health literacy is the foundation of mental health and underlies mental health promotion, interventions, care, and the changing of stigma. Although many significant developments have occurred in SMH over the past decades, the role of schools in addressing mental health literacy has proportionally been less visible. Ideally, mental health literacy should be part of every SMH framework, integrated into what is taught in schools and embraced by educators, students, and parents alike. Similarly to health literacy, improvements in mental health literacy can be expected to enhance mental health, improve mental health care and help to address health inequalities and the social determinants of health. Some important initiatives have begun in this domain, with demonstrated positive impacts that are similarly obtained in different settings and across high-income and low-income locations alike (Kutcher and Wei, 2014; Kutcher et al., 2013; pers. comm; Skre et al., 2013). These interventions are not difficult to implement, are not costly, do not require significant additional resources, and can be applied in any school setting by usual teachers working in usual classrooms. Further, they fit easily with whole-school approaches and models that focus on care interventions. As such, they may be a simple, useful, and sustainable approach toward SMH globally.

In conclusion, much has been achieved in SMH. Much has been learned. Now, as SMH goes global, we have much more to achieve and much more to learn – from our research and from each other.

References

Adolescent Health Research Group (2008). *Youth'07: The health and wellbeing of secondary school students in New Zealand, initial findings.* Auckland: The University of Auckland.

American Psychiatric Association (2014). *DSM-5 implementation and support. American Psychiatric Association DSM-5 Development.* Available at: www.dsm5.org/Pages/Default.aspx (accessed July 6, 2014).

Araya, R., Fritsch, R., Spears, M., *et al.* (2013). School intervention to improve mental health of students in Santiago, Chile: A randomized clinical trial. *JAMA Pediatrics*, 11, 1004–10.

Cohen, S. (1983). The mental hygiene movement, the development of personality and the school: The medicalization of American education. *History of Education Quarterly*, 23, 123–148.

Darr, C., Fisher, J., and Boyd, S. (2014). Wellbeing@School: Safe and caring schools. Available at: www.nzcer.org.nz/research/well being-at-school (Accessed July 15, 2014).

Gabhainn, S. N., O'Higgins, S., and Barry, M. (2010). The implementation of social, personal and health education in Irish schools. *Health Education*, 110, 452–470.

Gale Group (2008). *Mental hygiene: Encyclopedia of children and childhood in history and society.* Available at: www.faqs.org/child hood/Me-Pa/Mental-Hygiene.html http://www.faqs.org/childhood/Me-Pa/Mental-Hygiene.html (accessed July 15, 2014).

Global Fund (2014). Health systems strength-ening. Available at: www.theglobalfund.org/en/about/diseases/hss/ (accessed July 6, 2014).

Joint Consortium for School Health (2010). Schools as a setting for promoting positive mental health: Better practices and perspectives. Available at: www.jcsh-cces.ca/upload/PMH%20July10%202011%20WebReady.pdf (accessed July 15, 2014).

KidsMatter (2014). KidsMatter Early Childhood. Available at: www.kidsmatter.edu.au/early-childhood (accessed July 15, 2014).

Kutcher, S. and Wei, Y. (2014). School mental health literacy. Education Canada. Available at: www.cea-ace.ca/education-canada/article/school-mental-health-literacy (accessed July 15, 2014).

Kutcher, S., Wei, Y., McLuckie, A., *et al.* (2013). Educator mental health literacy: A programme evaluation of the teacher training education on the mental health and high school curriculum guide. *Advances in School Mental Health Promotion*, 6, 83–93.

Ontario Ministry of Education (2013). Supporting minds. Available at: www.edu.gov.on.ca/eng/document/reports/SupportingMinds.pdf (accessed July 2, 2014).

Patel, V., Flisher, A. J., Hetrick, S., *et al.* (2007). Mental health of young people: A global public-health challenge. *Lancet*, 9569, 1302–1313.

Prince, M., Patel, V., Saxena, S., *et al.* (2007). No health without mental health. *Lancet*, 9590, 859–877.

Richardson, T. (1987). *The century of the child: The mental hygiene movement and social policy in the United States and Canada.* Unpublished PhD thesis. University of British Columbia.

Richardson, T. (1989). *The century of the Child: The mental hygiene movement and social policy in the United States and Canada.* Albany, NY: State University of New York Press.

Rutter, M., Bishop, D., Pine, D., *et al.* (2008). *Rutter's child and adolescent psychiatry* (5th edn.). Malden, MA: Blackwell Publishing.

Shakespeare, W., Thompson, A., and Taylor, N. (2006). *Hamlet: the Texts of 1603 and 1623.* London: The Arden Shakespeare.

Skre, I., Friborg, O., Breivik, C., *et al.* (2013). A school intervention for mental health literacy in adolescents: Effects of a non-randomized cluster controlled trial. *BMC Public Health*, 13, 873–2458–13–873.

Social Hygiene Movement (1913). *American Journal of Public Health*, 3, 1154–1157.

United Nations Educational, Scientific and Cultural Organization (2010). Education for all goals. Available at: hwww.unesco.org/en/education-for-all-international-coordination/themes/efa-goals/ (accessed June 29, 2014).

United Nations Educational, Scientific and Cultural Organization (2014). Education for all movement. Available at: www.unesco.org/new/en/education/themes/leading-the-international-agenda/education-for-all/browse/1/ (accessed June 29, 2014).

University of Michigan Health & Well-Being Services (2012). Understanding U: Managing the ups and downs of life – what is mental health? Available at: http://hr.umich.edu/mhealthy/programs/mental_emotional/understandingu/learn/mental_health.html (accessed July 15, 2014).

Weare, K. and Nind, M. (2011). Mental health promotion and problem prevention in schools: What does the evidence say? *Health Promotion International*, 26, doi:10.1093/heapro/dar075.

Wei, Y., Hayden, J. A., Kutcher, S., Zygmunt, A., and McGrath, P. (2013). The effectiveness of school mental health literacy programs to address knowledge, attitudes, and help seeking among youth. *Early Intervention in Psychiatry*, 7 (2), 109–121.

Wei, Y. and Kutcher, S. (2012). International school mental health: Global approaches, global challenges, and global opportunities. *Child & Adolescent Psychiatric Clinics of North America*, 1, 11–27.

Wellbeing at School (2014). Wellbeing@School and inclusive practices self-review tools. Available at: www.wellbeingatschool.org.nz (accessed July 15, 2014).

Well-being Institute at the University of Cambridge (2011). A centre for the scientific study of well-being. Available at www.wellbeing.group.cam.ac.uk (accessed July 15, 2014).

World Bank Group (2014). Country and lending groups. Available at: http://data.worldbank.org/about/country-and-lending-groups#High_income (accessed July 15, 2014).

World Education Forum (2000). The Dakar framework for action. Available at: www.unesco.org/education/wef/en-conf/dakframeng.shtm (accessed June 28, 2014).

World Health Organization (1996). *Regional guidelines: Development of health-promoting schools: a framework for action*. Manila, WHO Regional Office for the Western Pacific. Available at: http://whqlibdoc.who.int/wpro/1994-99/a53203.pdf (accessed July 15, 2014).

World Health Organization (2001). *The world health report 2001: Mental health – new understanding, new hope*. Geneva: World Health Organization Publications.

World Health Organization (2005). *Mental health: facing the challenges, building solutions*. Copenhagen: World Health Organization Publications.

World Health Organization (2007). WHO health systems strategy. Available at: www.who.int/healthsystems/strategy/en (accessed July 6, 2014).

World Health Organization (2011). *Mental health atlas*. Geneva: World Health Organization Publications.

World Health Organization (2014a). Mental health: A state of well-being. Available at: www.who.int/features/factfiles/mental_health/en (accessed July 6, 2014).

World Health Organization (2014b). International statistical classification of diseases and related health problems, 10th revision. Available at: http://apps.who.int/classifications/icd10/browse/2010/en (accessed July 6, 2014).

World Health Organization (2014c). What is a health promoting school? Available at: www.who.int/school_youth_health/gshi/hps/en/ (accessed June 29, 2014).

World Health Organization (2014d). WHO Mental Health Gap Action Programme (mhGAP). Available at: www.who.int/mental_health/mhgap/en/ (accessed July 4, 2014).

World Psychiatric Association, World Health Organization, International Association for Child and Adolescent Psychiatry and Allied Professions (2005). *Atlas: Child and adolescent mental health resources*. Geneva: World Health Organization Publications.

Wyn, J., Cahill, H., Holdsworth, R., *et al.* (2000). MindMatters, a whole-school approach promoting mental health and wellbeing. *Australia & New Zealand Journal of Psychiatry*, 34, 594–601.

Index